A Skeptic's Investigation into Jesus

A Skeptic's Investigation into Jesus

J. P. HANNAH

WIPF & STOCK · Eugene, Oregon

A SKEPTIC'S INVESTIGATION INTO JESUS

Wipf & Stock
An Imprint of Wipf and Stock Publishers
199 W. 8th Ave., Suite 3
Eugene, OR 97401

www.wipfandstock.com

PAPERBACK ISBN: 978-1-5326-7461-7
HARDCOVER ISBN: 978-1-5326-7462-4
EBOOK ISBN: 978-1-5326-7463-1

Manufactured in the U.S.A. 10/05/20

Contents

Preface

As a skeptical agnostic with a passionate interest in the human condition, I spent many years exploring a fundamental question: do our lives have any meaning or are they random events that end with death? I searched for answers in a wide range of sciences, philosophies, and faiths and was prepared to reach any reasonable conclusion from the evidence.[1] Modern physics provides insights that are paradoxical and exhilarating, but no philosophy or faith system seemed ultimately convincing or satisfying. I initially ignored Christianity as an implausible story, but I often encountered references to the "Cosmic Christ" and finally decided that to be truly objective, I would have to develop an understanding of this enigmatic figure. So with the aim of identifying flaws in Christian doctrine, I listened critically to the New Testament while negotiating traffic on the way to deliver mathematics lectures.

But instead of hearing, as I had expected, a random collection of miracles, parables, and moralistic instructions to love one another, something else became increasingly apparent—a consistent voice of authority and wisdom that was strikingly different from anything I had yet encountered. So for the next few years, I thoroughly researched Old and New Testament Scripture, theological commentaries, and atheist critiques. The

1. My research included exploration into existentialism, idealism, Darwinism, quantum physics, cosmology, relativity theory, theosophy, anthroposophy, Taoism, Buddhism (Zen, Dzogchen, and Mahayana), Islam, Sufism, various forms of mysticism and meditation, Kashmir Shaivism, Kabbalah, Advaita Vedanta, the Hara Krishna movement, the Hindu Bhagavad Gita and Upanishads, the wisdom of Eastern gurus (particularly Paramahansa Yogananda, Ramakrishna, Nisargadatta Maharaj, Sri Aurobindo, and Ramana Maharshi), as well as eclectic combinations of faiths such as the *philosophia perennis* (perennial wisdom) and Gnostic-Christian-Kabbalah (yes, there is such a thing).

more I read, the more I realized that my initial view of Christianity was like judging the entire culture of a country from a few holiday snapshots.

The outcome of my extensive investigation was totally unexpected—the findings shook the foundations of my opinions and challenged many confident assumptions that have become an unquestioned part of our Western worldview. Having undertaken this research in the spirit of academic impartiality, I now offer these carefully verified facts to anyone who is interested in the universe and our place in it, whether atheist, agnostic, or follower of any faith. I have provided sources and additional information in footnotes, but these can be ignored for smoother reading without affecting the main arguments.

This book does not defend the Christian church, its creeds, or organized religion in general, which has undoubtedly been wielded as a tool of power.[2] Rather, it invites you on a journey of independent investigation into the latest relevant scholarship in science, mythology, history, archaeology, theology, and Judeo-Christian Scripture, in order to unearth and analyze facts relevant to the ongoing debate between atheism and faith in general, and Christianity in particular.

2. It is tempting to join atheists such as Richard Dawkins (*The God Delusion*) and Christopher Hitchens (*God is Not Great*) in identifying faith as the primary cause of the appalling inhumanity and violence in the world. However, although people have perpetrated deplorable acts in the name of religion, the absence of faith has had no humanitarian impact on regimes such as those of Mao Zedong, Pol Pot, Joseph Stalin, and Vladimir Lenin. Professor of political science Rudolph Rummel estimates that atheist totalitarian governments killed approximately 110 million people in the short period from 1929 to 1987 (*Death by Government*, 8) and concludes that "the problem is Power" (*Death by Government*, xxi). The real threat to humanity seems to be our lust for power and the corresponding inability to wield it with temperance and wisdom, whether in a religious or secular context.

Acknowledgements

MY THANKS GO TO family and friends who encouraged this project and helped shape the final product.

I would also like to express my profound gratitude to the community of scientists, theologians, and historians whose valuable work has made this book possible. I am not an expert in these fields but have striven to represent their opinions correctly, and I apologize for any misrepresentations, which I would hope to correct in any reprint should I receive suggestions.

In particular, I thank the following professors for generously providing invaluable feedback on certain chapters (which does not imply that they necessarily endorse all the opinions in this book): George Ellis (mathematician, cosmologist, and co-author with Stephen Hawking), Simon Conway Morris (who holds the Cambridge Chair of Evolutionary Paleobiology), and biblical scholars Michael Licona, Daniel Wallace and Larry Hurtado.[1]

1. Professor Hurtado kindly provided this feedback shortly before his tragic death from cancer.

Abbreviations

§	section
1QIsa	Great Isaiah Scroll of Qumran
1QS	Community Rule
Ant.	*Antiquities of the Jews*
b.	Babylonian Talmud
BZAW	*Beihefte Zur Zeitschrift Für die Alttestamentliche Wissenschaft*
ca.	circa (dated around)
CD	Damascus Document
CJB	Complete Jewish Bible
col.	column
COQG	Christian Origins and the Question of God
d.	died
DDD	*Dictionary of Deities and Demons in the Bible*
Dialogue	*Dialogue with Trypho*
EAH	*The Encyclopedia of Ancient History*
ed(s).	editor(s)
EPROER	Études Préliminaires aux Religions Orientales dans l'Empire Romain
esp.	especially
ESV	English Standard Version
frag.	fragment

JETS	*Journal of the Evangelical Theological Society*
JBL	*Journal of Biblical Literature*
JSNT	*Journal for the Study of the New Testament*
KJV	King James Version
LXX	Septuagint version of the Hebrew Old Testament
MSS	manuscripts
MT	Masoretic Hebrew Old Testament
m.	Mishna
n.	note
NIV	New International Version
NKJV	New King James Version
NT	New Testament
OCD	*Oxford Classical Dictionary*
OJB	Orthodox Jewish Bible
OT	Old Testament
p.	page
pp.	pages
PRL	*Physical Review Letters*
r.	reigned
RSV	Revised Standard Version
sic	intentionally so written
SNTSMS	*Society for New Testament Studies Monograph Series*
SPCK	*Society for Promoting Christian Knowledge*
STR	*Southeastern Theological Review*
t.	Tosefta
trans.	translator
vol.	volume
Wars	*The Wars of the Jews*

WEB	World English Bible
WUNT	*Wissenschaftliche Untersuchungen zum Neuen Testament*
YLT	Young's Literal Translation
ZNW	*Zeitschrift für die Neutestamentliche Wissenschaft*

OLD TESTAMENT

Gen	Genesis
Exod	Exodus
Lev	Leviticus
Num	Numbers
Deut	Deuteronomy
Josh	Joshua
Judg	Judges
1 Sam	First Samuel
2 Sam	Second Samuel
1 Kgs	First Kings
2 Kgs	Second Kings
1 Chron	First Chronicles
2 Chron	Second Chronicles
Ps	Psalms
Prov	Proverbs
Eccl	Ecclesiastes
Isa	Isaiah
Jer	Jeremiah
Ezek	Ezekiel
Dan	Daniel
Hos	Hosea
Mic	Micah
Zech	Zechariah
Mal	Malachi

NEW TESTAMENT

Matt	Matthew
Acts	Acts of the Apostles
Rom	Romans
1 Cor	First Corinthians
2 Cor	Second Corinthians
Eph	Ephesians
Phil	Philippians
Col	Colossians
Gal	Galatians
1 Tim	First Timothy
2 Tim	Second Timothy
Heb	Hebrews
Jas	James
1 Pet	First Peter
2 Pet	Second Peter
1 Thess	First Thessalonians
2 Thess	Second Thessalonians
Rev	Revelation

Introduction

A reflection on human existence and faith raises many questions:

- Is the universe the random result of physical laws?
- Do scientists know how life arose on Earth?
- Is atheism a conclusion from evidence, while faith is speculation?
- Is there any relationship between physical matter and human consciousness?
- Is our world governed by deterministic physical laws?
- Can we know anything for certain about Jesus of Nazareth?
- Do the gnostic gospels reveal suppressed information about Christianity?
- Does suffering contradict the existence of an omnipotent, loving God?
- Do any scientists believe that Jesus was resurrected?
- Are science and faith in opposition?

This book investigates evidence related to science, faith, and Christianity in the following way:

- Part A: The New Testament

This section explores whether Jesus was a myth or an exaggerated legend, whether the New Testament accounts contain any reliable information, and whether orthodox or alternative views of Jesus seem more credible.

- Part B: The New Science

The exploration in Part A raises questions about what might be possible in our world. To cast light on these issues, the second section discusses findings in quantum physics, relativity theory, cosmology, and biochemistry, which challenge our common-sense preconceptions about the universe. Scientists are puzzled about many aspects of reality, but these insights have still not permeated our cultural worldview although they have important implications for the question of faith.

- Part C: The Old Testament

This section reveals remarkable and significant links between the Old and New Testaments and surveys the broad tapestry of the Judeo-Christian message from Genesis to Revelation.

You are asked to approach the evidence like an ideal juror—setting aside all preconceptions and starting with a clean slate, to decide which explanations of the facts could be possible, which are plausible, and which seem the most probable. There will be regular opportunities to consider your verdict as part of the systematic analysis and comparison of arguments proposed by both atheism and faith. Individual facts can be judged in isolation, but it is ultimately the cumulative evidence as a whole that needs to be assessed. Each stage of the journey will provide an increasingly wider view until the complete picture is drawn, against which to formulate a personal answer to Jesus's question:

> "Who do you say I am?"

PART A

The New Testament

Investigation 1

Jesus of Nazareth—History or Myth?

An investigation into the veracity of the Christian faith has a logical starting point: was Jesus a historical person or a myth? These first three chapters will investigate possible historical references to Jesus, identify the earliest published sources of "Jesus-myth" claims, and explore suggested parallels between the gospel narratives and the mythologies of pagan gods.[1]

1.1 FOUR ANCIENT VOICES

The following four writers of antiquity made explicit references to a Jesus or Christ, which might support the historical existence of Jesus of Nazareth.

Cornelius Tacitus (ca. 55–ca. 120)

A devastating fire swept through Rome in AD 64. The Roman senator and historian Tacitus, who was young at the time, later recorded the rumor that Nero was partially responsible in that he had ordered an area to be burned to clear space for new building projects. Tacitus also mentioned Nero's attempt to deflect attention by accusing the unpopular Christians of being responsible for the fire, and his report includes a reference to the execution of "Christus" by the Romans:

1. The term "pagan" is used in this book to refer to a polytheistic worldview and does not have derogatory connotations.

> Consequently, to get rid of the rumor, Nero fastened the guilt and inflicted the most exquisite tortures on a class hated for their abominations, called Christians by the populace. Christus, the author of the name, suffered the extreme penalty during the reign of Tiberius at the hands of one of our procurators, Pontius Pilatus. And a most mischievous superstition, thus checked for the moment, again broke out not only in Judaea, the first source of the evil, but even in Rome.[2]

There are two main challenges to this reference as evidence of Jesus's historicity.

Challenge 1: It is alleged that Tacitus was merely repeating Christian legends. This claim is largely based on Tacitus referring to Pilate as procurator (*epitropos*) instead of prefect[3] and using the label "Christ" (or Christus) for Jesus. However, the Roman statesman Pliny also used this term for Jesus (see below), and it had probably become the most common name for Jesus by this time. There is also evidence that a Roman administrator could act as both prefect (military official) and procurator (financial administrator).[4] Tacitus is generally regarded as a reliable historian, and he wrote, "[It is] unbecoming the dignity of the task which I have undertaken to collect fabulous marvels and to amuse with fiction."[5] He encouraged his readers "not to catch eagerly at wild and improbable rumors in preference to genuine history"[6] and often explicitly identified stories that seemed to be merely hearsay, which he did not do in his report about Christus.[7] He also recorded conflicting traditions, as in his report of the burning of Rome: "A disaster followed, whether accidental or treacherously contrived by the emperor, is uncertain, as authors have given both accounts."[8] However, although Tacitus, like many Romans, was highly scornful of the Christian movement, he does not seem to have been aware of any belief that "Christus" had never existed.

2. Tacitus, *Annals* 15.44, translated by Church and Brodribb.

3. A first-century inscription from Caesarea Maritima identified Pilate as a prefect of Judea.

4. See Jones, *Roman Government*, 124.

5. Tacitus, *History* 2.50.

6. Tacitus, *Annals* 4.11.

7. For example, Tacitus introduced some accounts by writing, "according to some," "it was rumored," "as many said," and "was said to have" (*Annals* 1.76, 2.40, 12.7, 12.65).

8. Tacitus, *Annals* 15.38.

Challenge 2: The reference to Christus is claimed to be a later Christian addition. However, the terms "extreme penalty" and "procurator" are not typically Christian—the New Testament calls Pilate *hēgemōn* (governor). A historian has identified this passage as being "Tacitean in style, force, and prejudice,"[9] and there is no evidence of interpolation, so this is likely to be a reliable ancient reference to Christ. Atheist scholar Bart Ehrman expresses this opinion: "Some mythicists argue that this reference in Tacitus was not actually written by him . . . I don't know of any trained classicists or scholars of ancient Rome who think this, and it seems highly unlikely . . . Tacitus evidently did know some things about Jesus."[10] Many other scholars also consider this to be an authentic reference.[11]

Pliny the Younger (ca. 61–ca. 113)

Pliny the Younger was a Roman governor in Bithynia, Asia Minor. In one of his regular reports to Emperor Trajan, he described how he interrogated obstinate Christians who refused to worship the state gods:

> I put it to themselves whether they were or were not Christians. To each as professed that they were I put the inquiry a second and a third time, threatening them with the supreme penalty. Those who persisted I ordered to execution. For, indeed, I do not doubt, whatever might be the nature of that which they professed, that their pertinacity, at any rate, and inflexible obstinacy, ought to be punished. There were others afflicted with the madness, with regard to whom, as they were Roman citizens, I made a memorandum that they were to be sent for judgment to Rome . . . They affirmed, however, that this had been the sum, whether of their crime or their delusion: they had been in the habit of meeting together on a stated day, before sunrise, and of offering in turns a form of invocation to Christ, as to a god . . . This made me think it all the more necessary to inquire, even by torture, of two maid-servants who were styled deaconesses,

9. Durant, *Caesar and Christ*, 554.

10. Ehrman, *Did Jesus Exist?* 55.

11. See, for example, Meier, *Roots of the Problem*, 90; Bond, *Pontius Pilate in History*, xi; Eddy and Boyd, *Jesus Legend*, 127; Van Voorst, *Jesus Outside the New Testament*, 39–53.

> what the truth was. I could discover nothing else than a vicious and extravagant superstition.[12]

Although Pliny's letter does not prove the existence of Jesus, his use of the phrase "as to a god" suggests that he might have regarded Christ as a historical man who was being worshiped after his death through the "madness" and "extravagant superstition" of his followers.[13]

Gaius Suetonius Tranquillus (ca. 69–after 122)

The historian Suetonius wrote twelve biographies of the Roman Caesars, and he reported an action taken by the Emperor Claudius some time between AD 41 and 53:

> He banished from Rome all the Jews, who were continually making disturbances at the instigation of one Chrestus.[14]

According to the Acts of the Apostles, Paul met two Jewish Christians who had moved to Corinth "because Claudius had ordered all Jews to leave Rome" (Acts 18:2b). The question is whether the "Chrestus" in Suetonius's text was simply a local trouble-maker, or if Claudius had been trying to control violent Jewish-Christian disputes over the nature of Jesus Christ. Here are some relevant facts:

- The term "Christ" was often rendered as "Chrestus" in the first few centuries.[15]
- Not long after Jesus's death, the apostles converted many Jewish pilgrims who were visiting from Rome (Acts 2:10) and who would have returned with the message about Jesus.
- There were violent conflicts between Christians and Jews during this early period: around AD 35, Stephen was stoned to death by fellow Jews (Acts 7:59); around AD 44, Herod Agrippa had John's

12. Pliny, *Epistles* 10.96, translated by John Delaware Lewis.

13. This is the opinion of, among other scholars, Bart Ehrman (*Did Jesus Exist?* 52).

14. Suetonius, *Twelve Caesars, Claudius* 5 §528, translated by Alexander Thomson. According to the historian Cassius Dio (ca. 155–ca. 235), Claudius only banned Roman Jews from holding gatherings in Rome (*Roman History*, 60.6.6). If he was referring to the same incident, perhaps only key figures of the conflict were expelled.

15. For example, Tertullian (ca. 155–ca. 240) wrote that followers of Jesus were often called "Chrestianus" (*Apology* 3.5), and Lactantius (ca. 250–ca. 325) remarked that some non-Christians were calling Jesus, "Chrestus" (*Divine Institutes* 4.7.5).

brother James killed (Acts 12:2); the Apostle Paul wrote, "Five times I received from the Jews the forty lashes minus one . . . I have been in danger . . . from my fellow Jews" (2 Cor 11:24–26).

There is no clear explanation for what might have sparked these particular disturbances in the Roman Jewish communities, but it would have been a coincidence for another man with a name so similar to Christ to have been the cause of this major disruption. According to theologian James Dunn, "The broad consensus is that the disturbance referred to had been occasioned by some strong reactions within certain synagogues to Jewish merchants and visitors preaching about Jesus as the Christ."[16]

Flavius Josephus (ca. 38–after 100)

The Jewish historian Josephus was taken captive as a general in the First Jewish-Roman War (AD 66–70), and when he was freed, he took the emperor's family name of Flavius. His history of the Jewish nation, *Antiquities of the Jews*, contains the only non-Christian reference to the murder of John the Baptist by Herod Antipas,[17] and it also provides the following two reports that seem to refer to the Jesus of the New Testament.

Jesus in Antiquities 20

Josephus recorded an incident that took place in Jerusalem in AD 62, when the Roman governor died, and his replacement took some time to arrive:[18]

16. Dunn, *Jesus Remembered*, 142.

17. Josephus wrote, "Now some of the Jews thought that the destruction of Herod's army came from God, and that very justly, as a punishment of what he did against John, that was called the Baptist: for Herod slew him, who was a good man, and commanded the Jews to exercise virtue, both as to righteousness towards one another, and piety towards God, and so to come to baptism . . . Herod, who feared lest the great influence John had over the people might put it into his power and inclination to raise a rebellion (for they seemed ready to do any thing he should advise), thought it best, by putting him to death, to prevent any mischief he might cause . . . Accordingly he was sent a prisoner, out of Herod's suspicious temper, to Macherus, the castle I before mentioned, and was there put to death" (*Ant.* 18.5.2). Translations of Josephus's works in this book are by William Whiston.

18. The Apostle Paul had a hearing before this Roman governor, Porcius Festus (Acts 25).

> Festus was now dead, and Albinus was but upon the road; so [Ananus] assembled the sanhedrim of judges, and brought before them the brother of Jesus—the one called Christ—whose name was James, and some others; and when he had formed an accusation against them as breakers of the law, he delivered them to be stoned.[19]

Jesus and James were both very common names, which is presumably why Josephus added that this Jesus was "called Christ." This reference was not mentioned by the church until the third century, but this is not surprising as it only provided information about Jesus's existence, which was not questioned in this early period. It seems unlikely that the text is a Christian addition because they would have used the phrase "brother of the Lord" rather than "brother of Jesus."

Josephus's account confirms the Christian tradition that around this period, some religious leaders in Jerusalem instigated the death of Jesus's brother James, who was a leading figure in the Jerusalem Church. It would be a surprising coincidence if Josephus was referring to an entirely different incident involving the death of another James, who was the brother of another Jesus, at the hands of the Sanhedrin. Many scholars regard this as an authentic reference to the gospel Jesus.[20]

Jesus in Antiquities 18

In *Antiquities* 18, Josephus had already written about Jesus, so that two books later in *Antiquities* 20, he could identify James as the brother of this man. The underlined sections in this text (known as the *Testimonium Flavianum*) are almost certainly later Christian interpolations:

> Now there was about this time Jesus, a wise man, <u>if it be lawful to call him a man</u>; for he was a doer of wonderful works, a teacher of such men as receive the truth with pleasure. He drew over to him both many of the Jews and many of the Gentiles. <u>He was [the] Christ</u>. And when Pilate, at the suggestion of the principal men amongst us, had condemned him to the cross, those that loved him at the first did not forsake him; <u>for he appeared to them alive again the third day; as the divine prophets had foretold these and ten thousand other wonderful things concerning</u>

19. Josephus, *Ant.* 20.9.1 §200.

20. See, for example, Maier, *Josephus*, 284–85; Van Voorst, *Jesus Outside the New Testament*, 83; Painter, *Just James*, 139–142; Dunn, *Jesus Remembered*, 141.

> him. And the tribe of Christians, so named from him, are not extinct at this day.[21]

But how authentic is this text? At first glance, the passage seems to be an artificial insertion because it interrupts the flow of Josephus's story. However, writers of antiquity did not use footnotes and instead included their asides in the text. Josephus frequently did this, usually starting with "at (or about) this time," as in this case, so the extract is not suspicious on these grounds.[22] The entire text does not seem to be a Christian work because they would not have described themselves as a "tribe" or called Jesus a "wise man." The overall language is also typical of Josephus.[23]

On the other hand, the Jewish Josephus would not have claimed that Jesus "*was* the Christ" (the expected Messiah) rather than was "called Christ" (as in *Antiquities* 20), and he would certainly not have wondered "if it be lawful to call him a man." Interestingly, the tenth century Christian bishop and historian Agapius described a version of this text that did not include these two phrases.[24]

The text therefore seems to incorporate two styles, and there is no reason to reject it as an entirely Christian fabrication. Steve Mason points out that in all the writings of Philo and Josephus, "one is hard pressed to find a single example of serious scribal alteration. To have created the *testimonium* out of whole cloth would be an act of unparalleled scribal audacity."[25] As a result, "the vast majority of commentators hold a middle position between authenticity and inauthenticity, claiming that Josephus wrote *something* about Jesus that was subsequently edited by Christian copyists."[26]

21. Josephus, *Ant.* 18.3.3 §63–64.

22. According to historian Michael Grant, "Nowadays we have footnotes; the ancients did not, so that what would now be relegated to a footnote had to appear in the text" (*Greek and Roman Historians*, 53). Josephus used this technique in many places (see *Ant.* 13.7.5, 13.5.9, 13.10.4, 13.13.4, 13.15.4, 13.16.4).

23. For example, Josephus often referred to the "principal men" among the Jews (*Ant.* 17.6.3, 18.1.1, 18.3.3, 18.6.7), he used the term "wise man" for Solomon and Daniel (*Ant.* 8.2.7, 10.11.2), and he wrote about the "wonderful works" of Elisha (*Ant.* 9.8.6). See Meier, *Roots of the Problem*, 63.

24. See Pines, *Arabic Version of the* Testimonium, 16.

25. Mason, *Josephus*, 170.

26. Mason, *Josephus*, 173 (original emphasis). Others who support the authenticity of this reference (without the underlined interpolations) include Köstenberger et al., *Cradle*, 104–8; Vermes, *Jesus the Jew*, 51; Blomberg, *Jesus and the Gospels*, 434–35; Keener, *Historical Jesus*, 67; Ehrman, *Did Jesus Exist?* 60.

Argument from Silence

Apart from Jesus/Christus being mentioned by the above four writers, there is also a total lack of evidence that Jesus's existence was ever questioned in the early centuries. Pulitzer Prize-winning historians Will and Ariel Durant made this important observation:

> The denial of [Jesus's] existence seems never to have occurred even to the bitterest Gentile or Jewish opponents of nascent Christianity.[27]

The church fathers wrote extensive arguments for Jesus's divinity, but they never felt compelled to argue for his mere existence. And there is no indication of any accusation in antiquity that Christians revered an imaginary figure. In the second century, Lucian of Samosata ridiculed Christians for worshiping a crucified sage (in *The Passing of Peregrinus*), and the pagan critic Celsus criticized Christians for paying "excessive reverence to one who has but lately appeared among men."[28] Celsus described Jesus as "a most degraded man, who was punished by scourging and crucifixion" after having "gathered around him ten or eleven persons of notorious character, the very wickedest of tax-gatherers and sailors."[29] Celsus recorded rumors that Jesus was an illegitimate child of a Roman soldier and had studied satanic arts in Egypt, but his fierce condemnations of Christianity made no mention of any claim that Jesus had never been a real person. It is often pointed out that in a second-century work by the Christian Justin Martyr (named from his martyrdom), a Jewish character Trypho referred to Jesus as "this man who you say was crucified,"[30] and also commented: "If He has indeed been born." However, these phrases are taken out of context from a debate that was clearly *not* about Jesus's mere existence but about the claim that he was the expected Messiah.[31]

27. Durant, *Caesar and Christ*, 555.

28. Origen, *Against Celsus* 8.12, translated by Roberts and Donaldson. Celsus's work no longer exists, but around AD 248, Origen wrote detailed refutations of his arguments, using extensive quotations from Celsus's writings.

29. Origen, *Against Celsus* 2.31, 1.62.

30. Justin Martyr, *Dialogue* 8, 39.

31. Trypho was refuting the claim that Jesus could have been the expected Jewish Messiah, pointing out that "Christ—if He has indeed been born, and exists anywhere—is unknown, and does not even know Himself, and has no power until Elias come to anoint Him" (*Dialogue* 8). Trypho's arguments challenged the Christian claim about Jesus but not his existence: "Render us the proof that this man who you say was

It is sometimes claimed that the papacy must have regarded the Jesus narrative as a fiction because Pope Leo X is supposed to have said, "What profit has that fable of Christ brought us!" However, as with any evidence, it is important to note the source of this apparent admission. During the papacy of Leo X (from 1513 to 1521), Martin Luther launched his attack on the Catholic Church and denounced the sale of indulgences (church pardons). John Bale (1495–1563) was a supporter of Luther and a virulently anti-Papist Protestant, as is shown by the title of one of his works: *The Three Laws of Nature, Moses and Christ, Corrupted by the Sodymites, Pharisees and Papystes Most Wicked.* In his blistering work, *The Pageant of Popes*, Bale accused Pope Leo X of having accepted gifts in exchange for church pardons, and he made this further criticism of Leo:

> [He] had no care of preaching the Gospell, nay was rather a cruell persecutour of those that began then, as Luther and others, to reveale the light thereof: for on a time when cardinall Bembus did move a question out of the Gospell, the Pope gave him a very contemptuouse aunswere saiying: "All ages can testifie enough *howe profitable that fable of Christe hath ben to us* and our companie."[32]

So what is the significance of Leo's supposed statement about a "fable of Christe"? Did Pope Leo twist a gospel parable (fable) to suit his personal greed? If he was declaring that the entire Jesus-narrative had been invented, this would have been a startling and dangerous admission. But his severe antagonist John Bale did not even hint at this possibility. Instead, Bale linked the pope's "contemptuouse" answer directly to the accusation that Leo was a "cruell persecutour" of the reformists and abused Scripture to profit the Papacy.

There is no other evidence of this apparent quote by Leo X. We do not know if the alleged statement is accurate, whether the pope even said this, or what he might have meant by it. But considering its source, it does not prove that the Catholic Church fabricated the Jesus-figure.

---

crucified and ascended into heaven is the Christ of God . . . Show us that this man is He" (*Dialogue* 39). Translations of Justin Martyr in this book are by Roberts and Donaldson.

32. Bale, *Pageant of Popes*, 228 (original spelling).

Review the Evidence

Many scholars accept that there are some ancient, authentic references to a man named Christus or Jesus. Strictly speaking, these prove the existence of Christian beliefs rather than the historical Jesus, but as historian Will Durant pointed out, "Unless we assume the latter we are driven to the improbable hypothesis that Jesus was invented in one generation."[33]

Some skeptics insist there would be far more historical references to Jesus if he had existed. However, there are no extant records of Pilate's rule in Judea, and he is only mentioned by three writers (Tacitus, Josephus, and the Jewish Philo of Alexandria).[34] Josephus is not found in any Greco-Roman work, even though he was a historian under three Roman emperors. There is no reason to expect that Hellenic historians or Jewish writers such as Philo would have written about an executed criminal who was never involved in a political movement. And our historical records have other, far more surprising, gaps. For example, Josephus and the New Testament mention a revolt led by a Galilean named Judas,[35] but Tacitus does not record this event in his history of Roman-Judean conflict. And Josephus does not mention Claudius's actions against Jews in Rome. Other major gaps have been pointed out by professor of philosophy Timothy McGrew.[36]

Jewish professor Joseph Klausner made this categorical statement: "Of course, there can be no toleration whatever of the idea that Jesus never existed."[37] And Albert Einstein, who did not believe in a personal God, shared this impression of the New Testament accounts: "No one can read the Gospels without feeling the actual presence of Jesus. His personality pulsates in every word. No myth is filled with such life . . . No

33. Durant, *Caesar and Christ*, 555.

34. Philo (ca. 20 BC–ca. AD 50) appealed to Emperor Gaius to remove Pilate from office, complaining of his "continual murders of people untried and uncondemned, and his never ending, and gratuitous, and most grievous inhumanity" (*Embassy to Gaius* 302). Philo's works in this book are quoted from Yonge, *Works of Philo Judaeus.*

35. See Josephus, *Ant.* 18.1; Acts 5:37.

36. For example, Herodotus (ca. 484–ca. 425 BC) wrote nothing about the Romans; the historian Thucydides (ca. 460–ca. 400 BC) did not mention Socrates (ca. 470–399 BC), although they both lived in Athens; Aristotle (384–322 BC) did not mention Thucydides; Pliny the Younger and Suetonius recorded the eruption of Vesuvius but not the consequent destruction of Pompeii; Marco Polo wrote about his travels in China without mentioning the Great Wall; Grafton's *Chronicles* described King John's reign but did not include *Magna Carta.* See McGrew, "Inference," 37–38.

37. Klausner, *Jesus to Paul*, 107.

man can deny the fact that Jesus existed."[38] Historian Michael Grant, a translator of Tacitus's *Annals*, reached this conclusion:

> If we apply to the New Testament, as we should, the same sort of criteria as we should apply to other ancient writings containing historical material, we can no more reject Jesus's existence than we can reject the existence of a mass of pagan personages whose reality as historical figures is never questioned . . . To sum up, modern critical methods fail to support the Christ-myth theory.[39]

Consider Your Verdict

According to the evidence, what is the likelihood that Jesus did exist as a historical figure? What is your verdict?

- o It is highly probable that Jesus was a historical person.
- o This is a possibility.
- o It is unlikely.
- o It is impossible

1.2 WHAT ARE THE SOURCES OF THE "JESUS-AS-MYTH" CLAIMS?

There is no evidence that Jesus's historical existence was challenged in the first few centuries after his death. It has become popular to allege that he was a purely mythological figure compiled from stories of pagan gods, but this idea only gained credence in the eighteenth century when it was published by two Frenchmen.

Constantin Volney (1757–1820) and Charles François Dupuis (1742–1809)

When cries of "Liberté! Égalité! Fraternité!" were echoing in the chaotic streets of Paris, Constantin Volney and Charles Dupuis expressed the

38. Quoted by George Viereck, in "What Life Means to Einstein: An Interview by George Sylvester Viereck," *The Saturday Evening Post*, October 26, 1929.

39. Grant, *Jesus: Historian's Review*, 199–200.

spirit of Enlightenment by urging rational men to liberate themselves from the chains of religion. Dupuis described faith as "a shameful leprosy, infecting reason and causing it to wither."[40] He warned, "Who can depend on the liberties of one's country, as long as there is a priest in it? . . . We ought to exert ourselves to correct this malign influence . . . [through] reason over superstition."[41]

As part of their anti-faith argument, these authors claimed that Jesus was just another mythological sun-god. Volney described Christianity as "the allegorical worship of the Sun,"[42] and Dupuis remarked that "nobody was more ignorant and more credulous than the first Christians, with whom there was no trouble at all, to make them adopt an Oriental legend on Mithras or on the Sun."[43] However, in their desire to make all religions fit their theorized sun-worship, these authors made many incorrect and unfounded claims. For example, in *The Ruins*, Volney made these false statements:

- The Hebrew *tsur* in Deuteronomy 32:4 means Creator and must have referred to the Egyptian god Osiris (p. 159). Except that *tsur* means rock.
- The New Testament Peter was a mythological type of the god Janus "with his keys and bald forehead" (p. 167). However, in his authentic letters of the fifties, the Apostle Paul wrote about his interaction with this very real Jewish fisherman.
- The names Christos and Crishna are both based on the root word, "chris," which means preserver (p. 168). Except that the Greek *christos* means "anointed one," and the Sanskrit *Krishna* means "black" or "dark."
- Jesus was "the ancient and cabalistic name attributed to young Bacchus" (p. 168). Volney provided no evidence for this strange speculation.

In his *Origin of All Religious Worship*, Dupuis also claimed that the Apostle Peter was a form of the god Janus (p. 215) and made further incorrect and unsubstantiated statements. For example, he claimed that the

40. Dupuis, *Origin*, 301.
41. Dupuis, *Origin*, 339.
42. Volney, *Ruins*, 161.
43. Dupuis, *Origin*, 291.

Persian festival of Neuruz involved a celebration of the cross (although there is no cross symbolism in this spring festival), the Christian "hallelujah" was taken from the pagan *hilaries* days of rejoicing (although this word is a combination of the Hebrew word for praise—*hillel*—and the name of God), and the god Horus was dismembered (although this happened to Osiris, not Horus).[44]

Dupuis and Volney made numerous speculative and unfounded connections between Judeo-Christianity and ancient mythologies, which were repeated and supplemented by the following three English writers in the nineteenth century.

Godfrey Higgins (1772–1833)

Godfrey Higgins described his work as designed to "disabuse and enlighten mankind, and to liberate them from the shackles of prejudice."[45] In his opinion, a human Jesus had taught a perfect morality that over time had become "loaded by artful priests with the trash, the corruptions, of the ancient mythology."[46] Higgins theorized that all religions and all languages can be traced back to a single ancient source, and to create connections, he made many unfounded or blatantly false claims, such as these taken from his *Anacalypsis: An Attempt to Draw Aside The Veil of the Saitic Isis*:

- The Hebrew book of Genesis was a Buddhist text (p. 61).
- The gods and goddesses of Greece were all black (p. 138).
- The Tibetan word *lamh* means cross and is similar to the word lamb (p. 232).
- British Celts were originally a black nation of Buddhists, and Stonehenge was a Buddhist temple (p. 59).
- The Indian god Krishna was called Creechna in Ireland (p. 242).
- The language of the Saxons was almost pure Hebrew (p. 709).
- Every "Mohammedan" is also a Christian, but followers of Muhammed were also Buddhists, and Muhammed was the tenth avatar of the sacred Om (pp. 683–84).

44. Dupuis, *Origin*, 253, 255, 263.
45. Higgins, *Anacalypsis*, xiv.
46. Higgins, *Anacalypsis*, 562.

- The first Hebrew word in Genesis is *hokma* (p. 708). (No: it is *bereshit.*)
- The Jews became a nation of cannibals (p. 255).

Higgins also mistranslated many Hebrew words[47] and incorrectly stated that no extant gospel manuscripts predate the sixth century.[48]

Kersey Graves (1813–1883)

Kersey Graves regarded Christianity as entirely mythological. He wrote his *World's Sixteen Crucified Saviors* in an attempt to destroy "the blinding effect of this delusion," which has been "a serious obstacle to the progress both of the individual and of society."[49] In his opinion, the New Testament was written by Jews "possessing the strong proclivity to imitate and borrow,"[50] and he alleged that not even Christians believed that Jesus was a historical figure.[51]

Graves relied heavily on the work of Higgins. He regarded him as a "reliable and truthful writer"[52] and proudly admitted that he drew many of his important "facts" from Higgins's *Anacalypsis*.[53] Graves's central argument was that all pagan gods had once been historical men with known places of birth and death, and he offered this statement as evidence: "Mr. Higgins declares."[54]

Graves's work is full of errors. For example, he incorrectly claimed that the Jewish festival of Hanukkah celebrated the birthday of the pagan god Adonis,[55] and he seems to have been the first to publish the popular but false claim that a human Jesus was declared to be divine by

47. The following translation errors are found in Higgins's *Anacalypsis*: Bethel means "House of God," not "House of the Sun" (p. 71); Elisha means "my God is salvation," not "Lamb of God" (p. 199); *ram* means "high" or "exalted," not both "bull" and "ram" (p. 231); *sur* means "turn aside," not "sun" (p. 607) or "bull" (p. 671).

48. Higgins, *Anacalypsis*, 680.

49. Graves, *Crucified Saviors*, 5.

50. Graves, *Crucified Saviors*, 22–23.

51. Graves, *Crucified Saviors*, 100.

52. Graves, *Crucified Saviors*, 107.

53. Graves, *Crucified Saviors*, 11.

54. Graves, *Crucified Saviors*, 98.

55. Graves, *Crucified Saviors*, 68. This annual festival actually commemorates the purification and rededication of the Jerusalem temple that took place in the second century BC.

Emperor Constantine in the fourth century.[56] Some of his statements were decidedly eccentric: he claimed that some cultures had a scape-ox, scape-horse, scape-mouse, and scape-hen, like the Christian scape-God[57] and that "astronomers have recently discovered eighty-five millions of inhabited worlds."[58]

Graves's most blatantly false claim was that many pagan hero-gods were believed to have been crucified. In the conclusion to his book, he admitted that the mythologies do *not* depict these gods as being crucified but describe totally different deaths; he wrote: "Some readers, perhaps, will be surprised to observe that we have named so many crucified gods to whom some writers assign a different death. But we have followed, as we believe, the best authorities in doing so."[59] Unfortunately, Graves's preferred authority was merely Higgins's speculation, whose opinion was the only "evidence" he provided for claiming that Tammuz, Quirinius, Attis, Crite, Mithra, Bali, and Prometheus were all crucified.[60] Instead of being troubled by the complete lack of any crucifixion story in pagan mythology, Graves chose to regard this as evidence of a highly successful international conspiracy, building on the speculation of yet another writer: "Mr. Taylor informs us that some of the early disciples of the Christian faith demolished accessible monuments representing and memorializing the crucifixion of the ancient oriental sin-atoning Gods."[61] There is no foundation for any of Graves's crucifixion claims, and atheist writer Richard Carrier provides a thorough critique of his work on his website.[62]

Gerald Massey (1828–1907)

The spiritualist Gerald Massey was another admirer of Higgins. He believed that all events and characters in every religion and folk-tale were borrowed from Egyptian mythology, and therefore Jesus must have been a form of the Osiris-Horus myth. His *Ancient Egypt, the Light of the World* contains many false statements that he fabricated to support his theory:

56. Graves, *Crucified Saviors*, 216. We will explore this claim in chapter 2.2.
57. Graves, *Crucified Saviors*, 159.
58. Graves, *Crucified Saviors*, 131.
59. Graves, *Crucified Saviors*, 427.
60. Graves, *Crucified Saviors*, 121–27.
61. Graves, *Crucified Saviors*, 103.
62. See https://infidels.org/library/modern/richard_carrier/graves.html.

- Horus was born through the transformation of his father Osiris (p. 366). Except that Osiris did not transform into anything—he went to rule the realm of the dead.
- The British King Arthur was identical to Horus (p. 366). Massey provided no evidence for this innovative claim.
- The Buddha was no more historical than Christ (p. 431). But scholarship generally does accept that the Buddha existed.
- The biblical figures Jacob, Joseph, Moses, David, and Solomon were mythological gods (p. 524).
- The name Joseph means "God's son," which is a name of the Messiah (p. 508) Except that the Hebrew Yosef means "he increases."
- The ancient Mesha Stele records that the Israelites worshiped the pagan god Dodo (p. 524). But no such information appears in this inscription.[63]
- Horus reconstructed Osiris's dismembered body (p. 187). Except that the goddess Isis did this.
- Massey also made this bizarre claim: "The human race originated from the Mother-earth in Two Classes. They were the forest-folk and the Troglodites born of the Tree and the Rock" (p. 80), and these categories are apparently reflected in the New Testament reference to the sheep and the goats (p. 81).[64]

A review written soon after Massey's death was extremely critical of his work:

> Mr. Massey had in the course of a long life read much and noted much. Unluckily he had not read deeply enough. He never attempted to get his own knowledge, but depended on what others said. Hence in any case his book would be of no value except as a compilation. But, further, he had little idea of what is and what is not permissible in logical argument; very few of

63. A transcript of the Mesha Stele inscription can be read at https://en.wikipedia.org/wiki/Mesha_Stele.

64. Here is another sample of Massey's esoteric thinking: "Those who ascended from the netherworld were of the solar race who came into existence with the sun . . . They ascended from the under-world which had been hollowed out beneath the mount of earth for the passage of the sun . . . These, when born in Egypt, were the children of the sun-god Atum, who became the Hebrew Adam as the father of the human race" (*Ancient Egypt*, 629–30).

> his syllogisms are without a flaw; he had no perception of what is possible or impossible in respect of philological comparisons, and he was dominated by a fanatical belief with regard to the origin of Christianity which at once takes his book out of the realm of science.[65]

Review the Evidence

In the anti-religious spirit of Enlightenment and Rationalism, some authors of the eighteenth and nineteenth centuries claimed that Jesus was not a historical figure but a typical sun-god. However, their speculative writings contain many false statements that are not found in standard mythology texts, and modern scholarship does not recognize their works. In particular, all of their claims about crucified pagan gods were false: the second-century Christian Justin Martyr remarked that although some polytheistic cults were copying Christian rites, in no pagan tradition "did they imitate the being crucified; for it was not understood by them."[66]

Unfortunately, the unfounded speculations by these outdated writers continue to be presented as well-established facts by recent authors such as Alvin Kuhn,[67] Dorothy Murdock,[68] and Tom Harpur.[69] As a result, a statement that is said to be supported by, for example, Kuhn, Murdock, Graves, and Higgins, can usually be traced to a spurious claim by Higgins that never had any foundation. Atheist scholar Bart Ehrman criticizes Timothy Freke and Peter Gandy for repeating these false statements in their *Jesus Mysteries: Was the "Original Jesus" a Pagan God?* Ehrman makes this comment about their Jesus-myth claims:

> They have not even cited the available evidence, and for good reason. No such evidence exists . . . They "prove" it by quoting other writers from the nineteenth and twentieth centuries who

65. This extract is from the first page of a review of Massey's *Ancient Egypt* in *Nature* 77 (1908) 291–92.

66. Justin Martyr, *First Apology* 55. Justin mentioned some pagan traditions that were similar to Christianity, but this applied to second-century developments, long after the rise of Christianity.

67. Kuhn's *Lost Light* drew heavily from Gerald Massey's works, and it is interesting that his *Who Is This King of Glory?* opened with the dubious quote attributed to Pope Leo X.

68. See http://truthbeknown.com/.

69. See *The Pagan Christ: Recovering the Lost Light.*

> said so. But these writers too do not cite any historical evidence . . . The views they assert may have been believable more than a century ago, but no scholars hold to them today.[70]

Consider Your Verdict

The next chapter will explore specific parallels that are said to exist between Jesus and pagan gods. Most of these are drawn from claims made by Dupuis, Volney, Massey, Higgins, or Graves. Can these writers be trusted to provide reliable material that has been confirmed by objective evidence?

- o Yes
- o No

1.3 HOW VALID ARE THE PARALLELS BETWEEN JESUS AND PAGAN GODS?

You might have read this in Dan Brown's best-selling novel, *The Da Vinci Code*:

> Nothing in Christianity is original. The pre-Christian god Mithras—called the Son of God and the Light of the World—was born on December 25, died, was buried in a rock tomb, and then resurrected in three days. By the way, December 25 was also the birthday of Osiris, Adonis, and Dionysus. The newborn Krishna was presented with gold, frankincense, and myrrh.[71]

Unfortunately, although Brown's book is technically fiction, he has presented the work as being the result of scholarly research, and his incorrect claims have therefore come to be become widely accepted as historical facts. Many other books and websites also allege that the Jesus narrative was borrowed from pagan mythologies. But is this correct?

70. Ehrman, *Did Jesus Exist?* 26–27. The cover of the 2001 edition of Freke and Gandy's *Jesus Mysteries* showed a computer-enhanced image of an amulet depicting the crucified god Bacchus. But this (now missing) object has been dated to the third or fourth century AD (see Guthrie, *Orpheus*, 265), and there is still no evidence of crucifixion in pre-Christian mythology.

71. Brown, *Da Vinci Code*, 232.

What is the supporting evidence? It would take too long to investigate every supposed parallel between Jesus and ancient gods, but here is a sample to provide a general sense of their validity.

The Egyptian Osiris-Horus Myth

In the broad outline of the Osiris-Horus myth, Osiris becomes the husband of his sister Isis, but his brother Seth kills and dismembers him. Isis gathers Osiris's body parts together, and he is temporarily revived so that Isis can conceive Horus. Horus then becomes the king of the living, and Osiris rules the realm of the dead. The parallels that are supposed to exist between Jesus and Osiris or Horus are not found in the mythology: they are largely copied from Gerald Massey's incorrect claims, such as these from his *Ancient Egypt*:

- Claim: Horus was called the Krst or Messu, which is the Egyptian origin of the terms Messiah and Christ (pp. 215, 217–18). However, the Egyptian word *krst* meant burial and was not a name for Horus; Messiah is from the Hebrew *mashiach* (anointed one), which is *christos* in Greek.
- Claim: The god Anup was a baptizer like John (p. 218), and he baptized Horus (p. 215). Except that Anup was a funerary god, and there is no Egyptian tradition of gods being baptized.
- Claim: Osiris was "transubstantiated" (p. 225) and became "Horus of the resurrection" (p. 228). These Christian terms cannot be applied to any event in the mythology.
- Claim: The Book of Revelation depicts Jesus having many breasts, like Osiris (p. 237). This is incorrect—in Revelation 1:13 there is only a cloth wrapped around the figure's chest.
- More claims: Horus was born of a virgin, not begotten (p. 215); was thirty years old in his second advent (p. 509); turned water into wine, offered the bread of life, and rose at Easter (p. 229); was the logos and paraclete (p. 231) and rent the veil of the tabernacle (p. 225).

None of these "facts" are found in any text on Egyptian mythology. In *Natural Genesis*, Massey made the additional claims that Horus was called the Lamb of God, the Truth, and the Life (p. 404), was born on December 25 (p. 402), and had a father called Seb, which corresponds to

Joseph (p. 409). However, Horus had none of these titles, Seb was Seth's father, not Horus's, and Horus had no birthday in the mythology.

The popular claim that Horus was crucified and resurrected after three days is also a spurious invention.[72] And although Osiris was linked to natural cycles of renewal, he was never physically resurrected.[73] There are no specific parallels between the Osiris-Horus mythology and events in the Gospels.

The Mystery Cult of Mithra

The Roman cult of Mithraism only arose in the first century AD, and historians are uncertain about its connections with the older Indo-Persian god Mitra.[74] In the eighteenth century, Dupuis started the ball rolling with his claim that Christianity had originated within Mithraism,[75] and this theme has since gathered additional false speculations such as these:

- Claim: The child Mithra was born to a virgin. However, the Roman Mithra is always depicted emerging from rock as a fully grown adult. The Iranian Mitra has no clear birth story, and historian Franz Cumont commented that "he was said to have sprung from the incestuous intercourse of Ahura-Mazda with his own mother, and again to have been the offspring of a common mortal."[76] Some propose that Mitra's mother was the virgin Anahita, but she was

72. The closest description to Horus being "resurrected" is that, according to Egyptologist Wallis Budge, the Metternich Stella describes Horus being brought back to life after being stung by a scorpion (*Legends of the Gods*, 45). However, in modern translations, Horus is merely revived from unconsciousness. See *Ancient Egypt and Archaeology*, http://www.ancient-egypt.co.uk/metropolitan/pages/cippus,%20metropolitan%20museum.htm.

73. James Allen, a translator of the Egyptian Pyramid Texts, writes, "Osiris himself was envisioned as a mummy lying in the depths of the netherworld, the region through which the sun was thought to pass at night. In the middle of the night the Sun merged with Osiris's body; through this union, the Sun received the power of new life while Osiris was reborn in the Sun" (*Egyptian Pyramid Texts*, 8).

74. In a recent article, scholar of religions Aleš Chalupa concluded, "The hypothesis which places the proposed formative period of the Roman cult of Mithras in the years 75–125 CE can be considered confirmed" (*Roman Cult of Mithras*, 89).

75. Dupuis, *Origin*, 248.

76. Cumont, *Mysteries of Mithras*, 16.

a goddess of fertility, and although she was often associated with Mitra, she was not identified as his mother.[77]

- Claim: Mithra's followers were branded with the sign of the cross. However, "there is no evidence for branding or tattooing, nor for crosses or X-marks applied to the bodies of the initiates."[78] The second-century Christian Tertullian (ca. 155–ca. 240) did recall that Mithraic soldiers received some mark on the forehead, but this remark has a late dating and does not mention a symbol.[79]
- Claim: Mithra was "slain to make atonement for, and to take away, the sins of the world." This was Higgins's invention,[80] but Mithra *does not die at all* in the mythology. Historian Manfred Clauss also warns that regarding the beliefs of Mithraism, "we possess virtually no theological statements either by Mithraists themselves or by other writers."[81]
- Claim: Mithra was crucified. This is definitely not the case, despite Graves's confident assertion that "according to Mr. Higgins, he was 'slain upon the cross.'"[82]

The next four popular claims refer to evidence that appeared long after the rise of Christianity.

Claim 1: Mithra provided salvation through his sacrificial death, as is proven by a Mithraic inscription on the wall of the Santa Prisca Mithraeum in Rome, which translates: "you have saved us . . . shedding of the eternal blood." However, Mithra did not experience any death. And even more importantly, mythicists who circulate this quote fail to mention that this inscription is dated to *two hundred years after the time of Jesus*, so it does not provide evidence of Mithraic influence on Christian doctrines but rather the reverse.

Claim 2: Mithra said, "He who will not eat of my body and drink of my blood, so that he will be made one with me and I with him, the same

77. See *The Circle of Ancient Iranian Studies* at http://www.cais-soas.com/CAIS/Religions/iranian/anahita.htm.

78. Beskow, "Branding in the Mysteries of Mithra," 499.

79. Tertullian, *Prescription against Heretics* 40.

80. Higgins, *Anacalypsis*, 707.

81. Clauss, *Roman Cult of Mithras*, xxi.

82. Graves, *Crucified Saviors*, 123. Dupuis also incorrectly claimed that Mithra was crucified (*Origin*, 246).

shall not know salvation." The historian Maarten Vermaseren provided this intriguing quote,[83] which is often claimed to be the source for Jesus's teaching in John 6:54. However, these words (which were actually associated with Zoroaster, not Mithra) are found in a *medieval* Christian text about supposed pagan practices of the time. There is no evidence that this statement was ever part of any pagan ritual that predated Christianity.

Claim 3: Mithraic priests said to his followers, "Be of good cheer, sacred band of Initiates, your God has risen from the dead; his pains and his sufferings shall be your salvation." Dupuis associated this quote with Mithraism,[84] but we will soon see that it had no relation to Mithra and was, in any case, from a text of the fourth century AD.

Claim 4: Dupuis and Massey both alleged that Mithra was born on December 25,[85] but this is not supported by evidence. According to historian Steven Hijmans, pagan Saturnalia celebrations ran from December 17 to 23, and the traditional festival days of Sol were August 8, 9, and 28, and December 11, but there is no evidence of a pagan celebration on December 25 that predated Christian celebrations.[86] There is even no support for the claim that Emperor Aurelian established the feast of *Sol Invictus* (Unconquered Sun) on December 25, AD 274.[87] The Sol Invictus of the imperial cult was also different from Mithras Sol Invictus of the mystery cult.[88] The oldest written record of any religious celebration on December 25 is in the Christian Chronography of AD 354. In any case, the celebration of Jesus's birth was a late development and is not relevant to an investigation into the New Testament. (Interestingly, the Jewish Hanukkah was celebrated on the twenty-fifth day of Kislev, which fell in December or November.)

Other popular claims about Mithra include that he received gifts from the Magi, had twelve disciples, and was called the Way, Truth, and

83. Vermaseren, *Mithras*, 104. This quote is from the medieval manuscript *Ms. Syr.* 142 (Mingana collection).

84. Dupuis, *Origin*, 247.

85. Dupuis, *Origin*, 246; Massey, *Natural Genesis*, 402.

86. Hijmans, "*Sol Invictus*," 384–85. This is also the conclusion of Mithraic scholar Roger Beck ("Merkelbach's Mithras," 299 n. 12).

87. Inscription 580 ILS is usually cited as evidence that Aurelian established a feast day on December 25. However, the inscription does not mention any feast or a particular date. It translates as follows: "To the Holy Unconquered Sun for welfare and security of the perpetual Emperor Caesar Lucius Domitius Aurelian the Pius Auspicious Augustus Pontifex Maximus, earned title of consul 6 [times] 3 [times] proconsul."

88. See Mastrocinque, *Mysteries of Mithras*, 71.

Light, but these are not found in standard mythology texts. Even the vociferous second-century critic Celsus did not suggest that there was any connection between Mithraism and Christianity. Far from being similar to Christianity, Mithraism differed in fundamental ways, such as exclusively male membership, ritual handshakes, and a hierarchy of seven levels that involved wearing animal headdresses and passing initiation ordeals. Historian Manfred Clauss makes this clear statement about Roman Mithraism:

> The mysteries cannot be shown to have developed from Persian religious ideas, nor does it make sense to interpret them as a forerunner of Christianity.[89]

The Cult of Attis and Cybele

In the general outline of this myth, the jealous goddess Cybele appears at the wedding of the beautiful young Attis and drives him insane so that he emasculates himself. He then bleeds to death under a pine tree, and his spirit enters the tree. (In some versions, he is killed by a boar.) But contrary to popular claims, Attis did not have a birthday in December, did not die to save humanity, and was not crucified or resurrected. Only in the second century AD did the myth expand to have Zeus preserve Attis's body from corruption,[90] but even then, he was not revived and certainly not resurrected. Classical historian Jan Bremmer makes this comment:

> In our oldest testimonies, there seems to be no interest in his body . . . Attis's "resurrection" is not mentioned before the third century and seems closely connected with the rise of Christianity.[91]

Historian Guilia Gasparro agrees that "we cannot talk of the youth's return to life or 'resurrection' . . . rather what we would be entitled to call a subsistence 'in death.'"[92]

The Attis cult did have a festival in March (involving blood-letting and castration), but these dates were not relevant to early Christianity when Easter was still linked to the Jewish Passover. The following two claims again illustrate the importance of chronology.

89. Clauss, *Roman Cult of Mithras*, 7.

90. See Pausanias, *Description of Greece* 7.19.

91. Bremmer, "Attis," 550.

92. Gasparro, *Soteriology*, 42.

Claim 1: In the early nineteen hundreds, German historian Arthur Drews (pronounced "Drefs") alleged that the Christian concepts of baptism and salvation through blood were based on the Cybele-Attis *taurobolium* ritual, in which the blood of a slaughtered bull fell onto a person in the pit below. According to Drews, these cult members "obtained the forgiveness of their sins and were 'born again.'"[93] However, modern scholars assert that the taurobolium was originally a traditional animal sacrifice that only developed into the blood bath practice in the third and fourth centuries *in response* to the influence of Christianity.[94] Christian baptism is a natural development from Jewish rituals of purification and conversion rather than polytheistic practices.

Claim 2: Attis must have been a risen savior-figure because his priests said, "Be of good cheer, you of the mystery. Your god is saved; for us also there shall be salvation from ills." This is the quote that Dupuis seems to have paraphrased and incorrectly applied to Mithra, but it is found in a fourth-century work by the Christian Firmicus Maternus who was describing pagan practices long after the rise of Christianity.[95] In the same century, the philosopher Sallustius also described a ritual of rebirth at the end of the Attic celebrations,[96] which is often mentioned on websites but again referred to late developments. Gasparro's extensive study did not find evidence that early followers of Attis expected any form of new life: "The theory of a spiritual 'rebirth' achieved in the esoteric ritual practice by way of identification with an Attis 'resurrected' in his turn *has been rejected*."[97]

93. Drews, *Christ Myth*, 264. It is interesting to note that despite Josephus's account of the teachings and death of John the Baptist (*Ant.* 18.5.2), Drews insisted that John was a purely mythological figure (*Christ Myth*, 121).

94. According to Gasparro, rituals of personal renewal "reflect an extreme point in the evolution of the cult of Cybele . . . [manifested] in a lucid and lively effort to resist the ever more powerful advances of Christianity. The rite of the taurobolium was a major expression of this role" (*Soteriology*, 106). See also Duthoy, *Taurobolium*, 27. The claim that the taurobolium was a Mithraic ritual is incorrect.

95. See Willoughby, *Pagan Regeneration* 5.3.

96. Sallastius, *On the Gods and the World* 4.

97. Gasparro, *Soteriology*, 82 (emphasis added).

Other False Claims

Dionysus/Bacchus

The wine-god Dionysus was not born on December 25, as was incorrectly claimed by Graves,[98] was not laid in a manger as a child, did not turn water into wine at a wedding, as claimed by Dupuis,[99] and was certainly not crucified. It is often claimed that his followers symbolically consumed him in the form of a bull, which provided the basis for Jesus's teaching about eating his flesh. However, this has been questioned because "there is no sign that the initiated at Eleusis believed they were partaking through food of the divine substance of their divinity."[100] In an article in the *Oxford Classical Dictionary*, Heinrich argues that although poetry and painting depicted the mythical maenads (followers of Dionysus) eating raw flesh, this does not seem to have been an actual ritual, and the suggestion that they were sacramentally consuming Dionysus "has to be abandoned."[101]

Hercules/Heracles

The hero-god Hercules rode across the sea on a sacred bull but did not walk on water—the claim that he was probably able to do this is found in Emperor Julian's *Orations* 7.219 of the fourth century AD. Hercules

98. Graves, *Crucified Saviors*, 68.

99. Dupuis, *Origins*, 25. The following tenuously related facts are often offered as support for this claim. In Sophocles's ancient play, wine was said to have flowed from a rock at Bacchus's wedding without him doing anything (*Oedipus* § 487). According to Diodorus Siculus, a city claimed that Bacchus was their god because one of their fountains regularly ran with wine (*Library of History* 3.66.3). Pliny's *Natural History* 2.103 reported that a fountain in a temple of Bacchus annually ran with water that tasted like wine. In the second century AD, Pausanias skeptically reported that priests of Bacchus in the city of Elis would place empty pots in a locked building, and the next day these were found to be miraculously full of wine (*Description of Greece* 6.26). It has been claimed that Ovid described Bacchus as being able to transform anything into wine, but this is not correct—in Ovid's play, the god merely stated that everything his daughters touched turned into corn or wine (*Metamorphoses* 13.650). These stories do not seem to provide the basis for the gospel narrative of Jesus's work at the wedding in Cana.

100. Sheldon, *Mystery Religions*, 120.

101. Heinrich, "Dionysos," 480.

was not crucified or resurrected—his body was burnt on a pyre.[102] His last words, "It is completed" (echoing Jesus's dying words, "It is done") are found in the play *Hercules Oetaeus*, which was written in the late first century AD at the earliest.

Krishna

Kersey Graves invented many parallels between Jesus and the Indian god Krishna that continue to be repeated but are complete fabrications: wise men did not attend Krishna's birth; his mother was not a virgin (he was the eighth child); he was not called Jeseus; he was not born on December 25; his father was not a carpenter; he did not say, "I am the Resurrection," and he did not have a "Last Supper."[103] Godfrey Higgins insisted that "Cristna was put to death by being crucified,"[104] but Hindu tradition is clear that Krishna left this world after an arrow pierced his ankle (see Mahabharata 16.4). Higgins admitted that no other text mentions Krishna's crucifixion, but he offered this interesting and strangely confident response: "How very extraordinary that all of the writers in these works should have been ignorant of so striking a fact!"[105] Higgins was clearly determined to believe what suited him.

Review the Evidence

Some pagan gods were said to disappear and reappear, often linked to the seasonal cycles of nature. In *The Golden Bough* of 1890, James Frazer generalized these legends into an overarching motif of dying-rising gods. But many historians have since judged this to be inadequate for the variety of details found in different mythological traditions.[106] For example, concerning Attis as a dying-rising god, historian Jan Bremmer concludes that "the steady increase in new material from the Ancient Near East has refuted this traditional interpretation."[107] Gasparro agrees: "The vicissitudes of Attis, as we have seen, end once and for all in death . . . Attis does not 'return'

102. See Diodorus Siculus, *Library of History* 4.38.4–5.

103. For these false claims, see Graves, *Crucified Saviors*, 100, 109, 256, 259, 261.

104. Higgins, *Anacalypsis*, 131.

105. Higgins, *Anacalypsis*, 159.

106. This is the opinion of, for example, historian Gasparro (*Soteriology*, xvii).

107. Bremmer, "Attis," 534.

periodically."[108] There is little scholarly support for the claim that Jesus's death and resurrection was a form of this broad nature-god motif.

Over time, Christianity did adopt pagan practices such as painting eggs and decorating pine trees. But Jesus-mythicists go further in claiming that the Gospels drew their narratives from ancient mythologies and not from events in the life of a historical man. However, there are fundamental flaws in the supposed parallels between Jesus and pagan gods:

- Standard mythology texts do not contain these details.
- The parallels are largely drawn from outdated, discredited works that never provided supporting evidence.
- In particular, *all* of the crucifixion claims are inventions with no basis in the mythologies.
- Any valid commonalities with Christianity are found in texts written long after its rise, and there is substantial evidence of influence *from* Christianity on paganism rather than in the other direction. In particular, professor of ancient history Glen Bowersock comments on the "absorption of Christian elements in late antique paganism, especially soteriological elements" related to salvation.[109]

Professor of Jewish studies Susannah Heschel remarks that many writers have tried to claim "that Jesus's religious teachings originated in Hellenism, Buddhism, Hinduism, or Iranian culture—anything but Judaism . . . [However,] the bases of such arguments were weak if not non-existent, sources were read tendentiously or taken out of context, and solid data was replaced by fantasy."[110] In his extensive 2017 review of relevant ancient sources, professor of Roman history Attilio Mastrocinque made the adamant statement that "we should get rid of the preconceived idea that the mysteries of Mithra were a sort of pagan Christianity."[111] Scholars of mythology therefore reject the Jesus-as-sun-god theory. Unfortunately, their research is ignored by the writers of speculative websites and best-selling Jesus-myth books.

108. Gasparro, *Soteriology*, 125.

109. Bowersock, *Hellenism*, 44.

110. Heschel, *Aryan Jesus*, 27.

111. Mastrocinque, *Mysteries of Mithras*, 92.

Consider Your Verdict

In the eighteenth century, Dupuis wrote, "The author of the legend of Christ had made a collection of various marvellous fictions, which were current among the worshippers of the Sun under different names."[112] Many writers continue to allege that the Gospels copied the details of Jesus's life from ancient mythologies. How strong is the evidence to support this claim?

- o Very strong
- o Fairly strong
- o Weak

CONCLUSION 1
JESUS OF NAZARETH—HISTORY OR MYTH?

Human belief systems do not exist in self-contained isolation, so it is not surprising if they share common archetypal imagery and practices such as sacramental meals and purification rituals. But Jewish scholar Jacob Neusner warns that apparently common features in different religious practices are often superficial and not significant: "We identify a given component we deem common to both, e.g., rites of initiation, beliefs about God, practices of rite and cult . . . [But] commonly, extra-contextual comparison produces traits in common that prove illusory upon closer inspection."[113] Historian Suzanne Marchand also points out that there is very little evidence about what the ancient mystery cults taught and when these beliefs arose.[114] As a result, it is difficult to identify the direction of influence between these practices and Christianity. In general, the manuscript evidence for Jesus's historicity seems to be more substantial than the evidence that the gospel narratives were copied from pagan mythologies.

Two atheist professors of literature also argue that the New Testament is not typical of the genre of mythology. Holly Ordway comments, "I'd been steeped in folklore, fantasy, legend, and myth ever since I was a child, and I had studied these literary genres as an adult; I knew their

112. Dupuis, *Origin*, 259.

113. Neusner, "Contexts of Comparison," 67.

114. Marchand, *German Orientalism*, 290.

cadences, their flavor, their rhythm. None of these stylistic fingerprints appeared in the New Testament books that I was reading."[115] C. S. Lewis had a similar response: "I have been reading poems, romances, vision-literature, legends, myths all my life. I know what they are like. I know that not one of them is like this."[116] He admitted that he "was all agog for the Death and Rebirth pattern and anxious to meet a corn-king, [but] was chilled and puzzled by the almost total absence of such ideas in the Christian documents."[117] Both Lewis and Ordway converted to Christianity. Atheist Bart Ehrman offers this opinion:

> There is simply no way to convince conspiracy theorists that the evidence for their position is too thin to be convincing and that the evidence for a traditional view is thoroughly persuasive . . . [But] Jesus did exist, as virtually every scholar of antiquity, of bible studies, of classics, and of Christian origins in this country, and, in fact, in the Western world, agrees.[118]

115. Ordway, *Not God's Type*, 117.
116. Lewis, *Miracles*, 154.
117. Lewis, *Miracles*, 180.
118. Ehrman, *Did Jesus Exist?* 5.

Investigation 2

Was a Human Jesus Falsely Deified?

If Jesus did exist, could he have become a legendary figure over time? Does his narrative lie somewhere between myth and history? Greco-Roman culture deified many heroes, so perhaps Jesus's life was overlaid with fictions that exaggerated him from a human wisdom teacher to a deity. But who would have done this? His first Jewish disciples? An over-enthusiastic Apostle Paul? The Greco-Roman churches? Did the gospel writers borrow events from the lives of deified men? This investigation will explore these possibilities.

2.1 WAS THE JESUS NARRATIVE COPIED FROM DEIFIED MEN IN HISTORY?

It is often claimed that many men in history were believed to perform miracles and raise the dead and were worshiped after rising from death. Could the details of Jesus's life have been borrowed from these pre-Christian traditions? The lives of the following six men in particular are often alleged to have provided the basis for events in the gospel narratives. Let's consider the evidence.

Aristeas of Proconnesus (ca. Seventh Century BC)

The historian Herodotus (ca. 484–ca. 425 BC) recorded a story about an epic poet named Aristeas who dropped dead inside a shop but was nowhere to be found when the shop was reopened. He then reappeared seven years later and again after three hundred and forty years, when he claimed to have been visiting the god Apollo in the form of a crow.[1] This was one of many strange tales in Herodotus's *Histories*, which included water that wood could not float on (Book 3), Cambyses killing the cow-god Apis (Book 3), Hercules leaving a footprint in a rock (Book 4), a creature who was half woman half serpent (Book 4), and a mare that gave birth to a hare (Book 7). Pliny the Elder (AD 23–79) regarded some stories about Aristeas as mere fables,[2] and the respected historian Strabo (63 BC–AD 24) only noted that some people thought Aristeas might have been a teacher of Homer.[3]

Aristeas seems to have been a semi-legendary miracle worker, but his return from death is questionable, and his narratives provide no specific details in common with the Gospels.

Asclepius

Claims about this healer are drawn from traditions related to three figures:

- Asclepius in literature—Homer wrote the *Iliad* in the eighth century BC. In this epic tale about the Trojan War, one of Homer's characters was a physician called Asclepius who, along with his two sons, treated wounded soldiers.
- The god Asclepius—A cult of this god developed around the sixth century BC. In the mythology, the jealous god Apollo had the mortal woman Coronis killed, but he rescued their baby Asclepius from her womb. A centaur raised the child, taught him the art of healing, and gave him a magic potion from the blood of the Gorgon Medusa that could revive the dead.[4]
- A historical physician—Asclepiades of Prusa (ca. 124–40 BC) was a real doctor. Some writers claim that he was known to have resurrected a dead man, but this is not correct. Three authors of antiquity recorded that this skilled doctor simply stopped a funeral procession when he realized that the man being carried to his burial was

1. Herodotus, *Histories* 4.14–15.
2. Pliny, *Natural History* 7.52.
3. Strabo, *Geography* 14.1.18.
4. See Pindar, *Pythia* 3; Diodorus Siculus, *Library of History* 4.71.1–3.

not dead.[5] There was nothing miraculous about this physician who died in old age when he fell down the stairs.[6]

The identities of the first two Asclepius figures seem to have become confused over time, with uncertainty about whether the god was the doctor in Homer's epic, or if Homer's doctor came to be regarded as a god. For example, in the first century BC, Diodorus Siculus wrote that the semi-divine son of Apollo was also the healing doctor in Homer's *Iliad*.[7] But in the first century AD, the physician Celsus noted about Homer's doctor that "the superstition of those times gave him a place among the gods . . . It came at last to be doubted whether he was ever a mortal."[8] In the second century AD, Pausanias claimed that "Asclepius was considered a god from the first, and did not receive the title only in the course of time."[9]

An extensive healing cult developed around the merged hero-god figure of Asclepius. However, contrary to popular suggestion, there is no evidence whatsoever of a historical man called Asclepius who could bring the dead back to life and rose after his death to be worshiped.

Pythagoras (ca. 570–ca. 495 BC)

Godfrey Higgins noticed that there were substantial differences between the Gospels and the life of Krishna. In an attempt to explain these discrepancies, he alleged that early Christians had combined the life of Krishna with traditions about Pythagoras to form the gospel narratives.[10] To support his theory, Higgins incorrectly claimed that Pythagoras was

5. The physician Cornelius Celsus (25 BC–AD 50) wrote that Asclepiades, "when he met a funeral, cried out that the person whom they were about to bury was alive" (*Of Medicine* 2.6.13, translated by James Greive). The same story is also recorded in Pliny, *Natural History* 7.37, 26.8 and Apuleius, *Florida* 19.

6. See Pliny, *Natural History* 7.37.

7. According to Diodorus, "The myths relate: Asclepius was the son of Apollo and Coronis . . . He healed many sick whose lives had been despaired of, and for this reason it was believed that he had brought back to life many who had died . . . To Asclepius, we are told further, sons were born, Machaon and Podaleirius, who also developed the healing art and accompanied Agamemnon in the expedition against Troy," (*Library of History* 4.71, translated by C. H. Oldfather).

8. Celsus, *Of Medicine*, Preface to Book 1.

9. Pausanias, *Description of Greece* 2.26.10, translated by W. H. S. Jones.

10. Higgins, *Anacalypsis*, 150.

similar to Jesus in that he was born in Syria and was a "Nazarite" with no children;[11] however, he was born on the Greek island of Samos, and he did have children.

Pythagoras was believed to have had special powers and came to be regarded as a form of divinity. According to Aristotle (384–322 BC), he predicted the future, was greeted by a river, was at two different places at one time, and had a golden thigh that proved his divinity.[12] Centuries later, Porphyry (AD ca. 234–ca. 305) wrote that Pythagoras could interpret dreams, was regarded as a divinity in Italy, and could remember his previous lives.[13] Jamblichus (AD ca. 245–ca. 325) wrote that Pythagoras persuaded an ox to stop eating beans, could hear the music of the planets, and was identified with Apollo or with spirits that inhabit the moon.[14]

However, despite being revered as a form of deity, Pythagoras was not believed to have raised dead people, he did not rise after death, and none of his narratives share specific details with the Gospels.

Zalmoxis (Before Fifth Century BC)

Zalmoxis was said to have been a freed slave of Pythagoras who hid underground for three years before reappearing, and the Getae came to regard him as a god.[15] However, the historian Herodotus was uncertain whether this man had ever existed.[16] A modern article in an encyclopedia of religion also concludes, "Whether he is a figure of legend or of history is moot."[17] Zalmoxis might have been a historical man who was considered to be divine even during his lifetime, but his narratives provide no events related to the Gospels.

11. Higgins, *Anacalypsis*, 150. Higgins also incorrectly claimed that Pythagoras was called Zalmoxis and was persecuted (*Anacalypsis*, 563, 151).

12. See Ross, *Works of Aristotle*, 134.

13. Porphyry, *Life of Pythagoras* 11, 20, 45.

14. Jamblichus, *Life of Pythagoras* 13, 15, 6.

15. See Herodotus, *History* 4.94–95; Plato, *Charmides* 156e; Strabo, *Geography* 7.3.5; Porphyry, *Life of Pythagoras* 14; Jamblichus, *Life of Pythagoras* 30.

16. Herodotus, *History* 4.96.

17. "Zalmoxis," *Encyclopedia of Religion*. https://www.encyclopedia.com/environment/encyclopedias-almanacs-transcripts-and-maps/zalmoxis.

Gautama Buddha (ca. Fifth Century BC)

Gautama Buddha is generally considered to have been a historical person. But Godfrey Higgins was incorrect when he claimed that Buddha means shepherd (it means "enlightened one") and that the Buddha was crucified.[18] Indian tradition consistently records that something the Buddha ate made him ill; he died from this complaint and was cremated. Other false claims have been made about the Buddha, but he was not a carpenter, was not transfigured on a mountain, was not (as Graves claimed) born on December 25,[19] and was not the son of a virgin—his mother had been married for many years (although he was miraculously born from her side).

He and his disciples certainly outperformed Jesus regarding miracles. For example, the Buddha was said to perform the Twin Miracle "by producing a mass of fire from the upper part of his body and a shower of water from the lower."[20] And, like the Buddha, an advanced monk "goes unimpeded through walls, ramparts, and mountains as if through space. He dives in and out of the earth as if it were water. He walks on water without sinking as if it were dry land. Sitting cross-legged he flies through the air like a winged bird. With his hand he touches and strokes even the sun and moon, so mighty and powerful."[21] So yes, the Buddha and his advanced disciples could apparently walk on water.

The dating of incidents in the extensive Buddhist material is again important. For example, a disciple was said to sink while walking on water until he meditated on the Buddha, and a cake provided for the Buddha and his disciples never came to an end—but both of these stories are in a later commentary to an early text, so the direction of influence with the Gospels is difficult to determine.[22] Regarding the supposed parallels between the Buddha and Jesus, an author on Buddhism wryly

18. Higgins, *Anacalypsis*, 158, 159. Graves also falsely claimed that "Sakia, an account states, was crucified by his enemies for the humble act of plucking a flower in a garden" (*Crucified Saviors*, 115).

19. Graves, *Crucified Saviors*, 69.

20. From Paṭisambhidā-magga 128. http://zugangzureinsicht.org/html/lib/authors/nanadassana/wisdom_en.html.

21. From Iddhipada-vibhanga Sutta. https://www.accesstoinsight.org/tipitaka/sn/sn51/sn51.020.than.html.

22. See Thomas, *Life of Buddha*, 241, 246.

commented that "in proportion to the investigator's direct knowledge of the Buddhist sources, the number seems to decrease."[23]

Jewish scholar Susannah Heschel argues that nineteenth-century scholars claimed to find parallels between Jesus and the Buddha in their attempt to create an Indo-Germanic nature for Jesus and to sever Christianity from its Jewish roots.[24] She remarks that academic refutation did not check the rise of popular beliefs: "The Buddhist Jesus was received skeptically by scholars of Indian Buddhism, but that did not prevent the link between Buddha and Jesus in the popular imagination. Speculation soon formed a chain of tradition."[25] And unfortunately, this speculative, unscholarly tradition continues to find widespread support.

Apollonius of Tyana (AD ca. 40–ca. 120)

Apollonius is supposed to have led a life that was most similar to Jesus. Here are the earliest references to this historical man:

- Moeragenes (first or second century AD) referred to him as a philosopher and magician.[26]
- The second-century Lucian of Samosata was not flattering. He described a certain prophet as being taught by a "charlatan . . . a native of Tyana, a disciple and fellow-countryman of the notorious Apollonius, and familiar with the whole stage business of his master's magic."[27]
- The historian Cassius Dio described Apollonius as "a thorough juggler and magician."[28]

Apollonius was believed to have unusual powers, and Emperor Caracalla (188–217) erected a shrine to him a century after his death. Caracalla's mother commissioned Philostratus (ca. 170–ca. 250) to write a biography defending Apollonius against accusations of using dark magic.[29]

23. Thomas, *Life of Buddha*, 248.

24. Heschel, *Aryan Jesus*, 39.

25. Heschel, *Aryan Jesus*, 40.

26. See Origen, *Against Celsus* 6.41.

27. Lucian, *False Prophet* 5, translated by Augusta M. Campbell Davidson.

28. Cassius Dio, *Roman History* 78.18, translated by Herbert Baldwin Foster.

29. See Philostratus, *Life* 1.2. Philostratus's *Life of Apollonius of Tyana*, translated by F. C. Conybeare, can be read at https://www.sacred-texts.com/cla/aot/laot/index.htm.

But it is difficult to separate truth from fiction in Philostratus's *Life of Apollonius of Tyana*, which contained fantastic details: Apollonius was said to understand the languages of all people and animals (1.19); he chased away a hobgoblin by insulting it (2.4); he encountered a dragon hunt (3.6); he saw two jars that contained all the rain and winds of India (3.14); he met people who wore the skins of large fish and had cattle that looked like fish (3.55); he spoke with the ghost of Achilles (4.16); he identified a woman as a vampire (4.25), and he met an Egyptian king who had been transformed into a lion (5.42). Apollonius was also supposed to have seen the statue of Colossus at Rhodes (5.21), although this collapsed in the third century BC. Philostratus was uncertain about how and where Apollonius died, as there were at least three different traditions (8.30), but he commented that "no one ventured to dispute that he was immortal . . . Neither have the Emperors denied to him the honors of which they themselves were held worthy" (8.31).

Apollonius was believed to have joined the gods after death, but only Philostratus's inventive third-century work contains any details that are similar to Jesus's life in the Gospels. According to Philostratus, Apollonius healed blindness, lameness, and a paralyzed hand (3.39); he raised a young girl from her funeral bier by whispering to her (4.45); he exorcised a demon (4.20); he told a disciple to meet him at the seashore, "alive, but as you will believe, risen from the dead" (7.41)—a promised event that is not mentioned again in Philostratus's book. These direct parallels with the Gospels postdate the rise of Christianity, so when Bart Ehrman describes Apollonius as "casting out demons, and raising the dead,"[30] he is drawing from a very late tradition that could not have influenced the Gospels. Philostratus also reported that a visitor to Tyana had a dream in which Apollonius assured him that the soul was immortal,[31] but apart from the late dating, it is a reach to suggest that this is like Jesus being physically resurrected and appearing to his disciples after his death. And Graves's spurious claim that Apollonius was "reported in history as having died the death of the cross"[32] has no support from any text at all.

Various legends portrayed Apollonius as the son of the Egyptian god Proteus or the Greek god Zeus.[33] But apart from being credited with a

30. Ehrman, *New Testament*, 17.

31. Philostratus, *Life* 8.31.

32. Graves, *Crucified Saviors*, 128.

33. Philostratus, *Life* 1.4, 1.6.

supernatural healing ability, and ignoring Philostratus's late claims, there is very little in Apollonius's life that resembles that of Jesus. Researcher of classical literature James Francis comments that "little is known about the historical Apollonius . . . the most that can be said further both with certainty and without fear of 'contamination' from posthumous representations is that Apollonius appears to have been a wandering ascetic/philosopher/wonderworker of a type common to the eastern part of the early empire."[34]

Review the Evidence

This investigation has raised four important points about historical men who are supposed to have been pre-Christian Jesus figures:

- Apart from having unusual powers and being considered to be divine in some way, these hero-figures have very little in common with Jesus.
- The historicity of some of these men is uncertain.
- Events from myth and history often become muddled, as when the demi-god Asclepius's power to raise the dead is attributed to the human Asclepiades.
- Details about Apollonius that do match the Gospels only appear long after the rise of Christianity.

Consider Your Verdict

In ancient times, men and gods were not kept in distinct categories—heroes were often believed to have unusual births and special powers and to join the gods after death. But apart from this broad outline, how similar was Jesus to ancient hero-gods? Some skeptics allege that the Gospels drew directly from the lives of pre-Christian historical men to create specific events in Jesus's life, such as exorcism, miraculous feeding of the multitudes, giving sight to the blind, raising the dead, transfiguration, crucifixion, and resurrection. How strong is the evidence for this claim?

34. Francis, "Truthful Fiction," 419.

- There is indisputable proof.
- The evidence is quite strong.
- The evidence is inadequate.

2.2 WAS JESUS DEIFIED BY FOLLOWERS OUTSIDE PALESTINE?

The lives of historical god-men do not seem to provide much of the material in the Gospels, but they do reflect the tendency in antiquity to elevate heroes to divine status after or even before their death, through a process known as *apotheosis*. Could Jesus have been deified through this polytheistic practice? Who would have done this? When could this have taken place?

At the beginning of the second century, the Roman governor Pliny wrote that some Christians admitted to having worshiped Jesus twenty years previously,[35] and a letter written by the Roman Church at the end of the first century described Jesus as the Son of God who had died an atoning death.[36] It is therefore way out of the ballpark to claim (as some people still insist on doing) that Emperor Constantine was the first to declare Jesus to be divine in AD 325 at the (in)famous Council of Nicaea.[37] As atheist scholar Bart Ehrman points out, "Everyone at the Council—and in fact, just about every Christian everywhere—already agreed that Jesus was divine, the Son of God. The question being debated was how to *understand* Jesus' divinity in light of the circumstance that he was also human."[38]

At the time, Bishop Arius and others were teaching that Jesus was a lesser divinity between God and humanity, which other Christians regarded as dangerously polytheistic. Constantine apparently regarded the issue as unimportant,[39] but to settle the intensely divisive controversy and restore peace, he convened a Council of a few hundred bishops. After

35. Around 111–113, Pliny wrote, "They had been Christians, but had ceased to be so, some three years, some many years, more than one of them as much as twenty years, before" (*Epistles* 10.96).

36. See First Clement 36, 49.

37. This is one of the false claims in Dan Brown's novel: "Until that moment in history, Jesus as viewed by his followers was a mortal prophet" (*Da Vinci Code*, 233.)

38. Ehrman, *Truth and Fiction*, 14 (original emphasis).

39. See Eusebius, *Life of Constantine* 2.71.

a month, almost all agreed that Jesus was eternal and co-equal with the Father, although Constantine seems to have preferred the Arian position: he exonerated Arius in 335 and was baptized by an Arian bishop when he was dying.

Constantine certainly did not deify Jesus, so who is the most likely suspect? In his 1913 work, *Kyrios Christos*, Wilhelm Bousset (1865–1920) claimed that Jesus's first followers only revered him as a human messiah, but this attitude changed when Jewish preachers took the message outside Palestine to Greco-Roman cities such as Antioch, Damascus, and Corinth.[40] According to Bousset, the hellenized form of Judaism in these cities had been substantially corrupted by pagan beliefs. This influence shaped the development of Hellenistic Christianity and led to Jesus being transformed through apotheosis from a human teacher to a divine cult-Lord. Bousset's theory was accepted for many years, but modern scholars have identified the following four major flaws in the hypothesis.

Flaws in Bousset's "Messiah-to-God" Theory

The Background of Jesus's Titles "Son of God" and "Son of Man"

Bousset assumed that Jesus's title "son of God" must have been a Hellenistic term associated with pagan apotheosis. However, this has since been found to be a messianic title in ancient Jewish literature, so it is not essentially Hellenistic or non-Jewish.[41] It is also used in the Dead Sea Scrolls of Qumran, which, as James Dunn points out, "should have killed stone dead the old view that 'son of God' was not a messianic title in Second Temple Judaism."[42]

Bousset's theory also relied heavily on his claim that hellenized Jews deified Jesus because they expected the arrival of a heavenly redeemer called the "Son of Man." But scholars have found no evidence that this was a recognized title in pre-Christian Judaism. F. F. Bruce writes, "There

40. This use of the term "Palestine" does not have modern political connotations. The term was possibly derived from "Philistia" (land of the Philistines), and historians in antiquity used it to describe the region bounded by the Jordan River in the east, the Mediterranean in the West, Lebanon in the north, and the Negev in the south. This area included Galilee, Judea, and Samaria.

41. See Hengel, *Hellenization*, 55; Klausner, *Messianic Idea*, 354.

42. Dunn, *Jesus Remembered*, 709 n. 15. "Second Temple" Judaism covers the period from the sixth century BC (when exiles returned from Babylon to rebuild the second Jerusalem temple) to the Roman destruction of Jerusalem in AD 70.

does not appear to have been any existing concept of 'the Son of man' which Jesus could have taken over and used either to identify himself or to denote a being distinct from himself. The expression as Jesus used it was evidently original to himself."[43]

Bousset therefore misinterpreted the implications of both titles, and the correct understanding significantly weakens his hypothesis.

The Uniqueness of the Jewish Worship of Jesus

No Jewish sect—even outside Palestine—ever worshipped a contemporary man alongside God. Why did only Jesus receive this remarkable reverence that was otherwise reserved for God? And if hellenized Judaism had adopted the pagan practice of apotheosis, why did they stop with Jesus and not deify more men, in line with the polytheistic cultures around them? The worship of only one man alongside God the Father was a unique phenomenon. Hellenic influence therefore does not explain the Jewish worship of Jesus.

The Difference between Pagan Apotheosis and the Worship of Jesus

Polytheistic Romans such as Tacitus and Pliny regarded the worship of the crucified Jesus as a harmful, extravagant superstition,[44] which suggests that belief in his resurrection and ascension to heaven was not the result of the well-known process of pagan apotheosis.

Cotter points out two fundamental differences between apotheosis and the worship of Jesus. First, Roman emperors only wielded authority during their lifetime, and after their death, this control passed to their successor. By contrast, Jesus's power over heaven and earth was said to have been attained through his death.[45] Second, commitment to Jesus

43. Bruce, "Son of Man Sayings," 60. The Qumran Scrolls only used the general phrases "sons of men" and "the sons of men," and according to Fitzmyer, "In none of the phases of the Aramaic language has one been able to show that *bar 'enais* was ever used in a titular sense, for some 'apocalyptic' Son of Man" ("Aramaic Language," 21.) See also Hurtado, "Critique of Bousset's Influence," 312; Segal, *Two Powers*, xi; Dunn, "Messianic Ideas," 369.

44. See Tacitus, *Annals* 15.44; Pliny, *Epistles* 10.96.

45. Cotter, "Greco-Roman Apotheosis," 150. After his resurrection, Jesus was said to have claimed, "All authority in heaven and on earth has been given to me" (Matt 28:18b).

required far more than superficial rituals of tribute: it involved "a personal and community righteousness . . . [and] protectiveness towards the weak and sinful."[46] Martin Hengel agrees that the veneration of Jesus far exceeded the respect offered to deified pagan heroes:

> How did it come about that in the short space of less than twenty years the crucified Galilean Jew, Jesus of Nazareth, was elevated by his followers to a dignity which left every possible form of pagan-polytheistic apotheosis far behind? Preexistence, Mediation of Creation, and the revelation of his identity with the One God: this exceeds the possibilities of deification in a polytheistic pantheon.[47]

Fletcher-Louis also observes that Jesus's followers did not describe him in the typical pagan way as a separate divinity next to God: instead, glory given to Jesus went *through* him *to* God, and creation was *from* the Father *through* the Son (Col 1:16; Heb 1:2; John 1:3). Hence, "the birth of Christianity was not marked by the worship of a new Mediterranean god, but by the belief that the one unique God—*Yhwh-Kyrios*—had climactically, at the end of Israel's history, appeared in fully human and a highly personal form."[48] It is therefore highly doubtful that Jesus's deity could have been the result of pagan elevation.

The Lack of Two Distinct Forms of Judaism

The most crippling flaw in Bousset's theory is that he assumed there was a fundamental difference between pure Palestinian Judaism and corrupt hellenized Judaism. However, an extensive study by Martin Hengel has since established that by Jesus's time, Greco-Roman thinking had already influenced Palestine's culture, with the result that "even Palestinian Judaism must be regarded as Hellenistic Judaism."[49] This is now the accepted paradigm, and this lack of a profound distinction between Judaism inside and outside Palestine has critically undermined Bousset's hypothesis about the late deification of Jesus.

The influence of Greco-Roman thinking in Palestine therefore does not support Bousset's theory. But it does raise another logical

46. Cotter, "Greco-Roman Apotheosis," 150.
47. Hengel, "Christological Titles," 443.
48. Fletcher-Louis, *Jesus Monotheism*, 22.
49. Hengel, *Judaism and Hellenism*, 252.

possibility—that Jesus's first disciples in Palestine elevated him to cult-god status under this Hellenistic influence. However, it seems unlikely that they would have adopted such a pagan tradition for the reasons given below.

First century Judaism—monotheistic and separatist, but complex

Judas seems to have been the only one of Jesus's chosen twelve who was not from Galilee, and archaeologists have found widespread evidence of Torah-observant Judaism in first-century Galilee.[50] Historians have also concluded that hellenization was generally a superficial influence, which is unlikely to have affected the monotheistic beliefs and practices of Jesus's first Jewish disciples.[51] Judaism continued to be strongly separatist: the first-century Roman Tacitus complained that Jews "sit apart at meals, they sleep apart, and though, as a nation, they are singularly prone to lust, they abstain from intercourse with foreign women . . . They therefore do not allow any images to stand in their cities, much less in their temples. This flattery is not paid to their kings, nor this honour to our Emperors."[52]

Judaism was well-known for refusing to worship other gods or human beings, and thousands of first-century Jews offered to die rather than allow Emperor Gaius's statue to be placed in the Jerusalem temple.[53] Even the highly hellenized Philo in Egypt called the deification of men "excessive folly" and "preposterous impiety."[54] He warned against cultic "initiations, and mysteries, and all such trickery and buffoonery,"[55] and he urged his fellow Jews to "not worship those who are our brothers by

50. Archaeologist Jonathan Reed has found widespread evidence of four Jewish "identity markers" in Galilee: the use of ossuaries (burial chests for bones), stone vessels used for ritual purity, *mikveh* immersion baths, and the absence of swine bones (*Archaeology and Galilean Jesus*, 52–53). Mark Chancey's archaeological work in Galilee also revealed "impressive amounts of evidence for Judaism and very meagre evidence for paganism" (*Myth of Gentile Galilee*, vii).

51. According to Bowersock, "There was no more than a superficial Hellenization in much of Asia Minor, the Near East, and Egypt" (*Hellenism*, 6). Archaeologist Warwick Ball also describes Hellenistic influence as the "gloss of a Macedonian and subsequently Roman veneer" (*Rome in the East*, 1).

52. Tacitus, *History* 5.5, translated by Church and Brodribb.

53. See Josephus, *Ant.* 18.8.2; Philo, *Embassy to Gaius* 31 §207–10.

54. Philo, *Embassy to Gaius* 25 §163.

55. Philo, *Special Laws* 1.59 § 319.

nature . . . and let not the polytheistical doctrine ever even touch the ears of any man who is accustomed to seek for the truth."[56]

As biblical scholar Larry Hurtado remarked, "There is clear indication that devout Jews of the Roman era were characteristically concerned about the uniqueness of their God and held strong scruples about reserving worship for this God alone."[57] Richard Bauckham agrees that "most Jews of this period were highly self-consciously monotheistic . . . They drew a line of distinction between the one God and all other reality."[58] It is therefore unlikely that Jesus's first disciples in Palestine would have elevated him to divine status under polytheistic influence. This raises a critically important question: why *did* these Jewish people find it acceptable to worship their teacher?

Some scholars have suggested that this unprecedented devotion and veneration by Jewish disciples might be partly explained by the way Judaism described God as acting through "divine agents"—God's Spirit brooded over the waters at creation, his Wisdom participated in creation, and his Word went out to act.[59] These personifications were not regarded as separated figures but belonged within the unique identity of God himself. Richard Bauckham therefore remarks that the complex Judaic monotheism at the time of Jesus was not a simple "unitariness" but allowed for distinctions within the divine identity.[60] As a result,

> High Christology was entirely possible within the understanding of Jewish monotheism we have outlined. Novel as it was, it did not require any repudiation of the monotheistic faith . . . The New Testament writers did not see their Jewish monotheistic

56. Philo, *Decalogue* 14 § 64.

57. Hurtado, *One God*, xii.

58. Bauckham, *Jesus*, 3.

59. God's personified Wisdom was described in this way: "I have been established from everlasting . . . When He marked out the foundations of the earth, then I was beside Him as a master craftsman" (Prov 8:23–30). God's Word was also personified: "Thine Almighty word leaped down from heaven out of thy royal throne, as a fierce man of war into the midst of a land of destruction" (Book of Wisdom 18:15 KJV).

60. Bauckham, *Jesus*, 17. Interestingly, Judaism's ancient monotheistic declaration, "The Lord our God, the Lord is one" (Deut 6:4b), did not describe the One God as YHWH *yachid* (numerically one) but as YHWH *echad*. The word *echad* indicates unity in multiplicity, as when evening and morning form one day (Gen 1:5), and a man and wife become one flesh (Gen 2:24).

> heritage as in any way an obstacle to the inclusion of Jesus in the divine identity.[61]

However, it is also important to note that these personified agents of God's activity were never expected to appear in physical human form on Earth. Therefore, while these traditions might have helped to make Jewish worship of Jesus *possible*, they do not explain *why* God's presence would have been directly associated with any contemporary man, let alone an executed, failed messiah.[62] The Jewish worship of Jesus therefore cannot easily be traced to either pagan apotheosis or Judaic beliefs.

A Sobering Context

Before leaving this investigation into the earliest worship of Jesus, it is important to note that Bousset's messiah-to-God hypothesis was not developed in the rarefied air of disinterested academia but in a strongly anti-Semitic German context:

- In the late nineteenth century, German theologian Paul de Lagarde (1827–1891) of the University of Göttingen alleged that Jesus's disciples had misrepresented him as a Jewish messiah, and he called for the purging of Jewish influence from Christianity.[63]
- In 1902 the historian Friedrich Delitzsch (1850–922) gave a public lecture that was highly praised by Kaiser Wilhelm, in which he claimed that Jesus was partly Aryan and that Judaism was a pagan religion that should be expunged from German Bibles.[64]
- German theologian William Wrede (1859–1906) argued that Jesus's first Jewish disciples had only regarded him as a human teacher. James Charlesworth comments that Wrede's work is "sadly anti-Semitic . . . [and] we confront in these words the perennial attempt to remove Jesus and his followers from their Jewishness and from Judaism."[65]

61. Bauckham, *Jesus*, 19. See also Wright, "Jesus and the Identity," 42–56.

62. See Hurtado, *One God*, xvii.

63. See Head, "Nazi Quest for an Aryan Jesus," 63.

64. Delitzsch's 1902 lecture, "Babylon and the Bible," was published in 1921 as *The Great Deception.*

65. Charlesworth, "Messianology to Christology," 34.

- In 1937 Bishop Weidemann of Bremen produced an amended version of John's Gospel for Germans, which excluded all references to Moses, prophets, Jewish history, and Palestinian geography.[66]

As a leading figure of the "history of religions school" at the University of Göttingen, Wilhelm Bousset continued this trend of distancing Jesus from his Jewish background. He urged rational Germans to reject miracles, Jesus's divinity, and the Jewish concept of atonement for sin.[67] Theologian Anders Gerdmar points out that Bousset's writings were clearly prejudiced against Jews and Judaism, which is why he denied continuity between Christianity inside and outside Palestine, between Christianity and Judaism, and between Jesus and his Jewish context.[68] Historian Suzanne Marchand agrees that Bousset's theory of a paganized Hellenistic Judaism was motivated by the desire to separate Christianity from its Jewish roots,[69] and Susannah Heschel concludes that through such processes, "Jesus was transformed from a Jew prefigured by the Old Testament into an antisemite and proto-Nazi."[70]

Many German theologians opposed these and other anti-Semitic developments, which caused a deep rift in the German Protestant Church.[71] But this provides an important context against which to judge the alleged discontinuity between hellenized Christianity and Jesus's original teachings. This discontinuity continues to be supported by some groups, such as the history of religions school, through Rudolf Bultmann (1884–1976) and others,[72] and the Jesus Seminar. Theologian Peter Head comments bluntly that these scholars have "in effect de-Judaized Jesus and are, in some measure, guilty by association with those approaches to Jesus in Nazi Germany which denied that Jesus was Jewish."[73]

66. See Head, "Nazi Quest for an Aryan Jesus," 80.

67. Bousset, *What is Religion?* 241, 279, 282, 285.

68. Gerdmar, *Theological Anti-Semitism*, 162, 185, 147.

69. Marchand, *German Orientalism*, esp. 252–91.

70. Heschel, *Aryan Jesus*, 27. See also Perrin, *Jesus the Temple*, 2.

71. Members of the opposing Protestant "Confessing Church" included Karl Barth (a Swiss theologian), Marga Meusel, Martin Niemöller, who was imprisoned from 1938 to 1945, and Dietrich Bonhoeffer, who was hanged by the Nazis in 1945.

72. Gerdmar notes that Bultmann "is pleased with Bousset's fundamental distinction between Palestinian and Gentile early Christianity, as well as the breaking up of the straight line from Jesus to Paul" (*Theological Anti-Semitism*, 379).

73. Head, "Nazi Quest for an Aryan Jesus," 60.

Review the Evidence

Wilhelm Bousset theorized that a human Jesus was elevated to divinity outside Palestine, through the influence of polytheistic practices. This hypothesis became highly influential, but it rested heavily on central assumptions that scholars have since refuted: in particular, Jesus's "Son of God" title was found in Judaic messianism, not only in paganism; Judaism did not anticipate the arrival of a savior-figure known as the "Son of Man"; there was no substantial difference between Judaism inside and outside Palestine. Bousset also placed great emphasis on the influence of Gentiles in the development of early Christianity outside Palestine. But this ignored the dominant role of Jewish Christian leadership in the mission to the Gentiles as well as the fact that Jesus's deity was proclaimed in Matthew's Gospel and the book of Revelation, both of which have a strongly Jewish background.[74] Bousset's hypothesis also raises unanswered questions. Why was only Jesus ever worshiped alongside God in the "paganized" Hellenistic churches? And why did this worship far exceed that of heroes elevated through apotheosis?

It is also worth noting that the New Testament teaching about Jesus as both human and divine was not easily accepted in the Gentile world, and alternatives were developed, such as a purely human Jesus, a purely spiritual Jesus, or a human Jesus who was adopted to divine sonship. This does not suggest that his divine-human nature was the result of familiar pagan apotheosis. (Actually, no one finds it easy to comprehend a being that is both divine and human. The New Testament writers did not even try to explain how this was possible—they simply accepted that this was Jesus's nature.)

Larry Hurtado pointed out that "amid the diversity of earliest Christianity, belief in Jesus' divine status was amazingly common,"[75] and many scholars now reject Bousset's hypothesis about the later deification of Jesus. According to Fletcher-Louis, the new scholarly consensus is that Jesus was worshiped as divine very soon after his death[76] and that "NT Christology cannot be explained, as Bousset argued, with recourse to the

74. See Bauckham, *Jesus*, 130.

75. Hurtado, *Lord Jesus*, 650.

76. Fletcher-Louis, *Jesus Monotheism*, 4.

influence of a Greco-Roman model."[77] Even atheist Bart Ehrman agrees with this conclusion.[78] In the opinion of biblical scholar N. T. Wright,

> The earliest Christians very quickly came to the startling conclusion that they were under obligation, without ceasing to be Jewish monotheists, to worship Jesus. An older assumption, that this could only have happened insofar as they abandoned their Judaism and allowed pagan ideas to creep in surreptitiously, must now be abandoned. The evidence for the phenomenon I am describing is very early, very solid and quite unambiguous.[79]

Consider Your Verdict

According to Wilhelm Bousset (and others since), Jesus's first Jewish followers did not worship him but regarded him as merely human, and he was only deified later outside Palestine. How should this claim be classified?

- It is a well-founded theory with extensive supporting evidence.
- It is a sound hypothesis with some supporting evidence.
- It does not fit the evidence.

2.3 WAS CHRISTIANITY THE CREATION OF THE APOSTLE PAUL?

The German history of religions school proposed the "Paulism" theory, which claims that the Apostle Paul, who had not known the human Jesus, was largely responsible for elevating him to divine status. In this way, he is supposed to have contributed to the hellenization of the Jesus-message outside Palestine, creating the basis of the worship of Jesus.

We know that Paul was born outside Palestine in Tarsus (in present-day Turkey), but he described himself as a highly educated and motivated Pharisee: "I was advancing in Judaism beyond many of my own

77. Fletcher-Louis, *Jesus Monotheism*, 8.

78. Ehrman, *How Jesus Became God*, 3. Ehrman claims that Jesus's first Jewish followers in Palestine elevated him to divinity because even Judaism accepted that humans could become divine. See Ehrman, *How Jesus Became God*, 5. However, many scholars disagree with this suggestion, which we will explore in chapter 4.4.

79. Wright, *Challenge*, 106. See also Bauckham, *Jesus*, 130.

age among my people and was extremely zealous for the traditions of my fathers" (Gal 1:14). Paul's letters do not explain why he and others were keenly persecuting Jesus's followers, but this was probably sparked by their outrageous claim that the crucified Jesus had risen and was the promised Messiah, as well as by their challenge to Mosaic law, the temple, and religious leaders.[80]

Only a few years after Jesus's death, Paul set out to bring some of these apostate Jews back from Damascus to be disciplined by the Jerusalem Sanhedrin—a mission that seems to have had legal precedent.[81] We are told that on the way, a bright light blinded him and his companions, and he heard a voice saying, "Saul, Saul, why do you persecute me?" (Acts 9:4).[82] Paul interpreted this as an encounter with the risen Jesus, which convinced him that Jesus's disciples must have been correct about the resurrection after all. He would later write, "The gospel I preached is not of human origin. I did not receive it from any man, nor was I taught it; rather, I received it by revelation from Jesus Christ" (Gal 1:11–12).

Paul's change of opinion is as dramatic as Adolf Hitler deciding to wear a yarmulke and attend a synagogue! We cannot know exactly what he experienced on the Damascus road—suggestions include a weather phenomenon, an epileptic fit, a psychological crisis, or an authentic revelation. But the crucial question is whether he then taught his own doctrine of Jesus's divinity, which distorted the initial belief that Jesus was merely a human messiah. It will be useful to explore this "Paulism" claim directly through Paul's own letters, which are widely acknowledged to have been written in the fifties and sixties, only a few decades after Jesus's death.[83] These letters provide useful information relating to two questions:

80. According to the book of Acts, Jewish leaders denounced Jesus's disciples for preaching about his resurrection (Acts 4:2), blaming them for his death and defying the order to not teach in his name (Acts 5:28), and blaspheming against Moses, God, the temple, and the law (Acts 6:11–14).

81. For example, around 140 BC a Roman consul ordered Hellenic cities to hand over Judean Jews to the Jerusalem high priest for punishment under Jewish law (1 Macc 15:15–21). Josephus also wrote that Herod Agrippa (r. AD 41–44) had instructed officials at Ephesus that "such as steal that sacred money of the Jews, and fly to a sanctuary, shall be taken thence and delivered to the Jews, by the same law that sacrilegious persons are taken thence" to Jerusalem (*Ant.* 16.6.4 §168).

82. As a Roman citizen (Acts 22:25), Paul would have had a Roman and a Hebrew name. There is no indication that he adopted a new name after his Damascus experience.

83. Scholars almost unanimously accept that Paul wrote First and Second Corinthians, Galatians, Romans, First Thessalonians, Philippians, and Philemon. Most

- Did Paul teach new doctrines, including Jesus's divinity?
- What was the source of his doctrines?

Question 1: Did Paul Teach New Doctrines?

To decide if Paul was the first to deify Jesus, it is important to consider what he taught about Jesus, how his beliefs compared to those in other New Testament texts, and whether Jesus's first followers knew about and disputed his teachings.

What Did Paul Teach about Jesus?

According to the Paulism argument, Paul had no interest in the historical Jesus and regarded him as a purely spiritual being. For example, Arthur Drews alleged that "the Jesus painted by Paul is not a man, but a purely divine personality, a heavenly spirit without flesh and blood."[84] However, Paul's letters do not support this claim: he explicitly wrote that Jesus was born as a descendant of David (Gal 4:4; Rom 1:3), ate and drank (1 Cor 11:23–25), had brothers (Gal 1:19), and physically died (1 Cor 2:2). However, Paul also depicted Jesus as far more than a human messiah: he taught that Jesus had preexisted in the form of God before he took on human likeness (Phil 2:6–7) and that in him, "all the fullness of the Deity lives in bodily form" (Col 2:9b). Paul frequently referred to both Jesus and God the Father in equal terms,[85] and he directly applied Old Testament language about the Lord God to Jesus:[86]

---

regard Colossians, Second Thessalonians, and Ephesians as authentic. There is debate about the authorship of First and Second Timothy, and Titus.

84. Drews, *Christ Myth*, 180.

85. For example, Paul wrote about the churches of God and Christ (1 Cor 1:2; Rom 16:16), the glory of God and Jesus (1 Cor 10:31; 2 Cor 3:18), and the judgment seat of God and Christ (Rom 14:10; 2 Cor 5:10). He also described both God and Jesus as the Lord of Peace (1 Thess 5:23; 2 Thess 3:16) and urged believers to have faith in God and Christ (1 Thess 1:8; Col 2:5) and to ensure that their lives were worthy of God and also the Lord (1 Thess 2:12; Col 1:10).

86. The term "Old Testament" only arose around the second century, but I will use this familiar term for the Hebrew Bible even when discussing the time of Jesus.

Old Testament Words about God as Lord	Paul's Words about Jesus as Lord
"Whoever calls on the name of the Lord will be saved" (Joel 2:32b).	"If you declare with your mouth, 'Jesus is Lord,' and believe in your heart that God raised him from the dead, you will be saved . . . for 'Everyone who calls on the name of the Lord will be saved'" (Rom 10:9–13).
"To Me every knee shall bow, every tongue shall take an oath. He shall say, 'Surely in the Lord I have righteousness and strength'" (Isa 45:23b–24a).	"At the name of Jesus every knee should bow, in heaven and on earth and under the earth, and every tongue acknowledge that Jesus Christ is Lord" (Phil 2:10–11a).
"For what good is the day of the Lord to you? It will be darkness, and not light" (Amos 5:18b).	"For you know very well that the day of the Lord [Jesus] will come like a thief in the night" (1 Thess 5:2).
"I am the Lord, that is My name; And My glory I will not give to another" (Isa 42:8a).	Jesus is "the Lord of glory" (1 Cor 2:8b).
"The fear of the Lord is the beginning of wisdom" (Ps 111:10a).	"Since, then, we know what it is to fear the Lord [Jesus], we try to persuade others" (2 Cor 5:11a).
"Then the Lord my God will come, and all the holy ones with him" (Zech 14:5b NIV).	"When our Lord Jesus comes with all his holy ones" (Thess 3:13b).

These were astounding claims for a Pharisee to make about any human being. However, like other early Christians, Paul did not reject his monotheistic faith. The central creed of Judaism (the *Shema*) states, "The Lord our God, the Lord is one" (Deut 6:4b). Paul extended this core declaration to include Jesus and to associate him with the act of creation: "Yet for us there is but one God, the Father, *from* whom all things came and *for* whom we live; and there is but one Lord, Jesus Christ, *through* whom all things came and *through* whom we live" (1 Cor 8:6). Paul also wrote about "the Lord [Jesus], who is the Spirit" (2 Cor 3:18b) and about the one Spirit of both God and Jesus,[87] directly incorporating Jesus within God's unique identity.

As Richard Bauckham points out, Paul's "christological monotheism" was very different from polytheistic worship because he did not simply elevate Jesus to a position alongside the One God of Judaism: "In this unprecedented formulation of the Shema, the unique identity of the one God *consists* of the one God, the Father, *and* the one Lord, his Messiah."[88]

How Do Paul's Doctrines Compare to Other New Testament Teachings?

Paul certainly taught a "high" Christology about the divine Jesus Christ. But it does not seem that he was preaching radically new doctrines because his central teachings are also found in other New Testament writings:

- Jesus is the divine Son of God (Rom 1:4; 2 Cor 1:19; Col 1:13. See Mark 3:11; Matt 8:29; Luke 1:35; Heb 1:5).
- Jesus was involved in creation and gives life (1 Cor 8:6; Col 1:16. See John 1:4; Heb 1:2).
- Jesus is God's presence (Col 1:15, 19; Phil 2:6. See Matt 10:40; Mark 9:37; John 14:9; Heb 1:3).
- God's Holy Spirit was present in Jesus (Rom 8:2; 2 Cor 3:18. See John 14:15–18; Luke 3:22; Matt 28:19).
- Jesus's death atoned for sin (Gal 1:4; 1 Cor 15:3; 1 Cor 1:18. See Matt 1:21; John 1:29; Heb 1:3; 1 Pet 3:18; Rev 1:5).
- Jesus will return for final judgment (2 Cor 5:10. See Mark 13:26; Matt 24:27; John 5:22).

Like the writers of the Gospels, Paul taught that Jesus was humble and gentle (2 Cor 10:1; see Matt 11:20), came to serve (Phil 2:7; see Luke 22:27), instituted a Last Supper ceremony (1 Cor 11:23–25; see Luke 22:19–20), and fulfilled Old Testament prophecy (Rom 1:2; see Luke 24:44). And Paul's letters also included some of Jesus's specific teachings: divorce is not desirable (1 Cor 7:10–11; see Mark 10:11), the most

87. For example, Paul wrote, "You, however, are not in the realm of the flesh but are in the realm of the Spirit, if indeed the Spirit of God lives in you. And if anyone does not have the Spirit of Christ, they do not belong to Christ" (Rom 8:8–9).

88. Bauckham, *Jesus*, 101 (original emphasis).

important law is to love God and others (Gal 5:14; see Matt 22:39–40), you should be wise and yet innocent (Rom 16:19; see Matt 10:16), and you should bless those who persecute you (Rom 12:14; see Luke 6:28). Paul's core doctrines, including his belief in Jesus's divinity, are therefore consistent with the entire New Testament corpus.

Some of Paul's statements were also structured like formal creeds or church liturgies, which suggests he was transmitting an existing tradition rather than creating new ones. For example, he wrote, "For what I received I passed on to you as of first importance: that Christ died for our sins according to the Scriptures, that he was buried, that he was raised on the third day according to the Scriptures, and that he appeared to Cephas, and then to the Twelve" (1 Cor 15:3–5).[89] Nowhere in his letters did Paul try to persuade the churches to accept Jesus's divinity: he merely mentioned it in passing, in an almost formulaic way, as if it was already widely accepted. Theologian Gordon Fee points out that in many passages, "Paul is arguing for something else on the basis of a *commonly held belief* in Christ as the incarnate Son of God."[90] As Larry Hurtado argued, "nothing in Paul's letters indicates any awareness that his fundamental view of Christ was unique or that he had made any serious innovation in the way Christians before him had regarded the exalted Jesus."[91]

How Did the First Apostles View Paul's Teachings?

If Paul was distorting an original Palestinian tradition by deifying Jesus, he would surely have avoided interacting with Jesus's first disciples. But on the contrary, at a time when the Jerusalem apostles were still alive to contradict him, Paul wrote that he had met with them and had sought confirmation of his doctrines:

> Then after three years, I went up to Jerusalem to get acquainted with Cephas [Peter] and stayed with him fifteen days. I saw

89. See also Col 1:15–20; Phil 2:5–11. Among other scholars, Arthur Nock argued that "the style of the first passage from Colossians indicates that its writer is reproducing an earlier formulation of belief" (*Early Gentile Christianity*, 50). See also Köstenberger and Kruger, *Heresy of Orthodoxy*, 63; Jenkins, *Hidden Gospels*, 81; Keener, *Historical Jesus*, 151; Hurtado, *One God*, 4.

90. Fee, *Pauline Christology*, 500 (original emphasis). Fletcher-Louis agrees that "time and again, a high Christology . . . in Paul is presented as a presupposition that Paul assumes his readers will share" (*Jesus Monotheism*, 34).

91. Hurtado, *One God*, 4. See also Schweitzer, *Paul*, 79.

> none of the other apostles—only James, the Lord's brother. (Gal 1:18–19)
>
> Then after fourteen years, I went up again to Jerusalem, this time with Barnabas. I took Titus along also. I went in response to a revelation and, meeting privately with those esteemed as leaders, I presented to them the gospel that I preach among the Gentiles. I wanted to be sure I was not running and had not been running my race in vain . . . They added nothing to my message . . . James, Cephas, and John, those esteemed as pillars, gave me and Barnabas the right hand of fellowship when they recognized the grace given to me. (Gal 2:1–9)

Arthur Drews was therefore incorrect when he claimed that Paul instituted the worship of Jesus and then "strenuously avoided" Jesus's first apostles.[92] Instead, Paul acknowledged the authority of the Jerusalem apostles, and he seems to have received their support for his mission to the Gentiles. He clearly believed they were all teaching the same message: "I am the least of the apostles . . . Whether, then, it is I or they, this is what we preach, and this is what you believed" (1 Cor 15:9–11).

First-century Jerusalem was the center of an extensive network linking Jews inside and outside Palestine, with continuous communication and visitation between groups of Jesus's followers.[93] Paul also traveled and preached with men associated with the Jerusalem Church, such as John Mark (Phil 1:24; Col 4:10), Barnabas (Gal 2:2), and Silas (Acts 15:32). If Paul was falsely deifying a human Jesus, it is highly unlikely the first apostles would not have known about this, but there is no trace of a christological controversy in his letters or any other text.[94] Paul also did not form a breakaway sect but collected funds to support the Jerusalem Church (Rom 15:25–26; 1 Cor 16:1–3), and he preached passionately against divisive attitudes:

> One of you says, "I follow Paul"; another, "I follow Apollos"; another, "I follow Cephas [Peter]"; still another, "I follow Christ." Is Christ divided? Was Paul crucified for you? Were you baptized in the name of Paul? (1 Cor 1:11–13)

92. Drews, *Christ Myth*, 180.

93. See Köstenberger and Kruger, *Heresy of Orthodoxy*, 59; Wright, *Victory*, 63; McGrath, *Heresy*, 44–45. Judaic scholar Alfred Edersheim points out that specialist letter carriers seem to have been used for delivering communications (*Life and Times*, 92).

94. See, for example, Brunner, *Mediator*, 179; Fletcher-Louis, *Jesus Monotheism*, 67.

> So then, no more boasting about human leaders! All things are yours, whether Paul or Apollos or Cephas. (1 Cor 3:21–22)

There is no evidence that Paul was teaching something fundamentally different from Jesus's first apostles in Palestine.

Who Did Paul Come into Conflict With?

The fiery Paul did clash with some teachers, including Jesus's disciple Peter. Paul recorded an incident in which Jewish and Gentile followers of Jesus had been eating together in the church in Antioch, but when visitors arrived from the Jerusalem Church, Peter and some others separated themselves from non-Jews to fulfill Jewish purity laws. The furious Paul accused Peter of hypocrisy. He argued that "a person is not justified by the works of the law, but by faith in Jesus Christ" (Gal 2:16a), and "if righteousness could be gained through the law, Christ died for nothing!" (Gal 2:21).

Some of Jesus's Jewish followers were also insisting that Gentile believers had to be circumcised and convert to Judaism. But Paul was adamant that this was not necessary, arguing that Jesus's work had removed the distinction between Jew and Gentile (Eph 2:14). According to Paul, Mosaic law had only been a temporary guardian (Gal 3:24–25), and with the coming of Jesus, "whoever loves others has fulfilled the law" (Rom 13:8b). He did not instruct Jewish Christians to reject their traditions, but he did teach that "circumcision is nothing and uncircumcision is nothing. Keeping God's commands is what counts" (1 Cor 7:18–19). This seems consistent with Jesus teaching that he had come to fulfill Scripture but love was more important than mere observance of the law (Matt 5:17–44). Paul's main concern seems to have been that belief in Jesus should not be restricted to Judaism, and his zeal for the issue is reflected in his famous outburst that those who were trying to impose circumcision on others should go the whole way and emasculate themselves (Gal 5:12)!

In a letter to the church in Corinth, Paul also denounced "false apostles" (2 Cor 11:13) and expressed concern about immoral behavior that seemed to result from their teaching (2 Cor 12:21). But he called many preachers "apostles," and it is highly unlikely that he was criticizing leaders such as James, John, and Peter.[95]

95. Paul used the term "apostle" to describe Apollos (1 Cor 4:6–9), Barnabas (1 Cor 9:5–6), Silas (1 Thess 2:7), and Andronicus and Junia (Rom 16:7).

Paul's letters therefore do reveal that there were conflicts between himself and other teachers on certain issues. However, there is no evidence that he was ever in dispute with the Jerusalem apostles or any other preachers regarding Jesus's divinity.

Question 2: Where Did Paul Draw His Doctrines From?

If Paul did create his own doctrines that were fundamentally different from what was being taught by the first apostles, where would he have drawn his ideas from? It has been suggested that he could have been influenced by polytheistic religions in combination with Jewish expectations of the promised Messiah. Let's consider both possibilities.

Did Paul Borrow Concepts from the Pagan Mystery Cults?

Supporters of the Paulism argument claim that Paul deified a human Jesus to cult-Lord status under the influence of polytheistic mystery cults. However, the following facts make it unlikely that he would have developed a paganized form of faith:

- In Paul's eyes, he and other Jewish followers of Jesus were still faithful to the One God of Judaism, and he taught that the new faith was an extension of God's covenant with Abraham (see Romans 4).
- Paul made passionate appeals for his fellow Jews to accept Jesus as the promised Messiah, quoting extensively from the Old Testament to support his claim. As the Jewish scholar Daniel Boyarin points out, "We did not find the Paul of the Romans seeking to disassociate the new Christian movement from the synagogues, as many assume, but quite the opposite."[96] How would adopting pagan elements have furthered this aspect of Paul's mission?
- Paul repeatedly warned the new church to avoid polytheistic influences.[97]
- Paul described himself as "a Hebrew of Hebrews; in regard to the law, a Pharisee" (Phil 3:5b). It is unlikely that as a trained Pharisee,

96. Boyarin, *Radical Jew*, 338. The book of Acts confirms this: "As was his custom, Paul went into the synagogue, and on three Sabbath days he reasoned with them from the Scriptures" (Acts 17:12).

97. See Col 2:8; 1 Cor 8:4–6; 10:14–20; 12:2; 1 Thess 1:9–10; Rom 1:22.

Paul would have unconsciously incorporated polytheistic concepts in his teaching without noticing this influence.

- If he was consciously distorting the figure of Jesus, he would not have approached the Jerusalem apostles for approval of his doctrines.
- He does not seem the type of man who would have adapted his doctrines to attract followers: "Am I now trying to win the approval of human beings, or of God? Or am I trying to please people? If I were still trying to please people, I would not be a servant of Christ" (Gal 1:10).

Paul's intellectual environment was a complex mix of beliefs that included Second Temple Judaism, pagan religions and philosophies, mysticism, and Gnosticism.[98] It would therefore be overly simplistic to classify his theology as exclusively Hellenistic or Jewish. But when he used Greek terms that were also found in pagan gnostic-mystery cults, his concepts were far more strongly connected to his Jewish background. It is worth briefly noting his use of a few of these terms:

- Flesh: Paul's use of the Greek *sarx* (flesh) corresponded to the Hebrew *basar*, which referred to man's weakness and innate resistance to God's will. This use was very different from the Hellenistic-gnostic aversion to the body. Paul preached that Jesus was a physical human being and that believers would experience a final physical resurrection. His distinction between flesh and spirit is therefore not an expression of Hellenistic dualism.[99]
- Mystery: In the pre-Christian Greek translation of the Old Testament (the Septuagint), *mysterion* often referred to God's unknown plans, which Paul believed were being revealed through Jesus.[100] He did not need to borrow this term from pagan mystery cults because there were "from the Semitic world good parallels in thought and word for virtually every facet of the NT use of mystery."[101]

98. Gnosticism is a loose term for groups that stressed the importance of personal, esoteric spiritual knowledge (*gnosis*).

99. See Davies, *Paul and Rabbinic Judaism*, 17; Kennedy, *Paul*, 155.

100. Paul wrote, "We declare God's wisdom, a mystery that has been hidden and that God destined for our glory before time began" (1 Cor 2:7). See also Rom 11:25; Col 1:26–27. This revelation of God's plans is confirmed in the last book of the Bible: "But in the days when the seventh angel is about to sound his trumpet, the mystery of God will be accomplished, just as he announced to his servants the prophets" (Rev 10:7).

101. Brown, *Semitic Background*, 69. See also Nock, *Early Gentile Christianity*, 132; Kim, *Origin of Paul's Gospel*, 98–99; Kennedy, *Paul*, 123–24.

- Savior: Pagan emperors and gods were called saviors, but this was also a description of God in the Old Testament: "All flesh shall know that I, the Lord, am your Savior, and your Redeemer, the Mighty One of Jacob" (Isa 49:26b).
- *Kyrios*: Both Paul and the mystery cults called their Lords, *kyrios*. But the Septuagint used this term for YHWH[102] and as the translation of the Aramaic *mar*. In First Corinthians 16:22, Paul used the Aramaic phrase *Maranatha*: "Our Lord [Jesus] come,"[103] which suggests that the expectation of Jesus's return as divine Lord had a Palestinian origin. To support the Paulism theory, Bousset unsuccessfully tried to explain away this Aramaic tradition, even making the unfounded suggestion that the phrase was a Jewish curse formula.[104] In the opinion of Gordon Fee, Bousset's claim that Paul borrowed his *kyrios* theology from pagan cults was "one of the truly idiosyncratic moments in NT scholarship."[105] Paul's teaching about Jesus's return and the end times also corresponded to aspects of Palestinian Judaism[106] but had no connection to the mystery cults."[107]

Recent scholarship concludes that Paul's theology has a thoroughly Judaic background,[108] a fact that was not noticed by earlier "Paulism" supporters such as Richard Reitzenstein, who was a scholar of Gnosticism and Greek religion but not Judaism. And despite the implications of the title, in her book *Gnostic Paul*, Elaine Pagels reached this clear conclusion about the direction of influence between Paul and Gnosticism: "Some of what has been described as 'gnostic terminology' in the Pauline letters may be explained more plausibly instead as Pauline (and

102. See, for example, Joel 2:32; Jer 9:24; Isa 40:13.

103. This is the accepted translation of the phrase. See Fitzmyer, "Aramaic Language," 13. Fitzmyer traces the use of the Aramaic *mar* and argues that there is "a plausible Palestinian religious background for the title (*ho*) *kyrios* used of Jesus" ("Aramaic Language," 14). See also Hurtado, "Critique of Bousset's Influence," 315.

104. See Rawlinson, *New Testament Doctrine*, 235.

105. Fee, *Pauline Christology*, 41 n. 39.

106. See Sanders, *Paul*, 543. Sanders also points out that Paul's teaching about righteousness reflects Jewish rather than pagan thinking (*Paul*, 544).

107. Schweitzer noted that "of eschatology in the later Jewish or early Christian sense there is not a single trace to be found in any Greco-Oriental doctrine" (*Paul*, 228).

108. See Schweitzer, *Paul*; Boyarin, *Radical Jew*; Davies, *Paul and Rabbinic Judaism;* Sanders, *Paul*; Nock, *Early Gentile Christianity*, esp. 35–56; Hurtado, "Paul's Messianic Christology."

deutero-Pauline) terminology in the *gnostic* writings."[109] H. A. A. Kennedy represents the broad modern consensus when he makes this observation: "The evidence we have adduced from the Old Testament makes it wholly superfluous to seek for the explanation of Paul's use of any of these terms in Hellenistic Mystery-Religion."[110]

Did Paul Mistakenly Believe Jesus Was a Divine Messiah?

If Paul seemed to draw his concepts from Judaism rather than pagan cults, did his messianic expectations lead him to mistakenly believe that Jesus was divine? This was proposed by William Wrede, who in 1908 claimed that "Paul believed in such a celestial being, in a divine Christ, before he believed in Jesus."[111] However, although Second Temple messianism was a complex and fluid set of beliefs, the Messiah was not expected to be a divinity who would be worshiped alongside God. Jewish scholar Joseph Klausner argued that "the Messiah is only an instrument in the hands of God. He is a human being, flesh and blood, like all mortals."[112] He observed that "of the *divine* nature of the Messiah, there are perhaps certain indications in the later Midrashim; in the authentic writings of the Tannaitic period [first two centuries AD] there is not a trace."[113]

No messianic movement ever worshiped their leader as equivalent to God. The Parables (or Similitudes) of Enoch did depict a future heavenly Son of Man who would sit on a throne of glory and implement final judgment, but this was very rare in messianic expectations of the time, and Klausner pointed out that the Parables "add new features to the spiritual aspect of the Messiah."[114] Most scholars date the text to the first century AD, so its influence on or from Christianity is difficult to establish, and James VanderKam notes that "there remains widespread agreement that at least a few significant sections were added to the Similitudes during their textual history."[115] Matthew Black even suggests that

109. Pagels, *Gnostic Paul*, 164 (original emphasis).

110. Kennedy, *Paul*, 198. Schweitzer agreed that "real analogies both in the mysticism and the sacramental doctrine are surprisingly few" (*Paul*, 228).

111. Wrede, *Paul*, 151.

112. Klausner, *Messianic Idea*, 523.

113. Klausner, *Messianic Idea*, 466 (original emphasis).

114. Klausner, *Messianic Idea*, 299.

115. VanderKam, "Righteous One," 176. Darrell Hannah agrees that some sections are "best regarded as a later addition to the text of the *Parables*" ("Elect Son of

the uncertain dating leaves the text "open to the suspicion that Enoch as Son of Man was an invention of late esoteric cabbalistic Judaism, as a Jewish rival to the Gospel figure."[116]

Paul's teaching about Jesus's loving relationship with each believer is also unique in messianic literature. The Messiah was expected to usher in Israel's liberation, but there is no precedent for Paul's claim that "neither height nor depth, nor anything else in all creation, will be able to separate us from the love of God that is in Christ Jesus our Lord" (Rom 8:39).

In fact, it has been pointed out that it's surprising Paul and the other apostles thought that Jesus was the Messiah at all: Jesus performed many *non*-messianic acts, such as exorcisms and miracles, but did not direct his mission at defeating Israel's oppressors, which *was* a central messianic expectation. James Charlesworth goes so far as to state that "Jesus' message was certainly apocalyptic and eschatological; but it was not messianic," so "there is no smooth transition from messianology to christology."[117] D. H. Juel agrees that "there is no 'trajectory' within postbiblical Judaism that can account for the widespread confession of Jesus as the Christ."[118] Second Temple messianism therefore does not explain why Paul would have taught that the executed Jesus was also the divine presence of God. Some scholars suggest that his doctrines are more likely to have been formed by his personal experiences together with the teachings that he encountered in the existing churches.[119]

It is also significant that Paul's Damascus vision of Jesus was very similar to Old Testament encounters with the Glory of God. For example, the prophet Ezekiel saw a bright likeness of a man and fell to the ground; the Spirit of God entered him, and he was sent to prophesy to Israel (Ezek 1:26—2:3). Paul also experienced a blinding vision and believed he was sent to preach the risen Jesus. Jewish scholar Alan Segal

---

Man," 154).

116. Black, "Aramaic Barnāshā," 201. The ancient Enochian texts in the Dead Sea Scrolls do not contain the Parables section (1 Enoch 37–71). See Vermes, *Dead Sea Scrolls*, 17. Hengel comments about the Parables that "even its Palestinian origin is not certain" ("History of Isaiah 53," 99).

117. Charlesworth, "Messianology to Christology," 5, 29.

118. Juel, "Mark's Christology," 460. Nils Dahl agrees that when Jesus's disciples came to regard him as the Messiah, "their messianic ideas had undergone a radical transformation" ("Messianic Ideas," 403). See also Edersheim, *Life and Times*, 113.

119. See Dahl, "Messianic Ideas," 391; Hurtado, "Paul's Messianic Christology," 119–20; Kim, *Origin of Paul's Gospel*, 57–74; Chester, *Messiah and Exaltation*, 82; Beale, *Unfolding of the Old Testament*, 296.

offers this response to the two visions: "The theological implications of this hypothetical identification are staggering. Does Paul's Christianity stem from the identification of Jesus with the Glory of God, the Hebrew *Kavod*, God's sometimes human appearance in the visions of the Hebrew Bible?"[120] Andrew Chester agrees that if Paul did have a visionary experience of the glorified Christ, it would explain why he could speak of him as being in the form of God.[121]

But Chester also notes that Paul's interpretation of his vision was unique in Judaism: "No other visionary tradition had seen a *contemporary* figure as being exalted in this kind of way."[122] Seyoon Kim agrees that Paul's vision was "fundamentally different from the visions described in Jewish apocalyptic writings, in that for Paul it was not a vision of an exclusively future event but a vision of the one who had already come to earth . . . [so that] Paul's gospel that proclaims God's saving act in Jesus Christ bursts the apocalyptic schema."[123]

Paul's theology, and the corresponding doctrines in other New Testament texts, therefore cannot be explained by either pagan or Judaic beliefs of the time.

Review the Evidence

Paul's letters present powerful, indisputable evidence of the early Christian belief in a divine Jesus. To discredit Paul's testimony, skeptics have alleged that his teachings did not represent the understanding of Jesus's first followers but were an exaggerated and distorted view of Jesus's nature. The following seven points argue against this claim:

- Paul's Epistles do not provide any indication that he regarded his theology as being radically innovative.
- His central doctrines are consistent with the rest of the New Testament. It seems unlikely that he could have influenced all those writers to adopt his own theological creations.

120. Segal, "Conversion," 334.

121. Chester, *Messiah and Exaltation*, 90.

122. Chester, *Messiah and Exaltation*, 92 (emphasis added).

123. Kim, *Origins of Paul's Gospel*, 73.

- Paul structured his teachings around Old Testament promises, and there is no indication that he would have wanted to or did borrow from pagan concepts of a cult-Lord.
- Scholars have identified sound Jewish foundations for his central doctrines.
- Messianic expectations cannot explain why Paul would have elevated an executed, failed messianic figure to receive worship alongside God.
- By the time of Paul's conversion, there were followers of Jesus in widely dispersed cities such as Antioch and Rome, with extensive communication between the churches. How could he have persuaded those believers that a human Jesus was divine while the first apostles were teaching something fundamentally different?
- The first Jerusalem disciples and apostles would have noticed if Paul was preaching a substantially different message, but there is no evidence that they disputed Paul's doctrine of Jesus's divinity.

In the opinion of Nicholas Perrin, "The old story which holds Jesus and Paul radically asunder is not finally tenable; it requires us to suspend our disbelief indefinitely in regard to too many other stories."[124]

Consider Your Verdict

According to the Paulism argument, Paul was instrumental in transforming a human Jesus into a paganized divine-cult-Lord, and his distorted theology came to replace the first apostles' understanding that Jesus was only human. Is there convincing evidence to support this claim?

- Yes
- No

124. Perrin, *Jesus the Temple*, 2.

CONCLUSION 2
WAS A HUMAN JESUS FALSELY DEIFIED?

So far, our investigation into Jesus looks like this:

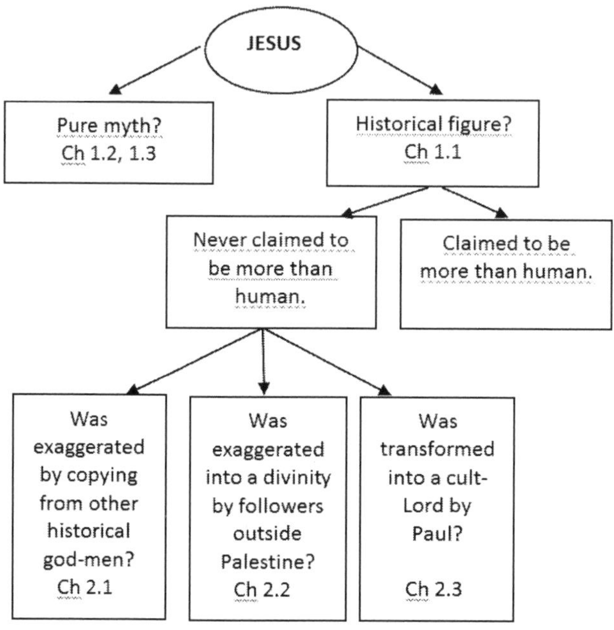

Figure 1: Outline of the investigation so far.

These arguments presume that if Jesus existed, he did not claim to be anything more than human. But could he have regarded himself as significantly different from other men? What is he supposed to have said about himself? How did he appear to his fellow Jews? Can we know anything about his acts and words? These questions lead naturally to an investigation into the New Testament Gospels.

Investigation 3

How Reliable are the Gospels?

Together with Paul's Epistles, the four gospels form the core of the New Testament message, so it is essential to explore their reliability.[1] Do they contain historical facts, or are they exaggerations or even complete fabrications? This investigation will explore evidence related to the four canonical gospels (Matthew, Mark, Luke, and John), starting from the time of Jesus and moving through to the existing New Testament manuscripts, to find answers to the following questions:

- Is there evidence of first-century Palestinian traditions in the Gospels?
- Is there reason to believe that some of this tradition was linked to eyewitness accounts of Jesus's life and teachings?
- What is the relationship between early oral traditions about Jesus and the later written gospels?
- Have the gospel texts been significantly altered over time?

3.1 PORTRAYAL OF JEWISH LIFE IN FIRST-CENTURY PALESTINE

It is often alleged that the gospel narratives of Jesus's life were late creations by the predominantly Gentile church outside Palestine, written by Christians with little connection to Jesus's life and original teachings. To

1. The other New Testament texts are the Acts of the Apostles, the book of Revelation, and the Epistles known as Hebrews, James, First and Second Peter, Jude, and First, Second, and Third John.

test this hypothesis, the following scenario of a day in Jerusalem has been compiled using gospel material. (The footnotes provide Old and New Testament references as well as confirmation of gospel details in other sources, but it might be best to ignore these notes in a first reading to get a sense of the world depicted by the gospel writers.[2])

Walking in Jerusalem

Smells and noises swirl around the busy streets of Jerusalem. The Hebrew idioms sound strange—someone speaks passionately about faith flowing like rivers from her bowels, which is the source of emotions in Hebrew culture.[3] A mother scolds her son for having a bad eye instead of a good eye, which means he is not behaving generously.[4] The young man responds, "What—to me and to thee, woman?" meaning, "What have I to do with you?"[5] Two men wash their hands in a front room, using water from stone jars that cannot become ritually impure.[6] There must have been a dispute because one is urging the other to find two or three witnesses as instructed in ancient tradition.[7] Above them, three young women are chatting on the flat roof—this is called being "on the housetop."[8]

A young woman at a well is being chided for not bringing anything for drawing water, which is necessary because there is no bucket for common use.[9] A passing group talks in shocked tones about Herod Antipas

2. Rabbinic material is taken from the Mishnah (*m.*); the Tosefta (*t.*); the Babylonian Talmud (*b.*), from the translation in Epstein, *Soncino Babylonian Talmud.*

3. Ps 31:9 KJV; Prov 20:27 KJV; John 7:3 KJV.

4. Prov 22:9; 28:22 OJB. Matthew's Gospel describes generosity using the metaphorical phrase about a good eye (Matt 6:22 CJB).

5. Jesus is said to have answered his mother in this way (John 2:4 YLT). See also Josh 22:24; Judg 11:12; 2 Sam 16:10; 1 Kgs 17:18; 2 Kgs 3:13.

6. John 2:6. The rabbinic text *b.* Shabbat 58a records that stone utensils were believed to not contract uncleanness. Archaeologists have found stone pots in Jewish areas, which seem to have been used for purification.

7. Matt 18:16; Deut 19:15.

8. "Let no one on the housetop go down to take anything out of the house" (Matt 24:17).

9. A woman pointed out that Jesus did not carry anything for drawing water at a well (John 4:11). Writing about his travels in the Middle East, James Neil observed that there was "no windlass, bucket, or rope attached to an Eastern well. Travellers carry their own bucket and rope about with them . . . a small one, much longer than it is broad, made of leather, so that it can be easily carried about without getting broken"

recently having the baptizer called John executed.[10] One man had even hoped he might have been the prophet like Moses whose coming was promised in the Old Testament.[11] Now they argue noisily about whether there will be an end-time resurrection or not—Sadducees do not believe this.[12] But they fall into a respectful silence as a wailing mourning party passes on its way to take down a crucified relative before sunset.[13] A nearby cliff is another ominous reminder of death—transgressors are pushed from the top before they are stoned.[14]

The impressive Jerusalem temple gleams in the sunlight. Herod has been rebuilding it for forty-six years.[15] Its structure represents increasing holiness and proximity to God: the enormous outer Court of Gentiles is the only area open to all people, the Women's Court is for Jews only, then there is an area for Jewish men, then the Holy Place for priests, and finally the inner Holy of Holies, which is hidden behind a thick curtain.[16] It will soon be Passover, so the Court of the Gentiles is buzzing with the exchange of money for animal sacrifices. Only shekels and half shekels are accepted, and there is some grumbling about the exchange rate. One man mutters angrily that according to Scripture, the temple should be a house of prayer, but it has become a den of robbers.[17]

(*Everyday Life*, 8).

10. Mark 6:27. Josephus recorded Herod's murder of John (*Ant.* 18.5.2).

11. John 6:14; Deut 18:18.

12. Mark 12:18. This Sadduccean opinion is also found in Josephus, *Ant.* 18.1.4.

13. Jesus had to be taken down from the cross before sunset (John 19:31). Josephus wrote, "The Jews used to take so much care of the burial of men, that they took down those that were condemned and crucified, and buried them before the going down of the sun" (*Wars* 4.5.2 §317).

14. According to the Talmud, a condemned man was pushed from a cliff that was the height of two men; if he survived the fall, he was then stoned to death (*m.* Sanhedrin 6.4). When Jesus's fellow Jews in Nazareth were outraged by his claims, they "got up, drove him out of the town, and took him to the brow of the hill on which the town was built, in order to throw him off the cliff" (Luke 4:29).

15. This period of forty-six years is mentioned in John 2:20. According to Josephus, Herod the Great started work on the temple around 20 BC (*Ant.* 15.11.1), which dates Jesus's cleansing of the temple in John's Gospel to around AD 27.

16. This curtain, or veil, was said to tear from top to bottom when Jesus died (Mark 15:38; Matt 27:51).

17. Mark 11:17. The phrase "house of prayer" is from Isaiah 56:7, and "den of robbers" is from Jeremiah 7:11, where it is directly connected to the destruction of the temple. Exchange rates for animals were sometimes excessive, and according to tradition, a rabbi once ordered the price of a pair of doves to be reduced from a golden

Ignoring the hubbub, a young man nods earnestly as his father reminds him that entering a Gentile home will render him defiled.[18] They have a distinctive Galilean accent[19] and are among thousands who have come up to Jerusalem for ceremonial purification before Passover.[20] A new mother passes by on her way to make the required purification offer of the value of two pigeons. There are thirteen treasure chests in the temple with inscriptions indicating the offerings: old and new shekels, bird-offerings, young pigeons for burnt-offerings, wood, frankincense, gold for the mercy-seat, and six chests for freewill-offerings.[21]

Some women are walking along the eastern porch called the colonnade of Solomon, which is believed to be built on the remains of an original colonnade of the first temple.[22] They console a weeping friend who has been given a bill of divorce according to Mosaic law,[23] and they quickly hustle her past a group of despised Samaritans who are discussing their own traditional worship on Mount Gerizim.[24] Suddenly, some leaders push forward a young man who claims to have been healed at the

---

dinar to half a silver dinar (*m.* Kerithoth 18a).

18. This is apparently why the Jewish leaders did not enter Pilate's court during the Passover week (John 18:28).

19. The Talmud comments on the distinctiveness of the Galilean accent (*b.* Erubin 53b), and Peter's speech identified him as Galilean (Matt 26:73).

20. John 11:55. In Jerusalem, archaeologist Eilat Mazar has found many "ritual baths dating to the Herodian period . . . Rock-cut channels directed water into the baths from the surplus in the colossal cisterns on the Temple Mount" (*Temple Mount Excavations*, 61).

21. See *m.* Shekalim 6.5. We are told that Mary made the traditional offering after Jesus's birth (Luke 2:24) according to ancient instruction (Lev 12:4–8). Jesus taught near the area where the offerings were placed (John 8:20).

22. Josephus wrote that "these cloisters belonged to the outer court . . . This was the work of king Solomon, who first of all built the entire temple" (*Ant.* 20.9.7). Jesus is said to have walked along Solomon's Colonnade (John 10:23).

23. Deut 24:3. Jesus taught that the Mosaic practice of divorce was only instituted because of the hardness of men's hearts (Matt 19:8). Interestingly, the Old Testament records that "the Lord God of Israel says that He hates divorce" (Mal 2:16a).

24. After King Solomon died, the nation split into southern Judah centered on Jerusalem and northern Israel centered on Samaria. Bitter enmity developed between these two groups, and around the fifth century, Samaritans built their own temple on Mount Gerizim, which Judean Jews destroyed in the second century BC. A Samaritan woman expressed surprise that the Jewish Jesus would speak to her, saying, "Our ancestors worshiped on this mountain, but you Jews claim that the place where we must worship is in Jerusalem" (John 4:20).

pool of Siloam,[25] and another man shouts that he has also been healed at the pool of Bethesda.[26] The skeptical leaders roughly demand that these men tell the truth about these strange incidents, using an ancient phrase of interrogation: "Give glory to God by telling the truth!"[27] The response seems to be the wrong one because a priest shouts, "He has blasphemed!" and tears his clothes in the traditional response.[28]

Arguing like a Rabbi

The above details from the Gospels are consistent with Old Testament traditions and independent information about Jewish culture and beliefs in first-century Palestine. Jesus's language and arguments in the Gospels also have strong links to rabbinic forms of debate. After the destruction of Jerusalem by the Romans in AD 70, Pharisaic traditions gradually developed into rabbinic Judaism, and these oral traditions were written down from the late second century onwards.[29] This rab-

25. John 9:7. Drainage work has exposed steps of a large pool thought to be the pool of Siloam, located at the end of the extensive ancient water system beneath Jerusalem.

26. Excavations have uncovered two connected pools with an intervening wall, believed to be the healing pool of Bethesda (from *beth-hesda*: house of mercy) where Jesus cured a crippled man (John 5:1–13). Archaeologist Shimon Gibson has noted features of these pools that are consistent with the gospel narrative: for example, there is evidence of five covered porches (colonnades) around and between the two pools; there are broad landings for the moving of disabled people; there is a sluice gate from the northern pool to the southern pool together with a drainage exit, which could have caused bubbling that some manuscripts of John described as the result of an angel stirring the waters. Gibson also notes that layers of bright red soil might explain early Christian remarks on the bloody color of the water in this double pool. See Gibson, "Excavations at the Bethesda Pool," 22–26.

27. John 9:24b. In the Old Testament, Joshua urged Achan to admit the truth, "My son, I beg you, give glory to the Lord God of Israel, and make confession to Him, and tell me now what you have done; do not hide it from me" (Josh 7:19b).

28. It was traditional to tear clothes in response to blasphemy (2 Kgs 18:37), and the high priest did this when Jesus promised to return on the clouds of heaven (Matt 26:65). In Mosaic law, the high priest was prohibited from rending his clothes (Lev 21:10), but in rabbinic tradition, this was how a judge was expected to respond to blasphemy (*m.* Sanhedrin 7.5).

29. Due to their late dating, rabbinic materials must be applied with care to New Testament times. However, Herbert Basser states confidently that some rabbinic literature predates the rabbis by centuries ("Gospels and Rabbinic Halakah," 82). And Jewish scholar Jacob Neusner agrees that it is valid to compare passages in rabbinic literature and the Gospels ("Contexts of Comparison," 59). See also Derrett, *Law in the*

binic material reveals direct similarities between the teachings of Jesus and the rabbis:

- Like Jesus, rabbis often started a parable with, "To what is this like?"[30] And they referred to Scripture by saying, "It is written."[31]
- Rabbis stood up to read Scripture and sat down to teach. Jesus also sat down to teach in the synagogue (Luke 4:16–21; Matt 23:55). He spoke about teachers of the law sitting in Moses's seat (*kathedras*; Matt 23:2), and a rabbi is said to have described Solomon's throne as being like the kathedras of Moses.[32] An ornate stone chair facing the congregation has been found in the excavated synagogues of Chorazin and Hammath-by-Tiberias.[33]
- Jesus is remembered as saying to his disciples, "Whatever you bind on earth will be bound in heaven, and whatever you loose on earth will be loosed in heaven" (Matt 16:19b). This is linked to the rabbinic terms *asar* (forbid) and *hitter* (permit), and Josephus reported that at one time, the Pharisees were "the real administrators of the public affairs: they banished and reduced whom they pleased; they bound and loosed [men] at their pleasure."[34]
- Jesus compared a rich man entering heaven to a camel passing through the eye of a needle (Mark 10:25). It has been suggested that he might have meant rope rather than camel because the Aramaic *gmla* can mean both. But talmudic texts record a similar idiom, using the largest animal outside Palestine: one rabbi argued that "a man is never shown in a dream a date palm of gold, or an elephant going through the eye of a needle," and another compared tortuous reasoning to trying to "draw an elephant through the eye of a needle."[35]

New Testament, xxxiv–xxxix.

30. *b.* Berachoth 31b; Mark 4:30; Luke 13:20.

31. *b.* Sanhedrin 91b; *b.* Rosh Hashanah 17b; John 10:34; Matt 4:4.

32. This is mentioned in Pesikta de-Rab Kahana. See Newport, "Note on the 'Seat of Moses,'" 55.

33. See Sukenik, *Ancient Synagogues*, 57–61.

34. Josephus, *Wars* 1.5.2.

35. See *b.* Berachoth 55b and *b.* Baba Mezi'a 38b respectively. The later Qur'an used the same comparison as the Gospels: "Nor will they enter Paradise until a camel enters into the eye of a needle" (Sura 7.40).

- The rabbinic form of logic known as *kal va-homer* (light and heavy) argues from lesser to greater. For example, the Old Testament taught, "If the righteous will be recompensed on the earth, how much more the ungodly and the sinner!" (Prov 11:31). And a rabbinic text taught, "If a grain of wheat, which is buried naked, sprouteth forth in many robes, how much more so the righteous, who are buried in their raiment!"[36] Jesus also used this familiar structure: "If you then, though you are evil, know how to give good gifts to your children, how much more will your Father in heaven give the Holy Spirit to those who ask him?" (Luke 11:13). Jesus similarly argued that if circumcision on the eighth day could override Sabbath restrictions, a man's entire body could be made whole on the Sabbath, which is also an opinion expressed in rabbinic literature.[37] And Jesus's teaching that man is not made for the Sabbath (Mark 2:27) is found in the Talmud.[38]

Drawing from the Old Testament

The writers of the Gospels must have had detailed knowledge of ancient Jewish Scripture because they often used Old Testament images and traditions:

- As in the Old Testament, Israel is depicted as God's vineyard.[39]
- Men are called a "stumbling block" when they resist God's will.[40]
- A kingdom is described as a large tree where subjects nest like birds.[41]
- Jesus was accused of being a glutton and a drunkard, which is the specific description in Mosaic law of a rebellious son who should be stoned to death.[42]

36. *b.* Sanhedrin 90b.

37. John 7:23; *t.* Shabbat 16.

38. "Shabbat is committed to your hands, not you to its hands" (*b.* Yoma 85b).

39. Mark 12:1–12; see Isa 5:1–7.

40. Matt 16:23; see Mal 2:8.

41. Matt 13:32; see Ezek 31:6.

42. Matt 11:19; Luke 7:34. In the Old Testament, God instructed: "And they shall say to the elders of his city, 'This son of ours is stubborn and rebellious; he will not obey our voice; he is a glutton and a drunkard.' Then all the men of his city shall stone him to death with stones; so you shall put away the evil from among you, and all Israel

- Jesus's promise that the meek will inherit the earth is from an ancient psalm.[43]
- Jesus echoed a Jewish proverb when he taught that it is better for the host to invite you to a higher position than to claim it for yourself.[44]
- Jesus drew from ancient prophecy when he warned that he had "come to set a man against his father, and a daughter against her mother, and a daughter-in-law against her mother-in-law. And a person's enemies will be those of his own household."[45]
- Jesus's words, "Do you have eyes but fail to see, and ears but fail to hear?" (Mark 8:18) was a traditional prophetic warning.[46]

Speaking Aramaic/Hebrew

Although the Gospels were written in Greek, they preserve aspects of an Aramaic/Hebrew tradition. For example, Jesus called Simon *Kepa* (rock; *Petros* in Greek) and labeled James and John *boanerges* (sons of thunder; Mark 3:17). Jesus said *talitha koum* (little girl, I say to you, rise; Mark 5:41) and *ephphatha* (be opened; Mark 7:34). The Gospels use the words *corban* (temple offering; Mark 7:11), *raca* (fool; Matt 5:22), *Gethsemane* (from the Hebrew *gath*: wine-press and *shemen*: oil; Matt 26:36; Mark 14:32). Jesus taught that not one jot or tittle would pass from the law (Matt 5:18 KJB)—yod is the smallest Hebrew letter, shaped like an apostrophe, and a tittle is an even smaller mark. The Gospels also contain Semitic idioms, syntax, parallelism, and Aramaic/Hebrew wordplay such as sons (*banim*) compared to stones (*abanim*) in Luke 3:8 and Matthew 3:9. And when Jesus said to his host, "Today salvation has come to this house" (Luke 19:9b), he was making an Aramaic pun, because *yesha* meant "salvation" and his Aramaic name was Yeshua.[47]

---

shall hear and fear" (Deut 21:20–21).

43. Matt 5:5; see Ps 37:11.

44. Luke 14:9–10; see Prov 25:7–8.

45. Matt 10:35–36. The related Old Testament prophecy is: "For son dishonors father, Daughter rises against her mother, Daughter-in-law against her mother-in-law; A man's enemies are the men of his own household" (Mic 7:6).

46. See Ezek 12:2; Deut 29:4; Prov 20:12; Isa 32:3.

47. The prefix Yeho means God, as in the names Yehonathan (Jonathan) and Yehoshua ("God saves"). Yeshua is a shortened form of Yehoshua.

Review the Evidence

To read the Gospels is to be immersed in a world of Jewish customs, idioms, and beliefs. The accounts also contain information about the Jerusalem temple that was destroyed in AD 70, and they draw heavily from Old Testament imagery and rabbinic conventions. As Herbert Basser concludes, "It is obvious that rabbinic literature is heir to the same culture that informs the Gospels."[48]

Most New Testament debates also involve specifically Jewish issues that would have been irrelevant to the later predominantly Gentile church, such as Sabbath restrictions, Mosaic law, fasting, and the temple tax. In addition, the church did not use Jesus's Semitic title "King of the Jews," which must have been part of an early tradition.[49] And Jesus's teaching that a person who would not accept correction should be rejected along with Gentiles and tax collectors (Matt 18:15) could not have been a late development. Such details place the gospel accounts firmly within a Jewish Palestinian context.

Consider Your Verdict

Does it seem likely that the gospel narratives could have been late creations by Gentile Christians with very little knowledge of Jewish customs and life in Palestine?

- Yes
- No

3.2 DO THE GOSPELS PRESERVE ANY EYEWITNESS TRADITIONS?

The strongly Jewish context of the Gospels does not in itself ensure that its narratives preserve original traditions about Jesus—it is a necessary but not sufficient condition. Could these accounts be fabrications by people who did have some knowledge of life in Palestine? Or was the

48. Basser, "Gospels and Rabbinic Halakah," 81–82.

49. Burton Easton commented that Christians always regarded "King of the Jews" as an inadequate title for Jesus, and the church found it increasingly embarrassing (*Christ*, 166).

writer of Luke's Gospel telling the truth when he claimed to draw from eyewitness traditions?

> Many have undertaken to draw up an account of the things that have been fulfilled among us, just as they were handed down to us by those who from the first were eyewitnesses and servants of the word. With this in mind, since I myself have carefully investigated everything from the beginning, I too decided to write an orderly account. (Luke 1:1–3a)

The authenticity of the gospel accounts is supported by the three criteria of embarrassment, dissimilarity to the norm, and historical plausibility.

The Criterion of Embarrassment

Writers do not usually invent embarrassing and negative details about themselves or their admired protagonist. However, the gospel narratives contain many such details about the disciples. For example, they express selfish ambition for positions of authority in the future kingdom (Mark 10:41; Luke 9:46). They often do not grasp Jesus's teachings (Matt 8:27; Mark 8:16) so that their frustrated teacher asks, "Do you still not see or understand?" (Mark 8:17b). In one instance, they cannot exorcise an evil spirit, and Jesus asks, "How long shall I put up with you?" (Mark 9:19b). Peter, James, and John fall asleep in the garden of Gethsemane, although Jesus repeatedly asks them to stay awake and keep watch (Mark 14:32–41). Jesus calls Peter a "stumbling block" and "Satan" (Matt 16:23). After Jesus's arrest, the disciples flee (Mark 14:50) and Peter denies even knowing him (John 18:27; Matt 26:74; Luke 22:57). After the crucifixion, the disciples lock themselves away in fear (John 20:19).

Jesus's life also contains unflattering details. For example, his mother was so poor that she could only offer two doves for the ritual purification after his birth,[50] and professor of the New Testament Craig Keener points out that "no one would have invented Jesus' Galilean background. Such a background was obscure to most people in the Diaspora, and Judean critics could employ it as a matter of scorn."[51] A doubting John the Baptist sends his disciples to check whether Jesus is after all the expected Messiah

50. Luke 2:24; Lev 12:4–8.

51. Keener, *Historical Jesus*, 178. Alfred Edersheim also argued that contemporary Judaism would never have expected the Messiah to be the son of a humble Galilean workman (*Life and Times*, 102).

(Matt 11:3; Luke 7:19). Jesus cannot work many miracles in Nazareth (Mark 6:5), is ignorant of the time of his return (Mark 13:32; Matt 24:36), and has to repeat his attempts to heal a blind man (Mark 8:22–26). He denies that he is a "good" teacher (Mark 10:18) and approves of the waste of expensive perfume to anoint him (Mark 14:3–9; John 12:1–8). His own family thinks he is out of his mind (Mark 3:20–21; John 7:5). His empty tomb is not discovered by leading disciples but by a woman who had been possessed by demons (Mark 16:1; Luke 8:2). In the opinion of Samuel Byrskog, the story of the women at the tomb is likely to be an original tradition that only survived because of their continued role in the church: "How else but through their influence in the early community would the account of their presence have endured the androcentric force of transmission and redaction?"[52]

Even Jesus's death is contrary to ancient ideals of martyrdom. For example, a Jewish tradition recorded that when seven brothers were tortured and killed for refusing to eat pork, one made this dying declaration: "The King of the world shall raise us up, who have died for his laws, unto everlasting life" (2 Macc 7:9b KJV). But Jesus offers no such heroic last words—he sweats blood at the thought of his coming ordeal and prays to be spared (Mark 14:36; Luke 22:42), and he dies with a cry of abandonment.[53]

Negative details such as these would not have provided any particular benefit to the later church, the early Christian communities, or Jesus's first followers. It seems reasonable to assume that they were preserved because they were part of an original, respected tradition that was based on eyewitness testimony.

The Criterion of Dissimilarity to the Norm

Although the gospel narratives are firmly set in a first-century Jewish context, they also depict Jesus acting against the norms of his time and culture. He is frequently described as challenging prevailing customs, and

52. Byrskog, *Story as History*, 81. James Dunn agrees that this tradition was probably recorded in the Gospels because "there was a persistent report within the communal memory of the earliest churches that the first witnesses had been women" (*Jesus Remembered*, 843 n. 75).

53. "And at three in the afternoon Jesus cried out in a loud voice, '*Eloi, Eloi, lema sabachthani?*' (which means 'My God, my God, why have you forsaken me?')" (Mark 15:34). See also Matt 27:46.

he preaches a distinctive and unusual message. According to the criterion of dissimilarity, this suggests that these recorded acts and teachings are more likely to be authentic than fabricated.[54] Here are a few examples:

- Jews who collected Roman taxes were despised by fellow Jews, but Jesus ate with tax collectors (Mark 2:15; Luke 15:1) and invited one (Levi/Matthew) to be his disciple.
- Jesus's association with sinners was not merely disreputable—it flouted respected religious principles. He also made the scandalous claim that sinners would enter God's kingdom before some respected religious leaders (Matt 21:31).
- There was bitter enmity between Jews and Samaritans. Jesus's Jewish opponents even accused him of being "a Samaritan and demon-possessed" (John 8:48). But in his parable, a Samaritan behaved more compassionately than a Levite and a Jewish priest (Luke 10:31–33).
- Judaism viewed financial success as a reward from God, but Jesus taught that it is almost impossible for a rich man to enter God's kingdom (Matt 19:24; Mark 10:25; Luke 18:25). His startled disciples asked, "Who then can be saved?" (Matt 19:25b).
- Jesus made physical contact with "untouchable" lepers and allowed a woman to wash his feet in public (Luke 7:36).
- He commanded a man to disregard the prescribed rituals for his dead father (Luke 9:60; Matt 8:22).
- He challenged Mosaic law. For example, he characterized marriage to a divorced woman as adultery, which his disciples had to ask him to explain again (Mark 10:10). He taught that food cannot defile a man (Matt 15:11) and allowed his disciples to "break the tradition of the elders" (Matt 15:2) by not fasting or washing hands (Mark 7:5; Luke 11:38; 5:33). He contradicted the Mosaic restriction on consuming blood when he taught that his followers should eat his flesh and drink his blood, which caused many to reject him (John 6:53–60).

As N. T. Wright observes, "these actions presented a challenge to certain aspects of the Jewish worldview . . . Almost all serious contemporary

54. The criterion of "double dissimilarity" judges Jesus's words to be authentic *only* if they disagree with both Judaic and later Christian traditions. But this approach has been heavily criticized, and the form used here simply regards challenges to respected Jewish traditions as likely to be authentic.

writers about Jesus would agree that something like this activity was indeed characteristic of him."[55] A first-century Jewish teacher would have been expected to uphold the law, and professor of oriental law J. Duncan Derrett remarks that Jesus's unconventional acts and teachings would have been embarrassing and awkward for his followers.[56] It therefore seems unlikely that his Jewish disciples would have invented these details, and it is unclear what advantage they might have offered the later Gentile church.

The Criterion of Historical Plausibility

The Gospels draw a historically plausible picture, which suggests a Palestinian origin for these traditions. Here are a few examples of historically accurate details:

- The desire of Jesus's followers to make him king (John 6:15) was consistent with messianic expectations.[57]
- Mary Magdalene's name probably indicated that she came from the ancient city of Magdala on the shore of the Sea of Galilee, in the modern Israeli municipality of Migdal.
- On the Sabbath day, people came for healing at sunset when restrictions would no longer apply (Luke 4:31–40; Mark 1:21–32).
- People farmed pigs in the Gadarene region (Matt 8:28–30), which was a Gentile area.[58]
- The New Testament reports that Herod Agrippa held a birthday banquet (Mark 6:21), and this practice has been independently confirmed.[59]

55. Wright, *Victory*, 150.

56. Derrett, *Law in the New Testament*, xxi.

57. According to Josephus, around AD 66 the messianic Menachem ben Judah "returned in the state of a king to Jerusalem" and went into the temple "adorned with royal garments" (*Wars* 2.17.8–9).

58. Josephus wrote, "As to Gaza, and Gadara, and Hippos, they were Grecian cities, which Caesar separated from his government, and added them to the province of Syria" (*Ant.* 27.11.4).

59. Josephus wrote, "When Agrippa was solemnizing his birthday . . . he gave festival entertainments to all his subjects" (*Ant.* 19.7.1).

- The reports of Jesus's crucifixion included the historically correct details of a notice of the crime being fixed to the top of the cross (Mark 15:26; Matt 27:37; Luke 23:38; John 19:19) and the victim's legs being broken to bring on death through suffocation (John 19:31–32).

Review the Evidence

The gospel accounts depict Jesus teaching an unpopular message and challenging cultural norms. They also often cast him and his disciples in an unflattering light. These details do not seem to provide any benefit to the later church or Jesus's early followers, so there would have been no reason to invent them. According to the criteria of dissimilarity and embarrassment, they are more likely to record eyewitness testimonies than to be fabrications. Together with historically plausible details, these aspects contribute to an overall impression of the authenticity of the gospel accounts. And Vincent Taylor made this observation about the continuing influence of Jesus's first Jewish followers:

> The one hundred and twenty at Pentecost did not go into permanent retreat; for at least a generation they moved among the young Palestinian communities, and through preaching and fellowship their recollections were at the disposal of those who sought information . . . When all qualifications have been made, the presence of personal testimony is an element in the formative process [of the Gospels] which it is folly to ignore.[60]

Experienced cold-case detective J. Warner Wallace describes himself as being an "angry atheist"[61] when he investigated the Gospels using linguistic analysis from his field of expertise. In his book, *Cold Case Christianity*, he discusses the evidence that led him to conclude that the Gospels *do* record eyewitness testimony. Those who allege that the Gospels do *not* contain any traditions based on eyewitness testimony are increasingly being challenged to meet the burden of proof.[62]

60. Taylor, *Formation*, 42–43.

61. Wallace, *Cold Case Christianity*, 16.

62. See Ellis, "Gospels as History," 6; Stein, "'Criteria' for Authenticity," 253.

Consider Your Verdict

How likely is it that at least some details in the Gospels are authentic and reflect an original eyewitness tradition?

- Very likely
- Possible
- Unlikely
- Impossible

3.3 HOW DID THE "GOOD NEWS" BECOME WRITTEN GOSPEL?

The claim of eyewitness traditions behind the Gospels is a two-edged sword—the accounts are worthless if they have no link to original testimony, but eyewitness evidence is notoriously unreliable. Every experience is shaped by perception, and stories are adapted in some ways as they circulate. It is therefore important to understand how early memories of Jesus's acts and words might have been preserved and transmitted.

Jesus is said to have sent out as many as seventy apostles (Luke 10:1; from *apostolos*: one sent forth), and many other believers would have spread the "good news" about Jesus.[63] Peter's first converts at the Jewish Feast of Weeks (Pentecost) included pilgrims from widely dispersed regions,[64] and each year after that, many thousands of visitors to the annual Jerusalem festivals would have heard and disseminated the message about Jesus. Jesus's brothers taught in other regions (1 Cor 9:5), and after the first martyr Stephen was killed, many believers left Jerusalem to preach in Phoenicia, Cyprus, and Antioch (Acts 11:19). There would therefore have been a vast pool of information about Jesus that would

63. The concept of "good news" has an Old Testament background: "You who bring good news to Zion . . . say to the towns of Judah, 'Here is your God!'" (Isa 40:9 NIV). "Good news" is *euangelion* in Greek and *gōd-spell* in Old English, which is the basis for the term "gospel."

64. According to the Acts of the Apostles, Peter preached to "Parthians, Medes and Elamites; residents of Mesopotamia, Judea and Cappadocia, Pontus and Asia Phrygia and Pamphylia, Egypt and the parts of Libya near Cyrene; visitors from Rome" (Acts 2:9–10).

have been transmitted through both written and oral traditions, which has implications for its preservation.

The Role of Written Texts

Not many people in antiquity were skilled writers, but there are reasons for believing that some of Jesus's early followers would have been able to make brief notes:

- It was common in the Greco-Roman world to carry notebooks and make shorthand notes, which would have influenced practice in Palestine.[65]
- First-century Jewish disciples kept written notes, and talmudic scholar Saul Lieberman considers it likely that some of Jesus's disciples would have done this.[66]
- The tax collectors Matthew and Zacchaeus (Luke 19:1–10) would certainly have been able to write. Jesus's calling of Matthew is similar to the use of a scribe by prophets such as Jeremiah in the Old Testament.
- Early Christians came from all levels of society, and even some slaves could write.[67]
- Early converts included educated priests and Pharisees (Acts 6:7; 15:5), and the wife of the manager of Herod's household (Luke 8:3) and presumably her husband.
- The Qumran Dead Sea Scrolls provide evidence that even a sect that thought they were facing imminent end times found it worthwhile to record their traditions.

65. See Gundry, *Use of Old Testament*, xii.

66. Lieberman, *Hellenism*, 20. See also Millard, *Reading and Writing*, 197, 223–24; Keener, *Historical Jesus*, 149.

67. According to Mendels, "Many of Jesus' followers came from among the poor, but the wealthy and 'middle class' also showed an interest in, and joined, Jesus' movement" ("Pseudo-Philo," 264). Eric Eve notes that "the tendency has been to emphasize that ancient literacy was confined to the educated elites, and that few if any people from that class belonged to the primitive Church. This needs some qualification. The fact that the educated sometimes had their slaves read to them or take dictation implies the existence of literary slaves" (*Behind the Gospels*, 13).

It is therefore highly likely that some brief records were made about Jesus's teaching and work at a very early stage, even during his lifetime. Graham Stanton is one of many scholars who consider it likely that "notebooks were used by the very first followers of Jesus for excerpts from Scripture, for drafts and copies of letters, and perhaps even for the transmission of some Jesus traditions."[68] The process of recording Jesus's teachings would have been spurred on by the devastating disruption of the Jewish-Roman War from AD 66 to 70 and the deaths of some of the apostles around this time.

It is also not surprising that the gospel manuscripts are written in Greek. The Greek Septuagint was in wide use in Palestine by this time, and Jesus's disciples Philip and Andrew spoke Greek, as did some members of the early Jerusalem Church (John 12:20–21; Acts 6:1). Martin Hengel concludes from physical and literary evidence that Greek-speaking Jews comprised 10 to 20 percent of the Jerusalem population at the time of Jesus, and he concludes that the Greek message about Jesus would have had its roots among his early followers in Jerusalem.[69] Oskar Skarsaune agrees that "there is nothing un-Jewish about the fact that the New Testament was written in Greek."[70]

The Role of Oral Transmission

The message about Jesus might have been partially written down at an early stage. But it was also preached in predominantly oral cultures, which has important implications for its preservation and reliable transmission.

Antiquity placed immense emphasis on the precise rote learning of large amounts of material, which would have helped to establish some of Jesus's teachings in a stable form within a short time. Birger Gerhardsson points out that first-century rabbinic teaching used both written notes and rote memorization, and he suggests that Jesus's disciples would have been expected to preserve his teaching and acts through both methods.[71] The gospel materials certainly include features that were traditionally

68. Stanton, *Jesus and Gospel*, 6. See also Gundry, *Use of Old Testament*, xii; Ellis, "Gospels as History," 7; Stein, "Early Recension," 178.

69. Hengel, *Hellenization*, 10–11, 18.

70. Skarsaune, *Shadow of the Temple*, 43. See also Stein, "Early Recension," 181; Easton, *Christ*, 37.

71. Gerhardsson, *Memory and Manuscript*, xii, 202, 326–32. See also Riesenfeld, *Gospel Tradition*, 26–29.

used to assist memorization, such as parables, vivid imagery, parallelism, metaphors, and proverbs.[72]

But when stories about Jesus started to spread outside his immediate followers, would they have spiraled out of control? Imagine this scene: a small group sits in the shade of a tree, listening intently to the familiar story of the lame man who was let down through the roof to reach Jesus. They know the story well, and there are some nods of approval. But then the speaker changes the tradition by using the alternative word *skimpous* for pallet (Mark 2:4), and someone calls out a challenge: "Are you superior to the one who said *krabattos*?"

Eta Linnemann records this incident in her study of modern Near Eastern oral tradition, and she suggests that this type of community control would have helped to preserve early Jesus-traditions.[73] Kenneth Bailey similarly describes a Middle Eastern oral tradition that he calls *informal but controlled*, in which recognized figures of authority in the community perform the tradition and the audience accepts minor, but not major, adaptations. Bailey regards this as "the 'braking system' that keeps that movement within limits and assures continuity and authenticity to what is being transmitted."[74]

Anthropologist Jan Vansina also provides some relevant insights. He studied the transmission of oral traditions in African cultures and believes that "all human thought and memory operate in the same way . . . and hence avoid limitations of place and time."[75] Therefore, although first-century Palestine is a very different context, Vansina's conclusions about the stability of oral tradition have important implications for early Christianity. He writes:

> When accounts of events have been told for a generation or so, the messages then current *may still represent the tenor of the original message*, but in most cases the resulting story has been fused out of several accounts and has acquired a stabilized form.[76]

> Recent oral tradition—one or two generations beyond the eldest living members in a community—suffers only small damage.[77]

72. See Stein, *Method and Message*, 27–32; Taylor, *Formation*, 89–104.
73. Linnemann, *Synoptic Problem*, 184.
74. Bailey, "Informal Controlled Oral Tradition," 10.
75. Vansina, *Oral Tradition*, xii.
76. Vansina, *Oral Tradition*, 17 (emphasis added).
77. Vansina, *Oral Tradition*, 192–93.

Stories about Jesus were retold within communities of believers, and when Vansina compared one-to-one transmission with community-based transmission, he reached this conclusion:

> The information was still passed on, in fact by more people and more continually than in the first model and *with a better control on the accuracy* of information than in the first model . . . Multiple flow does not necessarily imply multiple distortion only, rather perhaps the reverse.[78]

And Vansina makes these observations about adaptations to oral tradition:

> Memorized wording escapes these limitations . . . Poetry and song are excellent sources . . . A very few come to stand in the position of prayer formulas which cannot be changed, even if they are no longer understood.[79]

This strongly suggests that sayings such as the Lord's Prayer and Jesus's words at the Last Supper would have been preserved through regular use in the early church.

Cognitive psychologist David Rubin also concludes from his research that oral traditions "change little over long periods, although they do change from telling to telling . . . The transmission of oral traditions is remarkable to the modern, literate observer. Songs, stories, and poems are kept in stable form in memory for centuries."[80] According to findings such as these, the original Jesus-tradition would have suffered little distortion between the deaths of the last apostles and the writing down of the Gospels (discussed in the next chapter).

The three Synoptic Gospels seem to provide direct evidence of exact preservation of the Jesus-tradition through oral transmission. Biblical scholar Brooke Westcott discovered that although the gospels of Matthew, Mark, and Luke share many common narratives, they do *not* share a high percentage of verbal material (words and phrases) *except when recording spoken words*, where they have a very high percentage of common material.[81] And spoken words are precisely what oral transmission tends to preserve most accurately:

78. Vansina, *Oral Tradition*, 31 (emphasis added).

79. Vansina, *Oral Tradition*, 193.

80. Rubin, *Memory in Oral Traditions*, 3.

81. Westcott, *Introduction*, 202–3. See also Sanders, *Tendencies*, 1. The gospels of Mark, Matthew, and Luke are called *synoptic* ("seen together") because of their shared

	Common verbal material as a percentage of the total material in the three Synoptic Gospels	Percentage of common verbal material that records spoken words
In Matthew	17%	88%
In Mark	17%	80%
In Luke	10%	95%

Here are some examples of this shared tradition that seems to reflect memorized spoken words:

- Mark and Luke describe Jesus's trial in their own way, but they both record precisely the same dialogue: "So Pilate asked Jesus, 'Are you the king of the Jews?' 'You have said so,' Jesus replied" (Luke 23:3; Mark 15:2).
- All three gospels contain the words that Jesus spoke when he healed a paralyzed man: "Get up, take your mat and go home" (Mark 2:11; Matthew 9:6; Luke 5:24).
- In both Luke and Matthew, the centurion says to Jesus, "For I too am a man under authority, with soldiers under me. And I say to one, 'Go,' and he goes, and to another, 'Come,' and he comes, and to my servant, 'Do this,' and he does it" (Matt 8:9; Luke 7:8).

When John Rist analyzed parallel passages in Matthew and Mark, he concluded that these two gospels drew independently from a shared oral tradition,[82] although this would not necessarily exclude the influence of written texts.

Form critics such as Rudolf Bultmann assumed that different Christian communities could have and would have freely adapted the Jesus-tradition to suit their immediate needs. And Jan Vansina does note that a community will express its tradition according to its present situation: "All messages have some intent which has to do with the present, otherwise they would not be told in the present and the tradition would

material.

82. Rist argues this interpretation in his book, *Independence of Matthew and Mark.*

die out."[83] However, he offers this important counter-balancing perspective: "Some sociologists go further and hold that the total content of oral tradition is only a social product of the present. Oral tradition is created in the present for society, and when the impact of the present is assessed there remains no message at all from the past. This is exaggerated. Where would social imagination find the stuff to invent from?"[84] Although oral transmission does *shape* its tradition, it does not *create* it.

It is also relevant to note that a strongly oral community usually recognizes specific individuals as official guardians of the tradition. It is therefore highly probable that Jesus's first apostles would have intentionally trained others to transmit the precious message of salvation. Judas apparently had to be replaced by someone who had known Jesus before and after his resurrection (Acts 1:21), and Paul seems to have had to cite his Damascus experience to claim recognition because he had not been one of Jesus's disciples.[85] In the opinion of Gerhardsson, "we have good reason for believing that the young church in all its 'enthusiasm' was both ordered and organized, and that it recognized some men—and not others—as doctrinal authorities."[86] Regarding Bultmann's claim of uncontrolled adaptation of the Jesus-tradition, Vincent Taylor noted dryly that this would imply that "the disciples must have been translated to heaven immediately after the resurrection."[87] Eric Eve agrees:

> It would be odd indeed if the Twelve ceased to have any function within a year or two of Jesus' death or if certain persons did not come to have much more control over the tradition than others; the notion that folk tradition about Jesus simply emerged from an anonymous egalitarian community probably owes more to romanticism than to . . . social realities.[88]

Early Christians would also have been deeply committed to their new faith. The scattered communities faced increasing animosity from fellow Jews and Roman authorities, and Larry Hurtado described the implications of becoming a follower of Jesus: "To embrace Christian faith in earliest Christianity was to ally oneself with a small, vulnerable

83. Vansina, *Oral Tradition*, 92.

84. Vansina, *Oral Tradition*, 94.

85. "Am I not an apostle? Have I not seen Jesus our Lord?" (1 Cor 9:1b).

86. Gerhardsson, *Memory and Manuscript*, 12.

87. Taylor, *Formation*, 41.

88. Eve, *Behind the Gospels*, 45.

religious movement . . . [that] almost certainly courted various forms of disapproval, even hostility, from wider social circles . . . For Gentiles, embracing Christian faith certainly meant cutting themselves out of participation in the civic cults . . . There were costs involved in joining this particular 'voluntary association' with its exclusivist demands."[89] Believers would therefore have treasured the traditions that defined their unpopular identity and united them together, and they would have been highly motivated to preserve these teachings. The New Testament also indicates that many followers had intense conversion experiences, and it has been shown that groups with a high percentage of conversions tend to have high levels of cohesion and commitment.[90]

The well-established network of visits and communications between the churches, centered on the Jerusalem Church, would have provided these scattered groups with extensive corporate memory. They would therefore have had both the desire and the means to control their tradition and minimize corruption. It is highly probable that the collective memory about Jesus would have maintained a stable core rather than spiraling into uncontrolled myth-making within the time taken to set it down in the written gospels.

Possible Authorship

Who wrote the four canonical gospels? In the second century, the church father Irenaeus recorded the authorial tradition: "Matthew also issued a written Gospel among the Hebrews in their own dialect . . . Mark, the disciple and interpreter of Peter, did also hand down to us in writing what had been preached by Peter. Luke also, the companion of Paul, recorded in a book the Gospel preached by him. Afterwards, John, the disciple of the Lord, who also had leaned upon His breast, did himself publish a Gospel during his residence at Ephesus in Asia."[91] The author of Luke's Gospel also wrote the Acts of the Apostles, addressing both texts to a man called Theophilus and starting Acts from where his gospel had ended.[92]

89. Hurtado, *Lord Jesus*, 652.

90. See Segal, "Conversion," 301.

91. Irenaeus, *Against Heresies* 3.1.1–4, translated by Roberts and Donaldson.

92. The book of Acts begins: "In my former book, Theophilus, I wrote about all that Jesus began to do and to teach" (Acts 1:1).

It is difficult to confirm this tradition, and many scholars argue against it. However, there is no obvious reason for identifying Luke and Mark as two of the authors instead of better known figures such as Peter, Thomas, or James, and there is no evidence of alternative authorial claims. There are also no anonymous copies of the four gospels: all manuscripts that are sufficiently intact confirm the traditional authorship, and Martin Hengel argues against the suggestion that the gospels first circulated anonymously.[93] Hengel is one of many scholars who do accept the traditional authorship.[94]

Each gospel has its own particular style, language usage, and emphasis, which indicates a single author, but this comment in John's Gospel also suggests collaboration between an individual and a group: "This is the disciple who testifies to these things and who wrote them down. We know that his testimony is true" (John 21:24). Rafael Rodríguez makes this important observation:

> The question of the gospel's authorship becomes less critical than frequently thought. The distinction between eyewitness testimony of Jesus and the testimony of those who passed on Jesus stories without ever having seen or heard him directly begins to blur when we take into account the social aspects of oral history and collective memory.[95]

Review the Evidence

Stories about Jesus's work and teaching were disseminated by many followers after his death. But the following facts suggest that their shared tradition would have been carefully controlled and preserved:

- The predominantly oral cultures of the time extensively used rote memorization for the accurate transmission of their traditions, which did not undergo radical changes.

93. Hengel, *Four Gospels*, 48–56.

94. For example, Darrell Bock suggests that "the preponderance of the evidence, mostly external in nature, does suggest that [Mark's] gospel was written by a companion of Peter, John Mark, in Rome" ("Blasphemy", 58 n. 9). Other scholars who support the authorial tradition include Blomberg, *Historical Reliability of John's Gospel*; Rist, *Independence of Matthew and Mark*; Guthrie, *New Testament Introduction*; Köstenberger et al., *Cradle*; Riesenfeld, *Gospel Tradition.*

95. Rodríguez, *Early Christian Memory*, 6 n. 7.

- Jewish disciples used notes and memorization to faithfully preserve the words and acts of their teacher.
- Many gospel passages were structured to aid memorization.
- Some of Jesus's early followers and converts would probably have been able to write brief notes of his acts and teachings.
- The communities of persecuted believers would have been motivated to preserve the shared traditions that defined their identity.
- The first apostles and the Jerusalem Church were widely recognized as authorities, and frequent communication and visits between early Christian communities would have kept the tradition connected to its origins.

Instead of the Jesus-tradition developing from fluid oral forms to fixed written forms, evidence rather suggests there would have been a shared oral and written tradition that became less flexible as the four gospels were gradually accorded the status of Scripture.

This social-memory approach to the Gospels does accept that even the earliest memories of Jesus would have contained some conflicting details and would have been shaped over time, but this does not suggest that the accounts are unreliable. For example, all four gospels report that a woman anointed Jesus with perfume (Mark 14:3; Matt 26:6; Luke 7:37–38; John 12:1–3), but they provide different details about who she was and where and how this took place. These differences could be the result of faulty memory or the process of oral transmission, but it is still highly probable that an incident of this nature did take place. As Chris Keith puts it, "admitting that one cannot grasp the historical Jesus in full is not the same as saying one cannot approach him with a degree of confidence—lack of complete access to the past is not the same as a complete lack of access to the past."[96] Biblical scholar Daniel Wallace makes this comment regarding accusations that the Gospels are totally unreliable:

> At bottom, postmodern textual critics have confused absolute certainty—which we cannot have—with reasonable certainty—which we can. And they are even calling this reasonable certainty a "blind leap of faith" without recognizing that their own skepticism requires much more faith.[97]

96. Keith, "Memory and Authenticity," 174.

97. Wallace, "Challenges," 89.

As theologian Craig Keener reasonably asks: "Should not the burden of proof rest on the assumptions of radical skeptics, rather than on the assumption that Jesus' disciples were like other disciples in antiquity and hence sought to transmit their master's sayings accurately?"[98]

Consider Your Verdict

What is the likelihood that the writers of the Gospels could have extensively revised an existing Jesus-tradition and added radically innovative ideas that became widely accepted by the churches? In other words, how likely is it that the gospel traditions are substantially different from the early eyewitness memories of Jesus?

- Very likely
- Possible
- Not very likely
- Highly unlikely

3.4 WHAT IS THE MANUSCRIPT EVIDENCE FOR THE GOSPELS?

Having explored the oral-textual Jesus-tradition that became written gospel, this section will investigate the manuscript evidence for the Gospels with the aim of answering two questions:

- Do the Gospels contain traditions that were widely known to early Christian communities?
- Were the Gospels substantially corrupted over time?

Question 1: What Is the Earliest Evidence of the Gospel Teachings?

Written traditions about Jesus circulated among the early Christian communities in letters and other texts. Some of these letters were accepted into the canonical New Testament while others were not.[99] This chapter

98. Keener, *Historical Jesus*, 150.

99. The letters that were accepted into the New Testament canon are Paul's Epistles,

will trace the earliest evidence of the gospel teachings using two sets of sources: *indirect* evidence in noncanonical Christian letters and texts and *direct* evidence in the surviving manuscripts of the four gospels.

Indirect Evidence: Gospel Material in Early Christian Letters

Noncanonical church writings from the end of the first century and the early second century provide valuable evidence that numerous sayings, incidents, and doctrines found in the four gospels were already in wide circulation by that time:

- First Clement (ca. 95)—This letter was sent from the church in Rome to the church in Corinth at the end of the first century.[100] The writer reminded the Corinthians about Paul's earlier epistle to them: "He wrote to you concerning himself, and Cephas, and Apollos, because even then parties had been formed among you."[101] This important letter also contained material that is found in the Gospels, such as this: "Remember the words of our Lord Jesus Christ, how He said, 'Woe to that man! It were better for him that he had never been born, than that he should cast a stumbling-block before one of my elect. Yea, it were better for him that a millstone should be hung about [his neck], and he should be sunk in the depths of the sea.'"[102] "For thus He spoke: 'Be ye merciful, that ye may obtain mercy; forgive, that it may be forgiven to you; as ye do, so shall it be done unto you; as ye judge, so shall ye be judged.'"[103]
- Letters of Ignatius (ca. 105–115)[104]—On his way from Antioch (in modern-day Turkey) to his martyrdom in Rome, Ignatius wrote

Hebrews, James, First and Second Peter, Jude, and First, Second, and Third John.

100. Tradition associated this letter with Clement, although his name is not in the text. Many scholars support a late first-century dating for the letter. See, for example, Ehrman, *Apostolic Fathers*, 6.

101. 1 Clement 47.3 (referring to 1 Cor 1:11–13). Quotations from First Clement are taken from the translation by Roberts and Donaldson.

102. From 1 Clement 46. See Mark 9:42; 14:21; Matt 18:6; 26:24; Luke 17:2.

103. From 1 Clement 13. See Matt 7:2; Luke 6:38.

104. The letters of Ignatius exist in a shorter form and a longer form that contains later additions. The quotations in this section are from the shorter form, which most scholars regard as authentic. See, for example, Ehrman, *Apostolic Fathers*, 4, 325; Roberts and Donaldson, *Apostolic Fathers*, 134; Trebilco, "Christian Communities," 20. The translation is by Roberts and Donaldson.

letters to various churches using material that is found in the canonical gospels, such as: "the tree is made manifest by its fruit,"[105] and "be in all things wise as a serpent, and harmless as a dove."[106] Ignatius described how the risen Jesus invited the disciples to touch him to see he was not a spirit,[107] and he called Jesus the heavenly bread, the source of eternal life, and the Son of God who became the physical descendant of David.[108]

- The Letter of Polycarp (ca. 110–150)—From the city of Smyrna (Izmir in modern-day Turkey), Polycarp sent copies of Ignatius's Letters to the Philippian Church and added his own covering letter. This important text also shares some material with the Gospels: "[Be] mindful of what the Lord said in His teaching . . . 'Blessed are the poor, and those that are persecuted for righteousness' sake, for theirs is the kingdom of God'";[109] "[Beseech] the all-seeing God 'not to lead us into temptation,' as the Lord has said: 'The spirit truly is willing, but the flesh is weak'";[110] "Pray also for kings, and potentates, and princes, and for those that persecute and hate you."[111]
- The Letter of Barnabas (ca. 70–130)—This is an early Judeo-Christian text, which significantly used the Jewish term "the eighth day" to describe the Sunday "on which Jesus rose again from the dead" (15:9). It also applied the traditional Jewish phrase for Scripture ("as it is written") to material found in Matthew's Gospel: "Let us beware lest we be found [fulfilling that saying], as it is written, 'Many are called, but few are chosen.'"[112] This important letter called Jesus the Son of God who came "not to call the righteous, but sinners to repentance."[113] It also mentioned the remission of sins through

105. From Ephesians 14. See Matt 12:33.
106. From Polycarp 2. See Matt 10:16.
107. From Smyrnaeans 3. See Luke 24:39.
108. From Romans 7.
109. From Polycarp 2. See Matt 5:3. The translation is by Roberts and Donaldson.
110. From Polycarp 7. See Matt 6:13; 26:41; Mark 14:38.
111. From Polycarp 12. See Matt 5:44.
112. Barnabas 4.14. See Matt 22:14. The translation is by Roberts and Donaldson.
113. Barnabas 5.9. See Luke 5:32; Matt 9:13.

Jesus's blood,[114] Jesus choosing apostles to preach his gospel,[115] and Jesus drinking vinegar and gall on the cross.[116]

- The Didache/Teaching (ca. 80–130)—Bart Ehrman suggests a date before 110 AD for this important document.[117] It records material that is also found in the Gospels,[118] including the Lord's Prayer (8.3–10) and the prediction of Jesus's return on the clouds of heaven (16.2–3, 17).

These surviving Christian texts provide evidence of an early and widespread belief that Jesus was the resurrected Son of God who died to atone for human sin and promised to return in the future. These doctrines were therefore not late creations. It also suggests that radical changes to the tradition would have been recognized. As theologian James Dunn points out, "When the Synoptics were first received by the various churches, these churches already possessed (in communal oral memory or in written form) their own versions of much of the material. They would have been able to compare the Evangelist's version of much of the tradition with their own versions."[119]

Direct Manuscript Evidence of the Gospels

The oldest papyrus fragments of the Gospels (P52 and P104) are probably from the second century, containing verses from John and Matthew.[120] The manuscript P75 is typically dated to between 200 and 225 and contains roughly half of Luke and half of John. The oldest almost complete New Testament (in the Codex Vaticanus) is dated to the mid-fourth

114. Barnabas 5.1. See John 1:7.

115. Barnabas 5.9. See Luke 5:32; Matt 9:13.

116. Barnabas 7.3. See Matt 27:34.

117. Ehrman, *Apostolic Fathers*, 405.

118. For example, this gospel material is found in the Didache: "Bless them that curse you, and pray for your enemies. Fast on behalf of those that persecute you; for what thank is there if ye love them that love you? Do not even the Gentiles do the same?" (Didache 1.7–8; see Matt 5:47; Luke 6:28); "If anyone give thee a blow on thy right cheek, turn unto him the other also, and thou shalt be perfect; if anyone compel thee to go a mile, go with him two; if a man take away thy cloak, give him thy coat also" (Didache 1.10–12; see Matt 5:39–41; Luke 6:29); "Be thou meek, for the meek shall inherit the earth" (Didache 3.12; see Matt 5:5). The translation is by Roberts and Donaldson.

119. Dunn, *Jesus Remembered*, 250.

120. P52 contains John 18:31–33, 37, 38; P104 contains Matthew 21:34–37, 43, 45.

century, and its material agrees very strongly with P75. This similarity is highly significant because these documents are separated by approximately 125 years and, even more importantly, P75 is not a direct "ancestor" of the codex, so they indicate faithful copying from an even earlier common source.[121]

Frequent copying and the short life span of papyrus explain the lack of first-century gospel manuscripts; for example, Paul wrote his letters in the fifties and sixties, but the oldest manuscript evidence (P46) is dated to around 200 at the earliest. Many scholars believe that the Gospels were originally written in the first century. According to biblical specialist Bart Ehrman,

> Most historians think that Mark was the first of our Gospels to be written, sometime between the mid 60s to early 70s. Matthew and Luke were probably produced some ten or fifteen years later, perhaps around 80 or 85. John was written perhaps ten years after that, in 90 or 95.[122]

> By the year 80 or 85 we have at least three independent accounts of Jesus's life (since a number of the accounts of both Matthew and Luke are independent of Mark), all within a generation or so of Jesus himself.[123]

The first Christian communities regarded the Hebrew Bible (largely in its Greek translations) as their holy Scripture, and the concept of a "new" Testament only developed over time. But Justin Martyr records that by the middle of the second century, Christian communities were reading written works of Jesus's apostles alongside the Old Testament: "And on the day called Sunday, all who live in cities or in the country gather together to one place and the memoirs of the apostles or the writings of the prophets are read."[124] Justin Martyr, whose writings are accepted as authentic, quoted approximately one hundred and fifty times from the Gospels. For example, in *Dialogue with Trypho*, he wrote: "the Holy Ghost lighted on Him like a dove, [as] the apostles of this very Christ of ours wrote"; "we find it recorded in the memoirs of His apostles that

121. See Wallace, "Textual Reliability," 36.

122. Ehrman, *New Testament*, 40. For these dates, see also Hengel, *Four Gospels*, 113–14.

123. Ehrman, *Did Jesus Exist?* 76. Ehrman ends this sentence with the comment, "assuming he lived," but this extract is part of his argument *against* Jesus-mythicists.

124. Justin Martyr, *First Apology* 67, translated by Roberts and Donaldson.

He is the Son of God"; "He said, 'Father, into Thy hands I commend my spirit,' as I have learned also from the memoirs."[125] Around 170, Justin's student Tatian harmonized the four gospels into one account known as the *Diatessaron*.

Question 2: Have the Gospel Manuscripts Been Substantially Corrupted?

What does textual analysis reveal about possible alterations to the four canonical gospels? Were changes made over time, which distorted the early understanding of Jesus's nature? The comparison of many thousands of fragments and texts has revealed only a few significant variants, which do not affect any central doctrine. Here are some examples:

- The oldest version of Matthew (P104) does not contain verse 21:44, which is considered to be a later addition.[126]
- Not all manuscripts contain Luke 12:9 or John 5:4.[127]
- Early manuscripts of John do not include the story of the adulterous woman (John 7:53—8:11), which might have been incorporated from oral tradition.[128]
- The trinitarian reference in Matthew 28:19 is in all manuscripts, but a similar reference in First John 5:8 is a later addition.[129]
- The two oldest manuscripts of Mark end with the women at the empty tomb (Mark 16:8), while almost all others include a shorter or longer ending, or both.[130]

125. Justin Martyr, *Dialogue* 88, 100, 103, translated by Roberts and Donaldson.

126. "Anyone who falls on this stone will be broken to pieces; anyone on whom it falls will be crushed" (Matt 21:44).

127. "But whoever disowns me before others will be disowned before the angels of God" (Luke 12:9). "From time to time an angel of the Lord would come down and stir up the waters. The first one into the pool after each such disturbance would be cured of whatever disease they had" (John 5:4).

128. The Didascalia Apostolorum, written in the early to middle third century, refers to Jesus forgiving a sinful woman who the Jewish elders brought before him.

129. Earlier versions of First John read, "The Spirit and the water and the blood, and these three are in agreement" (1 John 5:8). The trinitarian version only appears in later centuries: "For there are three that testify in heaven: the Father, the Word and the Holy Spirit, and these three are one."

130. Scholars variously argue that Mark's Gospel had the longer ending, that the

- The phrase, "For thine is the kingdom, the power and the glory" (Matt 6:13) is not in the earliest manuscripts of Matthew or in Luke's version of the Lord's Prayer, but it is in the Didache version. It suggests a Jewish source, as the verse is similar to lines from an Old Testament prayer of King David.[131]
- Not all manuscripts contain the "Son of God" phrase in Mark 1:1, although some scholars regard this as authentic.[132] In the same gospel, a heavenly voice does call Jesus the Son of God (Mark 1:11; 9:7).
- In some cases, scribes might have deliberately omitted verses or words they disapproved of. For example, not all manuscripts have the full name Jesus Barabbas (Matt 27:17), Jesus's words, "Father, forgive them, for they know not what they are doing" (Luke 23:34a), Jesus sweating blood (Luke 22:44),[133] or Jesus not knowing the time of his return.[134]
- There is also evidence of scribal harmonizing. For example, in some manuscripts of Luke 3:22, the heavenly voice at Jesus's baptism says, "This day have I begotten thee" (from Psalm 2:7), but in others, the voice says, "In you I am well pleased," which agrees with Mark 1:11 and Matthew 3:17. This version might have become preferred in response to claims that Jesus was only adopted to divine sonship at his baptism or resurrection.[135]

Ancient Greek was not written with punctuation or spaces between the letters, so accurate copying was very difficult. As a result, there are

---

original ending was lost, or that the gospel was deliberately ended at verse 16:8. The two latter arguments seem to have best support.

131. David prayed, "Yours, O Lord, is the greatness, the power and the glory, the victory and the majesty; For all that is in heaven and in earth is Yours; Yours is the kingdom, O Lord, and You are exalted as head over all" (1 Chron 29:11).

132. See Boring, *Mark*, 30; Wasserman, "Son of God."

133. Justin Martyr recorded that the incident of Jesus sweating blood was in the "memoirs" of the apostles (*Dialogue*, 103). This process of excreting blood through the skin is called *hematidrosis* and is caused by blood capillaries rupturing into the sweat glands, often under extreme stress. Forensic pathologist Frederick Zugibe describes the physical and emotional causes of this phenomenon, provides known cases, and argues for its authenticity in Jesus's case (*Crucifixion of Jesus*, 8–15).

134. Some manuscripts do not have the phrase "nor the Son" in this verse: "But about that day or hour no one knows, not even the angels in heaven, nor the Son, but only the Father" (Matt 24:36).

135. See Streeter, *Four Gospels*, 143.

also thousands of minor manuscript variants caused by line-skipping, change of order, marginal commentaries, different spelling, and so on. However, when Johann Bengel compared thirty thousand variants from almost one hundred New Testament manuscripts, he concluded that no central Christian doctrine has been affected by these differences. This result is known as "the orthodoxy of the variants."[136]

Burnett Streeter's extensive comparison of "families" of New Testament manuscripts also identified a geographical pattern in the variations—early church texts from neighboring regions are far more similar than those from widely separated regions. Streeter commented that "the exactness of correspondence between the geographic propinquity and the resemblance of text exceeds anything we should have anticipated."[137] This strongly natural trend does not suggest that there was deliberate and widespread tampering with gospel manuscripts.

However, when the once evangelical Christian scholar Bart Ehrman discovered a possible error in Mark, he was shocked by the implication that the Bible is "a very human book."[138] His profound disillusionment then informed his textual analysis, so that in best-selling books, he now alleges that some variants provide evidence that New Testament texts were deliberately altered to introduce doctrines such as Jesus's divinity.[139] However, these variants are on the whole not new, and other biblical scholars disagree with this claim by the now-atheist Ehrman. They argue that his case "is frequently overstated in especially one of two ways: either his interpretation of the original text or his textual basis is a bit strained,"[140] that "too often he turns mere *possibility* into *probability*, and *probability* into *certainty*, where other equally viable reasons for

136. See Wallace, "Challenges," 92.

137. Streeter, *Four Gospels*, 106.

138. Ehrman, *Misquoting Jesus*, 11. Ehrman was concerned about a possible error in Mark regarding the name of a high priest in the time of King David (Mark 2:26). Interpretations of this verse can be found at https://bible.org/article/mark-226-and-problem-abiathar.

139. Ehrman argues for this deliberate textual corruption in *Misquoting Jesus* and *Orthodox Corruption of Scripture*.

140. Komoszewski et al., *Reinventing Jesus*, 288 n. 15. The subtitle of this book is: *How Contemporary Skeptics Miss the Real Jesus and Mislead Popular Culture.*

corruption exist,"[141] and that "there is much forcing of the evidence, and failure to see other possible lines of argument."[142]

In response to Ehrman's claims, Peter Head analyzed a passage from John's Gospel in P66 (dated to around 200), which contains many variants when compared to other manuscripts. However, unlike Ehrman, Head did not find evidence of a consistent trend in these scribal changes and instead reached this conclusion: "There is no cumulative pattern over a large number of examples. Attempts to discern a theological agenda in the work of our scribe generally involve over-interpreting the variations and, in any case, result in contradictory tendencies. I think it is preferable to see these as more or less directionless variations on the part of our careless, but committed scribe."[143] After a detailed analysis of Bart Ehrman's claims in *Misquoting Jesus* (which, incidentally, does not discuss any of Jesus's sayings), professor of New Testament studies Daniel Wallace reached this conclusion:

> Highly charged statements are put forth that Ehrman knows the untrained person simply cannot adequately process . . . Regarding the evidence, suffice it to say that *significant textual variants that alter core doctrines of the NT have not yet been produced*."[144]

Ehrman's position also seems somewhat inconsistent. For example, he alleges that scribes deliberately altered texts that could be interpreted as implying Jesus's adoption to the status of God's son, but he then admits that this was not a sustained trend, and he argues that Christians felt no pressure to change their texts:

141. Fee, "Review of *Orthodox Corruption*," 204 (original emphasis).

142. Birdsall, "Review of *Orthodox Corruption*," 460.

143. Head, "Scribal Behaviour," 73. In his article, Head critiques Ehrman's interpretations of the scribal variants in P66. For example, Pilate's statement, "Behold the man" (John 19:5) is omitted in P66, which Ehrman interprets as a deliberate attempt to downplay Jesus's humanity. In John 19:28, Jesus's thirst is not accompanied by the phrase, "in order to fulfill the scripture," which Ehrman suggests is designed to emphasize Jesus's human suffering; however, Head points out that this is the opposite tendency to the scribe's omission in John 19:5. P66 contains, "You, being a man, make yourself *the* God" (John 10:33b), and the italicized article is not in other manuscripts. Ehrman regards this as a deliberate attempt to claim absolute deity for Jesus, but Head points out that "God" without the article is still not an indefinite reference, and the scribe of P66 had marked this article for deletion, which does not suggest a deliberate, theologically motivated alteration.

144. Wallace, "Gospel According to Bart," 347 (original emphasis).

> None of these scribes appears to have made a concerted effort to adopt such readings with rigorous consistency. Almost certainly there was no attempt to create an anti-adoptionist recension of the New Testament. Indeed, the Christians of the proto-orthodox camp did not, on one level, *need* to change their texts . . . Most of the debates over Christology, then, centered on the correct *interpretation* of the texts rather than on their wording.[145]

Daniel Wallace makes this comment about Ehrman's *Misquoting Jesus*: "I wasn't sure exactly what he was saying. Reading it one way contradicted what he had written elsewhere, while reading it another way was hardly controversial."[146]

The Judaic Transmission of Tradition—Flexible yet Stable

A discussion of variations between gospel manuscripts should take into account the nature of the transmission of tradition within Judaism because this was the background for early Christianity, and there was an extended period of interaction between Christians and Jews.[147]

It is important to note that flexibility was a central feature of written Judaic tradition, and Birger Gerhardsson points out that "even the rabbis could rework their tradition, change formulations, cancel elements, and insert additions and new layers."[148] Torah scholar Martin Jaffee remarks that alongside the emphasis on exact memorization and preservation, rabbinic texts continued to be shaped by oral interpretation, and scribes considered it their responsibility to reframe a narrative where it seemed suitable.[149]

In his analysis of Old Testament manuscripts, including those found in the Dead Sea Scrolls of Qumran, Eugene Ulrich also identified two scribal trends: "faithful repetition of older text and creative reshaping . . . achieved through augmentation with additional material, rearrangement, [and] rewording" so that "the composition of the Scripture was dynamic, organic."[150] Scroll scholar James VanderKam agrees that while scribes did copy carefully, they also played a more constructive role and often blended

145. Ehrman, *Orthodox Corruption*, 116 (original emphasis).

146. Wallace, "Textual Reliability," 28.

147. See Skarsaune, *Shadow of the Temple*, 14.

148. Gerhardsson, *Memory and Manuscript*, xix.

149. Jaffee, *Torah in the Mouth*, 24–29.

150. Ulrich, *Dead Sea Scrolls*, 6, 8.

wording from parallel scriptural passages,[151] which is evident in the New Testament and other scriptural texts such as the Islamic Qur'an.[152]

So in general, "fixity and fluidity between texts *were part and parcel of the ways written texts were accessed in a traditional milieu*."[153] We should therefore expect that the oral-textual transmission of the early Jesus-tradition would have included some flexibility alongside careful preservation.[154] Against this background, textual variations do not provide evidence that the Gospels are unreliable or that any group deliberately manipulated the accounts. The fact that scribes could legitimately adapt Scripture also indicates that a text was not valued for its word-for-word *accuracy* so much as for its ability to express the correct *message* to its intended audience. According to Martin Hengel,

> Making a favourable impression on the reader was more important than "fidelity to the text" and historico-philological precision. This was true for most Jewish—also for early Christian—literature between the second centuries BCE and CE.[155]

It might therefore be wise not to revere the gospel texts themselves but to regard them as a finger pointing to the truth. Bart Ehrman's unfortunate disillusionment with Scripture is not the inevitable outcome of textual analysis, and very few biblical scholars have rejected Christianity as a result of textual fluidity.[156]

151. VanderKam, *Dead Sea Scrolls*, 11.

152. Sadeghi and Goudarzi identified scribal variants in Qur'anic manuscripts, including "additions, omissions, transpositions, and substitutions of entire words . . . [and] *assimilation of parallels*—whereby a scribe's writing of a verse is affected by his or her memory of a similar verse elsewhere in the Qur'ān" ("Origins of the Qur'ān," 20, original emphasis). Scholar of the Qur'an James Bellamy also identified more than two hundred meaningful variants and commented that "there was no solid oral tradition stemming directly from the prophet to prove which variant was correct" ("Textual Criticism of the Koran," 1). See also Daniel Brubaker, *Corrections in Early Qur'ān Manuscripts*.

153. Rodríguez, *Early Christian Memory*, 8 (original emphasis).

154. See Gerhardsson, *Memory and Manuscript*, xv; Bailey, "Informal Controlled Oral Tradition," 6–7.

155. Hengel, *Septuagint*, 87.

156. See Sanders, *Canon and Community*, 3.

Review the Evidence

Were the Gospels late creations without any connection to an original Jesus-tradition? Were they substantially distorted? Could they preserve any authentic information about Jesus?

The oldest extant manuscript evidence for the Gospels is dated to the second century. This is often claimed to be very late evidence, but by comparison, the oldest Buddhist manuscripts are dated to *four hundred years* after the Buddha's death and are still considered to preserve some of his original teachings. In general, regarding the date and quantity of copies, the New Testament has far better textual support than any other Greco-Roman literature.[157] Many scholars believe that the four gospels were written in the first century, and material in early second-century church texts provides evidence of an early and wide circulation of the traditions recorded in the Gospels, including belief in Jesus's deity and resurrection. This does not support claims that these doctrines were later inventions by the Gentile church or corruptions of Scripture.

There are a vast number of minor differences among the many thousands of gospel manuscripts, and in some cases, scribes did harmonize different accounts. However, variations between the gospel narratives were largely respected and left unchanged, which is why the manuscripts still contain these differences. There is some evidence of scribal adaptations for theological reasons, but even these do not indicate a sustained attempt to introduce new doctrines. It is interesting that in 1997, Bart Ehrman had already identified theologically motivated alterations in the Gospels, but at the time, he nonetheless stated confidently that "in spite of these remarkable differences, scholars are convinced that we can reconstruct the original words of the New Testament with reasonable (although probably not 100 percent) accuracy."[158] Nothing has changed since then except his personal perceptions. Burnett Streeter's textual analysis led him to a similar conclusion: "A text of the Gospels can be reached, the freedom of which from serious modification or interpolation is guaranteed by the concurrency of different lines of ancient and

157. As Daniel Wallace points out, "We have more than 1,000 times as many copies of the NT as we do of almost any Greco-Roman author. And the earliest of those copies come from within decades of the completion of the NT, while the average Greco-Roman author's surviving MSS do not show up for half a millennium" ("Challenges," 88).

158. Ehrman, *New Testament*, 415.

independent evidence."[159] Komoszewski et al. therefore accuse writers who exaggerate the implications of textual variants of being "sloppy and irresponsible."[160]

Consider Your Verdict

This investigation has considered evidence related to two questions.

What is the likelihood that the four canonical gospels recorded an early and widely known tradition?

- Very likely
- Possible
- Highly unlikely
- Impossible

What is the likelihood that the core doctrines of the four canonical gospels have been largely preserved since they were written?

- Very likely
- Possible
- Highly unlikely
- Impossible

CONCLUSION 3
HOW RELIABLE ARE THE GOSPELS?

What does the evidence from this investigation suggest about the authenticity of the gospel material? Let's see what decisions might be possible at this point:

159. Streeter, *Four Gospels*, 148.

160. Komoszewski et al., *Reinventing Jesus*, 279 n. 1. In particular, these authors characterize Freke and Gandy's *Jesus Mysteries* as "a good illustration of radical liberal's critical ignorance about, and abuse of, textual criticism" (*Reinventing Jesus*, 278 n. 1).

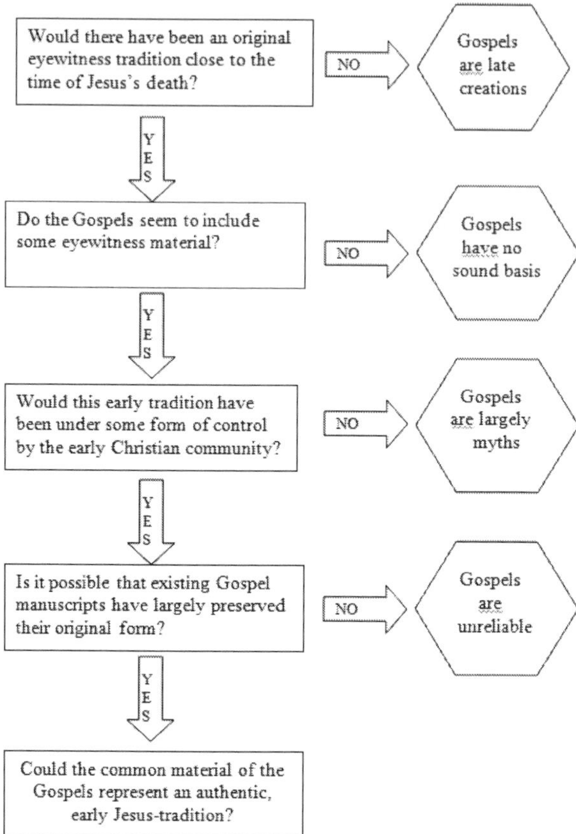

Figure 2: Making decisions about the Gospels.

If the answer to the last question is "No," there is no foundation for proceeding with an investigation into the orthodox Jesus-figure. This is a critical decision point, so it is worth carefully considering the argument of one scholar who returns a negative answer. Burton Mack, who studied at the University of Göttingen under a student of Rudolf Bultmann, claims that Jesus only taught the principles of Hellenistic Cynicism, his first followers merely admired him as a non-messianic wisdom teacher, and the gospel narratives of his life are late mythological additions. Christianity as we know it was therefore not based on Jesus's teachings, death, and resurrection but was the result of loosely formed groups "experimenting with new social relationships and experiences."[161] What is the evidence

161. Mack, "Christ," 217–18.

for this hypothesis? Mack dramatically declares that a newly discovered "Q-gospel" has confirmed his theory.[162] He writes:

> Its discovery in recent years has created a bit of consternation among Christian scholars . . . [because] the narrative gospels can no longer be viewed as trustworthy accounts.[163]
>
> [This] is hard evidence from the earliest period of Christian beginnings, a new text that has recently come to light.[164]

However, despite Mack's explicit claims, the apparently sensational Q-gospel is not a recent discovery and is not even a document, so it is not "hard evidence" of anything—it is merely an old theory. Scholars have long noticed that the gospels of Matthew and Luke share some material that is not found in Mark's Gospel. They suggest that this material might have been copied from a hypothetical written text dubbed "Q" (from the German *quelle*: source). Mack's so-called "lost Q-Gospel" is merely these familiar verses in Matthew and Luke. Following Rudolf Bultmann, Mack claims that these verses were written by Jesus's first followers (the "Q-people"), that they contain all the beliefs of this group, and that they prove there was no early belief in Jesus's resurrection or divinity.[165] According to Mack, all other gospel material must be regarded as later mythological additions, largely fabricated by Mark.[166] However, there are problems with Mack's Q-theory:

- Even if a Q-document did exist, which not all scholars believe, there is no consensus about which materials it would have included.[167]

162. Mack, *Lost Gospel*, 149.

163. Mack, *Lost Gospel*, 10.

164. Mack, *Lost Gospel*, 248.

165. This is similarly argued by John Kloppenborg (*The Formation of* Q) and Marcus Borg (*The Lost Gospel Q*).

166. Mack makes this comment about Mark's Gospel: "Mark's composition was a special case of mythmaking" ("Christ," 218).

167. Terence Mournet comments that "there is fundamental disagreement over the definition of Q and the scope, or boundaries of the source itself" (*Oral Tradition*, 10). Farrer agrees: "Q cannot be convincingly reconstructed. No one reconstruction, to say the least of it, is overwhelmingly evident, and no proposed reconstruction is very firmly patterned" ("Dispensing with Q," 57).

- Some supposed Q-material still implies that Jesus was more than a human wisdom teacher.[168] As a result, Mack and others have had to identify myth-making levels within Q itself, called Q2 and Q3. Even skeptical scholar Bart Ehrman does not support this speculation: "Q is a source that we don't have. To reconstruct what we think was in it is hypothetical enough . . . But to go further and insist that we know what was not in the source, for example, a Passion narrative, what its multiple editions were like, and which of these multiple editions was the earliest, and so on, really goes far beyond what we can know."[169]
- Like Wilhelm Bousset, Mack claims that Jesus's Jewish followers deified him because they expected the arrival of a figure of salvation known as the Son of Man.[170] However, there is no evidence of a pre-Christian belief in such a figure (see chapter 2.2).
- By definition, Q-material does not include verses that are found in Mark's Gospel. As a result, Burton Mack regards incidents that are found in all three Synoptic Gospels as fabrications.[171] However, there is no evidence that Mark unilaterally invented this material and that it later found its way into Matthew and Luke.
- The Q-people are supposed to have been Jewish disciples. However, there is no evidence that any group of first-century Palestinian Jews were committed to following a Hellenistic morality teacher.
- Mack alleges that core traditions such as the Lord's Supper and Jesus's divinity were the result of a "great change" when the Jesus-tradition moved outside Palestine, particularly into Syria where Mark could indulge in wild "myth-making."[172] However, our earlier investigations suggest that there would have been control over the

168. For example, in the Q-material, when John's disciples ask Jesus if he is the expected Messiah, he quotes from Isaiah's messianic promise that the crippled and blind are healed, and he adds that the dead are raised (Luke 7:22; Matt 11:5). Jesus also heals a centurion's servant (Luke 7:1–10; Matt 8:5–13) and predicts his return to implement final judgment (Luke 17:26; 18:8; Matt 16:27; 24:27).

169. Ehrman, *Jesus, Apocalyptic Prophet*, 133.

170. Mack, *Lost Gospel*, 149.

171. For example, these shared elements in all three Synoptic Gospels are not placed into the hypothetical Q-source: a heavenly voice declares Jesus to be God's son (Luke 3:22; Matt 3:17; Mark 1:11); Jesus tells his followers to take up their cross and follow him (Luke 14:27; Matt 10:38; Mark 8:34); women find the stone rolled away, and they are told that Jesus has risen (Mark 16:1–8, Matt 28:1–8; Luke 24:1–9).

172. Mack, "Christ," 215.

tradition even in these regions. In particular, Quispel points out that Syrian Christianity did not develop independently from Palestinian influence: "Scholarly research has shown convincingly that Jewish Christianity . . . was instrumental in bringing Christianity to Mesopotamia and further East, thus laying the foundations of a Semitic, Aramaic speaking, Syrian Christianity."[173]

Craig Keener points out that there is no historical basis for Mack's claim that Jesus's conduct and teaching were more Hellenistic than Jewish,[174] and he makes this comment:

> Many scholars recoil at Burton Mack's announcement that "Q is . . . a new text that has recently come to light." Scholars used the Q hypothesis through most of the twentieth century . . . But acknowledging and working from the hypothesis of Q is not the same as building a speculative hypothesis on a speculative reconstruction of a hypothetical document. Mack's particular *version* of Q is not a consensus document of NT scholarship . . . There is very much a *lack* of consensus about it.[175]

Mack's argument is another form of Wilhelm Bousset's late deification hypothesis, so it is important to assess its credibility.[176] Here is how Mack's "social experimentation" theory of Christianity compares to explanations in the New Testament:

According to the New Testament	**In Burton Mack's *Lost Gospel***
Jesus was a Jewish teacher who taught against the background of the OT and was regarded as the promised Messiah (Christ).	"Jesus was much more like a Cynic-teacher than either a Christ-savior or a messiah" (p. 245).

173. Quispel, "Judaic Christianity," 81. Jean Daniélou also argues that it was only later in the second century, when the Gospels were already in wide circulation, that Gentile Christian communities started to adapt their inherited Jewish Christianity to fit Hellenistic thought patterns (*Theology of Jewish Christianity*, 9–10).

174. Keener, *Historical Jesus*, 26.

175. Keener, *Historical Jesus*, 61 (original emphasis).

176. As N. T. Wright points out, "Mack's whole programme grows quite explicitly out of Bultmann and Wrede, with its emphasis on the fictitious (in every sense) work of Mark. His (Mack's) emphasis on primitive Palestinian Christianity as quite unlike the Christ-cult of Paul is straight out of Bultmann and Bousset" (*Victory*, 34–35).

According to the New Testament	In Burton Mack's *Lost Gospel*
Jesus's death was interpreted as an atoning work in the context of OT promises.	Belief in Jesus's atoning death arose because "a most unlikely mix of Jesus people was in need of 'justification,' or rationalization by means of a myth of origin" (p. 246).
The gospel message was a religious phenomenon, presented as the expansion of God's covenant with Israel.	The movement was "based on a new social anthropology" (p. 248). These beliefs arose because "the times were right for thinking new thoughts about traditional values" (p. 8).
The Jerusalem apostles did not dispute Paul's teaching of Jesus's divinity.	"The Christ myth . . . first emerged in northern Syria and the Pauline churches" (p. 246).
Jesus's followers were persecuted by Romans and fellow Jews, and some were martyred.	The new movement was exciting and appealing: "It was hardly the myth or the message that generated Christianity. It was the attraction of participating in a group experimenting with a new social vision" (p. 225).
Jesus's loving sacrifice and the promise of eternal life sustained his followers through persecution.	The Q-people "were sustained in their efforts to actualize their vision by a small selection of aphorisms, maxims, and images gathered from a profuse field of thought, lore, and mythology" (p. 256).
The Gospels contain some historically accurate information about first-century Jewish life in Palestine.	"The narrative gospels have no claim as historical accounts" (p. 247). They "were composed much later at crossroads in the history of the Jesus movements" (p. 246) and "must now be seen as the result of early Christian mythmaking" (p. 10).

In presenting his sociological hypothesis, Mack totally ignores the Judaic background of the New Testament material and the central role of the Old Testament in the early church. But he does not explain why Paul and other Jews would have associated a Hellenic morality teacher with Old Testament expectations. N. T. Wright criticizes Mack for "radically misreading first-century Judaism and completely marginalizing the theology and religion of Paul."[177] Mack's theory also does not explain why, as a wisdom teacher, Jesus would have aroused such hostility from some Jewish religious leaders and why the Romans would have crucified him. Mack's radical skepticism about the gospel material is a preferred interpretation rather than a conclusion from textual evidence, which is why he needs to incorrectly describe Q as an actual document, even though it is merely a hypothesis about the possible source of certain gospel verses.

Many scholars disagree with Mack, concluding that the Gospels do contain authentic descriptions of Jesus's life and teachings. James Dunn offers this opinion about the content of the Gospels:

> The probability is that the more constant material is the living heart of the earliest recollections of Jesus which has maintained the vitality of the tradition in all its variant forms.[178]

Critics like to produce long lists of discrepancies in the Gospels, but these differences are like leaves that cannot affect the branches, trunk, and roots of the central gospel message. In the opinion of historian Will Durant,

> The contradictions are of minutiae, not substance; in essentials the synoptic gospels agree remarkably well, and form a consistent portrait of Christ . . . The outline of the life, character, and teaching of Christ, remains reasonably clear.[179]

And historian Michael Grant reached this verdict about the reliability of the Gospels:

> The consistency, therefore, of the tradition in their pages suggests that the picture they present is largely authentic. By such methods information about Jesus *can* be derived from the Gospels.[180]

177. Wright, *Victory*, 43. Wright also suggests that "the existence of Q Christians, like that of Thomas Christians, may well turn out to be a modern myth" (*Victory*, 64).

178. Dunn, "Messianic Ideas," 371.

179. Durant, *Caesar and Christ*, 557.

180. Grant, *Jesus: Historian's Review*, 204 (original emphasis).

Investigation 4

Could the Orthodox View of Jesus Be Correct?

THE PREVIOUS INVESTIGATION SUGGESTS that the canonical gospels do record at least some authentic, early traditions about Jesus. These texts, together with the letters in the New Testament, present the teachings that came to be labeled as "orthodox" Christianity: that Jesus was the uniquely divine-human Son of God, his death provided atonement for humanity's rebellion against God, he rose physically after being crucified and will return for final judgment. But there is evidence of alternative beliefs about Jesus in texts such as the gnostic manuscripts found near Nag Hammadi in Egypt. Were these views just as valid as orthodox teachings? This investigation will explore three crucial questions regarding orthodox Christian doctrines:

- Were there equally valid "non-orthodox" beliefs about Jesus, which got bullied out of existence? In particular, do the gnostic gospels provide a more authentic picture of Jesus?
- Could Jesus have considered himself to be more than human? What claims did he make about himself?
- How should we regard the claim of his resurrection?

4.1 WERE "ORTHODOXY" AND "HERESIES" EQUALLY VALID VIEWS OF JESUS?

Given the appalling history of sectarian religious violence, the hair on the back of one's neck rises at the word "heresy." However, the deplorable actions of the later church are not relevant to an investigation into the validity of early Christian beliefs. The central question at this point is whether the New Testament presents the "correct" view of Jesus or if there was ever such a thing.

People seemed to struggle to classify Jesus's nature: "orthodox" teachings presented him as the eternal, divine-human Son of God; others believed he was a human being who was adopted as God's son at his baptism or resurrection; some regarded him as a created, semi-divine being between God and humanity; Gnosticism taught the docetic view that he was a purely spiritual being who only took on the appearance (*dokesis*) of a human being. When did these competing views arise? Do any of them represent Jesus more accurately? Did early Christianity even have a normative view of Jesus? It has become popular to claim that there were always many conflicting but equally legitimate beliefs about Jesus, a theory that can be traced to Walter Bauer.

Walter Bauer's Theory of Many Valid "Christianities"

In 1934 Walter Bauer, who taught at the University of Göttingen, identified a range of beliefs about Jesus in texts from the second to fifth centuries. He then projected these doctrines back into the first century and made the following claims, which challenged the legitimacy of Orthodox Christianity:[1]

1. According to Bauer, so-called heretical forms of Christianity arose earlier than orthodoxy in Asia Minor, Egypt, Edessa, and Rome, and heretics outnumbered the orthodox in these regions.
2. Bauer claimed that the Roman Church taught a minority form of Christianity, which it imposed on other Christians through political and financial power. It then suppressed valid alternative views and labeled them as "heresies."
3. This dominant winning sect then rewrote history to present itself as having always been the "orthodox" belief.

1. See Bauer, *Orthodoxy and Heresy*, xxii, 229–40.

According to Bauer, first century Christianity did not recognize a normative view of Jesus. Orthodox theology was just one view among many others, and all other conflicting claims about Jesus's nature and teachings should be regarded as being equally valid. This theory about the Roman Church's suppression of different but legitimate "Christianities" has become very popular, but modern scholars have challenged Bauer's evidence and conclusions. Below are six major criticisms.[2]

Heresies Were Not as Early or Extensive as Bauer Claimed

Some leaders of major heresies were initially part of the mainstream church, including Valentinus (a member of the church in Rome) and Marcion (who resigned from the church), so their "heretical" teachings did not precede orthodoxy. Bauer argued that Valentinian Gnosticism was the earliest and dominant form of Christianity in Rome, but this group's texts were based on New Testament materials, and they referred to themselves as a minority, so Bauer's conclusion is not valid.[3] Bauer had only very flimsy evidence to support his suggestion that the first form of Christianity in Edessa could have been Marcionite.[4]

Bauer claimed that Gnosticism was the original form of Christianity in Egypt, but of fourteen second- and third-century papyri found in Egypt, only the Gospel of Thomas shows some gnostic influence.[5] Bauer (and Rudolf Bultmann) alleged that New Testament Christology developed from gnostic redeemer myths, but recent scholarship has not found any evidence that this myth predated Christianity.[6] Paul Trebilco also points out that gnostic docetism seems to have developed *from* a high Christology of Jesus's divinity *to* a denial of his incompatible human nature so that docetism is unlikely to have been the original form of Christianity in any region.[7] Hengel agrees that gnostic systems were later attempts to hellenize existing Christian doctrines,[8] and professor of his-

2. Rodney Decker provided a very useful survey of some of these critiques in his article, "The Bauer Thesis: An Overview."

3. See McCue, "Orthodoxy and Heresy," 119.

4. See Turner, *Pattern*, 45.

5. See Köstenberger and Kruger, *Heresy of Orthodoxy*, 47. Some of these papyri were discovered after Bauer's time.

6. See Hengel, *Son of God*, 33; Bruce, *Paul*, 417; Segal, *Two Powers*, 15.

7. Trebilco, "Christian Communities," 23.

8. Hengel, *Crucifixion*, 16. See also Komoszewski et al., *Reinventing Jesus*, 303n. 22;

tory and religion Philip Jenkins reaches this conclusion: "What became the orthodox view has very clear roots in the first century, and indeed in the earliest discernible strands of the Jesus movement; in contrast, all the available sources for the Gnostic view are much later."[9]

Bauer's claim that early heretics were in the majority has also been challenged, and heresies have rather been identified as splinter factions on the periphery of the Church.[10] In particular, the Marcionite and Valentinian churches were minority groups among the Christian diversity in Rome.[11] Thomas Robinson's careful examination of Bauer's evidence led him to conclude that "Bauer's reconstruction of the history of the early church in western Asia Minor is faulty—not just in minor details—but at critical junctures."[12] In Robinson's opinion, "Heretics were neither early nor were they strong. The Bauer thesis requires that they be both."[13] Trebilco agrees:

> Where we can investigate the matter, what Bauer calls "heresy" is neither the earliest form of Christian faith, nor is it in the majority. None of this is to deny that there was significant diversity within earliest Christianity, both in the NT period and in the second century, nor that there was theological development from the NT period onwards. But in his reconstruction, Bauer has overlooked some key elements of the evidence.[14]

The Roman Church Was Not a Dominant Power during the First Two Centuries

Bauer's theory relied heavily on his claim that the early second-century Roman Church was powerful enough to impose its minority doctrines on the other churches. His central evidence was the letter known as First Clement (encountered in chapter 3.4), which was sent at the end of the first century from the Roman Church to the Corinthian Church in response to a leadership conflict. However, the letter extensively cited Old Testament

---

Segal, *Two Powers*, 15.

9. Jenkins, *Hidden Gospels*, 116.

10. See Turner, *Pattern*, 43, 57, 63.

11. See Thomassen, "Orthodoxy and Heresy," 255.

12. Robinson, *Bauer Thesis*, 204.

13. Robinson, *Bauer Thesis*, 199.

14. Trebilco, "Christian Communities," 43.

examples in an attempt to persuade the church to respect its leaders. It did not debate any specific doctrine and did not have a dictatorial tone.[15]

Köstenberger and Kruger argue that at the time of First Clement, Rome was not a central authority in Christianity.[16] For the first two centuries, Roman Christians met in private houses, and these groups were as diverse as in other areas.[17] In the second half of the second century, the church father Irenaeus found it necessary to write hundreds of pages refuting alternative views of Jesus (in *Against Heresies*), which strongly suggests that the Roman Church was not able to suppress these voices through autocratic action. By the end of the second century, the Roman Bishop Victor still could not impose his ruling about the date of Easter, and he had to withdraw his decision when other churches opposed him.[18] The authority of the Roman Church only started to develop towards the end of the second century and the beginning of the third.[19]

Bauer also claimed that the Roman Church imposed its doctrines by controlling the selection of canonical Scripture. It is often popularly alleged that gnostic-style gospels, in particular, were rejected because they depicted Jesus as too human. For example, in his influential novel *The Da Vinci Code*, Dan Brown claimed that "Constantine commissioned and financed a new Bible, which omitted those gospels that spoke of Christ's human traits and embellished those gospels that made Him godlike. The earlier gospels were outlawed, gathered up, and burned. But fortunately, some of these gospels survived and were found in 1945 in Nag Hammadi, Egypt."[20] However, although this claim has come to be widely accepted, it is blatantly false because, as Bart Ehrman points out, the Nag Hammadi gnostic texts portrayed Jesus as *far more divine* than human.[21]

By 180 the four canonical gospels were accepted as authoritative in widely dispersed churches without any particular action from Rome.[22] Contrary to popular conspiracy theories, the New Testament canon was

15. The letter First Clement can be read at http://www.earlychristianwritings.com/1clement.htm.

16. Köstenberger and Kruger, *Heresy of Orthodoxy*, 51.

17. See Lampe, *Paul to Valentinus*, 396 n. 29 (where Lampe rejects Bauer's theory).

18. See Eusebius, *Church History* 5.24.

19. See Ehrman, *Orthodox Corruption*, 40 n. 18; Norris, "Bauer Reconsidered," 42; Thomassen, "Orthodoxy and Heresy," 255.

20. Brown, *Da Vinci Code*, 234.

21. Ehrman, *Truth and Fiction*, 15.

22. See Streeter, *Four Gospels*, 7.

not selected by one dominant group but was a gradual and complex process of acknowledging the texts that were being used across a wide range of Christian communities. Theologian Alister McGrath comments that the rejection of alternative views of Jesus "generally has more to do with an emerging consensus within the church that they are inadequate, than with any attempt to impose an unpopular orthodoxy on an unwilling body of believers."[23] McGrath also provides a valuable caution about overestimating the role of the canon, pointing out that even without an officially recognized New Testament, the widespread traditions of worship and teaching in early Christianity would have been enough to establish a shared understanding of normative doctrines.[24]

Orthodoxy Was Widely Established outside Rome

Bauer ignored the fact that orthodox doctrines had wide acceptance outside Rome, long before the Roman Church developed its influence. For example, John's Gospel, Letters, and Revelation were probably written in Asia Minor, and Pliny recorded the worship of Jesus in that region, reaching back into the first century.[25] In the second century, five central aspects of orthodoxy seem to have originated outside Rome,[26] and men such as Ignatius in Antioch and Irenaeus in Lyons (in Gaul) were passionate defenders of orthodox teachings. Frederick Norris concludes that Bauer's thesis "fails to stand up to scrutiny because he underrated the strength and influence of centers in Asia Minor and Syria."[27]

There Was Early Awareness of a Normative Tradition

Bauer claimed that there was no sense of a normative Christian tradition until the Roman Church imposed its doctrines and rewrote history. However, the authors of early church letters written outside Rome clearly

23. McGrath, *Heresy*, 81–82.

24. McGrath, *Heresy*, 79.

25. Pliny, *Epistles* 10.96.

26. These five aspects were: control by a single bishop (probably arising in Jerusalem or Syria); theological support for the role of the bishop; differentiation between "orthodoxy" and "heresy"; recognition of canonical texts; use of liturgical texts. See Norris, "Bauer Reconsidered," 29–39.

27. Norris, "Bauer Reconsidered," 41.

regarded themselves as transmitting an original tradition. For example, Polycarp of Smyrna urged the Philippian Church: "Let us return to the word which has been handed down to us from the beginning."[28] The writer of First John wrote: "This is the message we have heard from him and declare to you" (1 John 1:5); "Dear friends, I am not writing you a new command but an old one, which you have had since the beginning" (1 John 2:7a). The educated Pharisee Paul used semi-technical terms of transmission, such as "traditions" (2 Thess 2:15), "you received" and "I delivered" (1 Cor 15:1–3). Gerhardsson observes that in Paul's letters, "we see that early Christianity had a tradition which was regarded as authoritative."[29] Trebilco reaches this conclusion:

> In the period from around AD 65 to 135, we can argue that there were strong and influential voices which stood for what later became "orthodoxy," notably voices in both the Pauline and Johannine traditions. Further, in the documents bearing witness to these traditions, we find a strong concern to discern what the authors regarded as acceptable belief and practice—which is in continuity with what later became orthodoxy. The situation in Western Asia Minor in the early second century thus supports a quite different scenario from that proposed by Bauer.[30]

Other scholars such as Köstenberger and Kruger agree: "The Bauer-Ehrman thesis is invalid . . . The trajectories spanning from the Old Testament to Jesus and to the apostles provided a clear and compelling infrastructure and mechanism by which the earliest Christians could judge whether a given teaching conformed to its doctrinal christological core or whether it deviated from it."[31] The early church leaders wrote passionately in support of their tradition, which Ehrman condemns as "a kind of spirited intolerance,"[32] but this intensity makes sense if they saw themselves as passing on a precious message of salvation.

28. From Letter to the Philippians.

29. Gerhardsson, *Memory and Manuscript*, 13.

30. Trebilco, "Christian Communities," 44.

31. Köstenberger and Kruger, *Heresy of Orthodoxy*, 233. See also Riesenfeld, *Gospel Tradition*, 17–20; Hultgren, *Normative Christianity*, 104–6.

32. Ehrman, *Orthodox Corruption*, 13.

Conflicting Teachings Were Not Lost

It is popularly believed that the Roman Church systematically suppressed valid alternative Christian texts, which over time became "lost gospels." However, historian Philip Jenkins argues that this theory is based on "a questionable historical narrative, or rather a myth. In reality, the lost gospels were never lost . . . It is wrong to suggest that all alternative scriptures ceased to exist. Nor did their ideas. Such an obliteration of texts would be a major task even with modern methods of repression and propaganda."[33] He points out that "dozens of 'non-lost' gospels persisted up to modern times in at least some major part of the Christian church,"[34] and even when action was taken against specific works, this did not necessarily have much impact.[35] Bart Ehrman also notes that there is little evidence of mass burnings of books in antiquity.[36]

Religious historian Elaine Pagels alleges that noncanonical texts were so successfully suppressed that she only encountered them in graduate school.[37] However, these teachings have always been available in extensive descriptions and quotations by the early church fathers, which recently discovered documents, such as the Nag Hammadi library, have largely confirmed to be accurate. And Pagels is simply incorrect when she claims that in his Easter letter of 367, the Christian Athanasius ordered Egyptian monks to destroy unauthorized writings: his letter was not addressed to monks and merely provided a list of officially accepted works with no instruction to destroy alternative texts.[38] Unfortunately, this false statement by a respected academic is now circulating as an established fact.

33. Jenkins, *Many Faces*, 6.

34. Jenkins, *Many Faces*, 12.

35. Jenkins, *Many Faces*, 18. For example, Emperor Constantine ordered works by Bishop Arius to be destroyed, but there is no evidence that this was implemented in a systematic or effective way.

36. Ehrman, *Truth and Fiction*, xxiv.

37. Pagels, *Beyond Belief*, 32.

38. Pagels, *Beyond Belief*, 97. Athanasius's *Letter* 39.6 can be read at http://www.ccel.org/ccel/schaff/npnf204.xxv.iii.iii.xxv.html.

Bauer's Methodology Was Flawed

Bauer's methodology has been heavily criticized: in particular, his tendencies to interpret texts in a way that supported his theory and to speculate where information is not available.[39] Norris remarks that Bauer's "basic error is in reading history backwards, imposing later events on earlier ones to support his interpretations. Frankly, he misreads the texts."[40] And Turner concluded that Bauer's "fatal weakness appears to be a persistent tendency to over-simplify problems, combined with the ruthless treatment of such evidence as fails to support his case."[41] In short, Bauer's thesis has not fared well against the evidence:

> The very infrastructure of Bauer's argument has been dismantled piece by piece.[42]

> Many of his specific arguments cannot stand in the face of the extant evidence.[43]

> The Bauer Thesis simply does not work for the area from which we have extensive and relevant data.[44]

Why Are Bauer-Based Books so Popular?

The public is intrigued by theories about the Roman Church's sinister motives and its suppression of "lost Christianities." Bryan Litfin notes that authors such as Elaine Pagels and Bart Ehrman have "helped a form of the Bauer Thesis attain the elusive aura of a reigning paradigm, despite

39. Hultgren writes, "Too often Bauer argues from silence and, in other cases, pushes aside evidence that works against his thesis" (*Normative Christianity*, 10). Trebilco points out that "Bauer's argument from silence—which he used extensively—is fragile. We cannot say that there were heretical communities in Colossae, Hierapolis, Pergamum, Thyatira, Sardis, and Laodicea simply on the basis that John and/or Ignatius did not write to these places" ("Christian Communities," 27).

40. Norris, "Bauer Reconsidered," 43.

41. Turner, *Pattern*, 79.

42. Litfin, "Apostolic Tradition," 142.

43. Hartog, "Walter Bauer," 59.

44. Robinson, *Bauer Thesis*, 204.

the many scholarly critiques levelled against it."[45] Köstenberger and Kruger make this somewhat prickly comment about the popular view:

> As even Bart Ehrman has conceded, Bauer's thesis has been largely discredited in the details, but, miraculously, the corpse still lives . . . [because] diversity, the "gospel" of our culture, has now assumed the mantle of compelling truth—and this "truth" must not be bothered by the pesky, obstreperous details of patient, painstaking research.[46]

Köstenberger and Kruger suggest that Bauer's theory is popular because it resonates with the following Western postmodern attitudes towards truth, authority, the individual, and power.[47]

Postmodern Rejection of "Truth" and Authority

Postmodernism generally rejects the belief in universal norms. Truth has become a matter of perspective so that any claim to *the* truth is taken as a sign of benighted ignorance or a sinister stratagem to gain power. Facts are no longer relevant to debate because all opinions are considered to be equally valid. For example, in a recently televised criminal investigation, a policeman and a judge provided conflicting evidence, to which an anthropologist responded: "There is no transcendent truth . . . Both are telling their truth."[48] In this light, it is argued that all early forms of Christianity *must* have been equally "true," regardless of any evidence of stronger or weaker connections to an earlier tradition.

Cognitive relativism even demands that the sciences must be inclusive in their approach. An eyebrow-raising example is the criticism by feminist Luce Irigaray that Einstein's famous equation $E=mc^2$ "privileges the speed of light over other speeds that are vitally necessary to us."[49] To critique such attitudes towards science, physicist Alan Sokal rattled some cages when he managed to publish a deliberately absurd article, using extensive postmodern jargon to make the outlandish claim that even

45. Litfin, "Apostolic Tradition," 141.

46. Köstenberger and Kruger, *Heresy of Orthodoxy*, 18.

47. Köstenberger and Kruger, *Heresy of Orthodoxy*, 233. See also Jenkins, *Hidden Gospels*, 13–15. "Postmodernism" loosely refers to prevailing views in the second half of the twentieth century.

48. Cited in Sokal and Bricmont, *Fashionable Nonsense*, 100.

49. Cited in Sokal and Bricmont, *Fashionable Nonsense*, 109.

physical reality is only a social and linguistic construct.[50] Sokal's hoax article was designed to highlight how science is often manipulated to support social and political agendas, but there is a similar trend in the field of history. As early as 1934, theologian Emil Brunner made this astute observation: "One of the characteristics of modern pseudo-history is the exaggeration of constructive interpretation . . . over against the primary process of listening to evidence . . . These constructions, or hypotheses, because they are in harmony with the general outlook of modern people, are regarded as more correct scientifically, from the historical point of view, than the evidence of the New Testament itself, which is not acceptable to the modern mind."[51]

Postmodernism is also anti-authoritarian and suspicious of the motives of mainstream institutions. Theologian Garett Green suggests that, in particular, mistrust of Christianity's motives reflects the impact of the theories of Marx (motives of power and economics), Nietzsche (vengeance of the resentful weak against the strong), and Freud (repressed aggression and sexuality).[52] Green comments that these ideas have had a profound impact on our worldview and that "under the suspicious eye of (post)modernist critique, every faith in scriptural authority appears as a false form of consciousness, every sacred text as a surreptitious rhetoric of power."[53]

Alister McGrath points out that unorthodox teachings about Jesus appeal to this fundamentally anti-establishment attitude: "Heresies are now to be seen as bold and brave statements of spiritual freedom, to be valued rather than avoided . . . Heresy has become fashionable."[54]

50. In his tongue-in-cheek hoax article, "Transformative Hermeneutics of Quantum Gravity," Sokal wrote: "Feminist and poststructuralist critiques have demystified the substantive content of mainstream Western scientific practice, revealing the ideology of domination concealed behind the façade of 'objectivity.' It has thus become increasingly apparent that physical 'reality,' not less than social 'reality,' is at bottom a social and linguistic construct" ("Transformative Hermeneutics," 217). Sokal's article can be read at https://physics.nyu.edu/sokal/transgress_v2_noafterword.pdf.

51. Brunner, *Mediator*, 163.

52. Green, *Theology*, 12–13.

53. Green, *Theology*, 20.

54. McGrath, *Heresy*, 1.

Postmodern Elevation of the Individual

Postmodernism encourages the search for personal meaning and individual truth. New-Age forms of Christianity therefore reject orthodox teachings and promote ancient gnostic-style thinking: Jesus is said to encourage believers to discover their divine nature, deny the existence of sin and guilt, and find salvation and forgiveness through their own acts. For example, Paul Ferrini teaches that "a true Christian does not worship Jesus . . . S/he internalizes his teachings and becomes the Christ,"[55] and seekers of truth should "reject the idea of evil as an idea created in fear."[56] Ferrini writes, "In my conversations with him, Jesus never claimed to be the only son of God. He has never claimed to have died for our sins."[57] Instead, Jesus apparently gave Ferrini this message to pass on: "I am not necessary to your salvation. You are the lamb of God. You are the one who has come to forgive yourself."[58] Glenda Green has received similar messages in her experiences of conversations with Jesus: "The God of all resides in oneness and perfection, knowing nothing of sin. It is from each other that you need to be asking forgiveness."[59] Principles such as these are fundamentally different from the New Testament doctrines of sin and atonement, and they are far easier to accept. The next chapter will explore whether early Gnosticism could have represented Jesus's original teachings.

The Appeal of Conspiracy Theories to Postmodern Beliefs

Lecturer in American studies Peter Knight remarks that "conspiracy has become the default assumption in an age which has learned to distrust everything and everyone . . . Narratives of conspiracy now capture a sense of uncertainty about how historical events unfold, about who gets to tell the official version of events."[60] Theories about suppressed knowledge therefore have great appeal, and popular critiques of Orthodox Christianity promise to share "sensational discoveries" and reveal "explosive

55. Ferrini, *Reflections*, 270.

56. Ferrini, *Reflections*, 167.

57. Ferrini, *Reflections*, 265.

58. Ferrini, *Reflections*, 212.

59. Green, *Love Without End*, 153. Similar gnostic teachings are found in theosophy, anthroposophy, the "I Am" movement, and Helen Shucman's *Course in Miracles*, received through an inner voice.

60. Knight, *Conspiracy Culture*, 3.

secrets." However, although such books usually make an impressive public splash, they lack academic support. Here are a few examples:

- Dead Sea Scroll scholar Barbara Thiering claimed these manuscripts proved that Jesus was an illegitimate child of Qumran who survived crucifixion by using snake-venom, married twice, had children, and died at an advanced age in Rome.[61] However, other scroll scholars have remarked that "her reconstruction of Jesus' life can only be described as eccentric or bizarre, reading into the [Qumran] Gospels material that is simply not there,"[62] and "these theories fail the basic credibility test: they do not spring from, but are foisted on, the texts. These—to say the least—improbable speculations . . . need not detain us any longer."[63]
- Lincoln, Baigent, and Leigh's *Holy Blood and Holy Grail* described a conspiracy around the physical descendants of Jesus and Mary Magdalene.[64] Historian Richard Barber describes this book as "a classic example of the conspiracy theory of history . . . It is essentially a text which proceeds by innuendo, not by refutable scholarly debate."[65]
- Dead Sea Scroll translator John Allegro claimed there was a conspiracy to suppress scrolls that threatened the doctrines of Orthodox Christianity. This led Baigent and Leigh to publish *The Dead Sea Scrolls Deception: Why a Handful of Religious Scholars Conspired to Suppress the Revolutionary Contents of the Dead Sea Scrolls*. However, no other members of the fifty-strong international scroll team supported these allegations, and in 2002 two scroll scholars expressed this opinion: "One wonders what anyone thought might damage Christianity or what the Vatican would be interested in and capable of suppressing. One of the beneficial side effects of full

61. Thiering presents these claims in *Jesus and the Riddle of the Dead Sea Scrolls* and *Jesus the Man*.

62. VanderKam and Flint, *Dead Sea Scrolls*, 326.

63. Vermes, *Dead Sea Scrolls*, 21.

64. The gnostic Gospel of Philip is supposed to prove that Jesus had a sexual relationship with Mary Magdalene because it states that he kissed her. However, a gap in the text leaves it unclear where he kissed her, and, in any case, in the gnostic Second Apocalypse of James, Jesus was also said to have kissed James on the mouth and to have called him "my beloved."

65. Barber, *Holy Grail*, 310.

access to the scrolls has been to show that the Baigent-Leigh conspiracy theory is without merit."[66]

Sadly, the extensive scholarly evidence in boring academic books makes little impression on public perception. People seem keen to believe that Orthodox Christianity was a power-hungry, intolerant minority group that never taught an authentic view of Jesus. This perception is linked to the rise of militant anti-theism, and Philip Jenkins expresses concern about the increasing disparagement of mainstream Christianity. He points out that this seems to be the last acceptable prejudice: "A statement that could be regarded as misogynistic, anti-Semitic, or homophobic would haunt a speaker for years, and could conceivably destroy a public career. Yet there is one massive exception to this rule."[67] Jenkins illustrates this attitude by comparing two recent incidents. In the one, a group disrupted a mosque service by playing the national anthem on bugles, and thousands of people gathered to demand a public apology. In another, a ski-masked group interrupted a Catholic service, spray-painted atheist graffiti on the altar, hurled condoms and sanitary towels, and destroyed or removed hundreds of hymn books—but there was hardly any public response at all.[68] Köstenberger and Kruger comment about this trend that "with the rise of postmodernism came the notion that the only heresy that remains is the belief in absolute truth—orthodoxy."[69]

Postscript on Adoptionism

It is often claimed that there must have been a very early belief that a human Jesus was adopted to be God's Son because Paul wrote that he was appointed (*horisthentos*) the Son of God through his resurrection (Rom 1:4). However, Paul could not have meant that the ordinary man Jesus was elevated to divine sonship because he explicitly taught that Christ Jesus had preexisted in the form of God before he took on human nature (Phil 2:6). The root word *horizó* means "determine horizons," which can be interpreted as declare, designate, ordain, determine, or appoint, sometimes indicating a predetermined event. In discussing Romans 1:3–4, Joshua Jipp argues that "whereas most modern readings have used the verses

66. VanderKam and Flint, *Dead Sea Scrolls*, 394.

67. Jenkins, *New Anti-Catholicism*, 4.

68. Jenkins, *New Anti-Catholicism*, 3–4.

69. Köstenberger and Kruger, *Heresy of Orthodoxy*, 39.

to support a two-*stage* enactment of Jesus' messianic career, ancient interpreters saw the verses as providing evidence for the two *natures* of Christ," and "the resurrection is precisely what publicly *reveals* Jesus, the Son of David, to be God's Son in power."[70] Michael Bird agrees that the change of Jesus's status after the resurrection "is not from mere human to divine sonship, as much as it is from a messianic role (Son of David) to heavenly regency (Son-of-God-in-power and Lord) . . . While Jesus's role as the Son changes, there is no beginning to his divine sonship."[71] Bird argues that adoptionism was a second-century phenomenon,[72] a conclusion also reached by Peter-Ben Smit in his recent article: "The End of Early Christian Adoptionism? A Note on the Invention of Adoptionism, its Sources, and its Current Demise."

Review the Evidence

Early Christianity was a diverse phenomenon with fluidity on some issues as people strove to comprehend and define Jesus's nature and work. But did some beliefs have a stronger connection to the teaching of Jesus and his first apostles than others? Many modern scholars have identified fundamental flaws in Walter Bauer's theory that all versions of Christianity should be regarded as equally valid, although some became suppressed and "lost." These criticisms include his incorrect assumptions about the early power of the Roman Church, his ignoring of early evidence of orthodox teaching outside Rome, and his flawed methodology.

In contrast to Bauer's hypothesis, McGrath argues that although Christian doctrine became more clearly articulated over time, "all the fundamental themes that would be woven into the fabric of orthodoxy were there from the beginning."[73] Martin Hengel agrees:

> Christological thinking between 50 and 100 CE *was much more unified in its basic structure* than New Testament research, in part at least, has maintained. Basically, the later developments are already there in a nutshell in the [Pauline] Philippian hymn

70. Jipp, "Romans 1:3–4," 242 (original emphasis), 258 (emphasis added).

71. Bird, *Eternal Son*, 29.

72. Bird, *Eternal Son*, 9.

73. McGrath, *Heresy*, 79.

> . . . More happened in the first twenty years than in the entire later, centuries-long development of dogma.[74]

Bryan Litfin is another of the many scholars who identify a connection between Jesus's teachings and later orthodoxy: "The historical evidence reveals a straight line of continuity (admittedly with some expansion) from the earliest apostolic preaching to the message confessed by the orthodox church fathers of later centuries."[75]

From the fourth century onwards, Roman orthodoxy would regrettably become an increasingly hierarchical tool of imperial power. But for the first two centuries, the Roman Church did not have the necessary power and influence to impose a minority doctrine on the widely spread Christian communities; supporters of orthodoxy could only combat alternative views through the written and spoken word. Michael Bird proposes that instead of one sect winning an outright power struggle, a gradual process of "christologizing" took place within the early Christian communities: "A cohesive mode of discourse and mutually recognized patterns of worship gradually emerged. Concurrently, seemingly incongruent beliefs and practices began to be pushed to the margins when they did not meet with consensus . . . These incongruent Christologies—later labelled as "heresies"—were regarded as invalid portrayals of Jesus."[76] And historian Philip Jenkins makes this comment about the texts of these marginal views of Jesus:

> The canonical gospels really are both more ancient and authoritative than virtually all of their rivals. Far from being the alternative voices of Jesus' first followers, most of the lost gospels should rather be seen as the writings of much later dissidents who broke away from an already established orthodox church.[77]

Bauer phrased his theory about early heresies quite cautiously.[78] But despite substantial contrary evidence, some academics continue to support his hypothesis. These scholars include Robert Funk of the Jesus

74. Hengel, "Christological Titles," 443 (original emphasis).

75. Litfin, "Apostolic Tradition," 164.

76. Bird, *Eternal Son*, 5.

77. Jenkins, *Hidden Gospels*, 12.

78. Bauer wrote, "Perhaps—I repeat, *perhaps*—certain manifestations of Christian life that the authors of the church renounce as 'heresies' originally had not been such at all . . . The possibility also exists that their adherents constituted the majority" (*Orthodoxy and Heresy*, xxii, original emphasis).

Seminar, James Robinson, Gerd Lüdemann, Elaine Pagels, and Helmut Koester, who regards Bauer's work as "a brilliant monograph" that is "essentially right."[79] These scholars are generally aligned with the history of religions school: Lüdemann studied at the University of Göttingen, Robinson and Koester studied with Bultmann (who supported Bauer's theory), and Pagels wrote her doctoral thesis under Koester.

Bart Ehrman also supports Bauer's hypothesis and dismisses the extensive scholarly criticisms with the offhand comment that "it has become somewhat fashionable to cast aspersions on Bauer's reconstruction."[80] He insists that only biased historians can accept the authenticity of orthodox teachings: "Many historians find this form of Christianity essentially compatible with the teaching of Jesus and his followers. We should not allow this consensus to blind our eyes to the impossibility of disinterested evaluation in the hands of contextually situated investigators: the postmodern world has seen in this modernist question for objectivity a myth of its own."[81] And yet, Ehrman has also made this statement in *agreement* with Philip Jenkins:

> The oldest and best sources we have for knowing about the life of Jesus . . . are the four Gospels of the New Testament, Matthew, Mark, Luke, and John. This is not simply the view of Christian historians who have a high opinion of the New Testament and its historical worth; it is the view of all serious historians of antiquity of every kind, from committed evangelical Christians to hard-core atheists.[82]

Consider Your Verdict

According to Bauer-type arguments, orthodox Christian doctrines had no stronger connection with the teaching of the first apostles than any other teaching about Jesus; orthodoxy was merely an inauthentic minority belief that only became widely accepted when it was imposed by the powerful Roman Church in the second century. How well-supported is this theory?

79. Koester, "*GNOMAI DIAPHOROI*," 114.
80. Ehrman, *Orthodox Corruption*, 39 n. 16.
81. Ehrman, *Orthodox Corruption*, 43 n. 40.
82. Ehrman, *Truth and Fiction*, 102–3.

- There is extensive supporting evidence.
- The evidence is quite strong.
- The evidence is inadequate.

4.2 HOW AUTHENTIC IS THE GNOSTIC JESUS?

Debates regarding the relationship between Orthodox Christianity and alternative doctrines often involve claims about the noncanonical gnostic gospels. The Greek *gnosis* means knowledge, and in Gnosticism, this referred to esoteric knowledge of secret spiritual truths. Gnosticism was a diverse way of thinking that arose in late antiquity within Christianity, Judaism, Neoplatonism, and Hermetism,[83] sometimes reflecting influence from Zoroastrianism and possibly Buddhism.

In 1945 a collection of ancient manuscripts was discovered near Nag Hammadi in Egypt, which included gnostic Christian texts such as the Gospel of Judas, the Gospel of Thomas, and the Secret Book of John, which present a very different view of Jesus from that of the New Testament. Although these manuscripts are dated to the third and fourth centuries, authors such as Elaine Pagels (*The Gnostic Gospels*) have argued that they represent a very early tradition and provide a more authentic picture of early Christian beliefs than the four canonical gospels of Orthodox Christianity. Do the gnostic texts confirm this claim? It is enlightening to read directly from these works to compare their worldview and depiction of Jesus with those of the New Testament and to decide which writings seem to provide more reliable information.[84]

The Gnostic Worldview in Nag Hammadi Christian Texts

Gnostic teachings varied among different groups, but in its broad outlines, the gnostic worldview was fundamentally different from that of the New Testament. Competing claims of authenticity can be assessed

83. See Robinson, *Nag Hammadi Library*, 10.

84. The interested reader can access the Christian Nag Hammadi library at http://www.earlychristianwritings.com/. Quotations from the Nag Hammadi texts in this book are from Robinson, *Nag Hammadi Library* (with square brackets indicating words inserted into textual gaps by the translator).

by deciding which view is more closely linked to Jewish beliefs in first-century Palestine.

Gnostic Views of Creation as a Mistake

The New Testament conforms to Old Testament teachings that the omnipotent One God of Judaism created the world and judged it to be good. By contrast, Gnosticism taught that matter is evil and the physical world was formed in error: "The world came about through a mistake."[85] Gnostics believed in a transcendent God who did not create the material world. The ignorant demi-god of Israel created the world through a foolish act, and gnostics therefore reviled him: "He is impious in his arrogance which is in him. For he said, 'I am God, and there is no other God beside.'"[86] The gnostic Jesus spoke directly against the God of Judaism: "I came . . . that I might reveal to you . . . the arrogance of the Arch-Begetter and his angels."[87]

Belief in the Duality of Good Spirit and Evil Matter

Gnostics despised matter as the evil opposition to pure spirit. They taught that human beings were sparks of divinity that became trapped in abhorrent physical bodies when the Jewish God ignorantly "commissioned the powers within his authority to mold mortal bodies. And they came to be from a misrepresentation."[88] Hence, in the semi-gnostic Gospel of Thomas, Jesus says, "Whoever has come to understand the world has found a corpse."[89] Contrary to Jewish expectations expressed in the New Testament, a physical resurrection was therefore rejected: "Some are afraid lest they rise naked. Because of this they wish to rise in the flesh, and [they] do not know that it is those who wear the [flesh] who are naked."[90] According to gnostic teachings, "none of those who have worn the flesh will be saved."[91]

85. From Gospel of Philip.
86. From Secret Book of John, quoting from Isaiah 45:5.
87. From Sophia of Jesus Christ.
88. From Letter of Peter to Philip.
89. Gospel of Thomas 56.
90. From Gospel of Philip.
91. From Secret Book of James.

Emphasis on Esoteric Knowledge

Judeo-Christian Scripture emphasized ethical conduct, and its message was openly taught to all. By contrast, gnostic salvation had no relation to moral behaviour but was achieved through esoteric knowledge that was only available to the spiritually elite. The Gospel of Thomas starts with these words: "These are the secret sayings which the living Jesus spoke and which Didymos Judas Thomas wrote down." The gnostic James wrote, "You asked that I send you a secret book which was revealed to me and Peter by the Lord . . . Take care not to rehearse this text to many—this that the Savior did not wish to tell to all of us."[92] And the gnostic Jesus taught, "I have said everything to you that you might write them down and give them secretly to your fellow spirits, for this is the mystery of the immovable race."[93]

Gnostic Ideas of Redemption

Gnostics did not believe that Jesus died an atoning death. They had no doctrine of redemption from sin but aimed to be redeemed from ignorance, which was gained through their own insight into esoteric truths. For example, the gnostic Philip wrote, "Ignorance is the mother of all evil . . . The word said, 'If you know the truth, the truth will make you free' . . . If we know the truth, we shall find the fruits of truth within us."[94] This phrase about the truth providing freedom is from John 8:32, but in John's gospel, this is linked directly to Jesus's instruction to follow his teachings, which is omitted in the gnostic interpretation that truth must be sought within one's own powers.

The gnostic James also taught, "Blessed will they be who have spoken out and obtained grace for themselves."[95] And in the Gospel of Thomas, Jesus says, "That which you have will save you, if you bring it forth from yourselves. That which you do not have within you [will] kill you if you do not have it within you."[96]

92. From Secret Book of James.

93. From Secret Book of John.

94. From Gospel of Philip. According to the gnostic Gospel of Truth, "It is within Unity that each one will attain himself, within knowledge he will purify himself from multiplicity into Unity, consuming matter within himself like fire."

95. From Secret Book of James.

96. Gospel of Thomas 70. I find it difficult to agree with Elaine Pagels's opinion that

Belief in the Innate Divinity of Man

The central gnostic goal was to use mystical insight to be liberated from the body and realize one's innate divinity. For example, the gnostic Jesus is supposed to have advised James: "Cast away from your blind thought, this bond of flesh which encircles you. And then you will reach Him-who-is. And you will no longer be James; rather you are the One-who-is."[97] And Jesus is said to have taught his disciples: "Become better than I; make yourselves like the son of the Holy Spirit."[98] Other gnostic texts also expressed this goal of deification:

> You saw the Spirit, you became spirit. You saw Christ, you became Christ.[99]

> Jesus said, "He who will drink from my mouth will become like me."[100]

Gnostic Attitudes Towards Women

It is often claimed that Gnosticism had high regard for women. However, although some gnostic sects might have encouraged women in leadership roles,[101] a scholar of Gnosticism observes that these predominantly male sects "generally regarded women with suspicion or contempt."[102] This claim is supported by statements such as these in gnostic texts:

> In this way the defect of femaleness appeared.[103]

> I am Christ, the Son of Man . . . Do not become female, lest you give birth to evil.[104]

---

this saying has "unexpected spiritual power" (*Beyond Belief*, 32).

97. From First Apocalypse of James.

98. From Secret Book of James.

99. From Gospel of Philip.

100. Gospel of Thomas 108.

101. See Pagels, *Gnostic Gospels*, 60.

102. Yamauchi, "Gnostics and History," 35.

103. From Eugnostos the Blessed.

104. From Second Treatise of the Great Seth.

> The perishable has gone up to the imperishable, and the female element has attained to the male element.[105]

> The Lord said, "Pray in the place where there is no woman". . . meaning "Destroy the works of womanhood."[106]

> Jesus said, "I myself shall lead her in order to make her male, so that she too may become a living spirit resembling you males. For every woman who will make herself male will enter the kingdom of heaven."[107]

By contrast, Paul taught that "there is neither Jew nor Gentile, neither slave nor free, nor is there male and female, for you are all one in Christ Jesus" (Gal 3:28). Women could also be deacons in the early church.[108] Paul specifically commended Phoebe who was a deacon in Cenchreae (Rom 16:1) and expressed his respect and appreciation for other women: Priscilla, one of his "co-workers in Christ," and Tryphena and Tryphosa "who work hard in the Lord" (Rom 16:3–12); Junia, who he regarded as "outstanding among the apostles" (Rom 16:7); Euodia and Syntyche, who had worked with him "along with Clement and the rest of my co-workers" (Phil 4:3b).[109] Tragically, this early egalitarian respect for women was not sustained in the developing church.

Jesus's Nature and Death in Gnostic Christianity

It is important to note that some gnostic gospels confirmed orthodox teachings about Jesus's divinity, atoning death, resurrection, and ascension, as well as the role of the Holy Spirit and miraculous healings by the apostles:

> [Jesus] was crucified on a tree and he was buried in a tomb. And he rose from the dead . . . For the Lord Jesus, the Son of the immeasurable glory of the Father, he is the author of our life . . .

105. From First Apocalypse of James.

106. From Dialogue of the Savior.

107. Gospel of Thomas 114.

108. The Roman Pliny mentioned deaconesses in the early church: "This made me think it all the more necessary to inquire, even by torture, of two maid-servants who were styled deaconesses" (*Epistles* 10.96).

109. The instruction in one of Paul's letters that women should be silent in church (1 Cor 14:34–35) might reflect his background in Jewish synagogues, or it might be a later addition to the letter.

> Then Peter and the other apostles saw him and they were filled with a holy spirit. And each one performed healings. And they parted in order to preach the Lord Jesus.[110]

The gnostic Gospel of Philip taught that the Holy Spirit brings about spiritual rebirth and that Christ existed before creation and came from heaven to ransom humanity from death.[111] In other gnostic texts, Jesus is said to have ascended to heaven to sit at the right hand of the Father,[112] and faith is expressed in the single name of the Father, Son, and Holy Spirit.[113]

However, unlike all of the New Testament writers, gnostics *denied Jesus's human nature*. Dan Brown and others allege that the gnostic gospels were not accepted into the New Testament canon because they depicted Jesus as too human, but this is a blatantly false claim, as any reading of these texts reveals.[114] Gnostic Christians regarded Jesus as a purely divine being without any human qualities: "He is immortal and eternal . . . He is unbegotten, having no beginning."[115] Gnostic texts therefore taught the docetic view that Jesus only appeared to have a physical body or was only temporarily joined to a human body. Hence, the gnostic Christ is said to have made statements such as these:

> I came from the infinite that I might tell you all things.[116]

110. From the gnostic Letter of Peter to Philip.

111. The gnostic Gospel of Philip contains these words: "Christ came to ransom some . . . He voluntarily laid down his life from the very day the world came into being"; "It was from that place that Jesus came and brought food. To those who so desired he gave [life, that] they might not die"; "Through the holy spirit we are indeed begotten again."

112. See Secret Book of James.

113. The gnostic Tripartite Tractate taught that there is "redemption into God, Father, Son and Holy Spirit, when confession is made through faith in those names, which are a single name of the gospel."

114. As mentioned in chapter 4.1, Brown made this false claim: "Constantine commissioned and financed a new Bible, which omitted those gospels that spoke of Christ's human traits and embellished those gospels that made Him godlike. The earlier gospels were outlawed, gathered up, and burned. But fortunately, some of these gospels survived and were found in 1945 in Nag Hammadi, Egypt" (*Da Vinci Code*, 234).

115. From Sophia of Jesus Christ.

116. From Sophia of Jesus Christ.

> I came down into their mortal mold. But they did not recognize me; they were thinking of me that I was a mortal man.[117]

> I visited a bodily dwelling. I cast out the one who was in it first, and I went in . . . And I am the one who was in it, not resembling him who was in it first. For he was an earthly man, but I, I am from above the heavens.[118]

The New Testament gospels describe Jesus as being hungry, tired, afraid, and suffering on the cross. But the gnostic Jesus was a superhuman spiritual being who had no human frailty, could not be humiliated, never felt pain, and did not die. The gnostic Jesus makes these triumphant claims:

> Never have I suffered in any way, nor have I been distressed. And this people has done me no harm.[119]

> I did not die in reality, but in appearance . . . It was another, Simon, who bore the cross on his shoulder. It was another upon whom they placed the crown of thorns. But I was rejoicing in the height over all the wealth of the rulers and the offspring of their error, of their empty glory. And I was laughing at their ignorance . . . For I was altering my shapes, changing from form to form.[120]

The Qur'an records a similar belief: "That they said [in boast], 'We killed Christ Jesus the son of Mary, the Messenger of Allah' but they killed him not, nor crucified him, but so it was made to appear to them" (Sura 4:157).[121]

117. From Letter of Peter to Philip.

118. From Second Treatise of the Great Seth.

119. From First Apocalypse of James.

120. From Second Treatise of the Great Seth. The Apocalypse of Peter similarly describes Jesus laughing above the cross while a substitute is crucified.

121. The Qur'an teaches that Jesus was born of a virgin (Surah 3:47; Surah 19:20–22), healed people and raised the dead to life (Surah 3:49; 5:110), and was raised up by God to heaven (Surah 3:55; Surah 4:158). But it also maintains that Jesus was not divine (Surah 5:116) but was only a human apostle and prophet (Surah 4:171; Surah 5:75; Surah 19:19, 30).

The Lack of Context in Gnostic Texts

The gnostic gospels therefore depict a very different Jesus from the figure described in the New Testament. In deciding which portrayal could be more valid, it is important to note the lack of context in the gnostic texts. The four canonical gospels describe Jesus debating contemporary Jewish issues with realistic characters in historically plausible first-century Palestinian settings. By contrast, the gnostic Jesus is not portrayed in any context at all. In particular, the Gospel of Thomas, which reveals some gnostic influence, is merely a list of one hundred and fourteen isolated sayings of Jesus that are not embedded in any narrative or context. Some of these sayings are also found in the New Testament gospels, so this text might provide independent evidence of these traditions. (The oldest fragments of the Gospel of Thomas, which are not from Nag Hammadi, are dated to the second century.) However, because Jesus's sayings in Thomas have no context and in many cases seem to be extracts or abbreviations, they do not provide a clear message. This limitation is illustrated by the following words (in italics) that are found in both Thomas and the New Testament gospels:

In the New Testament Gospels	**In the Gospel of Thomas's List of Sayings**
Jesus was accused of using satanic powers to exorcise demons. But he argued that this was not a logical claim, and he identified himself as the strong opponent of evil: "If Satan opposes himself and is divided, he cannot stand; his end has come. In fact, *no one can enter a strong man's house without first tying him up. Then he can plunder the strong man's house*" (Mark 3:26–27).	The parallel saying known as Thomas 35 contains only these words of Jesus, which provide no moral lesson about his conflict with evil: "*It is not possible for anyone to enter the house of a strong man and take it by force unless he binds his hands; then he will be able to ransack his house.*"
Jesus provided this warning about trying to follow both worldly ambition and God's will: "*No one can serve two masters.* Either you will hate the one and love the other, or *you will be devoted to the one and despise the other.* You cannot serve both God and money" (Luke 16:13).	The similar saying in Thomas 47 a, b contains no message about focusing on God. Jesus merely says, "It is impossible for a man to mount two horses or to stretch two bows. And *it is impossible for a servant to serve two masters, otherwise he will honor the one and treat the other contemptuously.*"

In the New Testament Gospels	In the Gospel of Thomas's List of Sayings
Jesus provided this teaching about the power of faith: "Have faith in God," Jesus answered. "Truly I tell you, *if anyone says to this mountain*, 'Go, throw yourself into the sea,' and does not doubt in their heart but believes that what they say will happen, *it will be done for them*" (Mark 11:22–23).	Jesus's corresponding saying in Thomas 48 has no message about faith: "If two make peace with each other in this one house, *they will say to the mountain, 'Move away,' and it will move away.*"
Jesus taught that one should not be charitable for the sake of reputation: "Be careful not to practice your righteousness in front of others to be seen by them . . . When you give to the needy, *do not let your left hand know what your right hand is doing*, so that your giving may be in secret. Then your Father, who sees what is done in secret, will reward you" (Matt 6:1–4).	Jesus's message about the correct motives for generosity does not appear in the parallel saying in Thomas 62, which merely presents this cryptic instruction: "It is to those who are worthy of my mysteries that I tell my mysteries. *Do not let your left hand know what your right hand is doing.*"
When Jesus was asked why his disciples did not fast, he used a parable to explain that his teaching required a new attitude: "*No one sews a patch of unshrunk cloth on an old garment. Otherwise, the new piece will pull away from the old, making the tear worse. And no one pours new wine into old wineskins. Otherwise, the wine will burst the skins, and both the wine and the wineskins will be ruined*" (Mark 2:21–22a).	Jesus's corresponding saying in Thomas 47 d, e does not include the debate about fasting. As a result, it simply sounds like household advice: "*And new wine is not put into old wineskins, lest they burst; nor is old wine put into a new wineskin, lest it spoil it. An old patch is not sewn onto a new garment, because a tear would result.*"

The much sensationalized Gospel of Thomas is popularly supposed to provide startling unorthodox truths about Jesus. However, Jesus's isolated sayings in this text do not present coherent teachings, and they are only rendered meaningful by the context that is provided in the New Testament gospels. If the canonical gospels later added false narratives to these shared sayings, they did so with astounding consistency and realism. Despite exaggerated claims, the Thomas text therefore does not provide new and profound insight into Jesus. Many of its sayings do not appear in the New Testament gospels, but the Jesus Seminar only classifies three as being possibly credible, and these provide no useful information about Jesus's teachings.[122] Many of Jesus's sayings in Thomas are also highly cryptic, such as these:

> Blessed is a lion that becomes man when consumed by man; and cursed is the man that a lion consumes, and the lion becomes man.[123]

> On the day when you were one you became two. But when you become two what will you do?[124]

> Jesus said to them, "When you make the two one, and when you make the inside like the outside and the outside like the inside, and the above like the below, and when you make the male and the female one and the same, so that the male not be male nor the female female; and when you fashion eyes in place of an eye, and a hand in place of a hand, and a foot in place of a foot, and a likeness in place of a likeness; then you will enter the Kingdom."[125]

And Thomas is not the only alternative gospel with inscrutable teachings. The gnostic Gospel of Philip offers this wisdom:

> Before Christ, some came from a place they were no longer able to enter, and they went where they were no longer able to come out. Then Christ came. Those who went in, he brought out, and those who went out, he brought in.

It's difficult to know what to make of this explanation from The Gospel of Truth, which starts reasonably enough:

> He is the shepherd who left behind the ninety-nine sheep which were not lost. He went searching for the one which had gone

122. See Funk et al., *Five Gospels*, 550–53. Only Thomas 42, 97, and 98 are accorded credibility by the Jesus Seminar. Jesus says, "Be passersby" (Thomas 42). Jesus says, "The Father's imperial rule is like a person who wanted to kill someone powerful. While still at home he drew his sword and thrust it into the wall to find out whether his hand would go in. Then he killed the powerful one" (Thomas 98). Jesus compares the kingdom of God to a woman who does not notice that her broken jar had leaked out all the flour that she was carrying (Thomas 97).

123. Gospel of Thomas 7.

124. Gospel of Thomas 11c.

125. Gospel Of Thomas 22b.

> astray. He rejoiced when he found it, for ninety-nine is a number that is in the left hand which holds it. But when the one is found the entire number passes to the right hand. As that which lacks the one—that is, the entire right hand—draws what was deficient and takes it from the left side, and brings it to the right, so too the number becomes one hundred. It is the sign of the one who is in their sound, it is the Father.

Such ramblings bear little relation to Jesus's typically Jewish methods of teaching in the canonical gospels.[126]

Review the Evidence

Gnostic Christian manuscripts date from the second century onwards and cannot be shown to predate the New Testament gospels.[127] These texts drew heavily from New Testament traditions, but while the four canonical gospels depict a historically authentic first-century Palestinian milieu, these alternative texts simply use the Jesus-figure as a mouthpiece for esoteric gnostic ideas.

Some writers have claimed that these works represent the authentic teachings of the Jewish Jesus, but gnostic attitudes towards Judaic traditions do not support this opinion. Gnostic writers showed no interest in Jewish messianic expectations, and they depicted Israel's God as an arrogant, foolish, minor demi-god. The Hebrew Bible was also sometimes reinterpreted: for example, according to the gnostic Secret Book of John, the creation of Eve was different from the way Moses described it in the Old Testament, and Jesus took on the form of an eagle to encourage Adam and Eve to eat from the forbidden tree of knowledge. The gnostic

126. Here is another bewildering example from the gnostic Secret Book of James: "The savior answered and said . . . Just as it is good that you be in want and, conversely, bad that you be full, so he who is full is in want, and he who is in want does not become full as he who is in want becomes full, and he who has been filled, in turn, attains due perfection. Therefore, you must be in want while it is possible to fill you, and be full while it is possible for you to be in want, so that you may be able to fill yourselves the more. Hence become full of the Spirit, but be in want of reason, for reason belongs to the soul."

127. See Keener, *Historical Jesus*, 47. The Nag Hammadi gnostic manuscripts date from the third and fourth centuries. Around 180 Irenaeus wrote that a Gospel of Judas and a Gospel of Truth had been "recently written" (*Against Heresies* 1.31.1, 3.11.9). Robinson identifies the Gospel of Philip as "undoubtedly a translation of a Greek text which was written perhaps as late as the second half of the third century" (*Nag Hammadi Library*, 141).

Second Treatise of the Great Seth made this claim about Jewish biblical heroes: "Solomon was a laughingstock, since he thought that he was Christ . . . Moses, a faithful servant, was a laughingstock . . . There is a great deception upon their soul."

In his attack on Christianity in *The God Delusion*, atheist biologist Richard Dawkins informs his readers that "the four gospels that made it into the official canon were chosen, more or less arbitrarily, out of a larger sample of at least a dozen including the Gospels of Thomas, Peter, Nicodemus, Philip, Bartholomew and Mary Magdalene."[128] Dawkins is clearly implying that these other works were equally authoritative testimonies to Jesus, but this claim ignores the nature and late dating of these gnostic texts as well as extensive scholarly commentary on Gnosticism and the development of the scriptural canon. As a historian of religions, Philip Jenkins argues against such popular claims for the value of the noncanonical gospels:

> It is amazing that these ideas have achieved the wide credence they have. One basic problem is the claim that the hidden gospels contain a wealth of information which is new and incendiary. To the contrary, much of what was uncovered is not relevant to Christian origins, while what is relevant is not new, still less inflammatory.[129]

> The vastly exaggerated claims made on behalf of these gospels are more revealing . . . about the interest groups who seek to use them today; about the mass media, and how religion is packaged as popular culture.[130]

New-Age forms of Christianity often promote gnostic principles that seem to promise personal fulfillment and liberation. But ironically, the ideals that appeal to modern spiritual seekers are found less in ancient gnostic teachings than in the New Testament: these ideals include an egalitarian[131] and caring community,[132] characterized by kindness towards

128. Dawkins, *God Delusion*, 121.

129. Jenkins, *Hidden Gospels*, 11–12.

130. Jenkins, *Hidden Gospels*, 5.

131. "Jesus called them together and said, 'You know that the rulers of the Gentiles lord it over them, and their high officials exercise authority over them. Not so with you. Instead, whoever wants to become great among you must be your servant'" (Matt 20:25–27a).

132. "But the fruit of the Spirit is love, joy, peace, forbearance, kindness, goodness,

others, including non-believers,[133] and offering joyous communion with the divine[134] and release from guilt and fear.[135] These features are at the heart of many Christian churches today, which emphasize Jesus's message of equality, love, and compassion.

Consider Your Verdict

How strong is the evidence for the claim that gnostic Christian texts provide a more authentic description of Jesus's nature and teachings than the four New Testament gospels?

- Convincing
- Strong
- Not very strong
- Weak

4.3 WHAT CLAIMS DID JESUS MAKE IN THE NEW TESTAMENT?

> *He is causing riots by his teaching wherever he goes—all over Judea, from Galilee to Jerusalem!*

---

faithfulness, gentleness and self-control" (Gal 5:22–23a). "Finally, all of you, be likeminded, be sympathetic, love one another, be compassionate and humble" (1 Pet 3:8). "And do not forget to do good and to share with others, for with such sacrifices God is pleased" (Heb 13:16). The fourth-century Emperor Julian (who hoped to revive polytheism) wrote to a pagan high priest: "It is disgraceful that, when no Jew ever has to beg, and the impious Galileans [Christians] support not only their own poor but ours as well, all men see that our people lack aid from us" (from Letter 22, in Wright, *Works of the Emperor Julian* 3).

133. "Opponents must be gently instructed, in the hope that God will grant them repentance leading them to a knowledge of the truth" (2 Tim 2:25). "Always be prepared to give an answer to everyone who asks you to give the reason for the hope that you have. But do this with gentleness and respect" (1 Pet 3:15b).

134. "Even though you do not see him now, you believe in him and are filled with an inexpressible and glorious joy" (1 Pet 1:8b). "May the God of hope fill you with all joy and peace as you trust in him, so that you may overflow with hope by the power of the Holy Spirit" (Rom 15:13).

135. "Therefore, there is now no condemnation for those who are in Christ Jesus" (Rom 8:1).

> *But why does this fellow talk like that? He's blaspheming!*
> *It is by the prince of demons that he drives out demons!*
> *No one ever spoke the way this man does.*
> *You mean he has deceived you also!*
> *One thing I do know. I was blind but now I see.*
> *If we let him go on like this, everyone will believe in him, and then the Romans will come and take away both our temple and our nation!* [136]

The Gospels depict a wide range of reactions to Jesus. They also portray him as making the following claims that would certainly have stirred up controversy.

Claims of Exalted Status and Authority

Jesus is remembered as making these extreme statements about his preeminence and authority:

- "You are from below; I am from above. You are of this world; I am not of this world. I told you that you would die in your sins; if you do not believe that I am he, you will indeed die in your sins" (John 8:23–24).
- "My Father's will is that everyone who looks to the Son and believes in him shall have eternal life, and I will raise them up at the last day" (John 6:40).
- "Whoever acknowledges me before others, I will also acknowledge before my Father in heaven" (Matt 10:32).
- "Anyone who loves their father or mother more than me is not worthy of me; anyone who loves their son or daughter more than me is not worthy of me" (Matt 10:37).
- "There is a judge for the one who rejects me and does not accept my words; the very words I have spoken will condemn them at the last day" (John 12:48).

Robert Stein points out that these claims "would appear to be evidence of gross egomania, for Jesus clearly implies that the entire world revolves around himself and that the fate of all men is dependent on their

136. See Luke 23:5 NLT; Mark 2:7; Matt 9:34; John 7:46; 7:47; 9:25; 11:48.

acceptance or rejection of him."[137] Jesus also claimed far greater authority than any Jewish teacher or prophet:

- Prophets introduced their message with: "Thus says the Lord," but Jesus said, "Truly, I tell you" (Luke 23:43; John 5:24; Matt 6:2). He also felt entitled to amend revered Mosaic instructions: "You have heard that it was said to the people long ago . . . But I tell you . . ." (Matt 5:21–22).
- Old Testament psalms and the Dead Sea Scrolls used the double "Amen, Amen" to confirm another person's statement,[138] but Jesus used this to ratify his own words, as in John 5:19.
- The Old Testament image of the "finger of God" signified God's direct action, as when God wrote his commandments on stone tablets (Exod 31:18) and unleashed plagues upon Egypt (Exod 8:19). Jesus used this divine image to describe his own work: "But if I drive out demons by the finger of God, then the kingdom of God has come upon you" (Luke 11:20). The authenticity of this saying is supported by the fact that no other Jewish literature associated exorcism with end-time expectations about God's kingdom.[139]
- Jesus claimed to have the power to lay down his life and take it up again (John 10:18).
- He assumed God's authority when he sent out prophets (Matt 23:34).

Jesus also depicted himself as the king of the future kingdom:

- "Then the King will say to those on his right, 'Come, you who are blessed by my Father; take your inheritance'" (Matt 25:34).
- "So that you may eat and drink at my table in my kingdom" (Luke 22:30).
- "Jesus answered, 'My kingdom is not of this world'" (John 18:35a).

And Jesus regarded his authority as absolute:

- "All things have been committed to me by my Father" (Luke 10:22a).
- "The Father loves the Son and has placed everything in his hands" (John 3:35).

137. Stein, *Method and Message*, 118.

138. See, for example, Psalms 89:52; 41:13 and Qumran scrolls 1QS and 4Q280.

139. See Keener, *Historical Jesus*, 198.

- "I have been given all authority in heaven and on earth" (Matt 28:18). Interestingly, a Qumran scroll predicted that "the heavens and the earth will listen to his anointed one."[140]

These claims far exceeded anything found in the Old Testament prophets and rabbinic literature.

Claim to Be the Unique Son of God

The Old Testament widely applied the title "son of God" to kings, prophets, righteous men, angels, and even the nation Israel. But Jesus's statements implied unique sonship: "No one knows the Father except the Son and those to whom the Son chooses to reveal him" (Matt 11:27b), and "He who does not honor the Son does not honor the Father, who sent him" (John 5:22b). His fellow Jews found these claims highly offensive: "For this reason they tried all the more to kill him; not only was he breaking the Sabbath, but he was even calling God his own Father, making himself equal with God" (John 5:18). Jesus spoke to his disciples about "your Father" but referred to God as "my Father," which was extremely rare in Judaism.[141] Cautious scholar Wolfhart Pannenberg concluded that even if Jesus's disciples only later explicitly called him "Son of God," this status would have been implied in his acts and teachings.[142]

Claim to Equivalence with God

Jesus is remembered as saying, "Anyone who has seen me has seen the Father" (John 14:9b),[143] and he seems to have frequently implied his equality with God through his statements that echoed God's words in the Old Testament:

140. 4Q521 frag. 2 col. 2, in Martínez and Tigchelaar, *Dead Sea Scrolls*.

141. Qumran scroll 4Q372 does contain this exceptionally rare phrase in a prayer by Joseph to "my Father and my God."

142. Pannenberg, *Jesus*, 40.

143. This saying seems to express Jesus's *ontological equality* with God the Father in his nature, while his saying, "The Father is greater than I" (John 14:28b) would express his *functional subordination* during his time on Earth.

God's Words in OT	Jesus's Words in NT
"You shall observe My judgments and keep My ordinances" (Lev 18:4a).	"If you love me, obey my commandments" (John 14:15 NLT).
"I will come to give rest to Israel" (Jer 31:2b).	"I will give you rest" (Matt 11:28b).
"When the poor and needy seek water, and there is none, and their tongue is parched with thirst, I the Lord will answer them" (Isa 41:17). "They have forsaken the Lord, the fountain of living water" (Jer 17:13b).	"Whoever drinks some of the water that I will give him will never be thirsty again, but the water that I will give him will become in him a fountain of water springing up to eternal life" (John 4:14 NET).
"You will seek me and find me when you seek me with all your heart" (Jer 29:13).	"Ask and it will be given to you; seek and you will find" (Luke 11:9a).
"Thus says the Lord God: 'Behold, I will kindle a fire in you, and it shall devour every green tree and every dry tree in you'" (Ezek 20:47b).	"I have come to bring fire on the earth, and how I wish it were already kindled" (Luke 12:49).

In the Greek Old Testament, God identified himself using the name "I am," or "*ego eimi*":

> And God said to Moses, "I AM WHO I AM." And He said, "Thus you shall say to the children of Israel, 'I AM has sent me to you.'" (Exod 3:14b)

Jesus might have been making an implicit claim to divinity through his own use of this phrase:

God's Words in OT	Jesus's Words in NT
"Indeed before the day was, I am He" (Isa 43:13a).	"Most assuredly, I say to you, before Abraham was, I am (*ego eimi*)" (John 8:58–59 NKJV). The crowd wanted to stone Jesus for this statement.

God's Words in OT	Jesus's Words in NT
"Do not fear, for I am (*ego eimi*) with you" (Gen 26:24b).	"It is I (*ego eimi*). Don't be afraid" (Mark 6:50b).
"Behold, I am with you and will keep you wherever you go" (Gen 28:15a).	"And surely I am with you always, to the very end of the age" (Matt 28:20b).

Claims to the Rights of Judgment and Forgiveness

The Old Testament taught that God is the only judge: "See, I myself will judge between the fat sheep and the lean sheep" (Ezek 34:20b). Jesus is remembered as claiming this divine right for himself:

- "For the Son of Man will come with his angels in the glory of his Father and will judge all people according to their deeds" (Matt 16:27 NLT).
- "And [the Father] has given him authority to judge because he is the Son of Man" (John 5:27).

Regarding the power of forgiveness, a rabbinic text taught that "David said to the Holy One blessed be He, There is no one but you who can pardon sin."[144] According to Daniel Johansson, "No firm evidence can be found which demonstrates that other figures than God forgave sins. Various strands of early Judaism conceived of human and angelic agents who interceded on behalf of others, expiated sin and mediated forgiveness from God, but they all seem to have shared the view that forgiveness is divine prerogative."[145] Even John the Baptist did not personally pardon

144. Midrash Psalm 17:3.

145. Johansson, "Who Can Forgive Sins," 351. Some scholars translate the Prayer of Nabonidus in Qumran scroll 4Q242 to read, "an exorcist pardoned my sins." See Vermes, *Dead Sea Scrolls*, 614; Martínez and Tigchelaar, *Dead Sea Scrolls*, 487. However, the scroll is in five separate fragments, and Wise et al. combine them in this form: "[I prayed to the Most High,] and He forgave my sins. An exorcist a Jew, in fact, a mem[ber of the community of exiles came to me and said . . ." (*Dead Sea Scrolls*, 342). Frank Cross offers a similar translation ("Fragments," 260–64). In *all* other Qumran texts, only God grants forgiveness.

sin, and although the Messiah would inaugurate the final era of atonement, he was not expected to directly grant forgiveness.[146]

Jesus therefore seems to have been unique in claiming that he could provide personal forgiveness for sin, a claim that led to accusations of blasphemy: "Why does this fellow talk like that? He's blaspheming! Who can forgive sins but God alone?" (Mark 2:7).[147] Jesus answered this challenge using the rabbinic *kal va-homer* form: "Which is easier: to say to this paralyzed man, 'Your sins are forgiven,' or to say, 'Get up, take your mat and walk'? But I want you to know that the Son of Man has authority on earth to forgive sins.' So he said to the man, 'I tell you, get up, take your mat and go home'" (Mark 2:9–11).

The Implications of Jesus as "Son of Man"

Jesus applied the Semitic phrase, "son of man," to himself. This was not a recognized title in Second Temple Judaism (see chapter 2.2), and many scholars regard this as an authentic tradition that traces back to Jesus.[148] In the Old Testament, "son of man" simply meant a human being, but it was also used in Daniel's important prophetic vision:

> In my vision at night I looked, and there before me was one like a son of man coming with the clouds of heaven. He approached the Ancient of Days and was led into his presence. He was given authority, glory and sovereign power; all nations and peoples of every language worshiped him. His dominion is an everlasting dominion that will not pass away, and his kingdom is one that will never be destroyed. (Dan 7:13–14)

146. Some scholars have claimed that Qumran scroll CD 14:18–19 describes a forgiving messiah. However, Martínez and Tigchelaar translate this text as: "Until there arises the messiah of Aaron and Israel. And their iniquity will be atoned through meal and sin-offerings" (*Dead Sea Scrolls*, 575).

147. See also Luke 5:21; Matt 9:3. Many scholars consider this to be an authentic accusation of blasphemy. See Collins, "Blasphemy," 397; Hooker, *Son of Man*, 173; Bock, "Blasphemy and Jewish Examination," 61.

148. Frederick Borsch argues that "by the two toughest standards of 'authenticity' with respect to the traditions (dissimilarity and multiple attestation), the Son of Man usage has much better than a prima facie case for being taken seriously" ("Further Reflections," 136). See also Segal, *Two Powers*, xi; Dunn, "Messianic Ideas," 369; Black, "Aramaic Barnāshā," 204.

A rabbinic text regarded this as a messianic prediction,[149] and Jesus is said to have identified himself directly with this ancient vision:

> Again the high priest asked him, "Are you the Messiah, the Son of the Blessed One?" "I am [*ego eimi*]," said Jesus. "And you will see the Son of Man sitting at the right hand of the Mighty One and coming on the clouds of heaven."[150] The high priest tore his clothes. "Why do we need any more witnesses?" he asked. "You have heard the blasphemy. What do you think?" They all condemned him as worthy of death. (Mark 14:61–64)

Jesus's promise that he would return on heavenly clouds was an early tradition, found in Paul and the Didache.[151] The Messiah was expected to sit at God's right hand (Ps 110:1), and clouds of heaven were associated with God's presence,[152] so Jesus's claim would have linked him directly with messianic promises and God's authority. Darrell Bock argues extensively for the authenticity of this incident and concludes that Jesus's Jewish audience would have regarded him as making the outrageous and blasphemous claim that God would exalt him to a shared place of honor.[153] Morna Hooker agrees: "To appropriate to oneself such authority and to bestow on oneself this unique status in the sight of God and man would almost certainly have been regarded as blasphemy."[154]

Jesus's Implied Claim of Divinity in His Parables

Apart from the above claims, Jesus also associated himself directly with God's role and authority in his numerous parables that used Old Testament themes and images, such as those below.

149. "One verse reads of the king Messiah that One, like the sun (*sic*) of man came to the Ancient of days, and they brought him near before Him" (Midrash Psalm 21:5).

150. Jesus's answer to this question is recorded in Matthew as, "You have said so." But this was also his answer when Judas asked if he would betray Jesus (Matt 26:25), so it was a form of affirmation, like our modern, "You said it!"

151. Paul wrote, "After that, we who are still alive and are left will be caught up together with them in the clouds to meet the Lord in the air" (1 Thess 4:17a). The Didache contained this teaching: "Then the world will see the Lord coming on the clouds of heaven with power and dominion" (Didache 16:8).

152. See Num 12:5; Jer 4:13; Ezek 1:4; Isa 19:1.

153. Bock, "Blasphemy and Jewish Examination," 76.

154. Hooker, *Son of Man*, 173.

Son of the Vineyard Owner

Israel was traditionally described as God's vineyard. When Jesus taught a parable about God's vineyard, he compared his religious opponents to tenant farmers who beat the vineyard owner's servants (the prophets)[155] and killed his only son (Mark 12:6–12). In this way, Jesus seems to have identified himself as God's only son and also predicted his death as a result of the antagonism of these religious leaders. Many scholars support the authenticity of this parable.[156]

Rock/Cornerstone

A rock was a common Old Testament symbol for God's faithfulness, and the prophet Isaiah linked God's redemptive work to a crucial cornerstone: "So this is what the Lord GOD says: 'See, I lay a stone in Zion, a tested stone, a precious cornerstone, a sure foundation; the one who believes will never be shaken'" (Isa 28:16). Isaiah also prophesied that this foundation stone would be a stumbling block and rock of offense to some people, which rabbinic tradition interpreted as a reference to the Messiah.[157] This cornerstone of God's work is also mentioned in the ancient Psalm 118:

> This is the gate of the Lord through which the righteous may enter. I will give you thanks, for you answered me; you have become my salvation. The stone the builders rejected has become

155. The Old Testament frequently described the prophets as God's servants: "Since the day that your fathers came out of the land of Egypt until this day, I have even sent to you all My servants the prophets" (Jer 7:25a).

156. Charles Kimball makes this observation: "A number of authorities have shown that the parable describes a realistic situation in light of the known conditions of first century Palestine and conclude that the parable is likely authentic. J. D. M. Derrett reconstructs the events of the parable in light of rabbinic law, and M. Hengel provides additional parallels from the Zenon papyri and from the rabbinic parables. Building on their essays, K. Snodgrass refutes in detail the eight charges of a lack of realism brought by some modern critics" ("Jesus' Exposition," 80–81).

157. Isaiah described a future figure: "He will be as a sanctuary, but a stone of stumbling and a rock of offense to both the houses of Israel" (Isa 8:14a). The Talmud applied Isaiah's prophecy to the expected Messiah: "The son of David cannot appear ere the two ruling houses in Israel shall have come to an end . . . for it is written, And he shall be for a Sanctuary, for a stone of stumbling and for a rock of offense to both houses of Israel" (*b*. Sanhedrin 38a).

> the cornerstone . . . Blessed is he who comes in the name of the Lord!" (Ps 118:20–26a)

Jesus is said to have associated himself directly with these messianic images of rock, cornerstone, and gate:

- Jesus claimed, "I am the gate; whoever enters through me will be saved" (John 10:9a).
- He taught that to obey his teaching was to lay a foundation on rock (Luke 6:48; Matt 7:24).
- In his parable about the vineyard owner's son (who symbolized himself), Jesus quoted from Psalm 118: "Haven't you read this passage of Scripture: 'The stone the builders rejected has become the cornerstone'" (Mark 12:10). Charles Kimball suggests that in this way, Jesus made "an indirect yet pointed claim to be the messianic Son of God, who has been rejected by the Jewish religious leaders."[158]

It seems significant that in Hebrew, *ab* means father, *ben* means son, and *eben* means stone. The implication is that Father and Son together form this foundation stone of redemptive work.

Shepherd

In the Old Testament, the Messiah and God are both depicted as shepherds of God's people:

- "I will establish one shepherd over them, and he shall feed them—My servant David. He shall feed them and be their shepherd" (Ezek 34:23).
- "I will feed My flock, and I will make them lie down . . . I will seek what was lost" (Ezek 34:15–16a).

Jesus applied this redemptive imagery directly to himself:

- "For the Son of Man came to seek and to save the lost" (Luke 19:10).
- "I am the good shepherd . . . and there shall be one flock and one shepherd" (John 10:14–16).

158. Kimball, "Jesus' Exposition," 90.

Bridegroom

The Old Testament described God as the husband and bridegroom of his people,[159] and Jesus associated himself with this divine imagery. For example, when he was asked why his disciples did not fast, he answered, "How can the guests of the bridegroom fast while he is with them?" (Mark 2:19a). In speaking about his return, he warned that "the Son of Man will come at an hour when you do not expect him" (Matt 24:44b), and he then taught a parable about the bridegroom arriving when some of the reception party were unprepared (Matt 25:12).

Many scholars conclude that the New Testament parables represent Jesus's original teachings,[160] and Philip Payne points out that Jesus's self-portrayal in these parables is unique: "In the vast corpus of rabbinic parables there seems to be none in which a rabbi depicts himself. This is strong evidence that the parables recorded in the gospels are authentic to Jesus."[161] Payne provides additional examples of Jesus identifying himself with imagery that was traditionally associated with God, such as the sower, director of the harvest, and returning Lord and king, and he concludes that through these parables, Jesus was making implied claims of divinity.[162]

Review the Evidence

Karen Armstrong confidently asserts that "even though Paul and the evangelists all called Jesus the 'son of God,' they were not making divine claims for him. They would have been quite shocked by this idea," and "Jesus was not asking people to 'believe' in his divinity, because he was making no such claim."[163] Does the evidence support this opinion? We have seen that Paul directly applied Old Testament Yahweh language to Jesus and taught that he had existed before creation. And although the Gospels do not describe Jesus openly declaring to be divine, they

159. See Jer 31:32; Isa 62:5.

160. For example, Craig Blomberg remarks that "most of the parables and most parts of each parable are among the most indisputably authentic sayings of Jesus in the Gospels" (*Interpreting the Parables*, 18). See also Streeter, *Four Gospels*, 228.

161. Payne, "Jesus' Implicit Claim," 3.

162. Payne, "Jesus' Implicit Claim," 4–17. See also Blomberg, *Interpreting the Parables*, 313–324.

163. Armstrong, *Case for God*, 88, 90.

do record him making claims of unprecedented status and authority. Through his unique use of parables and Old Testament imagery, Jesus associated himself directly with God's work and messianic expectations. If he made even a few of the above claims, it would certainly explain why he became the center of controversy and aroused the anger of religious leaders. And the following facts make it unlikely that these claims could all be later inventions by his followers:

- Previous investigations suggest there would have been some measure of control to preserve Jesus's words and prevent radical additions.
- The entire fabric of the Gospels is saturated with acts, words, and images that imply unique authority and sonship. Doriani argues that "this Christology so suffuses the synoptics that one cannot alter the gospels' Christology by excising a few 'post-Easter insertions.'"[164]
- Jesus's direct and implied claims far exceeded contemporary messianic expectations, so there was no precedent or reason to invent these outrageous statements and expect that fellow Jews would accept them.
- Many of Jesus's claims have a strongly Semitic background, which does not suggest they were later developments in the Hellenistic Gentile churches.
- In all four gospels, there is a strong coherence between Jesus's acts and words, which would have been very difficult to invent.
- If Jesus never made any of these claims and, as Burton Mack suggests, merely taught moral principles, it is difficult to explain why he encountered such hostility from the Jewish leadership and was crucified by the Romans.

Richard France makes this observation about Jesus's claims in the Gospels:

> The whole of this evidence can hardly be dismissed as later Christian creation in view both of its varied and pervasive nature and of its very unobtrusiveness. It does not look as if it was designed to make a theological point. But if even some of this material is genuine, and if we may assume that Jesus' disciples, however gradually, were able to discern its implications, then we have the raw material in Jesus' own teaching for an increasing

164. Doriani, "Deity of Christ," 338–39.

> awareness that He was more than a prophet, and for that attitude to Him which could ultimately result in worshipping Him as God.[165]

Fletcher-Louis expresses the opinion of many scholars when he concludes that Jesus did make the above remarkable claims, which show that "the historical Jesus believed himself to be uniquely included . . . within the identity of the one God."[166]

Consider Your Verdict

How should we interpret Jesus's claims to unprecedented authority in the Gospel accounts? Could any of them be authentic? Is it possible that he regarded himself as different from other men in some fundamental way?

- Yes
- No

165. France, "Worship of Jesus," 27.

166. Fletcher-Louis, *Jesus Monotheism*, xiv.

4.4 HOW SHOULD WE VIEW JESUS'S RESURRECTION?

Figure 3: A burial cave at Emmaus Nicopolis.
(Photograph by Dr. Avishai Teicher; CC BY-SA 4.0.
https://commons.wikimedia.org/wiki/File:Emmaus_Nicopolis,_burial_cave.jpg)

Figure 3 shows an existing first-century tomb at Emmaus Nicopolis, not far from Jerusalem. Rocks that covered tomb entrances were commonly a rough plug shape as shown here, and only a few tombs have been found that used disc-shaped covers. It is understandable that the women would have wondered who could help them roll away such a large stone from Jesus's tomb (Mark 16:3). But how should we regard the bizarre claim that the tomb was empty because Jesus had risen from death? This investigation aims to find a simple and convincing explanation for the following widely accepted facts:

- Jesus was crucified.
- His disciples believed they interacted with a risen Jesus soon after his death.
- A few years later, their adversary Paul had an experience that he interpreted as an encounter with the risen Jesus.

- Jesus's brother James, who had rejected his claims, became a leader of the Jerusalem Church.
- Many of these people died for preaching that Jesus had risen.

In assessing these events, this chapter will explore the following aspects: beliefs about the afterlife that were prevalent at the time of Jesus, alternative explanations that have been offered for the resurrection story, and whether the resurrection claim meets any criteria for a valid hypothesis.

Contemporary Beliefs in the Afterlife

Paul's Epistles show that there was a very early belief in Jesus's resurrection, so it is worth identifying prevailing contemporary beliefs about the afterlife.

Greco-Roman culture often exalted dead heroes to the realm of the gods, but our earlier investigation into Bousset's theory (chapter 2.2) does not suggest that this would have been a dominant influence on Jesus's first disciples.

Second Temple Judaism had developed a mystical tradition in which biblical figures such as Job and Moses were believed to have been exalted to heaven after their death.[167] There was also a reverence for transcendent figures such as archangels, the eternal priest Melchizedek, and God's personified Wisdom and Word.[168] If Jesus's disciples had wanted to exalt their dead leader, they could therefore have drawn from an extensive pool of Jewish rather than pagan traditions. However, it is important to note why Jesus's resurrection and exaltation could *not* have been drawn directly from any contemporary Judaic belief:

- Jesus's exaltation to God's right hand of power was directly linked to humiliation, sacrifice, and atonement, which were not features of Jewish exaltation mysticism.[169]

167. For example, in the Testament of Job of the first century BC or AD, Job's body is buried, but God takes his soul to heaven; Philo also wrote about how God transformed the dead Moses, "into a most sun-like mind" (*Life of Moses* 2.51 §288).

168. Philo also adapted the abstract Greco-Roman principle of reason (*logos*) to form a figure that he sometimes identified with God's Wisdom. Like Jesus in Arian thinking, Philo's logos was somewhere between God and humanity, but he was an inconsistent figure with no atoning role.

169. See Chester, *Messiah and Exaltation*, 31. Prophetic themes of messianic humiliation and suffering in the Old Testament will be discussed in chapter 7.1.

- Judaism never elevated a contemporary man to God's side. In considering Paul's exalted depiction of Jesus, Andrew Chester remarks, "What should still strike us as astounding is the fact that Paul can apply these terms and traditions to a human figure not from the remote past (or biblical tradition) but from contemporary history and experience. This is something that is unique to the New Testament, in the context of Jewish usage."[170]
- Exalted figures in Second Temple Judaism were not accorded equal status alongside God. As Larry Hurtado observed, "Even the angelic figures . . . and also the great human heroes in the Bible (e.g., Moses) . . . were not treated as rightful recipients of cultic worship in any known Jewish circles of the time."[171] Fletcher-Louis agrees that the reverence offered to God "is specifically denied to other figures (mediatorial beings such as angels or exalted patriarchs) but is now given to Jesus."[172] Chester therefore concludes that Jesus's enthronement alongside God transformed the Jewish concept of exaltation to a degree that was no longer acceptable to monotheistic Judaism.[173]
- Jesus's resurrection was different to the raising of Lazarus and similar traditions in the Old Testament (1 Kgs 17:22; 2 Kgs 4:35) because those people finally died, but the risen Jesus was said to have conquered death.
- Regarding messianic expectations, atheist scholar Bart Ehrman makes this categorical statement: "In no surviving Jewish text—whether in the Hebrew Bible or later, up to the time of Christianity—is the Messiah said to die and be raised."[174] Martin Hengel agrees: "In the light of all our present knowledge, the suffering and dying Messiah was not yet a familiar traditional figure in the Judaism of the first century AD."[175] Despite sensational claims, VanderKam

170. Chester, *Messiah and Exaltation*, 393.

171. Hurtado, *Lord Jesus*, 31.

172. Fletcher-Louis, *Jesus Monotheism*, 20. See also Bauckham, *Jesus*, 14. These conclusions undermine Bart Ehrman's claim, mentioned in chapter 2.2, that Jesus's Jewish followers deified him because, as ancient Jews, they "believed that human beings could become divine" (*How Jesus Became God*, 5).

173. Chester, *Messiah and Exaltation*, 121.

174. Ehrman, *Apocalyptic Prophet*, 218.

175. Hengel, *Atonement*, 40. See also Charlesworth, "Messianology to Christology," 8; Wright, *Resurrection*, 25.

and Flint confirm that there is no evidence of a suffering or dying-rising messiah in the Qumran Scrolls.[176] In addition, Jesus's death by crucifixion would have placed him under the Old Testament curse on a hanged person (Deut 21:23), which Paul admitted was a "stumbling block" (*skandalon*) to the Jews (1 Cor 1:23; Gal 3:13). As Martin Hengel points out, a crucified son of God would have been an unacceptable contradiction in both Hellenic and Judaic cultures of the time.[177] The idea of a crucified hero was distasteful, and by the middle of the second-century, Justin Martyr could still remark that in no pagan story or tradition "did they imitate the being crucified; for it was not understood by them."[178]

As a result of these fundamental differences, Chester concludes that the veneration of the crucified Jesus as the risen Messiah "was completely without precedent,"[179] an opinion that is supported by scholars such as Endsjø[180] and Pannenberg.[181] Theologian N. T. Wright undertook an extensive investigation into afterlife beliefs in the Old Testament, post-biblical Judaism, and pagan texts, and concluded that the claim of Jesus's physical resurrection would have been just as controversial in his time as in ours:

176. VanderKam and Flint, *Dead Sea Scrolls*, 345. Eisenman and Wise claimed to find a dying messiah in Qumran scroll 4Q285 frag. 7.4, which they translated as, "they will put to death the Prince of the Congregation, the Branch of David" (*Scrolls Uncovered*, 29). However, many other scholars translate this as, "the Prince of the Congregation will kill him." See García Martínez and Tigchelaar, *Dead Sea Scrolls*, 643. Geza Vermes makes this comment: "The recently and groundlessly advanced theory that 'the Prince of the Congregation, Branch of David' of 4Q285 is a suffering and executed Messiah is contradicted both by the immediate context and the broader exegetical framework" (*Dead Sea Scrolls*, 12). John Collins agrees: "The more sensational claims about fragments, such as the discovery of a dying messiah in a pre-Christian Jewish text . . . turned out to be short-lived" (*Scepter*, vi). See also Chester, *Messiah and Exaltation*, 235.

177. Hengel, *Crucifixion*, 10.

178. Justin Martyr, *First Apology* 55.

179. Chester, *Messiah and Exaltation*, 121.

180. Endsjø writes, "Jewish beliefs on the afterlife were never identical with what Christians held to be true" (*Greek Resurrection Beliefs*, 121).

181. Pannenberg maintained that "the primitive Christian news about the eschatological resurrection of Jesus—with a temporary interval separating it from the universal resurrection of the dead—is, considered from the point of view of the history of religions, something new" (*Jesus*, 92).

> Nothing in Jewish beliefs about the Jewish god, and certainly nothing in non-Jewish beliefs about non-Jewish gods, would suggest to devotees that they should predicate resurrection of their object of worship. Some sort of new life beyond the grave, quite possibly: resurrection, certainly not.[182]

So *why did* Jesus's disciples believe that their executed leader had risen from his tomb? The simplest explanation is that they encountered him in some form after his death. However, this is difficult to accept, so we must explore alternative explanations—first, for the reports of Jesus's appearances and then, for the empty tomb tradition.

Alternative Explanations for Jesus's Appearances after Death

Suggestion 1: Jesus Did Not Die on the Cross and Later Recovered

We are told that Jesus was identified as dead by a Roman centurion. He is unlikely to have survived the combined effects of severe flogging (with flails tipped with bone and metal to strip flesh) and crucifixion, which leads to fluid in the lungs, shock, suffocation, and the trauma-related failure of the blood to clot. Forensic pathologist Frederick Zugibe also points out that Jesus would already have been weakened by sweating blood, leading to dehydration and low blood volume.[183] It is sometimes argued that Josephus knew of a man who had survived crucifixion; however, in this case, the process was interrupted and the man was taken down and carefully treated by a doctor—he was not mistaken for dead and buried.[184] In any case, if Jesus had survived, he would have been critically wounded when his disciples saw him. Why would they have concluded that he had miraculously defeated death? Theories of Jesus using healing herbs are unconvincing.

182. Wright, *Resurrection*, 25.

183. Zugibe, *Crucifixion of Jesus*, 15.

184. Josephus wrote, "I saw many captives crucified, and remembered three of them as my former acquaintance. I was very sorry at this in my mind, and went with tears in my eyes to Titus, and told him of them; so he immediately commanded them to be taken down, and to have the greatest care taken of them, in order to their recovery (*sic*); yet two of them died under the physician's hands, while the third recovered" (*Life of Flavius Josephus* 75 § 420–21).

Suggestion 2: The Resurrection Story Was a Hoax

Matthew's Gospel and the second-century Justin Martyr reported a Jewish accusation that Jesus's disciples had stolen his body and lied about him rising.[185] But what would have been the motive for such a bizarre conspiracy? As N. T. Wright points out, there were many failed messianic figures in Judaism, but "in not one case do we hear of any group, after the death of its leader, claiming that he was in any sense alive again, and that therefore Israel's expectation had in some strange way actually come true."[186]

In the opinion of Geza Vermes, "The rumour that the apostles stole the body is most improbable. From the psychological point of view, they would have been too depressed and shaken to be capable of such a dangerous undertaking. But above all, since neither they nor anyone expected a resurrection, there would have been no purpose in faking one."[187] There is no clear explanation for why any of Jesus's first disciples would have wanted to concoct this conspiracy in the first place, why they would have continued to insist it was true, despite Jesus's horrific death and in the face of growing antagonism from Roman authorities and fellow Jews, and why some of them chose martyrdom rather than admitting to the hoax. The conspiracy claim therefore lacks evidence and a convincing motive.

If the resurrection story was fabricated to extol and deify the human Jesus, the reports could also have been more expansive and creative. As it is, the New Testament contains no information about Jesus's actual rising. By contrast, the later noncanonical Gospel of Peter dramatically describes two men walking out of the tomb with their heads reaching up into the clouds, accompanied by a third man (Jesus) whose head reaches even beyond the clouds, and a cross that also exits the tomb and answers a voice from heaven.

Suggestion 3: Jesus's Followers Experienced Hallucinations

Perhaps the distraught, grieving disciples had hoped to see Jesus again and experienced a hallucination of his return. But this proposal has severe problems:

185. Matt 28:12–15; Justin Martyr, *Dialogue* 108.

186. Wright, *Victory*, 110.

187. Vermes, *Jesus the Jew*, 40.

- The disciples do not seem to have been in an excited state of anticipation but apparently hid behind locked doors (John 20:19). When the women reported the empty tomb, the disciples "did not believe the women because their words seemed to them like nonsense" (Luke 24:11).
- If Jesus's disciples did have a collective hallucination of him, why would they have interpreted this as meaning that he had returned in physical form, rather than being immediately translated to the divine realm? This was not consistent with prevailing Hellenic or Judaic beliefs.
- At a time when the people involved could have challenged his statement, Paul wrote that Jesus had appeared to them at different times—first to Peter, then the twelve, then a larger group of disciples, and then James (1 Cor 15:5–8). No case study provides evidence that different people can experience a consistent hallucination at different places and times.
- What explains Paul's vision a few years later? As an opponent of Jesus's teaching, he was not grief stricken and had no desire to see a risen Jesus. Gerd Lüdemann claims that he must have been suffering from subconscious doubt and guilt about his persecution of Jesus's followers, and "analysis would probably have shown a strong inclination to Christ in his subconscious; indeed, the assumption that he was unconsciously Christian is then no longer so far-fetched."[188] However, there is no evidence, least of all in his own letters, that this self-righteous Pharisee suffered from any such doubt or guilt before his Damascus experience. And although psychological stress can be converted into physical symptoms such as Paul's blindness, these "conversion disorder" episodes are not associated with hallucinations, and it is highly improbable that Paul could have experienced two profound psychological disorders at the same time.

There is no evidence in Scripture or psychiatry to support the hallucination hypothesis. Many scholars therefore agree with this conclusion by medical doctor Joseph Bergeron:

> Psychiatric hypotheses for the disciples' belief in Jesus' resurrection are found to be inconsistent with current medical

188. Lüdemann, "Resurrection," 26.

understanding and do not offer plausible explanations for the biblical story of Easter.[189]

Suggestion 4: The Resurrection Narrative Was Only a Metaphor

Perhaps the resurrection story was only a metaphor to describe the immortality of Jesus's teachings. However, there is no example of such figurative language being used at the time, and it does not explain why the disciples started to preach the *new* message that Jesus was now at the right hand of God, interceding for humanity.

Alternative Explanations for the Empty Tomb

If Jesus did not rise, what could explain the reports of the empty tomb?

Suggestion 1: Jesus Was Never Placed in a Tomb

It has been suggested that as an executed criminal, Jesus might have been buried in a shallow grave where his body decomposed or was eaten by animals. However, there is evidence that even victims of crucifixion were given a proper burial: Josephus reported that customary burials did take place after crucifixion,[190] and the bones of a crucified man have been found gathered together after burial according to tradition and placed in an ossuary (a chest for bones, used from the first century BC to the first century AD).[191] All four gospels also report that the Sanhedrin member Joseph supervised Jesus's entombment, and it is unlikely that the later church would have invented this detail at a time of increasing conflict with Judaism.

It might be relevant that according to the Talmud, criminals who had been convicted by the Sanhedrin were buried in disgrace in designated tombs until the bones were clean enough to be reburied.[192] The Sanhedrin

189. Bergeron and Habermas, "Resurrection: A Clinical Review," 157.

190. Josephus, *Wars* 4.5.2 §317.

191. The legs of this man had been broken, and an iron spike that was driven through both heels is still embedded in the bone. See Tzaferis, "Crucifixion: The Archaeological Evidence."

192. See *m.* Sanhedrin 6.5–6; *b.* Sanhedrin 47b.

had condemned Jesus for blasphemy (Matt 26:66, Mark 14:64; Luke 23:13–15), so Joseph might have undertaken the official interment of Jesus's body, possibly motivated by secret respect.[193]

Suggestion 2: No One Could Locate Jesus's Tomb

It has been suggested that the women went to a different, empty tomb. But why would they have just given up without continuing to search for the correct tomb? Why would their mistake have led to the unprecedented claim that Jesus had physically risen? Why did Jesus's opponents not find his tomb and display his body to quash rumors of his resurrection? Particularly if the Sanhedrin member Joseph knew where his body had been placed. The suggestion of the "wrong tomb" raises many unanswered questions.

Suggestion 3: Someone Else Moved Jesus's Body

Who would have benefited from hiding Jesus's body? Neither the Roman officials nor the Jewish religious leaders would have wanted Jesus's followers to believe that he was alive. It has been suggested that Jesus might have been temporarily placed in a nearby tomb because of the urgency to bury him before the start of the Sabbath, and his body could have been moved afterward for permanent burial. But again, why did none of Jesus's followers or opponents know the new location of the body? This seems to lead back to unsatisfactory conspiracy theories.

Suggestion 4: The Empty Tomb Story Was a Later Fabrication

There are problems with the suggestion that the story of the empty tomb only developed later outside Jerusalem:

- Late traditions usually have alternative versions, as in the different traditions about Apollonius's death recorded by Philostratus. But there are no competing stories about Jesus's tomb. Not even the numerous noncanonical gospels offer a different story, such as the

193. According to the Gospels, Joseph of Arimathea had not supported the Sanhedrin's condemnation of Jesus (Luke 23:51) and was also "waiting for the kingdom of God" (Mark 15:43). Only Matthew's Gospel states that the tomb belonged to Joseph.

disciples revering the tomb, making regular pilgrimage to its site, or later gathering Jesus's bones in the traditional way.

- Mark's Gospel records that the women went to the tomb on "the first day of the week" (Mark 16:2). This Semitic description for Sunday indicates a Palestinian tradition.
- If the story was fabricated later by followers of Jesus outside Jerusalem, it would be even more likely to have had figures such as Peter and John first discovering the empty tomb, rather than women.

Paul's Epistles provide evidence of a very early belief in Jesus's death, burial, and resurrection. Paul did not write about the empty tomb, but he also never mentioned where Jesus was buried or where his bones had been gathered and kept. And his explicit teaching that "he who raised Christ from the dead will also give life to your mortal bodies" (Rom 8:11b) does not suggest that he imagined Jesus's body to be decomposing in a tomb.

In general, alternative explanations do not convincingly explain the tradition of the empty tomb or the reports of Jesus's appearances to his disciples after death.

Testing the Resurrection Using Criteria for a Credible Hypothesis

The claim that a dead person can live again is unreasonable and contrary to natural laws. But what does logical analysis suggest? Let's set aside preconceptions and test the resurrection hypothesis according to three criteria of credibility provided by historian C. Behan McCullagh: explanatory scope and power, lack of additional required assumptions, and plausibility.[194]

Criterion 1: Explanatory Scope and Power

A valid hypothesis should have explanatory *scope* (explain a variety of facts) and explanatory *power* (make the facts more probable). Jesus's resurrection certainly explains a range of facts and makes them more probable: the detested Roman cross was transformed from a brutal tool of oppression to a revered symbol of faith; Sunday came to be regarded

194. McCullagh, *Justifying Historical Descriptions*, 19.

as the "Lord's Day"; Torah-observant Jews such as Paul believed that salvation no longer depended on the observance of Mosaic law because Jesus's death and resurrection had provided atonement; Jesus's disciples experienced a dramatic change from terror to defiant courage. Jewish theologian Pinchas Lapide made this observation:

> When these peasants, shepherds, and fishermen, who betrayed and denied their master and failed him so miserably, suddenly could be changed overnight into a confident mission society, convinced of salvation and able to work with much more success after Easter than before, then no vision or hallucination is sufficient to explain such a revolutionary transformation.[195]

The evidence led Lapide to this conclusion: "I accept the resurrection of Easter Sunday not as an invention of the community of disciples, but as a historical event."[196]

There seem to be more unexplained facts if Jesus was not resurrected than if he was, and historian McCullagh therefore concludes that the resurrection hypothesis has greater explanatory scope and power than alternative hypotheses.[197]

Criterion 2: Few Additional Assumptions

A valid hypothesis should not require additional assumptions. The resurrection hypothesis certainly does require two enormous assumptions—that God exists and that he can reverse physical death. However, each alternative hypothesis also involves at least one improbable assumption: for example, that a man could survive crucifixion and reappear soon after in perfect health; that men would be prepared to die to protect a hoax; that different people can experience the same hallucination at different times, or that no one knew where Jesus's body lay.

Criterion 3: Plausibility

A hypothesis is considered to be plausible if it is implied by some accepted truths and contradicted by very few. This is a tricky criterion

195. Lapide, *Resurrection*, 125.

196. Lapide, *Resurrection*, 131.

197. McCullagh, *Justifying Historical Descriptions*, 21.

because if Jesus's resurrection did take place, it would be a unique event with no preexisting "accepted truth" to support its plausibility. As C. S. Lewis pointed out, "If the story is true, then a wholly new mode of being has arisen in the universe."[198] James Dunn explains:

> The historical method inevitably works with some application of the principle of analogy. The resurrection of Jesus as "understood" in the beginning, however, broke through the analogies . . . The interpretation that God had raised Jesus from the dead became itself paradigmatic, *that which defines rather than that which is defined.*[199]

A judgment about the resurrection is therefore strongly linked to preconceptions: if the existence of an omnipotent Creator is regarded as an "accepted truth," then the hypothesis of his Son being raised from death becomes plausible. And as biblical scholar Michael Licona points out, the attitude that rejects the supernatural is "no less a philosophical construct than supernaturalism and theism."[200]

Licona undertook an objective and extensive review of the evidence in a wide range of early Christian and non-Christian sources, and he applied historical methodology to six alternative hypotheses about the resurrection. This is the conclusion he reached from his analysis: "If one brackets the question of worldview, neither presupposing nor a priori excluding supernaturalism, and examines the data, the historical conclusion that Jesus rose from the dead follows."[201] It is interesting that in a public debate on the resurrection in 1985 between theologian Gary Habermas and well-known atheist Anthony Flew, the two judging panels voted for Habermas's arguments.[202] Flew converted to belief in a Creator God in 2004, for reasons related to science.

198. Lewis, *Miracles*, 240.

199. Dunn, *Jesus Remembered*, 877 (emphasis added).

200. Licona, *Resurrection*, 604.

201. Licona, *Resurrection*, 608.

202. Three out of five professional debate judges and four out of five philosophers voted for Habermas. See Habermas and Flew, *Did Jesus Rise?*

Review the Evidence

It is difficult to find a convincing, rational explanation for the tradition of Jesus's resurrection. If Jesus did *not* rise, the alternative explanations for the story look something like this:

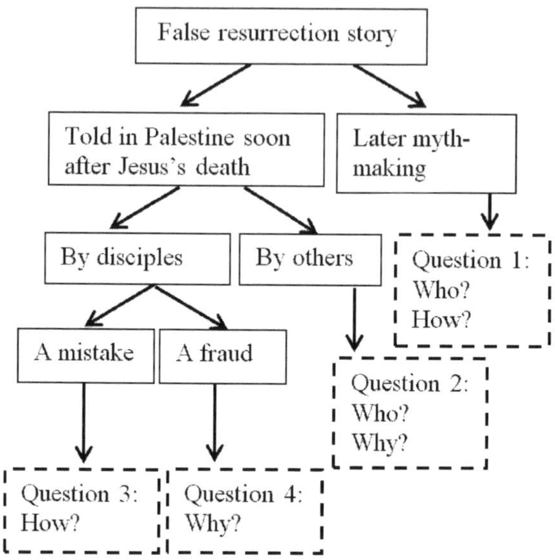

Figure 4: Decisions about the resurrection.

But these possibilities raise questions that require further explanations.

- Question 1: Who were these myth-makers, and how did they get others to believe their bizarre story? Our earlier investigations raised serious doubts about uncontrolled mythologizing in Christian communities.
- Question 2: Which non-followers of Jesus would have hidden his body and concocted the resurrection story? Why would they have done this?
- Question 3: How could so many of Jesus's followers have been fooled into believing that their dead leader had returned to physical life?
- Question 4: Why would his disciples have fabricated such a bizarre tale, which they continued to defend even in the face of persecution and death?

The wealth of details from Scripture and early church history forms a coherent picture only if Jesus did rise from death. As N. T. Wright argues, "The proposal that Jesus was bodily raised from the dead possesses unrivalled power to explain the historical data at the heart of Christianity."[203] If this key piece of the puzzle is rejected, the others fly apart into fragments that can only be explained by separate, sometimes conflicting hypotheses that have little supporting evidence.

Consider Your Verdict

Like other miracles and the question of God's existence, perhaps the resurrection event is simply not accessible to rational analysis—its very uniqueness would place it outside analogy and logical explanation. But what does the evidence suggest about the story of Jesus's resurrection?

- It has been proven to be false.
- It does not fit the facts.
- It provides the best explanation of the facts, although it is difficult to accept.
- It probably took place.

CONCLUSION 4
COULD THE ORTHODOX VIEW OF JESUS BE CORRECT?

Is it possible that the teachings of Orthodox Christianity are more closely connected to the beliefs of Jesus's first followers than alternative interpretations of Jesus and his work? The evidence has suggested that the central doctrines of orthodoxy (Jesus's divinity, atoning death, and resurrection) were in place at least by the time of Paul's letters, which were written only a few decades after Jesus's death. It also strongly suggests that these doctrines were not different from the beliefs of the Jerusalem apostles and were largely preserved in the New Testament. Many scholars therefore believe that canonical Scripture represents Jesus's acts and teachings more reliably than alternative theories such as adoptionism, Arianism, or Jesus as a human wisdom teacher. In particular, the gnostic gospels do not depict a more authentic Jewish Jesus than canonical materials.

203. Wright, *Resurrection*, 718.

However, despite the evidence that supports the greater validity of orthodox doctrines, Komoszewski et al. remark wryly that "it's simply easier to pretend all interpretations are created equal. The radical scepticism sown in the media and rooted in postmodernism has been cultivated in an environment of biblical ignorance."[204]

It is relevant to take note of a challenge that historians Schermer and Grobman have issued to people who deny central aspects of the World War II Holocaust: they write, "It is not enough for deniers to concoct an alternative explanation that amounts to nothing more than denying each piece of free-standing evidence. They must proffer a theory that not only explains all of the evidence but does so in a manner superior to the present theory."[205] Similarly, if orthodox doctrines were not based on Jesus's claims and resurrection, there must be *one* coherent alternative hypothesis, supported by substantial evidence, that can convincingly account for the following generally accepted facts:

Jesus taught a specific message in Palestine.

Some Jewish leaders regarded this teaching as blasphemous and subversive.

Jesus was crucified.

His death was very soon believed to have atoning value.

His followers became inspired and active within a short time of his death.

He was the only contemporary Jewish figure to be elevated to equality with God.

As N. T. Wright argues, hypotheses that explain some of these facts cannot adequately account for others.[206] The simplest explanation, which accounts for all known facts, is that Jesus did rise after death.

But at this critical point in the investigation, evidence becomes irrelevant. No matter what information we have about early manuscripts, or the process of oral transmission, or Second Temple beliefs about the afterlife, the modern mind instinctively rejects the outrageous claim that a man rose from death, and any other explanation seems more acceptable. Like Dupuis, Higgins, and Bousset before us, we are a product of Enlightenment and Rationalism, with the additional influence of postmodern skepticism. The only reasonable response seems to be to deny the possibility of any

204. Komoszewski et al., *Reinventing Jesus*, 15.

205. Schermer and Grobman, *Denying History*, 172.

206. Wright, *Victory*, 91–116.

supra-natural event. But what is this decision based on? Is it the inevitable result of scientific knowledge and rigorous laws of logic? Or is it merely an opinion? McCullagh points out that whenever we draw a conclusion from evidence, we are also making three assumptions about this process:

- That our perceptions provide an accurate impression of reality.
- That reality is structured according to the concepts by which we describe it.
- That our rules of inference are reliable means of arriving at new truths about reality.[207]

McCullagh remarks that rejecting any one of these assumptions "would introduce a quite massive dislocation into our system of beliefs about the world."[208] However, he points out that the truth of these underlying assumptions is not provable because we do not have access to reality apart from our beliefs and experiences of it.[209] So can we safely rely on these assumptions? Perhaps reality is *not* structured according to our concepts, and perhaps our rules of inference are *not* "reliable means of arriving at new truths about reality." Perhaps Jesus's resurrection really *was* a "massive dislocation" of our understanding of the world. Andrew Chester uses this same term when he describes Paul's conversion experience as a "dramatic, socially and cognitively dislocating experience."[210]

Our assessment of the resurrection story therefore rests on untestable assumptions. And *only one fact* makes it impossible to accept: the fact that resurrection after death contravenes the laws of nature. It is therefore essential to understand the role of physical laws in our world. John Polkinghorne, who is a physicist and a Christian, urges an objective assessment of the evidence:

> We know the physical world is very surprising, and we cannot guess beforehand what it is going to be like. Who would have guessed quantum theory beforehand? The answer is nobody! Similarly, in our encounter with God, we must expect surprises.

207. McCullagh, *Justifying Historical Descriptions*, 1. McCullagh provides four assumptions, but these three are most relevant to this discussion.

208. McCullagh, *Justifying Historical Descriptions*, 1.

209. McCullagh, *Justifying Historical Descriptions*, 2.

210. Chester, *Messiah and Exaltation*, 394–95.

> In a search for motivated belief, we ask: What is the evidence? What are the things that might make us think this was the case?[211]

He writes:

> My conclusions are that a belief in the raising of Jesus that first Easter Day, and an adherence to a modified form of kenotic Christology as a means of affirming the meeting of the divine and the human in him, are tenable beliefs in a scientific age.[212]

Why does Polkinghorne find the physical world so surprising? How can he reconcile his scientific work with belief in a resurrection? To answer these and other questions, our exploration will now move into the realm of modern science. The next few mind-opening investigations challenge our preconceptions about the nature of the physical world and what is possible in our universe.

211. Polkinghorne, *Serious Talk*, 2–3.

212. Polkinghorne, *Faith of a Physicist*, 2.

PART B

The New Science

Investigation 5

What Do Scientists Know about Space, Time, and Matter?

As I type these words, I am aware that the chair on which I am sitting is mainly empty air—the protons and electrons of its atoms could be compressed into a tiny speck. The same is true for my body, so what stops me from falling through the chair? Seeds on the sunflower outside my window are arranged in a pattern that shares mathematical features with the bronchi in my lungs and the pulsating light of some stars. According to relativity theory, the passengers in a passing airplane are aging slower than me, and the faster the airplane travels, the shorter it gets! Science has revealed unusual aspects of our world, and it seems the more we know, the more we realize we don't know. Our judgments are directly shaped by our beliefs about what is "real" and what is possible in our world, so to check the validity of our conclusions, we need to check the validity of our beliefs. How well do we know our universe and how it functions?

5.1 SPACE AND TIME—IT'S ALL RELATIVE

The "new" physics of relativity has been with us for almost a hundred years. However, its counter-intuitive results are still difficult to comprehend, and experienced physicist Brian Greene makes this admission: "The relativity of space and time is a startling conclusion. I have known about it for more than twenty-five years, but even so, whenever I quietly sit and think it through, I am amazed."[1] Let's find out what is so counterintuitive about the nature of time and space.

The Findings of Relativity Theory

Motion Destroys Simultaneity

Here is one of Albert Einstein's thought experiments regarding the nature of time.[2]

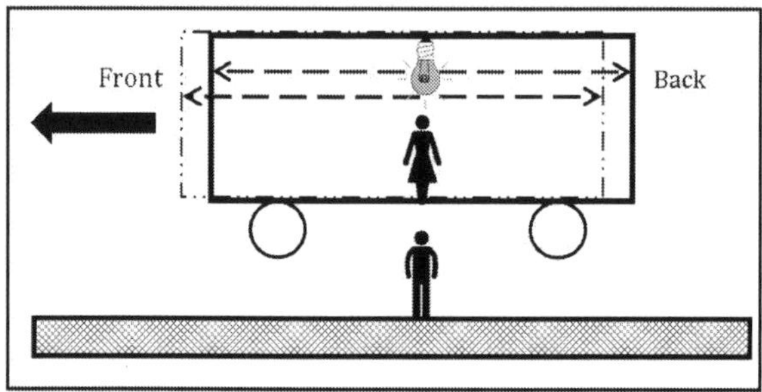

Figure 5: Light rays in a moving train carriage.

Imagine that Sue is standing in the center of a train carriage. A ceiling light directly above her flashes once, and she sees the light rays reach the front and back walls of the carriage at the same time. (See the top arrows in figure 5.) But if the light flashes as the carriage passes Joe standing on the platform, the front wall will be racing *away* from the flash of light, and the back wall will be racing *towards* the flash. As a result, the carriage will have traveled a minuscule distance before the light reaches the walls, which means that for Joe, the light rays reach the back wall *before* they reach the front wall. As a result, two events that are simultaneous for Sue are not simultaneous for Joe.

Let's have the train pass Joe again, this time with Sue taking her hat off. To another passenger on the train, Sue is in the same location with her hat on and with it off. But Joe sees her in one location with her hat on and in a different location with her hat off. Simply put, the above results mean that two events that for one person seem to happen at the same time (or place) can seem to happen at two different times (or places)

1. Greene, *Fabric of the Cosmos*, 47.
2. See Einstein and Infeld, *Evolution of Physics*, 187–88.

for a person in a different state of motion.[3] Relativity theory therefore destroys the concept of simultaneity.

Time Slows with Motion

Sue and Joe now each have an identical timing box in which a signal bounces off a plate and returns exactly one second later. Joe stays stationary with his timer, while Sue travels away with her timer.

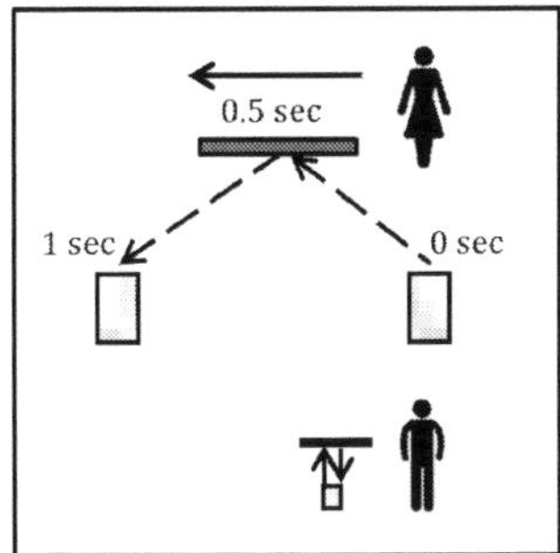

Figure 6: Joe and Sue with two identical timers.

From Joe's perspective, the signal in Sue's moving timer must travel a longer distance in each bounce, as shown in figure 6. (This is like Sue bouncing a ball vertically on the floor of a moving train; Joe on the platform would see the ball moving along diagonal paths.) But if the signal speed is constant, each longer bounce must also take a longer time. Sue doesn't notice this difference because she is traveling with her timer, but one second on her timer will be a longer time interval than one second on Joe's timer. Her clock therefore ticks slower than Joe's, and she will age more slowly than him. This phenomenon is known as time dilation, which has been experimentally confirmed. For example, when a short-lived particle called a muon passes through our system, the faster it travels, the longer it lives. As a result, if two equivalent timers start at one event and travel along different *paths* to a second event, they will record different *times* between the same two events.[4] A clock therefore does not measure absolute time—the interval that it measures depends entirely on its reference system. Time really is relative.

3. See Gamow, *One, Two, Three—Infinity*, 88.

4. See Malament, *General Relativity*, 137.

Distances Shrink in the Direction of Travel

If two observers in relative motion measure different times, they must also measure different distances for speed to remain the same. As a result, distance contracts in the direction of motion. A stick measuring one meter will remain one meter long if it travels at right angles to its length, but it will shrink if it travels in the direction of its length. The distance from one planet to another *really decreases* for a space traveler in a speeding rocket. (But this effect is extremely small at normal speeds, so the distance to the office won't be much shorter if you drive very fast.)[5]

Acceleration and Gravity Are Equivalent

Imagine standing on a weight-scale fixed to the floor of a stationary rocket on Earth. You look down and note your weight, which is the result of gravity. The rocket then shoots off into outer space, and after a while, you float weightlessly without gravity. You place your feet against the scale just as the rocket accelerates in your direction. The scale is forced against your feet and once again gives a reading of your weight. Floating objects also seem to fall to the floor. If you didn't know where you were, how could you decide whether "falling" and "weight" were caused by gravity or acceleration? Einstein reached the remarkable conclusion that there is no difference in these effects because gravity is *equivalent* to acceleration.[6]

The fact that acceleration affects time means that gravity should also affect time, and time does pass more slowly in the presence of mass. For example, an extremely accurate timer at the bottom of a tower will run very slightly slower than a similar timer at the top, and you will age infinitesimally faster at the top of a tall building than at ground level. Once again, there is no absolute time.

5. The shortening effect is called Lorentz-FitzGerald contraction. If the length of an object is L_0 (for an observer traveling with the object), then its contracted length to a stationary observer is $L = L_0\sqrt{1-\frac{v^2}{c^2}}$, where v is the object's speed and c is the speed of light. The fraction $\frac{v^2}{c^2}$ will be very close to zero unless the object has an exceptionally high speed.

6. See Einstein and Infeld, *Evolution of Physics*, 230–32.

Implications for the Nature of Time and Space

The findings of relativity theory suggest that our universe is stranger than we might realize.

Spacetime Must Be Four-Dimensional

The phenomena of time dilation, length contraction, and non-simultaneity would not be possible in a world with only three dimensions.[7] Time and space are therefore considered to be two related aspects of a unified four-dimensional realm. As Einstein's lecturer Hermann Minkowski said, "From now onwards space by itself and time by itself will recede completely to become mere shadows and only a type of union of the two will still stand independently on its own."[8] Minkowski regarded four-dimensional space-time as "a major discovery about the world, not a discovery of a mathematical abstraction."[9]

Is it possible to imagine four dimensions? Start by moving a dimensionless point through space to form a one-dimensional line. Now move the line at right angles to itself to form a two-dimensional square, then move the square at right angles to itself to form a three-dimensional cube. A four-dimensional hypercube is formed by moving the cube in a new direction that is "perpendicular" to itself. In the same way that a flat cross of six squares can fold up to form a three-dimensional cube, a cross of eight cubes (four vertical cubes and four around the second cube) can in theory "fold up" to form a four-dimensional hypercube or tesseract (figure 7).[10]

7. See Petkov, *Space and Time*, 34.

8. Quoted in Petkov, *Space and Time*, 39.

9. Petkov, *Space and Time*, 31.

10. In Salvador Dali's exceptional painting, *Corpus Hypercubus*, Jesus is shown crucified on an unfolded eight-cube tesseract.

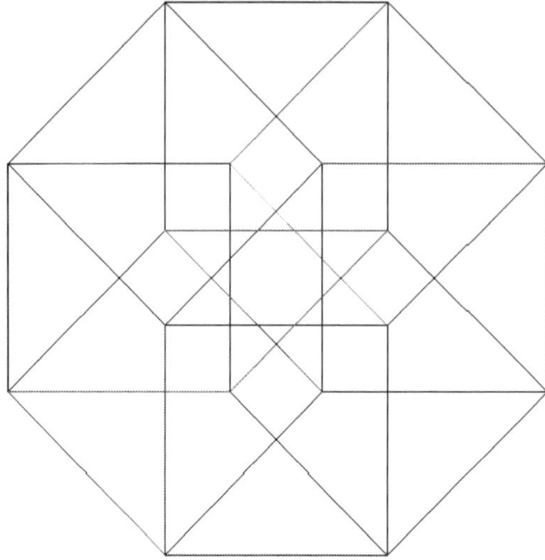

Figure 7: Representation of a four-dimensional hypercube (tesseract).

Spacetime Participates in the Unfolding of Events

> It is one of the fundamental ideas of relativity theory that spacetime structure is not a fixed backdrop against which the processes of physics unfold, but instead participates in that unfolding.[11]

Our four-dimensional spacetime is a connected, unified interaction of matter, force, energy, and motion, which all continuously affect each other. There is therefore no such thing as empty "space" with "things" in it. Spacetime is distorted by mass and energy so that light rays follow curved paths in gravitational fields, and the Earth orbits the sun because of these distortions in the spacetime fabric.[12] Gravity is not a pulling force but the result of the curvature of four-dimensional spacetime.[13] This effect of mass creates gravitational ripples in spacetime that travel at the speed of light, so if our moon suddenly disappeared, it would take

11. Malament, *General Relativity*, 159.
12. See Greene, *Fabric of the Cosmos*, 71.
13. See Gamow, *One, Two, Three—Infinity*, 109.

one and a half seconds for us to stop seeing its light and the same length of time for the moon's effect on ocean tides to cease.[14]

Time and Distance Are Interchangeable

If we represent three-dimensional space on a horizontal axis and time on a vertical axis, then the path of an object through space and time is represented by its worldline on the graph. A remarkable result is that if the axes are rotated to represent acceleration, this "may result in partial transformations of distances into durations and vice versa."[15] In other words, *distance and time are partially interchangeable.*[16] As a result, one person's interval of time can correspond to another person's interval of time *and* space. For example, when Sue moves away from Joe, who remains stationary, he only travels through time, but some of Sue's motion through time is diverted into motion through space.[17] When she returns to Joe, some of her total worldline will have been allocated to space, so her progress through time will be less than Joe's, and she will have aged less.

All Aspects of Time Might Exist Together

If time is relative to each observer, then the past and future are also relative. Einstein explained the implication: "In classical physics . . . such words as 'simultaneously,' 'sooner,' 'later,' had an absolute meaning . . . Relativity theory force[s] us to give up this view."[18] The physicist Vesselin Petkov is even more daring:

> The very essence of time flow is that *only one moment of time exists* which constantly changes. But it is a well known fact

14. See Greene, *Fabric of the Cosmos*, 72.

15. Gamow, *One, Two, Three—Infinity*, 84.

16. To create equivalent units for these two quantities, one second is treated as a distance of 3×10^8 meters (from the speed of light). The interval between two events is then calculated using three space dimensions and one time dimension: $D^2 = \Delta x^2 + \Delta y^2 + \Delta z^2 - \Delta t^2$.

17. See Greene, *Fabric of the Cosmos*, 48. Greene points out that "the combined speed of any object's motion through space and its motion through time is always precisely equal to the speed of light" (*Fabric of the Cosmos*, 49). Traveling through distance at the speed of light would therefore leave no motion for traveling through time, so time would stand still.

18. Einstein and Infeld, *Evolution of Physics*, 188.

> that there does not exist any physical evidence whatsoever that only the present moment exists. On the contrary, all relativistic experimental evidence confirms Minkowski's view that all moments of time have equal existence due to their belonging to the entirely given time dimension.[19]

Spacetime is often represented as a loaf-shaped "block" universe, with each vertical slice containing all events taking place at one time. But acceleration changes the angle of the cut so that observers with different motions have different events on their "now"-slice, and therefore they have different perceptions of what is "past" and "future." As a result, relativity theory suggests that all times have equal existence, and there is no fundamental difference between past, present, and future. Brian Greene maintains that this totality of spacetime is not merely conceptual but real: "Just as we envision all of space as *really* being out there, as *really* existing, we should also envision all of time as *really* being out there, as *really* existing, too."[20]

Review the Evidence

The findings of relativity theory have had a profound impact on how scientists view reality. Ancient man believed that the sun moved around the earth because that was his perceptual experience. Until recently, we believed that time and distance were absolute quantities because that was our perceptual and experimental evidence. But now, only spacetime is regarded as absolute, while time and distance are relative. Might there be even further developments in our understanding? If a two-dimensional surface is embedded in three-dimensional space, and our three-dimensional world is embedded in four-dimensional spacetime, perhaps this, in turn, is embedded in higher dimensions. According to astronomer James Jeans,

> Just as the shadows on a wall form the projection of a three-dimensional reality into two dimensions, so the phenomenon of

19. Petkov, *Space and Time*, 37 (original emphasis).

20. Greene, *Fabric of the Cosmos*, 139 (original emphasis). The paradoxical nature of time is still under debate, and cosmologist George Ellis suggests that spacetime should rather be regarded as an *evolving* block universe, in which the future is not the same as the past. According to Ellis, there is an instant along our worldline where the indefinite future changes to the definite past, including more spacetime events as time passes. See Ellis, "The Evolving Block Universe and the Meshing Together of Times."

> the spacetime continuum may be a four-dimensional projection of realities which occupy more than four dimensions.[21]

Modern science is seriously considering the possibility that our world lies within a higher dimensional realm, which has important implications for our perceptions of reality.[22] For example, in his 1884 satire, *Flatland*, Edwin Abbot described two-dimensional beings that live on a flat world and are mystified by the behavior of three-dimensional beings. For example, when Sphere passes through Flatland, he first appears to be a point, then a growing circle, and then a shrinking circle until he disappears completely. These puzzling beings can also escape from Flatland's secure two-dimensional jails. Abbott's intention (apart from satirizing aspects of society) was to illustrate that human perception is completely determined by our limited experience in a three-dimensional world. As a result, we cannot rely on our "common sense" to interpret phenomena that might lie outside our experience.

To use another analogy, a small section of a very large circle looks like a straight line—mathematicians say the curve is "locally linear." A small area of the Earth's curved surface is "locally flat" so that a triangle drawn on the ground seems to have an angle sum of 180 degrees.[23] At speeds much slower than that of light, our world is "locally Newtonian," so we do not notice the peculiar effects of relativity. If our four-dimensional spacetime is embedded in a more complex reality, perhaps it is only "locally relativistic," and even stranger laws might apply beyond this. Perhaps from a higher dimensional realm, all events on our spacetime loaf can be viewed at once—our apparent past, present, and future. For example, Page and Wootters theorized that time only flows for observers inside the universe, which will appear to be unchanging to any "outside" observer. In 2013 this strange hypothesis received some experimental verification when scientists proved that an internal observer who becomes correlated

21. Jeans, *Mysterious Universe*, 149.

22. For example, according to Dahia and Romero, "The old idea that our universe is fundamentally higher-dimensional with n = A + d space-time dimensions seems to be gaining grounds very rapidly in recent years" ("Embedding Spacetime in Five Dimensions," 4287). See also Matej Pavšič, *Landscape of Theoretical Physics*.

23. On a flat, two-dimensional surface, a triangle has an angle sum of 180 degrees—the three corners can be torn off and put together to form a straight line. But this is not the case in spherical geometry: a triangle formed on a globe by two lines of longitude and a section of the equator will have an angle sum that is greater than the two right angles at the equator and therefore more than 180 degrees.

with a clock photon sees the system *evolve*, while an external observer can establish that the system is *static*.[24] Professor of physics Peter Galison makes this intriguing suggestion:

> Beyond the divisions of time and space which are imposed on our experience, there lies a higher reality, changeless, and independent of observer.[25]

Consider Your Verdict

Given the counter-intuitive results of relativity, is it safe to rely on our common sense when deciding how our universe functions?

- ◦ Yes, definitely
- ◦ Perhaps not

5.2 ABSTRACT HUMAN CONCEPTS AND THE PHYSICAL WORLD

We have seen that space and time are related in ways that are not obvious to our five senses. Another intriguing aspect of physical reality is that it can be modeled by abstract mental concepts that are created by human beings in ivory tower *isolation from that reality*. The laws of physics are generally developed by taking measurements and developing formulae to match the experimental data, but most mathematical concepts are created with no reference at all to the physical world.[26] The remarkable fact is that so many of these abstract concepts have been found embedded in nature. Nuclear physicist Eugene Wigner called this the "unreasonable effectiveness of mathematics" and concluded, "It is difficult to avoid the impression that a miracle confronts us here."[27] This astonishing relationship between human consciousness and the physical world is illustrated

24. See Moreval et al., "Time From Quantum Entanglement."

25. Galison, *Minkowski's Space-Time*, 98.

26. The traditional difference between three mathematical sciences is illustrated by this tongue-in-cheek observation: the engineer is happy when his theories match the real world; the physicist is happy when the real world matches his theories; the mathematician asks, "What real world?"

27. Wigner, "Unreasonable Effectiveness," 7.

by the predominance in nature of three mathematical concepts: fractals, phi, and Fibonacci numbers.

Relationships between Fractals, Phi, and Fibonacci Numbers

The Number Phi as the "Golden Mean"

A "golden" rectangle is special in that when a square is added or cut off, the new rectangle is the same shape as the original. In other words, the length and breadth are in the same proportion. It has become popular to see the golden rectangle everywhere, but astrophysicist Mario Livio points out that trying to find this shape in, for example, the Great Pyramid and the Parthenon, requires specific selection and manipulation of the dimensions.[28] But mathematics provides a particularly interesting result about these special rectangles. Figure 8 shows a square AMND added to rectangle MBCN to form a second rectangle ABCD.

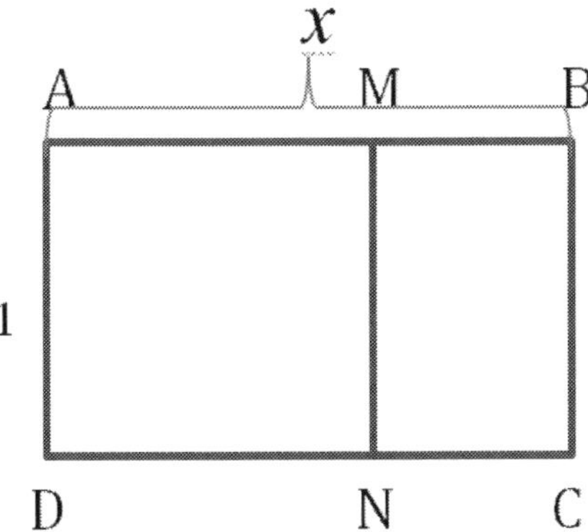

Figure 8: Two golden rectangles.

Some simple mathematics[29] proves that the two rectangles will be golden if they both have sides in the ratio "length : width = ϕ : 1," where the Greek letter ϕ (*phi*) denotes the number 1.618 (correct to three decimal places). The number phi is called the golden ratio or golden mean.

28. Livio, *Golden Ratio*, 58, 74.

29. The two rectangles in figure 8 are golden if the ratio $\frac{length}{width}$ is the same in both, which means that $\frac{x}{1} = \frac{1}{x-1}$. This relationship forms the equation $x^2 - x - 1 = 0$, which has the positive solution $x = \frac{1+\sqrt{1^2-4(1)(-1)}}{2} = \frac{1+\sqrt{5}}{2} = 1.618$, correct to three decimal places.

This is an interesting result because phi is also related to Fibonacci numbers and some fractal patterns.

Fractals and Phi

A fractal is an infinite self-replicating pattern that looks the same at all scales. Mathematical fractals describe many natural phenomena such as the branching systems shown in figure 9.

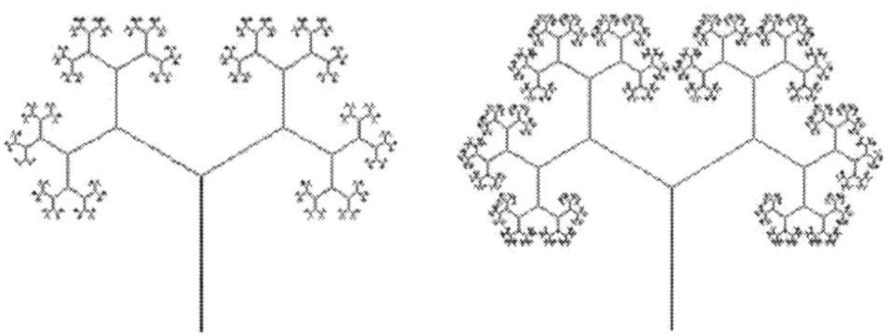

Figure 9: Two fractal branching systems.

The left tree in figure 9 repeatedly forms two branches that are half the length each time, using a scaling factor of $\frac{1}{2}$ or 0.5. This scaling factor creates a sparse and inefficient branching system, but a larger scale factor, say 0.7, would cause the branches to eventually overlap. The most efficient branching system is shown in the right tree, which fits in as many branches as possible without any overlapping. This is called a "golden" tree because the lengths of consecutive branches are in the same ratio as the sides of a golden rectangle: "larger branch : smaller branch = ϕ : 1." The branching scale factor of $\frac{1}{\phi}$ is approximately 0.6, which lies between the factor that is too small (0.5) and the factor that is too large (0.7). So the number phi produces the most efficient fractal designs in many cases.

Fibonacci Numbers and Phi

The number phi is also related to the Fibonacci sequence of numbers. Imagine a hypothetical pair of breeding rabbits that takes one month to mature and produce another breeding pair (one male and one female each time).

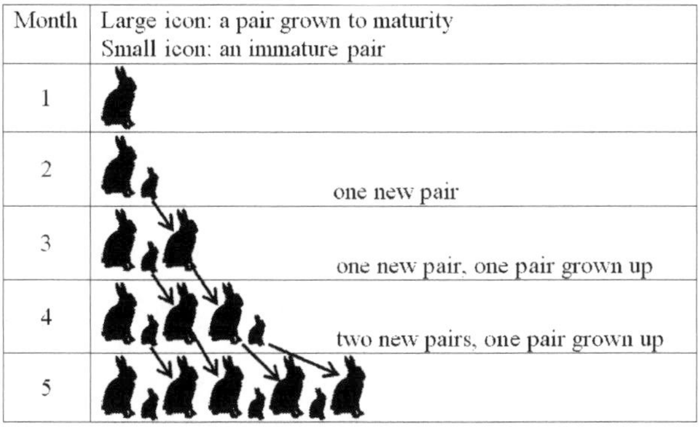

Month	Large icon: a pair grown to maturity Small icon: an immature pair
1	
2	one new pair
3	one new pair, one pair grown up
4	two new pairs, one pair grown up
5	

Figure 10: A breeding pattern that follows the Fibonacci number pattern.

Figure 10 shows the number of rabbit pairs each month, which illustrates the famous Fibonacci sequence: 1; 2; 3; 5; 8; . . . Can you work out the next three numbers in the sequence?[30] Ratios of consecutive Fibonacci numbers look like this: $\frac{2}{1}; \frac{3}{2}; \frac{5}{3}; \frac{8}{5};$ . . . These ratios get increasingly close to the number 1.618, correct to 3 decimal places. (You can check this on a calculator.) In other words, the number phi is also the "limit" of the ratios of consecutive Fibonacci numbers.

Fibonacci Numbers, Phi, and Fractals in the Natural World

It is perhaps not surprising to find links between the mathematical concepts phi, Fibonacci numbers, and fractals. What is far more astonishing is that these purely theoretical and mental constructs, which were developed by mathematicians without any reference to the natural world, have been found to describe *real* structures and behaviors in the physical world. This truly amazing phenomenon can be likened to creating a mental image or poem and then finding it embedded in the real world. This "unreasonable effectiveness of mathematics" is so extraordinary that Eugene Wigner compared it to a miracle. Here are some examples of where researchers have found these mathematical constructs in the physical world:

- In human lungs—Human lungs are not very large, but the total internal surface area of a pair of adult lungs is approximately fifty

30. Each number is the sum of the two previous numbers, so the next three numbers are 5 + 8 = 13, 8 + 13 = 21, and 13 + 21 = 34. (Strictly speaking, the Fibonacci number sequence is 1; 1; 2; 3; 5; 8; . . .)

square meters.[31] A primary reason for this exceptional optimization is that the branching of the bronchi uses the golden ratio $\phi : 1$.[32]

- In brain activity—Neural networks in the brain use fractal branching structures,[33] and EEG brain activity reveals fractal self-similarity that involves the golden mean.[34]
- In DNA—In each cycle of the double helix spiral, the DNA molecule is 34 angstroms long and 21 angstroms wide (two Fibonacci numbers). The Fibonacci sequence is also found in the genetic codes of amino acids,[35] and genetic code is determined by the golden mean.[36] DNA packing is so efficient that two meters of DNA can be coiled inside a single microscopic nucleus, possibly achieved by using fractal packing.[37]
- In botany—Phyllotaxis is the process by which leaves and florets are arranged on plants for the most efficient packing and maximum exposure to sunlight, and this process involves Fibonacci numbers.[38] Fibonacci numbers are also related to the seed packing efficiency on a sunflower,[39] and if there are eight clockwise floret spirals on a pine cone, there will be thirteen anticlockwise spirals (two Fibonacci numbers). In general, there is a "predominance in botany of the Fibonacci series."[40]

31. This internal surface area includes the surfaces of the bronchi, bronchioles, alveolar sacs, and capillaries.

32. See Goldberger et al., "Bronchial Asymmetry and Fibonacci Scaling," 1537.

33. See Bieberich, "Recurrent Fractal Neural Networks," 145.

34. See Vitiello, "Coherent States, Fractals and Brain Waves"; Pletzer et al., "The Golden Mean and the Resting EEG."

35. See Négadi, "Genetic Code(s) Based on Fibonacci Numbers," 259.

36. See Rakočević, "Genetic Code as a Golden Mean Determined System," 283; Perez, "Codon Population in Single-stranded Whole human Genome DNA are Fractal and Fine-tuned by the Golden Ratio."

37. See Lieberman-Aiden et al., "Folding Principles of the Human Genome," 289; Grosberg et al., "Crumpled Globule Model of the Three-Dimensional Structure of DNA."

38. Mitchison reports that "Fibonacci phyllotaxis follows as a mathematical necessity . . . for positioning new leaves" ("Phyllotaxis and the Fibonacci Series," 275).

39. See Shipman et al., "How Universal are Fibonacci Patterns?" 5, 7.

40. Douady and Couder, "Phyllotaxis as Dynamical Self Organizing," 255.

- In physics—The ratio of bond lengths in some hydrogen bonds is $\phi : 1$.[41] And ferrofluid droplets in a magnetic field arrange themselves in spirals that correspond to Fibonacci numbers.[42] Fractals, Fibonacci numbers, and phi have also been identified in processes involving quasicrystals[43] and resistors.[44]
- In astrophysics—The brightness of some stars pulsates at primary and secondary frequencies with ratios close to the golden mean.[45] Astrophysicist Carlos Castro comments that some spacetime models "belong to families of fractal strings whose scaling ratios are powers of the Golden Mean,"[46] and he suggests that nature's code seems to involve the golden mean at its core.[47]

Scientists continue to discover areas in which the abstract mental concepts of fractals, phi, and Fibonacci numbers seem to guide the natural processes of the physical world.

Review the Evidence

Mathematician Richard Hamming comments that "we have tried to make mathematics a consistent, beautiful thing, and by so doing we have had an amazing number of successful applications to the real world."[48] Scientist Roger Penrose even claims that the mathematical Mandelbrot fractal is not simply a mental construct but is as real as Mount Everest.[49] Physicist Paul Davies points out that our brain is

41. See Yu et al., "Golden Ratio and Bond-valence Parameters," 212.
42. See Douady and Couder, "Phyllotaxis as Physical Self-organized Growth," 2101.
43. At the microscopic level, some quasicrystal surfaces have flat terraces with heights in the ratio $\phi : 1$. See Livio, *Golden Ratio*, 209. Grushina et al. report that in diffraction experiments with quasicrystals, the resulting patterns are self-similar "with the fractal geometry obeying the principle of the Golden ratio" ("Diffraction of Light on Optical Fibonacci Gratings," 123).
44. According to Srinivasan, "The ratio of the effective resistance of an infinite network of identical resistors to the resistance of a constituent resistor is equal to the golden ratio" ("Fibonacci Sequence, Golden Ratio, and a Network of Resistors," 461).
45. See Lindner et al., "Strange Nonchaotic Stars," 1.
46. Castro, "Fractal Strings," 1341.
47. Castro, "Fractal Strings," 1348.
48. Hamming, "Unreasonable Effectiveness," 87.
49. Penrose, *Emperor's New Mind*, 95.

> the most complex system known in nature. And yet the mathematics it produces finds its most spectacularly successful applications in the most basic processes in nature, processes that occur at the subatomic level. Why should the most complex system be linked in this way to the most primitive processes of nature?[50]

Davies suggests this relationship might indicate that there is a resonance between the human mind and the organization of the physical world.[51] Astronomer James Jeans observed that the universe reveals "the tendency to think in the way which, for want of a better word, we describe as mathematical,"[52] and more recently, physicist Max Tegmark argues the extreme view that our physical world *is* an abstract mathematical structure.[53]

Is it just a lucky coincidence that some purely theoretical mathematical concepts model the real world? Or could there be a fundamental connection between human consciousness and the way the physical universe functions? The next exploration into quantum physics sheds more light on a possible relationship between matter and the human mind.

Consider Your Verdict

Does the discovery of abstract mathematical constructs in nature suggest that there might be a link between human mental concepts and the physical world?

- Yes
- No

5.3 THE ENIGMA OF MATTER

Scientists have discovered strange phenomena on the cosmic scale and astounding connections between mathematical constructs and the natural world. There are also startling results at the sub-atomic level. In 1900 Max Planck proposed that electromagnetic energy is not continuous but

50. Davies, *Mind of God*, 156.
51. Davies, *Mind of God*, 20.
52. Jeans, *Mysterious Universe*, 186–87.
53. Tegmark, "Mathematical Universe," 101.

is transferred in quantized packets (now called photons), a concept that ushered in the era of quantum mechanics. But this field of science has encountered such unexpected behavior that physicist Richard Feynman has made this dramatic statement:

> The theory of quantum electrodynamics describes Nature as absurd from the point of view of common sense. And it agrees fully with experiment. So I hope you accept Nature as She is—absurd.[54]

To explore why scientists are so puzzled, try this thought experiment. Figure 11 represents a laboratory double-slit system in which a light source shines through two narrow slits in a piece of card.[55] When the light is switched on, which pattern will the light rays cast on the screen on the other side? Would you expect to see two strips of light as in figure 11a or more strips as in figure 11b?

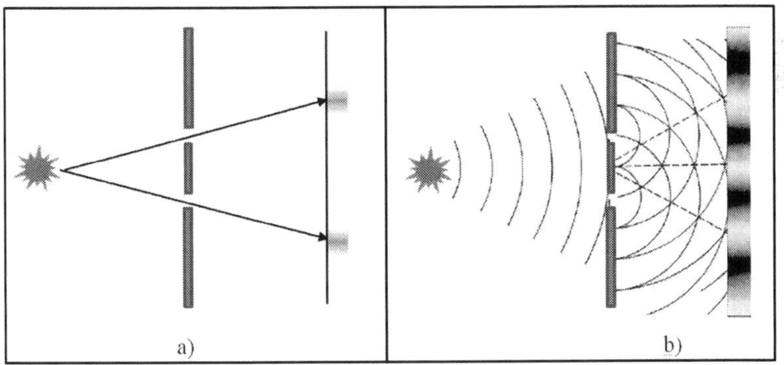

Figure 11: Two double-slit patterns.

You would be correct if you chose pattern b). The light waves set up this interference pattern because they interact like waves in water: two crests combine to create a strip of bright light, and a crest and a trough cancel out to give no light. But if we shoot bullets at a similar bullet-proof system, apart from a few deflections, they will create pattern a). So how do electrons, which are fundamental particles of matter, travel through the double-slit system? Physicists have been perplexed by their quirky behavior.

54. Feynman, *QED*, 10.

55. In this experiment, the light source first passes through a single slit to send only one light wave through the double-slit system. The slits should also be approximately the same dimension as the wavelength of the light.

Are Electrons Particles or Waves?

Here are some experimental results that shattered the world of Newtonian physics and had scientists scratching their heads.[56]

Experiment 1: Use an electron gun to fire a beam of electron particles at a double-slit system, with a detection screen on the other side to register where each electron lands. Do you expect to see pattern a) or pattern b) on the screen?

Surprising result 1: The electrons do not travel like bullets through the two slits—they form interference pattern b) as if they are waves interfering with each other.

Experiment 2: Set the gun to fire just one electron each second so that they cannot "interfere" with each other. If you walk away and return about two hours later, what pattern will the individual electrons have formed on the screen?

Surprising result 2: Over time, the individual electrons still collectively form the wave interference pattern b)! An online time-lapse video shows this interference pattern developing as each electron strikes the detection screen.[57] But how can one electron "interfere" with itself? Or how does each electron "know" where to land to form the interference pattern?

Experiment 3: Again fire one electron at a time, but this time, place a monitoring device in front of the double-slit barrier, which will tell you which slit each electron passes through.

Surprising result 3: Now that you are monitoring the experiment, the electrons behave differently: like bullets, they form only two strips on the detection screen, with no interference pattern. Somehow the act of observation has changed the behavior of the electrons.

Experiment 4: Erase the monitor information just before each electron hits the detection screen.

Surprising result 4: The electrons again go through the slits like waves and form the familiar interference pattern!

These puzzling experimental results, which are very well established, reveal that electrons sometimes behave like particles (when they are fired or detected) and sometimes like waves, and this behavior seems to depend on *whether there is an observer or not*. It is no wonder that, like Richard

56. See Gribbin, *Schrödinger's Cat*, 170–71; Greene, *Fabric of the Cosmos*, 85–88, 192–99.

57. The time-lapse video, made by experimental physicists Bach, Pope, Liou, and Batelaan, is available at https://www.youtube.com/watch?v=hv12oB_uyFs.

Feynman, atomic scientist Werner Heisenberg once asked, "Can nature possibly be as absurd as it seemed to us in these atomic experiments?"[58]

To explain these peculiar and counter-intuitive results, quantum theory proposes that an electron (and every other fundamental particle) is represented by a wave function, and the amplitude of this wave at any point indicates the *probability* of finding the particle there. An unobserved electron will behave like a wave, with its location "smeared out" in space, but a measurement "collapses" its wave function, and the electron is then found in one specific location.[59] Physicist Nick Herbert remarks that this alternating identity between particle and wave is characteristic of all quantum entities and is the major cause of the "reality crisis" in physics.[60] He also points out that as a result of the measurement effect, we cannot engage directly with reality because our observation affects it by a kind of Midas touch:

> The measurement act does not passively reveal some preexisting attributes of quantum entities, but actively transforms "what's really there" into some form compatible with ordinary experience . . . We can't directly experience the true texture of reality because *everything we touch turns to matter.*[61]

A particle does not even have a specific position between two measurements but takes *every possible path simultaneously*. Its wave function is then the sum of all these probabilities. As a result, when one electron is fired at a double-slit system, there is a probability that it will pass through either one of the slits—its wave function therefore passes through *both* slits and creates an interference pattern.[62]

The startling implication of these scientific results is that the quantum world is not made of objects but of wave functions that determine probabilities. Nick Herbert makes this comment about the significance of this finding:

> The world we see around us is real enough, but it floats on a world that is not as real. Everyday phenomena are themselves

58. Heisenberg, *Physics and Philosophy*, 16.

59. In the alternative "many-worlds" interpretation, every event instead splits into multiple universes in which all possibilities are realized.

60. Herbert, *Quantum Reality*, 66.

61. Herbert, *Quantum Reality*, 194 (original emphasis).

62. See Greene, *Fabric of the Cosmos*, 179.

> built not out of phenomena but out of an utterly different kind of being.[63]

Physics therefore cannot predict what an individual electron will do, and Davies and Gribbin comment that there has been "a breakdown of determinism in nature . . . There is thus an intrinsic uncertainty in the subatomic world."[64] This uncertainty leads to bizarre results such as *quantum tunneling*, in which a particle vanishes from one position and appears instantaneously somewhere else *without moving through the intervening space.*

Another unexpected property of reality is *nonlocality*. The common-sense principle of locality states that objects in different places cannot directly affect each other. However, Bell's Theorem has proven that our reality is nonlocal. For example, in the well-established phenomenon known as *quantum entanglement*, particles become permanently correlated with each other so that they form a single system even when they are extremely far apart. As a result, measuring a property of one particle instantly affects the related property of the other. Erwin Schrödinger classified quantum entanglement as "*the* characteristic trait of quantum mechanics."[65] Einstein never accepted this bizarre concept, and in a letter to fellow scientist Max Born, he famously complained that "physics should represent a reality in time and space, free from spooky actions at a distance."[66] Physicists Davies and Gribbin make this observation:

> This property of "nonlocality" has sweeping implications. We can think of the Universe as a vast network of interacting particles, and each linkage binds the participating particles into a single quantum system . . . There is a strong holistic flavour to the quantum description of the Universe.[67]

63. Herbert, *Quantum Reality*, 16. This is according to the Copenhagen interpretation of quantum physics.

64. Davies and Gribbin, *Matter Myth*, 202.

65. Schrödinger, "Probability Relations," 555 (original emphasis).

66. Einstein to Born, March 3, 1947, in *Born Einstein Letters*, 158. The correspondence between Einstein and Born provides a fascinating insight into the work and experiences of these exceptional scientists during the Second World War. Their letters can be read at https://archive.org/details/TheBornEinsteinLetters.

67. Davies and Gribbin, *Matter Myth*, 217.

The strange phenomenon of nonlocal entanglement is also not restricted to fundamental particles but has been shown to apply to larger objects and to operate at the microbiological level.[68]

What Is Matter?

What is a brick made of? Atoms, we could say—all fine and well. But protons and electrons make up an extremely small fraction of an atom's volume. If a hydrogen atom were the size of St Paul's cathedral, its nucleus would be the size of a fist and its single electron would be like a moth fluttering around inside.[69] So why can't we push our hand through a brick? Quantum mechanics explains that each atom is filled with the probability wave functions of its electrons, which have electrical charges that repel each other and provide a force that prevents compression or one solid passing through another.[70]

Does a particle of matter even have a continuous existence? Physicist Vesselin Petkov suggests not. He remarks that an electron is "an ensemble of constituents which appear-disappear $\sim 10^{20}$ times per second . . . Such a quantum object can pass simultaneously through *all* slits at its disposal. In Minkowski's four-dimensional language . . . an electron is not a worldline but a 'disintegrated' worldline whose worldpoints are scattered all over the spacetime region."[71]

Fundamental particles can also be transformed: "All the elementary particles can, at sufficiently high energies, be transmuted into other particles, or they can simply be created from kinetic energy . . . They are just different forms in which matter can appear."[72] This means that *all* elementary particles, and therefore *all* objects, are simply forms of energy as represented by Einstein's famous equation $E=mc^2$ (energy = mass × light-speed squared).[73] Einstein described the relationship in this way:

68. See Lee et al., "Entangling Macroscopic Diamonds"; Julsgaard et al., "Experimental Long-lived Entanglement of Two Macroscopic Objects"; Sarovar et al., "Quantum Entanglement in Photosynthetic Light Harvesting Complexes."

69. This was Tom Stoppard's analogy, in his play, *Hapgood.*

70. This resistance also involves Pauli's exclusion principle for electrons.

71. Petkov, *Space and Time*, 18 (original emphasis).

72. Heisenberg, *Physics and Philosophy*, 134.

73. This concept of matter as a form of energy is reminiscent of the claim by the ancient Greek Heraclitus that fire is the fundamental element of the universe. But a vast amount of energy is equivalent to an extremely small amount of matter. Einstein

"What impresses our senses as matter is really a great concentration of energy into a comparatively small space . . . A thrown stone is, from this point of view, a changing field, where the states of greatest field intensity travel through space with the velocity of the stone."[74]

Matter and force are also merely different views of the same reality: the "dualism of waves and particles makes the same entity appear both as matter and as force."[75] The apparent differences between aspects of reality are increasingly disappearing because "everything in the world is pure quantumstuff."[76] As if this isn't mysterious enough, approximately 23 percent of the universe is "dark" matter, which cannot be directly measured,[77] has no electrical charge, does not absorb or emit light, and does not interact with ordinary matter. A huge 73 percent of the universe is a type of "dark" energy that no one understands but is thought to cause the accelerating expansion of the universe. Only approximately *4 percent* of the universe is what we call normal, observable matter, and a vast 96 percent is completely inaccessible to our senses. This is an astonishing and humbling fact—we can only perceive a tiny fraction of the mysterious "reality" that surrounds us and forms our world.

Implicate Order and Consciousness

Given the strange connectedness of fundamental particles, theoretical physicist David Bohm has proposed that "reality" should be viewed as a unified, multi-dimensional sea of energy, which he calls the *implicate order*. According to this concept, what appear to our five senses as separate physical objects are actually connected expressions of this one energy, which forms "separable projections into a three-dimensional explicate

and Infeld noted that "the quantity of heat able to convert thirty thousand tons of water into steam would weigh about one gram! Energy was regarded as weightless for so long simply because the mass which it represents is so small" (*Evolution of Physics*, 209). For readers interested in units of measure, 1 joule of energy is the amount of force used to move an object one meter, so energy = force × distance, and force = mass × acceleration, so energy = mass × acceleration × distance, which gives the units $kg \times \frac{m}{s^2} \times m = \frac{kg.m^2}{s^2}$. If we measure the speed of light in *m/s*, then both sides of Einstein's famous equation have the same units.

74. Einstein and Infeld, *Evolution of Physics*, 257–58.

75. Heisenberg, *Physics and Philosophy*, 134.

76. Herbert, *Quantum Reality*, 64.

77. Dark matter can only be detected indirectly by effects such as gravitational lensing (light deflection) and the rotational velocities of some galaxies.

order of manifestation."[78] In the same way that two-dimensional Flatlanders would perceive five fingers of a hand as five disconnected circles, we perceive the connected expressions of the implicate reality as separate, unrelated objects.

To explain the strange phenomenon of quantum entanglement, Bohm uses the analogy of two cameras filming a fish from different angles—the two images seem to be directly correlated to each other because a movement of the one image appears to instantaneously affect the other. However, this is only because they are different two-dimensional representations of the same three-dimensional fish.[79] In a similar way, electrons might be connected manifestations of a higher-dimensional reality. Bohm even suggests that matter and consciousness might both be expressions of this unified underlying reality:

> The more comprehensive, deeper, and more inward actuality is neither mind nor body but rather a yet higher-dimensional actuality, which is their common ground and which is of a nature beyond both. Each of these is then only a relatively independent sub-totality . . . [There is a] higher-dimensional ground in which mind and body are ultimately one.[80]

According to this way of thinking, human consciousness and physical matter are not unrelated to each other: the same reality is expressing itself in both ways. This proposed interconnectedness could help to explain why our minds can create abstract mathematical constructs that model behaviors and structures in the physical world.

The hidden connectedness that underlies our visible world might be illustrated by stereograms such as the one in figure 12. On the surface, the image appears to be a meaningless two-dimensional collection of random, disconnected dots, but the correct focus brings into view a hidden, underlying three-dimensional "reality." (The footnote provides some guidance to this process. It is worth taking the time to achieve the dramatic effect.)[81]

78. Bohm, *Wholeness*, 243.

79. Bohm, *Wholeness*, 238.

80. Bohm, *Wholeness*, 265.

81. To view the hidden image, focus through the page (a little cross-eyed). Move the page slowly closer and then further away, and without trying too hard, let your eyes focus lazily beyond the surface until a three-dimensional image springs into view. It might take a while, but you should see the symbol "3 D" appear against a background of circular ripples.

Figure 12: A stereogram image.
(Martin Hawlisch, CC BY-SA 3.0; https://commons.wikimedia.org /wiki/File:Mh_stereogramm_sirds.png)

Review the Evidence

It seems that matter is not as simple as we might think: there is no clear distinction between matter, energy, and force; apparently solid objects are merely excitations in a field of energy; electrons are probability waves rather than particles with predictable behavior. As Werner Heisenberg pointed out, all elementary particles "form a world of potentialities or possibilities rather than one of things or facts."[82] Astronomer Arthur Eddington provided these reflections on quantum reality:

> The external world of physics has thus become a world of shadows. In removing our illusions we have removed the substance, for indeed we have seen that substance is one of the greatest of our illusions.[83]

> To put the conclusion crudely—the stuff of the world is mind-stuff.[84]

82. Heisenberg, *Physics and Philosophy*, 160.
83. Eddington, *Physical World*, xiv.
84. Eddington, *Physical World*, 140.

> Something unknown is doing we don't know what—that is what our theory amounts to.[85]

More recently, scientists continue to express a similar uncertainty. For example, theoretical physicist Lee Smolin writes:

> Quantum theory contains within it some apparent conceptual paradoxes that even after eighty years remain unresolved . . . There are many experts who are convinced that quantum theory hides something essential about nature.[86]

James Glattfelder, who holds degrees in theoretical physics and complex systems, makes this observation:

> For centuries, people hoped that science, the abstract mathematical understanding of the physical world, would shed light on the true nature of reality . . . However, in an act of cosmic irony, this expanding continent of knowledge found itself surrounded by ever longer shores of ignorance. We have been able to probe the unseen subatomic world, only to discover quantum weirdness at its heart.[87]

And scientist Nick Herbert assures us that these counter-intuitive results are not just abstract speculation: "Physicists, for all their odd notions, are basically a conservative lot . . . However, new quantum facts forced them to admit that the world almost certainly rests on some bizarre deep reality."[88]

85. Eddington, *Physical World*, 291. Physicist Wolfgang Pauli provided an amusing comment in 1958 on the uncertainty of quantum theories. Heisenberg had claimed that a unified field theory had been found, although he admitted that some technical details were still missing. In a letter to George Gamow, Pauli responded by drawing an empty rectangle along with the comment that this showed he could paint like the famous artist Titian except that some technical details were missing!

86. Smolin, *Trouble with Physics*, 6.

87. Glattfelder, *Information—Consciousness—Reality*, 2.

88. Herbert, *Quantum Reality*, 55.

Consider Your Verdict

Can we be certain that we understand what matter is, how it must behave, and what is possible in the physical world?

- Yes
- No

CONCLUSION 5
WHAT DO SCIENTISTS KNOW ABOUT SPACE, TIME, AND MATTER?

The insights of science are thoroughly exhilarating. On both the subatomic and cosmic scales, our world is fuzzier, more connected, more relative, more complex, more fluid, and less predictable than it appears to our senses. There is also a surprising and "unreasonable" link between abstract human constructs and the physical world. James Jeans remarked that "the universe begins to look more like a great thought than like a great machine . . . The old dualism of mind and matter . . . seems likely to disappear . . . through substantial matter resolving itself into a creation and manifestation of mind."[89]

In the peculiar quantum world, our observations even seem to affect outcomes, and quantum physicist Henry Stapp has remarked that the most exciting aspect of the new physics is that human consciousness plays a causal role in the unfolding of reality.[90] As a result, physicists such as John Polkinghorne consider it possible that physical matter and the human mind are not separate phenomena: "The only possibility appears to be a complementary world of mind/matter in which these polar opposites cohere as contrasting aspects of the world-stuff, encountered in greater or lesser states of organization."[91] James Glattfelder asks, "Can information, consciousness, and reality be braided into a unified fabric of existence?"[92] and he provides reasons for returning a positive answer.

Theoretical physicist Matej Pavšič suggests that when we perceive an event, such as an electron on a screen, the collapse of its wave function

89. Jeans, *Mysterious Universe*, 186.

90. Stapp, *Mindful Universe*, 6.

91. Polkinghorne, *Science and Creation*, 71.

92. Glattfelder, *Information—Consciousness—Reality*, 6.

correlates with an event in our consciousness, with the implication that the wave function *is* someone's consciousness.[93] He then makes this bold statement:

> There is no longer a psychological barrier to accepting the idea that the wave function (of the universe) is actually closely related, or even identified, with the consciousness of an observer who is part of that universe. After becoming habituated with such, at first sight perhaps strange, wild, or even crazy ideas, one necessarily starts to realize that quantum mechanics is not so mysterious after all. It is a mechanics of consciousness. With quantum mechanics the evolution of science has again united two pieces, matter and mind, which have been put apart by the famous Cartesian cut . . . Quantum mechanics . . . cannot be fully understood without bringing mind and consciousness into the game."[94]

It is also worth taking note of the Incompleteness Theorem of mathematician Kurt Gödel, which challenges our assumption that we can fully explain events in our universe. Gödel's theorem proves that a logical system that is founded on basic axioms (assumptions) will always contain statements that cannot be proven true or false within that system. As a result, any finite system cannot be self-contained but will always require facts from outside itself to prove its statements. Stephen Hawking acknowledged the implications of this theorem for physics:

> We are not angels, who view the universe from the outside. Instead, we and our models are both part of the universe we are describing. Thus a physical theory is self-referencing, like in Gödel's theorem. One might therefore expect it to be either inconsistent, or incomplete. The theories we have so far, are both inconsistent, and incomplete . . . Some people will be very disappointed if there is not an ultimate theory that can be formulated as a finite number of principles. I used to belong to that camp, but I have changed my mind.[95]

And logician Rudy Rucker has formally extended Gödel's theorem to apply to the natural world:

93. Pavšič, *Landscape of Theoretical Physics*, 322.

94. Pavšič, *Landscape of Theoretical Physics*, 337.

95. Hawking, "Gödel and The End of Physics." http://www.hawking.org.uk/godel-and-the-end-of-physics.html.

> *Every* possible complex natural process is going to have undecidable sentences associated with it! Undecidability is everywhere, and all of our theories about nature must remain incomplete.[96]

Gödel's theorem and the findings of physics therefore pose a serious challenge to our belief that we can reach definite conclusions about our universe and how it functions. Our perceptions and theories are thoroughly conditioned by our three-dimensional experience, so we cannot rely on them to understand reality if our world is embedded in a higher-dimensional realm. We can measure, observe, and interact with only approximately 4 percent of the physical universe, and matter itself is only a set of unpredictable probabilities that seem to be affected by human observation.

Perhaps fundamental particles are a form of information or even intelligence.[97] Some scientists propose that the physical universe might be a hologram in which the total cosmic information is contained in every part—including each particle and each human brain. These developments should make us cautious about judging what is ultimately possible in our world. And those who insist that matter must be separate from mind and subject to deterministic laws should explain what they mean by "matter."

The new physics therefore impacts powerfully on questions of faith. How can we know for certain that a higher-dimensional Being cannot exist, or that such a being could not interact with human consciousness, appear in some form in three-dimensional space, or modify matter and override the natural laws of our world? Can we even conclude with certainty that the resurrection hypothesis, which has superior explanatory scope and power, must be rejected as an impossible event? What is the basis for this rationalist, materialistic confidence? Are we using "Flatlander" thinking when we make judgments according to our limited three-dimensional experience? The unexpected results of modern physics have prompted mainstream scientists to warn us that our intuitions,

96. From http://www.rudyrucker.com/blog/2012/02/12/an-incompleteness-theorem-for-the-natural-world/ (original emphasis).

97. Biologist Lynn Margulis proposes a form of intelligence at least at the cellular level: "The evolutionary antecedent of the nervous system is 'microbial consciousness.' In my description of the origin of the eukaryotic cell via bacterial cell merger, the components fused via symbiogenesis are already 'conscious' entities" ("Conscious Cell," 55).

common sense, and beliefs about what is reasonable are of no use when trying to comprehend and define "reality":

> The reality exposed by modern physics is fundamentally alien to the human mind.[98]
>
> The very notion of what we mean by truth and reality must go into the melting pot.[99]
>
> Trying to squeeze Nature into our pre-set and deceivingly comfortable views of the world should not be an option for anyone in the 21st century.[100]

It would be wise to take heed of these warnings whenever we are tempted to make sweeping generalizations about what is possible in our universe.

98. Davies and Gribbin, *Matter Myth*, 104.

99. Davies and Gribbin, *Matter Myth*, 11.

100. Petkov, *Space and Time*, 37.

Investigation 6

Are We and Our Universe the Result of Random Events?

Most of us have at some time pondered the existence of the universe and human life. Is it merely a random accident? Could there be a guiding intelligence behind it all? The latest findings in cosmology, genetics, and biochemistry provide interesting insights into these questions.

Scientific results cannot be used to prove or disprove the existence of a Creator—this is not the function of science. It is also not useful to propose that whatever we do not yet understand must indicate some form of supernatural intervention. But at the same time, it is important to note that there is much debate in the mainstream scientific community about whether purely random, deterministic processes can fully explain the existence of the universe and the arising of intelligent life. This investigation will explore recent research evidence and its implications.

6.1 THE BIG BANG—A FINELY-TUNED EXPLOSION?

NASA launched the Wilkinson Microwave Anisotropy Probe (WMAP) in 2001. Its data helped scientists to develop the Standard Model of Cosmology (figure 13) and confirmed that approximately 96 percent of our universe is composed of mysterious, unknown material. The Standard Model has important implications for our understanding of how the universe arose and developed.

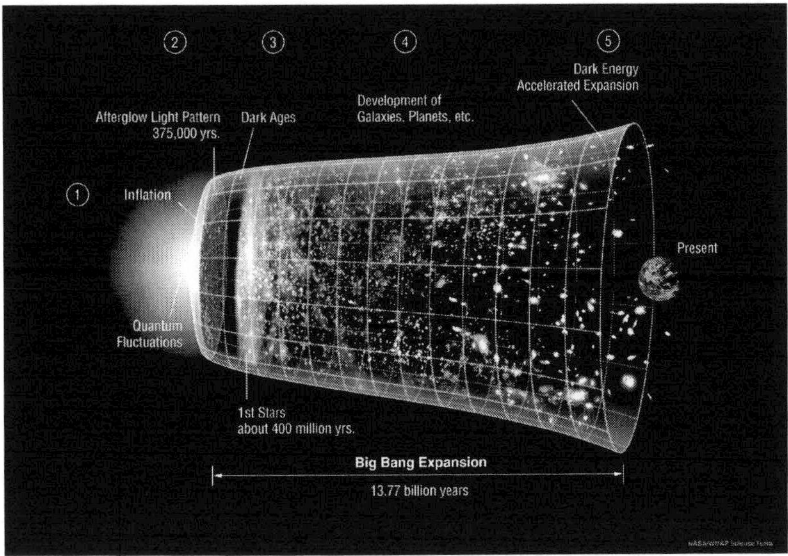

Figure 13: The Standard Model of Cosmology.
(Image courtesy of NASA/WMAP Science Team.
https://lambda.gsfc.nasa.gov/education/graphic_history
/images/Universe_Timeline_2016_4096.jpg)

Initial Creation

Some scientists once thought that our universe had always existed, but this theory encountered three major difficulties: new energy cannot be endlessly created; if starlight had been traveling for an infinite time, our sky would never be dark; an eternally existing universe contradicts the Second Law of Thermodynamics, which states that the disorder of a closed system will keep increasing.[1] Most cosmologists now accept that our universe had a point of creation, which skeptical cosmologist Fred Hoyle mockingly called the "big bang."

The general form of the "big bang" theory states that through quantum uncertainty, even apparently "empty" space is filled with quantum field fluctuations. These are thought to have caused the very brief appearance and disappearance of exceptionally small "bubbles" of space-time. An unknown repulsion force termed "dark energy" then caused

1. Disorder (entropy) can never decrease in a closed system and can only stay the same if all processes are reversible, which is not the case in our universe.

the incredibly rapid and very brief inflation of one of these bubbles, and the energy of this process created particles: "At the end of inflation, the intense energy released would have heated the Universe to around a thousand trillion trillion degrees—more than sufficient to create all 10^{50} tonnes of matter in the observable Universe."[2]

So what existed before this event? Apparently, only the laws of nature, which had to be in place. So nothing "banged"—matter, space, and time came into being together.[3] And nothing expanded *into* space—space itself is expanding so that galaxies move away from each other like dots on the surface of an expanding balloon. This expansion and cooling allowed gravity to form stars, planets, and galaxies. Nuclear processes within stars fused light elements into heavier elements that were distributed through supernovae explosions. Our galaxy formed after about five billion years, our solar system after about nine billion years, and the first life forms appeared on Earth after about ten billion years. It took an exceptionally long time for the universe to be ready to support intelligent carbon-based life.

Finely-Tuned Constants

But the big bang was not merely an uncontrolled expansion. For human life to be possible, the universe had to develop according to a very precise balance of many finely-tuned physical constants such as these:[4]

- Gravitational attraction—This had to be in perfect balance with the rate of expansion to enable structures to form.
- The ratio of gravitational force to electromagnetic force—A slightly different ratio would have created stars that were either white dwarfs or blue giants, neither of which can support complex life.
- The electrical charge of electrons—If this were slightly different, stars would not be able to burn hydrogen and helium, or would not explode to distribute heavy elements.

2. Davies, *Goldilocks Enigma*, 70.

3. This is an ancient idea: the first-century Jewish Philo and the Christian Augustine (AD 354–430) proposed that time came into existence with creation.

4. See Hawking, *Brief History of Time*; Greene, *Fabric of the Cosmos*; Davies, *Cosmic Blueprint*; Barnes, "Fine-Tuning"; Penrose, *Emperor's New Mind.*

- The strong nuclear force—A slightly weaker force would have prevented the formation of heavy elements, but a stronger force would have converted all hydrogen into other elements, resulting in no water and no fuel for stars to burn.
- Formation of carbon—Stars can only produce carbon from helium because the carbon nucleus has very specific values of spin and resonance energy.
- Initial entropy (disorder)—The entropy of our very old universe continues to increase but is still not at its maximum. As a result, its initial value must have been exceptionally small, with an extremely low probability of 1 out of $10^{10^{123}}$. This ridiculously large number has more zeros than the total number of protons and neutrons in the entire universe.[5]

The universe also has other specific properties that are necessary for carbon-based life:

- If the classical laws of physics applied at all levels, with no subatomic quantum behavior, electrons would radiate their energy and spiral into the nucleus.[6]
- Exactly three dimensions of space are necessary for the development of our world.[7]
- During the big bang, every created particle would have had an antiparticle with opposite charge and spin. These matter-antimatter pairs annihilate each other (producing energy), and matter only exists because *one* extra matter particle somehow came to be formed for every billion pairs.[8] Scientists still do not understand how or why this imbalance could have arisen.

Approximately twenty-six physical constants had to have very specific values for human life to be possible. And as astrophysicist Luke Barnes points out, *all* of these had to be in place: "Juggling five balls one-at-a-time isn't really juggling. For a universe to be life-permitting, it must satisfy a number of constraints simultaneously . . . One cannot refute FT [fine-tuning] by considering life-permitting criteria one-at-a-time and

5. See Greene, *Fabric of the Cosmos*, 175.
6. See Barnes, "Fine-Tuning," 18.
7. See Linde, "New Inflationary Universe Scenario."
8. See Davies and Gribbin, *Matter Myth*, 152.

noting that each can be satisfied in a wide region of parameter space."[9] Along with many other scientists, Paul Davies regards this fine-tuning as

> powerful evidence that there is something going on behind it all . . . It seems as though somebody has fine-tuned nature's numbers to make the Universe . . . The impression of design is overwhelming.[10]

Physicist Frank Wilczek makes this observation: "It is logically possible that parameters determined uniquely by abstract theoretical principles just happen to exhibit all the apparent fine-tunings required to produce, by a lucky coincidence, a Universe containing complex condensed structures. But that, I think, really strains credulity."[11]

What about an Infinite Number of Universes?

Perhaps our apparently finely-tuned universe is merely the result of random events after all. If there was an infinite number of universes with different physical laws, surely one must have eventually arisen that just happened to have the properties required for human life. There is some scientific support for this hypothesis, but many scientists argue against it.

- Paul Davies is critical of the multiverse theory. He writes, "It flies in the face of Occam's razor, by introducing vast (indeed infinite) complexity to explain the regularities of just one universe. I find this 'blunderbuss' approach to explain the specialness of our universe scientifically questionable."[12] Stephen Hawking commented: "In what sense can all these different universes be said to exist? If they are really separate from each other, what happens in another Universe can have no observable consequences in our own Universe. We should therefore use the principle of economy and cut them out of the theory."[13]

9. Barnes, "Fine-Tuning," 6.

10. Davies, *Cosmic Blueprint*, 203.

11. Wilczek, "Absolute Units," 10–11.

12. Davies, *Mind of God*, 218–19. The principle known as Occam's (or Ockham's) Razor states that the most likely explanation should require the least number of assumptions and conditions.

13. Hawking, *Brief History of Time*, 132.

- The multiverse theory cannot be scientifically proven because it does not provide testable predictions. In the opinion of physicist Peter Woit, the theory therefore does not lie within the domain of science: "Maybe we really live in a 'multiverse' of different possible universes . . . [But] this way of thinking about physics does not seem to lead to any falsifiable predictions, and so is one that physicists have traditionally considered to be unscientific."[14]
- As cosmologist George Ellis and others point out, universes that actually exist, rather than merely being theoretically possible, would still require specific laws and would probably share a common causal connection.[15]
- Some scientists argue that any inflationary (or cyclical) universe must have a beginning in time, which would still need to be explained.[16]

There are also serious difficulties with trying to apply the mathematical concept of infinity to a physical situation. As mathematician David Hilbert pointed out, "The infinite is nowhere to be found in reality."[17] George Ellis notes that the multiverse theory is "the only scientifically based way of avoiding the fine-tuning required to set up the conditions for our seemingly very unlikely Universe to exist."[18] However, he and others argue that the concept of an infinite collection of really existing universes is highly problematic and does not solve the problem of origins:

> Can there really be an infinite set of really existing universes? We suggest that, on the basis of well-known philosophical arguments, the answer is no. The common perception that this is possible arises from not taking seriously enough the difficulties associated with this profoundly difficult concept . . . Many universes in the ensemble may themselves have infinite spatial extent and contain an infinite amount of matter, with the paradoxical conclusions that entails . . . The phrase "everything that

14. Woit, *Not Even Wrong*, xi. The title of Woit's book is taken from the physicist Wolfgang Pauli who sometimes rejected a scientific theory as being "wrong" or "completely wrong" but flatly condemned one particular article as being "not even wrong" (*Not Even Wrong*, xii).

15. Ellis et al., "Multiverses and Physical Cosmology."

16. Borde and Vilenkin assert that inflationary spacetimes "must necessarily possess initial singularities; i.e., the inflationary Universe must have had a beginning" ("Eternal Inflation," 1).

17. Hilbert, "On the Infinite," 151.

18. Ellis et al., "Multiverses and Physical Cosmology," 921.

> can exist, exists" implies such an infinitude, but glosses over all the profound difficulties implied.[19]

> Existence of the hypothesized ensemble remains a matter of faith rather than proof. Furthermore, in the end it simply represents a regress of causation. Ultimate questions remain.[20]

In general, there is a problem with the belief that infinity renders anything possible. In the classic illustration, monkeys typing for an infinite length of time are supposed to eventually type out any given text. But mathematics provides an important insight into this hypothesis. For example, if a typewriter has 50 keys, the probability of randomly hitting one specific key is 1 out of 50, so the probability of producing just one specific five-letter word is

$$\frac{1}{50} \times \frac{1}{50} \times \frac{1}{50} \times \frac{1}{50} \times \frac{1}{50} = \frac{1}{312{,}500{,}000}$$

This is a tremendously low probability—less than one in three hundred million—and this decreases exponentially when letters are added. A computer program that simulated random typing eventually produced nineteen consecutive letters and characters that appear in a line of a Shakespearean play, but this result took 42,162,500,000 billion billion monkey years to achieve.[21] According to two scientists, the probability of randomly typing out *Hamlet* is therefore zero in any operational sense, and the claim of any meaningful result "gives a misleading conclusion about very, very large numbers."[22] Against this background, what is the probability that all the universe's finely-tuned laws arose by chance?

There is no way to prove or disprove the theory that our universe arose randomly as one of an infinite number of universes, a proposal that remains a contested, untestable hypothesis. But its validity is severely affected by the problems associated with physical infinities and the extremely low probabilities of meaningful results from random events.

19. Ellis et al., "Multiverses and Physical Cosmology," 927–28.

20. Ellis et al., "Multiverses and Physical Cosmology," 935.

21. This combination was finally typed: "VALENTINE. CeasetoIdor:eFLPoFRjW K78aXzVOwm." The first nineteen characters are found in Shakespeare's *Two Gentlemen of Verona*. This experimental result was provided in Wershler-Henry's *History of Typewriting*, reported in Acocella, "The Typing Life."

22. Kittel and Kroemer, *Thermal Physics*, 53.

Review the Evidence

Cosmologists generally agree that our universe came into being at some stage, but as Brian Greene points out, there is a "continuing ignorance of fundamental origin."[23] The fine-tuning of the universe has led some scientists to suggest that its development might have required more than the random operation of physical laws.

Fred Hoyle, atheist astrophysicist:

> A common sense interpretation of the facts suggests that a superintellect has monkeyed with physics, as well as with chemistry and biology, and that there are no blind forces worth speaking about in nature.[24]

Freeman Dyson, theoretical physicist:

> The more I examine the Universe and study the details of its architecture, the more evidence I find that the Universe in some sense must have known we were coming.[25]

Stephen Hawking (in his forties):

> The initial state of the Universe must have been very carefully chosen indeed if the hot big bang model was correct right back to the beginning of time. It would be very difficult to explain why the Universe should have begun in just this way, except as the act of a God who intended to create beings like us.[26]

Allan Sandage, one of the most prominent cosmologists of the twentieth century, who converted to Christianity:

> The world is too complicated in all its parts and interconnections to be due to chance alone.[27]

A discussion of the fine-tuning of the universe is often accused of being an attempt to "smuggle in" the concept of a Creator, but many atheist scientists find this situation to be truly remarkable and inexplicable. Science might one day develop a broadly accepted theory for the origin of the universe that requires only random events, but at present,

23. Greene, *Fabric of the Cosmos*, 286.
24. Hoyle, "The Universe," 12.
25. Dyson, *Disturbing the Universe*, 250.
26. Hawking, *Brief History of Time*, 133–34.
27. Sandage, "A Scientist Reflects on Religious Belief," 57.

interpretation of the evidence seems to rest on personal preference. Professor of astronomy George Greenstein is an interesting example of the instinctive reaction against suggestions of deliberate design. He makes this admission about the fine-tuning of the universe: "As we survey all the evidence, the thought insistently arises that some supernatural agency—or, rather, Agency—must be involved."[28] But he passionately and viscerally rejects this implication:

> The more I read the more I became convinced that such "coincidences" could hardly have happened by chance. But as this conviction grew, something else grew as well . . . It was intense revulsion, and at times it was almost physical in nature.[29]

> I will have nothing to do with it. My conviction is that the world obeys laws, the laws of nature, and that nothing can ever occur that stands outside those laws.[30]

Greenstein speaks for many people who are offended by suggestions of any influence beyond blind physical laws. But as Garrett Green points out, "Whether we get things right or not is a function not only of our intelligence and powers of observation, but also of the lenses through which we observe."[31]

Consider Your Verdict

Does evidence from cosmology and physics strongly suggest that the existence of our universe can be explained as the result of purely random events?

- Yes
- No

28. Greenstein, *Symbiotic Universe*, 27.
29. Greenstein, *Symbiotic Universe*, 24.
30. Greenstein, *Symbiotic Universe*, 87.
31. Green, *Theology*, 17.

6.2 SCIENTIFIC FINDINGS ON THE ORIGIN AND INCREASING COMPLEXITY OF LIFE

No investigation into our place in the universe would be complete without considering the contentious issue of the origin and development of life.[32] As with the fine-tuning of the universe, the interpretation of research results varies widely, and the conclusion of one scientist is likely to be challenged by a dozen others. Let's hear what scientists are saying about problems that have arisen in research into abiogenesis (the arising of life from non-living matter) and evolution.

Problems with Life Arising from Random Prebiotic Processes

In 1953 Miller and Urey sent sparks through a mixture of gases to produce amino acids, which are the building blocks of proteins.[33] This seemed to support the theory that life arose on Earth when prebiotic (non-living) chemicals randomly combined to form organic compounds, which then spontaneously developed the ability to replicate. However, this process of abiogenesis has been difficult to confirm and model for the following reasons.

Many Steps Are Still Not Understood

Biologist Richard Dawkins provides this vague explanation: "The account of the origin of life that I shall give is necessarily speculative . . . At some point a particularly remarkable molecule was formed by accident."[34] He admits that "nobody knows how it happened but, somehow, without violating the laws of physics and chemistry, a molecule arose that just happened to have the property of self-copying."[35] George Whitesides,

32. In this chapter, the term "life" refers to organisms with attributes such as metabolism, growth, adaptation, and replication.

33. It is often pointed out that Miller and Urey used a base of methane and ammonia, although it is now believed there was probably more carbon dioxide and nitrogen on early Earth. However, amino acids have been formed using a nitrogen-carbon dioxide mixture, when the acidity is carefully controlled and oxidation inhibitors are added. See Kitadai and Maruyama, "Origins," 1125.

34. Dawkins, *Selfish Gene*, 14–15.

35. Dawkins, *Climbing Mount Improbable*, 259.

who was awarded the Priestley Medal for Chemistry in 2007, also frankly expresses uncertainty about how life arose on Earth:

> Most chemists believe, as do I, that life emerged spontaneously from mixtures of molecules in the prebiotic Earth. How? I have no idea.[36]

As recently as 2018, geoscientists Kitadai and Maruyama published an extensive review of research results in abiogenesis and were forced to conclude that several steps in the process are still unconfirmed and remain highly hypothetical.[37]

The First Self-Replicating Molecule Has Not Been Identified

The replication of living cells requires protein and DNA (deoxyribonucleic acid), which poses a chicken-or-egg problem—DNA holds the genetic code for building proteins, but this information can only be accessed if proteins are already present. Philosopher of science Karl Popper explained the problem:

> What makes the origin of life and of the genetic code a disturbing riddle is this: the genetic code is without any biological function unless it is translated; that is, unless it leads to the synthesis of the proteins whose structure is laid down by the code. But . . . the code cannot be translated except by using certain products of its translation. This constitutes a really baffling circle.[38]

Microbiologist Jack Trevors and cyberneticist David Abel point out that this DNA-protein problem has not been solved and remains a scientific enigma.[39]

To avoid this dilemma, scientists are trying to identify a molecule that arose *before* DNA, which could have provided genetic information and also promoted self-replication. This might be RNA (ribonucleic acid), but there are some uncertainties: "The most promising candidate is RNA *if* a mechanism existed on the primitive Earth for the formation of

36. Whitesides, "Revolutions in Chemistry," 15.

37. Kitadai and Maruyama, "Origins," 1117, 1142.

38. Popper, "Scientific Reduction," 270. Popper also argued that consciousness itself has no demonstrable survival value, so it is not clear how natural selection could have led to its emergence ("Scientific Reduction," 231).

39. Trevors and Able, "Chance and Necessity," 734.

oligoribonucleotides, and *if* some of these polymers acquired, *by chance*, the ability to copy their sequences."[40] (Nucleotides are the building blocks of DNA and RNA.) In Whitesides's opinion, the proposed RNA world "is so far removed in its complexity from dilute solutions of mixtures of simple molecules in a hot, reducing ocean under a high pressure of CO_2 that I don't know how to connect the two."[41] Kitadai and Maruyama describe many problems that remain unresolved regarding the spontaneous arising of RNA,[42] and molecular scientists Robertson and Joyce express this opinion:

> The myth of a small RNA molecule that arises de novo and can replicate efficiently and with high fidelity under plausible prebiotic conditions . . . [is] unrealistic in light of current understanding of prebiotic chemistry.[43]

Research chemist Leslie Orgel agrees: "It is possible that all of these, and many other difficulties, will one day be overcome and that a convincing prebiotic synthesis of RNA will become available. However, many researchers in the field, myself included, think that this is unlikely."[44]

As a result, some scientists are now looking for an even simpler molecule that preceded RNA. For example, Nobel-winning biochemist Christian de Duve writes: "Contrary to what is sometimes intimated, the idea of a few RNA molecules coming together by some chance combination of circumstances and henceforth being reproduced and amplified by

40. Kitadai and Maruyama, "Origins," 1138 (emphasis added).

41. Whitesides, "Revolutions in Chemistry," 15.

42. According to Kitadai and Maruyama, these problems include the fact that a large, continuous supply of activated monomers is unlikely to have been available on the primitive Earth, as well as "the slow rate and insufficient fidelity of RNA template-copying, the hydrolysis of activated nucleotides on the same timescale as polymerization, and the fast reannealing of separated RNA strands" ("Origins," 1141).

43. Robertson and Joyce, "Origins of RNA World," 7.

44. Orgel, "Prebiotic Chemistry," 114. Orgel points out that "there is at present no convincing, prebiotic total synthesis of any of the nucleotides" ("Prebiotic Chemistry," 108). See also Kolomiytsev and Poddubnaya, "Diffuse Organism," 69. Two RNA ribozymes were synthesized in 2009, but this process used preexisting RNA sections that were too complex to have formed spontaneously. See Ricardo and Szostak, "Life on Earth," 59. In 2016 Nobel Prize-winner Jack Szostak and his team published a paper identifying a peptide that could copy RNA, but they found they had misinterpreted the results and they retracted the paper. (The article was "Oligoarginine Peptides Slow Strand Annealing and Assist Nonenzymatic RNA Replication," published in *Nature Chemisty* 8.)

replication simply is not tenable . . . The development of RNA replication must have been the second stage in the evolution of the RNA world."[45] However, this precursor of RNA has not yet been identified,[46] and in any case, "all of the arguments concerning the relationship between the fidelity of replication and the maximum allowable genome length would still apply to this earlier genetic system."[47]

Professor of chemistry Robert Shapiro also pointed out that there is still no explanation for *how* the first self-replicating molecule could have been formed.[48] It cannot have arisen through natural selection because this process can only operate on an existing self-replicating system, which results in another chicken-or-egg problem.[49] Shapiro and others therefore propose an alternative "metabolism-first" approach in which a collection of organic molecules is able to multiply through reaction cycles. However, this theory has its own critics: Vasas et al. argue that such systems would lack evolvability,[50] and in Orgel's opinion, there is no hard evidence for the theory, so its acceptance "can only be based on faith."[51]

Laboratory Experiments Might Not Replicate Conditions on Early Earth

Experiments that synthesize living molecules might be using processes that could not have occurred on the primitive Earth.[52] For example, it is not known whether ribozymes (a type of RNA molecule) could have developed from materials that would have been abundant on early Earth.[53] Kolomiytsev and Poddubnaya reach this conclusion:

45. De Duve, "Beginnings of Life," 432.

46. See Orgel, "Prebiotic Chemistry," 117.

47. Robertson and Joyce, "Origins of RNA World," 9.

48. Shapiro, "Small Molecule Interactions," 106.

49. Robertson and Joyce write, "Without evolution it appears unlikely that a self-replicating ribozyme could arise, but without some form of self-replication there is no way to conduct an evolutionary search for the first, primitive self-replicating ribozyme" ("Origins of the RNA World," 8).

50. Vasas et al., "Lack of Evolvability," 1470.

51. Orgel, "Implausibility of Metabolic Cycles," 10.

52. See Kitadai and Maruyama, "Origins," 1142.

53. See Robertson and Joyce, "Origins of RNA World," 12.

> No one has found conditions as yet that could result in the formation of ribonucleotides on the primitive Earth . . . Darwin's "warm little pond" as well as a pond filled with self-copying RNA molecules and concentrated solutions of all the biochemical precursors of RNA could scarcely exist.[54]

Various sites are being researched for the possible arising of the first reproductive molecule, including geothermal and hydrothermal systems, or mineral surfaces, but these all suffer from severe shortcomings.[55] As a result, some scientists suggest that organic molecules were formed somewhere else in the universe and were carried to Earth on meteors to provide the biological basis for life. But this merely transfers the problem of life's origins to a different location. Despite the advances made in synthesizing molecules in laboratories, a plausible route from prebiotic chemicals to replicating nucleotides on the ancient Earth remains, in Orgel's terms, "the Molecular Biologist's Dream."[56]

Probabilities Are Low

According to Kitadai and Maruyama, the proposed chemical evolution of living molecules requires at least eight different reaction conditions: (1) reductive gas phase, (2) alkaline pH, (3) freezing temperature, (4) fresh water, (5) dry/dry-wet cycle, (6) coupling with high energy reactions, (7) heating-cooling cycle in water, and (8) extraterrestrial input of life's building blocks.[57] The proposed process is therefore extremely complex. Regarding one suggested process for the random arising of adenine (a nucleobase of DNA), Robert Shapiro remarks: "While no single reaction or location in this sequence violates the possibilities of chemistry or geology, the need for them to occur in an exact order creates an implausibility

54. Kolomiytsev and Poddubnaya, "Diffuse Organism," 69–70.

55. Kitadai and Maruyama write, "Various sites for the origin of life have been proposed, including transient melt zones in a frozen ocean, hydrothermal systems within volcanos, and subterranean lithic zones. Although each setting has advantages in some stages of chemical evolution, *unsolved problems also remain*" ("Origins," 1121, emphasis added). Regarding the role of meteorite impacts, these two chemists agree that "amino acids could have been formed on the primitive Earth through meteorite impacts and comets. However, yields of amino acids from nonreducing gas mixtures (e.g., CO2 and N2) are extremely low . . . [and] the contribution of the impact event to the origin of life on Earth would therefore be minor" ("Origins," 1126).

56. Orgel, "Prebiotic Chemistry," 119.

57. Kitadai and Maruyama, "Origins," 1117.

comparable to that involved in generating a particular English sentence by hitting word processor keys at random."[58] George Whitesides makes this admission about the random arising of living molecules: "Perhaps it was by the spontaneous emergence of 'simple' autocatalytic cycles and then by their combination. On the basis of all the chemistry that I know, it seems to me astonishingly improbable."[59] Nobel Prize-winning chemist Ilya Prigogine expressed a similar opinion:

> The probability that at ordinary temperatures a macroscopic number of molecules is assembled to give rise to the highly ordered structures and to the coordinated functions characterizing living organisms is vanishingly small. The idea of spontaneous genesis of life in its present form is therefore highly improbable, even on the scale of the billions of years during which prebiotic evolution occurred.[60]

Of course, improbability is not the same as impossibility, and many scientists believe that a self-replicating molecule could have arisen through a stupendous number of random events.[61] But there is much that is still unknown about the arising of life on Earth.

Challenges to Neo-Darwinian Theories

After living cells eventually appeared on Earth, what processes could have led to the increasing complexity of life? According to the neo-Darwinian Modern Synthesis model, random errors in DNA-copying caused mutations, and only some resulting forms survived through environmental natural selection. It is generally agreed that these gene-driven processes do account for certain aspects of development, but many scientists are questioning whether they can explain all evolutionary change. Eugene Koonin, an evolutionary biologist at the National Center for Biotechnology Information who does not propose any form of supernatural Designer, makes this blunt observation:

> The summary of the state of affairs on the 150th anniversary of the *Origin* is somewhat shocking: in the post-genomic era, all major tenets of the Modern Synthesis are, if not outright

58. Shapiro, "Small Molecule Interactions," 110.
59. Whitesides, "Revolutions in Chemistry," 15.
60. Prigogine et al., "Thermodynamics of Evolution," 23.
61. See, for example, Kolomiytsev and Poddubnaya, "Diffuse Organism," 69.

> overturned, replaced by a new and incomparably more complex vision of the key aspects of evolution. So, not to mince words, the Modern Synthesis is gone.[62]

Standard evolutionary theory is being challenged in the following three major areas.

Only Small, Continuous Changes?

Microevolution involves minor genetic mutations and natural selection. But these processes do not seem to account for dramatic periods of development. According to geneticists Baguñà and Garcia-Fernàndez, repeated microevolution cannot account for major evolutionary transitions, and as a result, "even to the most unbounded optimist, we are still far from understanding morphological diversity and evolution."[63] Evolutionary biologist Stephen Jay Gould argued that there was a fundamental difference between minor adaptations and the formation of new species,[64] an opinion that is also expressed by paleobiologist Douglas Erwin of the Smithsonian Institute, in his article, "Macroevolution is More Than Repeated Rounds of Microevolution."[65] Anthropologist Jeffrey Schwartz points out that some major groups "appear in the fossil record as Athena did from the head of Zeus—full-blown and raring to go, in contradiction to Darwin's depiction of evolution as resulting from the gradual accumulation of countless infinitesimally minute variations."[66] Eugene Koonin reaches this conclusion:

> The idea of evolution being driven primarily by infinitesimal heritable changes in the Darwinian tradition has become untenable.[67]

62. Koonin, "*Origin* at 150," 474–75.

63. Baguñà and Garcia-Fernàndez, "Evo-Devo," 706.

64. Gould, "New and General Theory of Evolution," 124.

65. Erwin argues that "microevolution provides no satisfactory explanation for the extraordinary burst of novelty during the late Neoproterozic-Cambrian radiation, nor the rapid production of novel plant architectures associated with the origin of land plants during the Devonian, followed by the origination of most major insect groups" ("Macroevolution," 81). He concludes that these discontinuities in evolution "impart a hierarchical structure to evolution, a structure which impedes, obstructs, and even neutralizes the effects of microevolution" ("Macroevolution," 82).

66. Schwartz, *Sudden Origins*, 3.

67. Koonin, "*Origin* at 150," 474.

Only Random Mutations and Natural Selection?

Some scientists are also questioning the purely random nature of evolutionary change. For example, Gerd Müller, Head of the Department of Theoretical Biology at the University of Vienna, argues that developmental systems seem to have innate tendencies or bias towards certain solutions, and these tendencies have as strong an influence on development as random DNA variations.[68] Molecular geneticist James Shapiro makes this observation: "It is difficult (if not impossible) to find a genome change operator that is truly random in its action within the DNA of the cell where it works. All careful studies of mutagenesis find statistically significant non-random patterns of change."[69] According to genetic biologists Thornton and DeSalle,

> It remains a mystery how the undirected process of mutation, combined with natural selection, has resulted in the creation of thousands of new proteins with extraordinarily diverse and well optimized functions. This problem is particularly acute for tightly integrated molecular systems that consist of many interacting parts . . . It is not clear how a new function for any protein might be selected for unless the other members of the complex are already present, creating a molecular version of the ancient evolutionary riddle of the chicken and the egg.[70]

Gould pointed out that many evolutionists now doubt the exclusive role of natural selection in genetic change,[71] and Andras Pellionisz, an expert in genome informatics, suggests that the theory of natural selection should be extended to include goal-directed aspects.[72] Professor of evolutionary biology Kevin Laland explains the newer approach to evolution, which is not deterministic or gene-driven:

> Much variation is not random because developmental processes generate certain forms more readily than others . . . Rather than selection being free to traverse across any physical possibility, it is guided along specific routes opened up by the processes of development . . . "Niche construction," like developmental bias, means

68. Müller, "Extended Evolutionary Synthesis," 4, 7.
69. Shapiro, *Evolution*, 82.
70. Thornton and DeSalle, "Gene Family Evolution," 64.
71. Gould, "New and General Theory of Evolution," 121.
72. Pellionisz, "Principle of Recursive Genome Function," 349.

> that organisms co-direct their own evolution by systematically changing environments and thereby biasing selection.[73]

Simon Conway Morris, who holds the Chair in Evolutionary Paleobiology at Cambridge, agrees that adaptation does not seem to be an undirected, random walk through all possibilities, and instead, evolutionary choices seem to be restricted, if not inevitable.[74] This view is supported by numerous examples of evolutionary *convergence* in which organisms evolve similar traits even if they are not closely related. A striking example of this convergence is when muscle tissue develops into organs that produce electricity. Conway Morris points out that this requires a very precise process of amino acid replacements at key sites, along with accelerated evolution of the new function, and he concludes that "there is little doubt that these changes are very far from random."[75] He therefore suggests that while the underlying principles of Darwinian evolution are correct, they do not provide a complete explanation of development, and there is a need for a more comprehensive theory of evolution.[76] He also comments that convergent forms of behavior such as toolmaking and social play suggest that intelligence is "evolutionarily inevitable,"[77] so that evolution is not merely a mechanism by which forms adapt to the environment, but can be regarded as a process through which the universe becomes increasingly self-aware.[78]

What about the Complex Genetic Code?

It is generally accepted that the modern genetic code evolved from a simpler form. However, there is no agreement about when or how this initial code evolved.[79] In their article, "Chance and Necessity Do Not Explain the Origin of Life," Trevors and Abel explain why they believe natural selection cannot be the primary mechanism for developing DNA coding:

73. Laland et al., "Evolutionary Theory," 162.

74. Conway Morris, *Runes of Evolution*, 31.

75. Conway Morris, *Runes of Evolution*, 38.

76. Conway Morris, *Runes of Evolution*, 24.

77. Conway Morris, *Runes of Evolution*, 19.

78. Conway Morris, *Runes of Evolution*, 286.

79. See Lenstra, "Evolution of the Genetic Code," 96; Knight and Landweber, "Early Evolution of the Genetic Code," 569–70.

> Without the machinery and protein workers, the [DNA] message cannot be received and understood. And without genetic instruction, the machinery cannot be assembled . . . It is not reasonable to expect hundreds to thousands of random sequence polymers to all cooperatively selforganize into an amazingly efficient holistic metabolic network.[80]

> All of the above problems pale in comparison to the difficulty of explaining the origin of (1) an operating system, (2) genetic programming, and (3) encryption/decryption coding. Natural processes, mechanisms, and chemical catalyses do not explain any of these emergent conceptual phenomena. . . . Even "meaningful" RNA or DNA inserted into a lifeless physical world such as the ancient Earth, would not be "readable." It could not communicate its coded message for protein synthesis unless a language (operating system) context already existed.[81]

> Contentions that offer nothing more than long periods of time offer no mechanism of explanation for the derivation of genetic programming. No new information is provided by such tautologies. The argument simply says it happened. As such, it is nothing more than blind belief.[82]

In other words, "time made it happen" might be science's version of "God made it happen."

Review the Evidence

After their comprehensive review of recent research findings, Kitadai and Maruyama reached this frank conclusion: "When, where, and how did life on Earth originate? These questions on the origin of life are among the biggest unsolved problems in natural science."[83] After more than seventy years of international research into abiogenesis, there is still "no plausible scenario that can explain all the stages of the origin of life,"[84]

80. Trevors and Abel, "Chance and Necessity," 735.
81. Trevors and Abel, "Chance and Necessity," 734.
82. Trevors and Abel, "Chance and Necessity," 735.
83. Kitadai and Maruyama, "Origins," 1117.
84. Kitadai and Maruyama, "Origins," 1121.

and there remains an "insuperable gap between prebiological chemistry and the first living systems."[85]

As with the fine-tuning of the universe, different scientists offer varying interpretations of the research results in biogenesis and evolutionary biology, with many (perhaps most) continuing to propose purely deterministic theories. However, in the opinion of atheist geneticist and evolutionist Richard Lewontin, dominant scientific theories have been strongly influenced by the prevailing materialistic worldview:

> Our willingness to accept scientific claims that are against common sense is the key to an understanding of the real struggle between science and the supernatural. We take the side of science in spite of the patent absurdity of some of its constructs . . . because we have a prior commitment, a commitment to materialism. It is not that the methods and institutions of science somehow compel us to accept a material explanation of the phenomenal world, but, on the contrary, that we are forced by our a priori adherence to material causes to create an apparatus of investigation and a set of concepts that produce material explanations, no matter how counter-intuitive, no matter how mystifying to the uninitiated. Moreover, that materialism is absolute, for we cannot allow a Divine Foot in the door.[86]

The biochemist Christian de Duve exemplifies this commitment to materialism: he admits about the arising of life that "how this momentous event happened is still highly conjectural," but he is adamant that the relevant processes must have been purely deterministic "because the processes are chemical and are therefore ruled by the deterministic laws."[87] Similarly, Richard Dawkins believes that there is only an "illusion of design in the living world,"[88] and he insists that "*cumulative selection*, by slow and gradual degrees, is the explanation, the only workable explanation that has ever been proposed, for the existence of life's complex design."[89] However, Lewontin points out that this adamant claim ignores an enormous amount of recent research:

> Dawkins's vulgarizations of Darwinism speak of nothing in evolution but an inexorable ascendancy of genes that are selectively

85. Kolomiytsev and Poddubnaya, "Diffuse Organism," 76.

86. Lewontin, "Billions of Demons," 30.

87. De Duve, "Beginnings of Life," 428, 437.

88. Dawkins, *God Delusion*, 25.

89. Dawkins, *Blind Watchmaker*, 317 (original emphasis).

> superior, while the entire body of technical advance in experimental and theoretical evolutionary genetics of the last fifty years has moved in the direction of emphasizing non-selective forces in evolution . . . What worries me is that they [the public] may believe what Dawkins and Wilson tell them about evolution.[90]

Adaptation and natural selection do play a role in the development of some life forms, but in Gould's assessment, the Modern Synthesis theory "is effectively dead, despite its persistence as textbook orthodoxy."[91] Computational physiologist Denis Noble argues that the highly reductionist view of neo-Darwinism is not a necessary conclusion from scientific evidence,[92] and he expresses the desire of many biologists to "distance [themselves] from the biased conceptual scheme that neo-Darwinism has brought to biology, made more problematic by the fact that it has been presented as literal truth."[93] He therefore suggests that evolutionary biology needs to broaden its approach:

> I believe that in the future, the Modern Synthesis . . . will be seen as only one of the processes involved, a special case in certain circumstances, just as Newtonian mechanics remains as a special case in the theory of relativity. The mathematics of evolutionary theory is developing to take additional processes into account.[94]

Gerd Müller points out that this is not the view of only a handful of fringe scientists and that an increasing number of publications argue for a major revision of the standard evolutionary theory.[95] These scientists are not suggesting a supernatural origin of life, but they are questioning the reductionist aspects of neo-Darwinism, and they propose that various nonrandom processes should be taken into account.[96] However, Laland et al. remark that there is passionate resistance to the proposals of the newer Extended Evolutionary Synthesis (EES):

90. Lewontin, "Billions of Demons," 29–30.

91. Gould, "New and General Theory of Evolution," 120.

92. Noble, "Evolution Beyond Neo-Darwinism," 7.

93. Noble, "Evolution Beyond Neo-Darwinism," 12.

94. Noble, "Rocking Foundations of Evolutionary Biology," 1240.

95. Müller, "Extended Evolutionary Synthesis," 2.

96. Proposed contributing factors include nonrandom mutations; spontaneous tendencies toward increased diversity and complexity; variation through mechanisms that are designed to adapt to the environment; systems dynamics, and feedback loops.

> The number of biologists calling for change in how evolution is conceptualized is growing rapidly . . . Yet the mere mention of the EES often evokes an emotional, even hostile, reaction among evolutionary biologists . . . This is no storm in an academic tea-room, it is a struggle for the very soul of the discipline.[97]

Anthropologist Jeffrey Schwartz relates that the early founders of evolutionary theory made deliberate decisions to support certain developmental hypotheses and reject others, and he makes this sobering observation: "As a result, the alternative theories, which had kept the possibility of intellectual novelty alive through the debates they provoked, were submerged. The synthesis that emerged was, by stark contrast, largely intolerant of criticism and resistant to change."[98] Schwartz is one of the growing number of scientists who propose that the time has come for a new look at how evolution functions.[99] Marcos Eberlin is a winner of the Thomson Medal in Chemistry, and he summarized recent scientific findings in his 2019 book *Foresight: How the Chemistry of Life Reveals Planning and Purpose*, which is endorsed by three winners of Nobel Prizes in science. Here is Eberlin's conclusion about the cumulative evidence regarding the development of life on Earth:

> [It] seems to point beyond any blind evolutionary process to the workings of an attribute unique to minds—foresight. And yes, I know: We're told that it's out of bounds for science to go there . . . [but] I urge you to inspect the evidence.[100]

Consider Your Verdict

Has scientific research provided convincing evidence that life's origins and development can be fully explained by unguided, random events?

- Yes
- No

97. Laland et al., "Evolutionary Theory," 162.

98. Schwartz, *Sudden Origins*, 275. Schwartz was referring to a group known as the Committee on Common Problems of Genetics, Paleontology, and Systematics, which was established in 1943.

99. Schwartz, *Sudden Origins*, ix–x.

100. Eberlin, *Foresight*, 13–14.

6.3 LOGIC AND FAITH

Some scientists interpret their research results as indicating foresight and deliberate design in the development of the universe. If this is correct, what could be the source? The modern mind might be prepared to consider impersonal concepts such as Cosmic Intelligence (as Einstein did), or Brahman, or the Tao, but it generally regards the notion of a personal God as superstitious and irrational. In particular, Christianity is considered to be logically unsound on three fronts: the incompatibility of an omniscient God and people with free will; the impossibility of the miraculous; the paradox of suffering under a loving, omnipotent God. The final investigation of this section will analyze these arguments to identify assumptions that might lie behind the reasoning.

Argument 1: God's Omniscience Is Incompatible with Humanity's Free Will

This argument is usually structured as follows:

> Statement 1: An omniscient, all-knowing God would know about every act in advance.
> Statement 2: Free will means that a person can choose to act in any way.
> Conclusion: There cannot exist an omniscient God and people with free will.

Here are two implicit assumptions behind this argument:

> God has the same relationship to time as we do.
> God's knowledge would determine how we act.

An omniscient God might be able to predict how each person would act in a particular situation without causing them to behave in that way. In that case, each person would still be free to choose their actions. But another possible solution to this paradox lies in the nature of time itself. If spacetime exists in a single block so that "all moments of time have equal existence,"[101] and if God is part of a higher-dimensional realm that encompasses all of creation, then perhaps his "present" includes all of our times, including our future. Philosopher Ludwig Wittgenstein suggested that eternity is not an infinite extension of time but timelessness, in which case, our timeline from past to future could be a single "no-time" point

101. Petkov, *Space and Time*, 37.

for God. Then, as Ken Wilber suggests, perhaps "God, who knows all things by non-dual insight, knows all times—past and future—as existing in this Eternal Moment."[102] C. S. Lewis explained it in this way:

> Suppose God is outside and above the timeline. In that case, what we call "tomorrow" is visible to Him in just the same way as what we call "today." All the days are "Now" for Him. He does not remember you doing things yesterday; He simply sees you doing them, because, though you have lost yesterday, He has not. He does not "foresee" you doing things tomorrow; He simply sees you doing them, because, though tomorrow is not there for you, it is for Him. You never supposed that your actions at this moment were any less free because God knows what you are doing. Well, He knows your tomorrow's actions in just the same way—because He is already in tomorrow and can simply watch you. In a sense, he does not know your action till you have done it: but then the moment at which you have done it is already "Now" for Him.[103]

If a higher-dimensional Creator does exist, with a fundamentally different relationship to time than ours, then the relationship between his perfect knowledge and our freedom to act, which are incompatible in our limited realm, might not be a paradox in that higher realm. James Jeans made this comment about the impact of the new physics on the concepts of time and causality in science:

> The theory of relativity goes at any rate some distance towards stigmatising this steady onward flow of time and the cause-effect relation as illusions . . . And if time is so fundamental that an understanding of its true nature is for ever beyond our reach, then so also in all probability is a decision in the age-long controversy between determinism and free-will.[104]

Argument 2: Miracles Are Not Possible

The argument against the miraculous usually takes a form such as this:

> Statement 1: Events in our world conform to natural laws.
> Statement 2: Miracles do not conform to natural laws.

102. Wilber, *Spectrum of Consciousness*, 87.

103. Lewis, *Mere Christianity*, 144.

104. Jeans, *Mysterious Universe*, 37.

Conclusion: Miracles cannot be events in our world.

These are some underlying assumptions:

Physical processes are completely deterministic.
The world is closed to any influence that can supersede natural laws.

It might not be possible to assess the concept of miracles through logic. Even the brilliant philosopher David Hume could only construct this argument against miracles: they are not part of our daily life, and "as a uniform experience amounts to a proof, there is here a direct and full *proof*, from the nature of the fact, against the existence of any miracle."[105] However, this simply states that because miracles do not happen often, they cannot happen at all, which is an opinion, not a logical conclusion. Hume also stated adamantly that records of miracles are only found "among ignorant and barbarous nations," and hence, "no testimony is sufficient to establish the miracle."[106] Timothy McGrew, a specialist in philosophical applications of probability theory, remarks that recent work on probabilistic analysis of testimony has exposed flaws in Hume's reasoning.[107]

Hume's attitude is not only found among atheists, and Craig Keener notes that research into Jesus has been strongly shaped by the Enlightenment's prejudice against the supernatural.[108] For example, theologian Rudolf Bultmann made this claim: "The historical method includes the *presupposition* that history is a unity in the sense of a closed continuum of effects . . . This closedness means that the continuum of historical happenings *cannot* be rent by the interference of supernatural, transcendent powers and that therefore there is no "miracle" in this sense of the word."[109]

But what is this "presupposition" based on? How can we be certain that a higher, transcendent power cannot exert any influence in our universe and override or supersede the laws of nature? This confident assumption has been radically undermined by the paradoxical and indeterminate behavior that characterizes "reality" at the quantum level. After all, Einstein was wrong when he instinctively rejected counter-intuitive phenomena such as quantum entanglement. Max Born recorded this

105. Hume, *Enquiry* 10.2 (original emphasis).

106. Hume, *Enquiry* 10.20, 13.

107. McGrew, "Inference," 34.

108. Keener, *Historical Jesus*, 4.

109. Bultmann, "Exegesis," 291–92 (emphasis added).

bitter reflection on Einstein's dismissal of some of his (correct) ideas: "Einstein's verdict on quantum mechanics came as a hard blow to me; he rejected it not for any definite reason, but rather by referring to an 'inner voice.'"[110] Science provides ample evidence that our intuition of how the universe should function is not a reliable indication of how it does function or what might be possible within it. C. S. Lewis reasoned as follows:

> [A miracle's] peculiarity is that it is not interlocked with the previous history of nature. And this is just what some people find intolerable. The reason they find it intolerable is that they start by taking nature to be the whole of reality. And they are sure that all reality must be interrelated and consistent. I agree with them. But I think they have mistaken *a partial system within reality*, namely nature, for the whole . . . The great complex event called nature, and the new particular event introduced into it by the miracle, are related by their common origin in God . . . but you must go back as far as their common Creator to find the interlocking. You will not find it *within* nature.[111]

While most so-called miracles are undoubtedly exaggerations, illusions, or fabrications, can we be absolutely certain that not one has ever been authentic? For example, Forster and Marston write about a friend who was diagnosed with amyloidosis, but after group prayer, there was astoundingly no remaining trace of the condition except in the original medical samples.[112] Roger Forster has a Cambridge degree in mathematics and theology, and Paul Marston has degrees in economics, statistics, and the philosophy of science, so this is not a tale told by "ignorant and barbarous" people. If we reject it, we must provide a plausible alternative explanation involving a conspiracy or technical medical error, which would require suitable evidence. But following the warnings of science, we should be careful not to deny the miraculous simply because it does not suit our comfortable preconceptions.

110. *Born Einstein Letters*, 91. In his earlier letter to Born, dated December 4, 1926, Einstein had written, "An inner voice tells me that it is not yet the real thing. The theory says a lot but does not bring us any closer to the secret of the 'old one.' I, at any rate, am convinced that *He* is not playing at dice" (*Born Einstein Letters*, 91, original emphasis).

111. Lewis, *Miracles*, 95 (original emphasis).

112. Forster and Marston, *Reason, Science, and Faith*, 154. Appendix 1 relates my own exposure to unusual events.

Argument 3: A Loving, All-Powerful God Would Not Allow Evil and Suffering

This is the broad argument:

> Statement 1: Evil and suffering exist.
> Statement 2: An omnipotent God could prevent evil.
> Statement 3: A loving God would not allow suffering.
> Conclusion: There cannot exist an omnipotent and loving God.

These are some underlying assumptions:

> God's love must necessarily express itself by preventing all human pain.
> Humankind has no responsibility for the state of the world.
> God's ultimate plan is that we be comfortable in this world.

George Carey suggests that "when we talk in terms of omnipotence or goodness but not both, we are smuggling in a value system which has its own inbuilt assumption that if God exists he must exist to make us all happy in this life."[113] But is there a sound basis for this belief?

A related assumption is that there cannot be any morally acceptable reason for God to permit evil and its resulting suffering. Philosopher J. L. Mackie expressed this assumption in the form: "a good thing always eliminates evil."[114] Arguing from this basis, Mackie claimed that God could have (and therefore would have) created people with free will who would always choose the good and therefore avoid suffering.[115] But logician and philosopher Alvin Plantinga disagrees, arguing that because only God is perfect, it is logically impossible to create a truly free being that *cannot* choose evil; he also proposes that God considers a world *with* moral freedom to be more valuable than one *without* it, despite the resulting suffering.[116]

John Feinberg even suggests that the existence of evil might be necessary for mankind's development: "To build souls there must be evil, so [God] can't both build souls and remove evil. If he removes evil, he can't create human beings and let them function as they were intended to function."[117] Feinberg also makes the significant point that atheist

113. Carey, *Great God Robbery*, 28.

114. Mackie, "Evil and Omnipotence," 201.

115. Mackie, "Evil and Omnipotence," 209–10.

116. Plantinga, *God, Freedom, and Evil*, 29–30.

117. Feinberg, *Faces of Evil*, 490.

critiques about suffering are formulated outside Christian theology and therefore do not establish inconsistency *within* that belief system.[118] The biblical view of suffering takes into account the profound consequences of humanity's rebellion against God and their resultant responsibility for the present state of creation, in which light, there is no logical contradiction between suffering and the existence of an all-powerful, loving God.

After his conversion to faith, atheist philosopher Anthony Flew decided that he had rejected the existence of God too quickly, for what he later judged to be the wrong reasons.[119] One of these reasons was his belief that the problem of evil contradicted the existence of an all-good, all-powerful God—a conclusion that he came to regard as "clearly inadequate."[120] He later wrote, "Certainly, the existence of evil and suffering must be faced. However, philosophically speaking . . . the existence of God does not depend on the existence of warranted or unwarranted evil."[121] Skeptics argue that human suffering under an omnipotent, loving God is a logical paradox, but Christianity offers this alternative perspective:

> God is all-powerful and can destroy evil.
> God is all-good and desires to destroy evil.
> Evil is not yet destroyed.
> Therefore, *God's work is not yet complete.*[122]

Review the Evidence

Three central atheist arguments against the Christian God that appear to be logically sound actually involve unproven assumptions. Regarding miracles, if matter is merely a form of energy and probability rather than fixed "stuff," which might even be connected to human consciousness, how can we be certain that a superior mental power could not influence the physical world? Our generally "non-miraculous" world might be embedded in a higher dimensional realm that *can* exert unusual influences. In that case, we might be like Flatlanders in rejecting events simply

118. Feinberg, *Faces of Evil*, 20.
119. Flew and Varghese, *There Is a God*, 12–13.
120. Flew and Varghese, *There Is a God*, 42.
121. Flew and Varghese, *There Is a God*, 156.
122. See Zacharias and Geisler, *Who Made God?* 38.

because they are outside our experience and comprehension. Perhaps with the availability of higher dimensions, even apparent paradoxes relating to free will and suffering might be resolvable or simply fall away. As an analogy, it is meaningless to ask, "What two-dimensional object is a rectangle and also a circle?" But if we add a third dimension, the object is simply a cylinder seen from different perspectives.

Modern logic has also become more complex through the recognition of *quantum superposition*, in which a particle can exist in different states at the same time and even be in two places at once. Paul Davies points out the implications of this unusual result:

> Even the use of standard logic has been questioned by some. In so-called quantum logic, the rule that something cannot both be and not be such-and-such is dropped. The motivation for this is that in quantum physics the notion of "to be" is more subtle than in everyday experience: physical systems can exist in superpositions of alternative states.[123]

It is worth taking note of the strange, counter-intuitive developments of science before we make categorical statements about what must be logically contradictory or impossible in our world.

Consider Your Verdict

Are miracles and the existence of an omnipotent, omniscient, caring God strictly logical impossibilities?

- o Yes
- o Perhaps
- o Perhaps not
- o No

123. Davies, *Mind of God*, 26.

CONCLUSION 6
ARE WE AND OUR UNIVERSE THE RESULT OF RANDOM EVENTS?

Science cannot prove or disprove the existence of a creative Intelligence at work through the physical laws of the universe. But its findings do continue to hint at something beyond the iron grip of random, deterministic events. As James Glattfelder points out, "A series of taboos is being broken and blind spots exposed, all inherently contained within the current materialistic and reductionist scientific worldview."[124]

Religion that does postulate the guiding hand of a Creator is often dismissed as a crutch for those who are intellectually or emotionally weak, and there is a popular assumption that science and religion are in direct opposition. But atheist philosopher Anthony Flew cited scientific reasons for his conversion to faith, including the fine-tuning of the cosmos and the complexity of DNA.[125] He wrote, "The journey to my discovery of the Divine has thus far been a pilgrimage of reason. I have followed the argument where it has led me. And it has led me to accept the existence of a self-existent, immutable, immaterial, omnipotent, and omniscient Being."[126] Scientist John Polkinghorne also finds no incompatibility between his scientific research and his faith: "Christians do not have to close their minds, nor are they faced with the dilemma of having to choose between ancient faith and modern knowledge. They can hold both together."[127]

We can decide to function within a deterministic, naturalistic worldview, and we can claim to know for certain that no Supreme Being can be involved in the creation and development of our universe. However, this is not the inevitable result of scientific research or logical analysis—it is a preferred interpretation, as the philosopher Thomas Nagel frankly admits:

> I want atheism to be true and am made uneasy by the fact that some of the most intelligent and well-informed people I know are religious believers. It isn't just that I don't believe in God and, naturally, hope that I'm right in my belief. It's that I hope there is

124. Glattfelder, *Information—Consciousness—Reality*, 22.
125. Flew and Varghese, *There Is a God*, esp. 75, 119–21.
126. Flew and Varghese, *There Is a God*, 155.
127. Polkinghorne, *Faith of a Physicist*, 5.

> no God! I don't want there to be a God; I don't want the universe to be like that. [128]

But even as a committed atheist, Nagel rejects "the ludicrous overuse of evolutionary biology to explain everything about human life, including everything about the human mind."[129] He argues that these deterministic theories have been incorrectly presented as the only intellectually acceptable explanation, with the result that "almost everyone in our secular culture has been browbeaten into regarding the reductive research program as sacrosanct."[130] It is surprising that our postmodern skepticism, which criticizes so many other claims to absolute "truth," is generally not being applied to the rigidly deterministic aspects of neo-Darwinist thinking.

The "new" ideas from science have therefore still not permeated our worldview, despite the extensive research evidence. Physicist Henry Stapp makes this astute observation: "The notion of mechanical determinism still dominates the general intellectual milieu . . . You are influenced by what you are told by pundits who expound as scientific truth a mechanical idea of the universe that *contravenes precepts of contemporary physics*."[131] Stapp is concerned about the effect of this influence and "the social consequences of the misrepresentation of contemporary scientific knowledge that continue to hold sway, particularly in the minds of our most highly educated and influential thinkers."[132] Atheist evolutionist Michael Ruse, director of the history and philosophy of science at Florida State University, also expresses unease in his article, "Curb Your Enthusiasm: How did Humanism End Up Acting Like a Religion?" He points out that instead of being characterized by openness and adaptability, the New Atheism (or anti-theism), as represented by writers such as Richard Dawkins, has become as intolerant and self-righteously condemnatory as any conventional religion.[133]

128. Nagel, *Last Word*, 130.

129. Nagel, *Last Word*, 130.

130. Nagel, *Mind and Cosmos*, 7. The full title of Nagel's book is, *Mind and Cosmos: Why the Materialist Neo-Darwinian Conception of Nature Is Almost Certainly False.*

131. Stapp, *Mindful Universe*, vii–viii (emphasis added).

132. Stapp, *Mindful Universe*, viii.

133. Ruse's thought-provoking article was printed in *Aeon*, October 2012. https://aeon.co/essays/how-humanism-lost-its-way-in-a-charismatic-crusade.

Our judgments are powerfully shaped by our preconceptions and the prevailing worldview of our culture. But those who do consider the possibility of a guiding, creative Power in the universe are in good company: the 2009 Pew Survey found that 51 percent of scientists believed in some form of deity while 41 percent did not.[134] Physicist Paul Davies makes this personal declaration:

> I belong to the group of scientists who do not subscribe to a conventional religion but nevertheless deny that the universe is a purposeless accident . . . There must, it seems to me, be a deeper level of explanation. Whether one wishes to call that deeper level "God" is a matter of taste and definition. Furthermore, I have come to the point of view that mind—i.e., conscious awareness of the world—is not a meaningless and incidental quirk of nature, but an absolutely fundamental facet of reality.[135]

It is therefore not intellectually weak, scientifically ignorant, or logically unsound to consider the possibility of a directing Intelligence in the universe. However, this could be an impersonal, organizational form of energy or consciousness that requires nothing from us. Why should anyone believe that this guiding force is a personal God who cares for creation? To answer this question, we now turn our attention to the precursor of the Christian story—the ancient Hebrew Bible.

134. See http://www.pewforum.org/2009/11/05/scientists-and-belief/.

135. Davies, *Mind of God*, 16.

PART C

The Old Testament

Investigation 7

What Light Does the Old Testament Shed on Jesus?

THE OLD TESTAMENT SHARES some traditions and themes with other ancient writings. However, this does not imply that it is simply a collection of myths. As historian Will Durant pointed out, "The story of the Jews as unfolded in the Old Testament has stood the test of criticism and archaeology; every year adds corroboration from documents, monuments, or excavations . . . We must accept the Biblical account provisionally until it is disproved."[1] A recent encyclopedia of ancient history also notes that "from the early eighth century onwards . . . there is relatively good agreement between the biblical accounts on the one hand and the archaeological evidence and extra-biblical texts on the other."[2] (Appendix 2 provides some examples of this confirmation.)

However, the focus of this investigation is not biblical history but the relationship between Christianity and the Old Testament. This ancient Jewish Scripture played a central role in the church's interpretation of Jesus's work, and Thomas Torrance commented that "the whole historico-redemptive movement in the Old and New Testaments is to be regarded as essentially one . . . The Old Testament is stretched out in expectation, and the New Testament looks back in fulfillment."[3] It is therefore impossible to develop a comprehensive understanding of Jesus and his work without opening the Jewish Bible. In the words of Wolfhart Pannenberg,

1. Durant, *Oriental Heritage*, note on page 300.
2. Maeir, "Israel and Judah," 3523.
3. Torrance, *Space, Time and Incarnation*, 44–45.

> To the extent that the concept of the incarnation cuts itself loose from the Old Testament and Jewish theology of history, it becomes mere myth, a myth of a divine being descending from heaven and ascending again . . . On the other hand, within the horizon of the Old Testament and apocalyptic idea of history, the formation of the Christological tradition in primitive Christianity becomes understandable.[4]

The extensive Old Testament writings reveal a remarkable unity of themes, images, and prophecies that are said to have prefigured Jesus in some way, so that he is remembered as saying, "If you believed Moses, you would believe me, for he wrote about me" (John 5:46). This investigation will determine whether there is support for this claim, by exploring the following aspects of the Old Testament:

- messianic prophecies of a triumphant and a suffering figure
- the seven holy feasts of Judaism
- the fulfillment of Old Testament promises as finally depicted in Revelation, the last book of Judeo-Christian Scripture.[5]

7.1 MESSIANIC PROPHECIES OF A TRIUMPHANT AND A SUFFERING FIGURE

Jesus claimed to have been prefigured in the Old Testament:

> You study the Scriptures diligently because you think that in them you have eternal life. These are the very Scriptures that testify about me. (John 5:39)

> And beginning with Moses and all the Prophets, he explained to them what was said in all the Scriptures concerning himself. (Luke 24:27)

The Old Testament contains hints and predictions of a Christ-like individual in its prophetic descriptions of a victorious figure and a suffering figure. These prophecies used the "prophetic perfect" tense, which blurred the distinction between present and future by describing a predicted event as if it had already recently taken place. In this way, a single

4. Pannenberg, *Jesus*, 166.

5. These last three chapters will not have a "Consider Your Verdict" section.

prophecy could partially apply to a present situation and also predict a complete fulfillment in the future. For example, Joseph Klausner identified two kinds of messianic hopes in the prophetic text Isaiah 40–48: hopes that were "near, grounded in the nature of the time and the environment, and therefore . . . were fulfilled and hopes that "remained promises for the distant future."[6]

Modern rationalism dismisses the concept of someone having insights into the future. But what if our material world is like a sponge immersed in a realm of divine consciousness in which "we live and move and have our being"?[7] An omniscient, omnipresent Creator Being, who inhabits a higher-dimensional realm and has access to all human times, would surely be able to communicate with human consciousness and deliver prophetic messages that foreshadow coming events.[8] At this stage, let's allow this to be a possibility and assess the supporting evidence.

This investigation will consider verses that were (or came to be) interpreted as messianic prophecies within Judaism. These verses will be taken from different translations and interpretations of the Jewish Bible: the Greek Septuagint (LXX) was written between the third and first centuries BC; modern synagogues use the Hebrew Masoretic Text (MT), which was largely copied and edited between the sixth and ninth centuries AD;[9] ancient oral rabbinic commentaries were collated in the Babylonian Talmud around the fifth and sixth centuries AD; the Targums were Aramaic interpretations that accompanied readings of the Hebrew Bible and were probably written down from the second century AD onwards (in some places, possibly being altered in response to Christian claims). These biblical texts and commentaries describe a messianic figure that will triumph and also a figure that will suffer for others, both of which have strong links to Jesus's work.[10]

6. Klausner, *Messianic Idea*, 150.

7. Paul was said to use this quote from the Cretan philosopher Epimenides when he preached to the Athenians (Acts 17:28).

8. A prophet is one who speaks for God, from *pro* (for) and *phanai* (to speak).

9. Depending on the particular text, either MT or LXX can be considered to be the superior translation. See Gentry, "Septuagint," 194, 205; Hengel, *Septuagint*, 49 n. 79.

10. Babylonian Talmud (*b.*) quotations are from Epstein, *Soncino Babylonian Talmud*; Midrash Psalm quotations are from the translations at https://www.matsati.com.

Prophecies of a Triumphant Figure

The Old Testament described a future victorious figure that would usher in God's time of liberation and peace.

The Messiah Will Ride a Donkey

Zechariah predicted the arrival of a king who would be "lowly and riding on a donkey, a colt, the foal of a donkey" (Zech 9:9b), and this verse has a messianic interpretation in Judaism.[11] According to the Jewish scholar Joseph Klausner, "The Jews wait for one 'lowly and riding upon an ass' *who is to come*, and the Christians affirm that the Messiah *has already come* as one 'lowly and riding upon an ass.'"[12]

The patriarch Jacob also predicted the coming of a significant figure that was associated with a donkey and was connected to the vine that represented God's chosen people:[13] "The scepter shall not depart from Judah, nor a lawgiver from between his feet, until Shiloh comes; And to Him shall be the obedience of the people. Binding his donkey to the vine, and his donkey's colt to the choice vine" (Gen 49:10–11a). The word Shiloh was a name for the Messiah, and this figure in Jacob's prediction is regarded as messianic in a Qumran scroll[14] and in rabbinic interpretation.[15] Jesus was said to make his final entrance to Jerusalem riding a donkey, and it might be significant that the later Targum Jonathan removed the reference to a donkey in its messianic interpretation of Jacob's prediction.[16]

11. "If they [Israel] are meritorious, [Messiah will come] with the clouds of heaven; if not, lowly and riding upon an ass" (*b.* Sanhedrin 98a, original brackets).

12. Klausner, *Messianic Idea*, 203–4 (original emphasis).

13. "For the vineyard of the Lord of hosts is the house of Israel, And the men of Judah are His pleasant plant" (Isa 5:7a).

14. "The sceptre shall not depart from the tribe of Judah . . . until the messiah of righteousness comes, the branch of David" (4Q252, col. 5.1–3).

15. "If one sees a choice vine, he may look forward to seeing the Messiah, since it says, Binding his foal unto the vine and his ass's colt unto the choice vine" (*b.* Berachoth 57a). Also, "Rabbi Johanan said: For the sake of the Messiah. What is his name?—The School of Rabbi Shila said: His name is Shiloh, for it is written, until Shiloh come" (*b.* Sanhedrin 98b).

16. The Targum Jonathan has this interpretation of Genesis 49:10–11: "Kings shall not cease, nor rulers, from the house of Jehuda, nor sapherim teaching the law from his seed, till the time that the King the Meshiha, shall come, the youngest of his sons;

Old Testament prophets also expressed the expectation of God's future arrival on Earth.[17] N. T. Wright suggests that Jesus "saw his journey to Jerusalem as the symbol and embodiment of YHWH's return to Zion"[18] and that his "riding on a donkey over the Mount of Olives, across Kidron, and up to the Temple mount spoke more powerfully than words could have done of a royal claim."[19] Jesus's arrival in Jerusalem and his visit to the temple bring to mind God's promise of a future figure who would be Lord and messenger of the covenant:

> "Behold, I send My messenger, and he will prepare the way before Me. And the Lord, whom you seek, will suddenly come to His temple, even the Messenger of the covenant, in whom you delight. Behold, He is coming," says the Lord of hosts. (Mal 3:1)

A Special Child Will Be Born

Isaiah predicted the birth of an unusual child:[20]

> The people who walked in darkness have seen a great light . . . For unto us a Child is born, unto us a Son is given; and the government will be upon His shoulder. And His name will be called Wonderful, Counsellor, Mighty God, Everlasting Father, Prince of Peace. (Isa 9:2–6)

The Septuagint does not apply all of these titles to the child,[21] but the Masoretic Text writes them as one name: "his name is called Pele-joez-el-gibbor-Abi-ad-sar-shalom."

---

and on account of him shall the peoples flow together. How beauteous is the King, the Meshiha who will arise from the house of Jehuda." Translation by Etheridge.

17. "For behold, the Lord is coming out of His place; He will come down and tread on the high places of the earth" (Mic 1:3). "Thus the Lord my God will come, and all the saints with You" (Zech 14:5b). "For I know that my Redeemer lives, and He shall stand at last on the earth" (Job 19:25).

18. Wright, *Victory*, 639.

19. Wright, *Victory*, 490.

20. In the pre-Christian Septuagint, this child is said to be born of a virgin (*parthenos*; Isa 7:14). MT uses the Hebrew *almah*, which means young maid rather than virgin (*betulah*), but in those times an unmarried Jewish girl would be expected to be a virgin. Isaiah also called the birth a "sign" (Hebrew: *ot*), which was the Old Testament term for a miraculous act of God (Isa 7:14).

21. This is the Brenton Septuagint translation: "For a child is born to us, and a son is given to us, whose government is upon his shoulder: and his name is called the

It has been suggested that Isaiah was applying these titles to the future king Hezekiah of Judah. However, he used remarkably exalted language, and the Talmud records some rabbis disagreeing that Hezekiah could have been the Messiah.[22] This might be an example of a prophecy that applied to both the present and the future: Klausner comments, "I, along with most modern scholars, consider this whole prophecy messianic. The prophet *wished and longed* that Hezekiah would be a 'wonderful counsellor' and a 'prince of peace'; but Hezekiah was such a person only in a limited way. Hence the wish and longing of the prophet to see his ideal *completely* realized are his Messianic expectations."[23]

The names given to the promised child are highly significant. Isaiah's promised Prince of Peace would also be mighty God[24] and eternal Father—Jesus was said to be the divine Son of God but also to be equal with the Father, and he promised to be a "Counsellor" in the form of the Holy Spirit.[25] This expected child is also called Immanuel—"God with us" (Isa 7:14).

The Messiah Will Be Filled with the Spirit of God

Isaiah's prophecy included the expectation of a messianic son of Jesse (the father of King David):

> There shall come forth a Rod from the stem of Jesse, And a Branch shall grow out of his roots. The Spirit of the Lord shall rest upon Him, the Spirit of wisdom and understanding, the Spirit of counsel and might . . . But with righteousness He shall judge the poor, and decide with equity for the meek of the earth

Messenger of great counsel: for I will bring peace upon the princes, and health to him. His government shall be great, and of his peace there is no end: it shall be upon the throne of David, and upon his kingdom, to establish it, and to support it with judgment and with righteousness, from henceforth and forever."

22. "This was said *in opposition to* R. Hillel, who maintained that there will be no Messiah for Israel, since they have already enjoyed him during the reign of Hezekiah" (*b.* Sanhedrin 98b; emphasis added). An extra-biblical text from the first or second century AD explicitly depicted Hezekiah as a different figure from the Messiah. See 2 Baruch 63.

23. Klausner, *Messianic Idea*, 64–65 (original emphasis).

24. *El Gibbor* is a title for God. See Isa10:21; Jer 32:18; Neh 9:32.

25.. "And I will ask the Father, and he will give you another *paraklēton* to help you and be with you forever—the Spirit of truth . . . I will not leave you as orphans; I will come to you" (John 14:16–18). The term *paraklēton* means advocate or counselor.

> . . . And in that day there shall be a Root of Jesse, Who shall stand as a banner to the people; For the Gentiles shall seek Him, And His resting place shall be glorious. (Isa 11:1–10)

A rabbinic text interprets this prophecy as messianic,[26] and this figure is reminiscent of Jesus: he is filled with God's Spirit, speaks for the meek, and draws in God's people, including the Gentiles.

The Messiah Will Bring Healing and Liberation

Isaiah's promised figure was associated with the freedom of the year of the Lord:

> The Spirit of the Lord God is upon Me, Because the Lord has anointed Me To preach good tidings to the poor; He has sent Me to heal the brokenhearted, To proclaim liberty to the captives, And the opening of the prison to those who are bound; To proclaim the acceptable year of the Lord, And the day of vengeance of our God; To comfort all who mourn. (Isa 61:1–2)

We are told that Jesus read this text in the synagogue of Nazareth and identified himself directly with its prophecy:

> Then he rolled up the scroll, gave it back to the attendant and sat down. The eyes of everyone in the synagogue were fastened on him. He began by saying to them, "Today this scripture is fulfilled in your hearing." (Luke 4:20–21)

Prophecies of a Suffering Figure

A question that arose earlier remains unanswered: why did Jesus's followers continue to proclaim him as the promised Messiah even after his mission seemed to have failed? The answer might lie in Old Testament depictions of a pierced, forsaken figure associated with vicarious suffering and atonement.

26. "In that day there will be a root of Jesse, which will stand for an ensign of the peoples, unto him will the nations seek, that is, seek the king Messiah, David's son, who will remain hidden unto the time of redemption" (Midrash Psalm 21.1–3).

A Figure Is Pierced, Forsaken, and Cut Off

In Psalm 22, a person cries out in acute suffering and despair:

> My God, My God, why have You forsaken Me? . . . I am poured out like water, and all My bones are out of joint; My heart is like wax; It has melted within Me. My strength is dried up like a potsherd, and My tongue clings to My jaws . . . They pierced My hands and My feet . . . All the ends of the world Shall remember and turn to the Lord, And all the families of the nations Shall worship before You . . . It will be recounted of the Lord to the next generation, they will come and declare His righteousness to a people who will be born, that He has done this. (Ps 22:1–31)

This description of terrible thirst, piercing, and bones being pulled out of joint, is strongly reminiscent of Jesus's suffering on the cross.[27] However, the psalm ends on a positive note with all nations worshiping God. Three gospel traditions directly link the opening and closing lines of this psalm to Jesus's words on the cross: he cried out, "My God, my God, why have you forsaken me?" (Mark 15:34b; Matt 27:46b), and his last words were recorded in Greek as *tetelestai*—"It is done/finished" (John 19:30b), echoing Psalm 22:31: "He has done this."

Zechariah also predicted the piercing of a significant figure: "When they look on him whom they have pierced, they shall mourn for him, as one mourns for an only child" (Zech 12:10b RSV). The Talmud and Tosefta regard this as a messianic prophecy and apply the piercing to a future Messiah ben Joseph and Messiah bar Ephraim respectively.[28] The Hebrew MT also predicts that this person will be "thrust through," but Targum Jonathan renders this line as, "And they will inquire of me because they were exiled."[29]

27. The Hebrew words for "pierced" and "lion" are very similar, and some manuscripts of the Masoretic Text use the phrase "like a lion my hands and my feet" (Ps 22:16). However, the Septuagint uses "dug/pierced," and the oldest manuscript of Psalm 22 (Qumran scroll 5/6 HevPsalms) seems to use the word "pierced." See Abegg et al., *Dead Sea Scrolls Bible*, 519.

28. See *b*. Sukkah 52a; Mitchell, "Messiah bar Ephraim," 223.

29. See Mitchell, "Messiah bar Ephraim," 223. Martin Hengel regards the targumic version as a deliberate change in reaction to Christian quotations of the piercing verse ("History of Isaiah 53," 89) as does Mitchell ("Messiah bar Ephraim," 230). But this is not a unanimous point of view, and the pre-Christian Septuagint translated the "pierced" section of this verse as, "they shall look upon me, because they have mocked me." Christian interpretations of Zechariah 12:10 are found in John 19:37 and Revelation 1:7.

The book of Daniel also contains a prediction about an anointed prince who will be "cut off, but not for himself" (Dan 9:26b KJV), or "cut off, and will have nothing" (Dan 9:26b WEB). Joseph Klausner states that "almost all of Daniel is Messianic in spirit; but Chapters 2, 6–9, and 12 are Messianic in essence."[30]

Is it possible that these ancient texts contain hints of Jesus's crucifixion and atoning death, which would bring people to God?

God's Suffering Servant Predicted in Isaiah 53

Isaiah predicted a future servant of God who would be a light to the Gentiles (Isa 49:6) and who would suffer and be cut off in order to accomplish God's will and save others. The oldest version of Isaiah's prophecy is found in the ancient Great Isaiah Scroll (1QIsa) of Qumran, dated to around the end of the second century BC, which is very similar to the Masoretic Text. The "arm of the Lord" represented God's work of salvation,[31] and Isaiah used this symbol in his prophecy of God's Suffering Servant.

> Who has believed our message? And to whom has the arm of the Lord been revealed? . . . He was wounded [pierced][32] for our transgressions, and he was crushed for our iniquities, and the punishment that made us whole was upon him, and by his bruises we are healed . . . For he was cut off from the land of the living, he was stricken for the transgressions of my people . . . The will of the Lord will triumph in his hand. Out of the suffering of his soul he will see light, and find satisfaction . . . He bore the sins of many, and made intercession for their transgressions. (1QIsa 53:1–12) [33]

This prediction, written in the prophetic perfect tense, describes a man whose vicarious suffering and death brings healing and who intercedes for forgiveness. Isaiah's prophetic figure therefore provides an

30. Klausner, *Messianic Idea*, 228.

31. "Awake, awake, put on strength, O arm of the Lord! Awake as in the ancient days, In the generations of old . . . Are You not the One who dried up the sea, The waters of the great deep; That made the depths of the sea a road For the redeemed to cross over?" (Isa 51:9–10).

32. Klausner points out that the Masoretic Text uses here the same Hebrew word that is translated as "pierced" in Isaiah 51:9 (*Messianic Idea*, 165 n. 25).

33. The scroll translation is from Ulrich and Flint, *Qumran Cave 1. II*. Strictly speaking, this scroll is 1QIsa a, as opposed to the shorter 1QIsa b.

important background for Jesus's atoning work. But is this text about an individual messiah or not? The servant is sometimes clearly the entire nation of Israel (Isa 43:10) but is also identified with the prophet Isaiah (Isa 49:3) and in places is described as a highly exalted individual (Isa 52:13).

Judaism variously interpreted Isaiah's servant figure as being the nation of Israel, the prophet Jeremiah or Isaiah, King Hezekiah, Job, Moses, or a dying Messiah ben Joseph and a victorious Messiah ben David.[34] It is often claimed that the Christian interpretation of Jesus as God's Suffering Servant is incorrect because Isaiah's prophecy clearly identified the nation of Israel as the servant. However, although Targum Jonathan changed this text in significant ways so that the suffering applied to the entire nation of Israel, not to an individual,[35] rabbinic tradition did interpret these verses as messianic,[36] as do modern Jewish prayers for the Day of Atonement.[37]

Jewish philosopher George Kohler points out that "the Talmud had no difficulty reading the famous passages about God's 'suffering servant'

34. See Driver and Neubauer, *Fifty-third Chapter of Isaiah*, lxi–lxii.

35. The Targum Jonathan changed the text to apply the suffering directly to collective Israel: "We are in contempt and not esteemed, as a man of pain and appointed to sickness," and "we are considered crushed, smitten of the Lord, and afflicted" (Isa 53:3–4). Bruce Chilton points out that in making these alterations, the Targum interpreter had to change singular grammatical constructions to plural ones (*Glory*, 92). Targum Jonathan also made other significant changes to Isaiah's text: the individual servant figure does not bear the nation's sins but merely prays for them (Isa 53:5, 12, 13); he does not suffer like a lamb but delivers "the mighty of the nations as a lamb to the slaughter" (Isa 53:8); forgiveness is the result of his teachings, not his death: "Through the teaching of his words, our sins shall be forgiven us" (Isa 53:6). Quotations are from Pauli, *Chaldee Paraphrase*.

36. "Another explanation—he is speaking of the king Messiah . . . this refers to the chastisements, as it is said, 'But he was wounded for our transgressions, bruised for our iniquities'" (*m*. Ruth Rabbah 2.14). See Driver and Neubauer, *Fifty-third Chapter of Isaiah*, 9. The Talmud also contains this messianic reference to Isaiah 53:4: "The Rabbis said [of the messiah]: His name is 'the leper scholar,' as it is written, Surely he hath borne our griefs, and carried our sorrows: yet we did esteem him a leper, smitten of God, and afflicted" (*b*. Sanhedrin 98b).

37. "Our righteous anointed is departed from us: horror hath seized us, and we have none to justify us. He hath borne the yoke of our iniquities, and our transgression, and is wounded because of our transgression. He beareth our sins on his shoulder, that we may find pardon for our iniquities. We shall be healed by his wound, at the time that the Eternal will create him (the Messiah) as a new creature." See *Mahzor la-Yom Kippur* (Prayers for the Day of Atonement), 282–84 (original brackets). https://archive.org/details/maohzorlayomkippoounknuoft.

from the 53rd chapter of Isaiah in a Messianic light."[38] Judaic scholar Joel Rembaum also argues that the dominant rabbinic interpretation of Isaiah 53 was that Isaiah's servant figure was an individual messiah, and he asserts that Judaism only emphasized the collective-Israel interpretation in the Middle Ages, in response to Christian claims.[39] Talmud specialist Daniel Boyarin agrees with this conclusion.[40]

But it is not necessary to interpret Isaiah's servant figure as exclusively an individual figure or the nation of Israel. A more comprehensive approach might be indicated by the Hebrew understanding of corporate identity.

The Jewish Concept of Corporate Identity

According to the ancient Jewish concept of corporate identity, "the *one* who represents the group and the *many* who are represented are equally a part of the same single meaning intended by the author . . . [expressed in] concepts such as the 'seed,' the 'servant of the Lord,' the 'branch,' the 'firstborn' and the like."[41] For example, the high priest represented all Israel by wearing a breastplate with twelve gems inscribed with the names of the tribes (Exod 28:21). And the name Israel/Jacob could variously refer to the son of Isaac, the tribe of Jacob, or the entire nation of Israel. In general, "an oscillation between a group and an individual within the group as its representative is certainly common in the Tanakh."[42]

This collective identity can be applied to the prophecies of Isaiah, as the fourteenth-century Rabbi Shlomoh Astruc argued: "When [Isaiah] speaks of the people, the King Messiah is included in it, and when he speaks of the King Messiah, the people is comprehended with him."[43] Martin Hengel agrees that both individual and collective interpretations of Isaiah's servant figure are possible "because a messianic figure is always

38. Kohler, "Renewed Messianic Thought," 9.

39. Rembaum, "Jewish Exegetical Tradition," 291–93.

40. Boyarin, *Jewish Gospels*, 152.

41. Kaiser, *Messiah in Old Testament*, 25 (original emphasis).

42. Dempster, *Dominion and Dynasty*, 69 n. 26. The Hebrew Bible is called the *Tanakh*, an acronym of Torah, Nevi'im and Ketuvim (Law, Prophets, and Writings).

43. Quoted in Driver and Neubauer, *Fifty-third Chapter of Isaiah*, 129.

at the same time a representative of the whole people. This still holds even in early Christianity."[44] Stuhlmacher concurs:

> In Judaism the individual figure of the Servant-Messiah is the prince appointed by God, a prince who rules over the people of God and simultaneously represents them before God. So also with Jesus. He is the Son of God who leads the people of God; yet that people also constitutes his body.[45]

Overview

The New Testament teaches that Jesus fulfilled ancient Jewish prophecies, which were interpreted as messianic within Judaism. Some of these prophecies predicted a future triumphant figure, but there were also scattered hints of vicarious suffering as part of God's redemptive plan. These marginal expectations of atoning suffering might help to explain why Jesus's disciples could have proclaimed him as the Messiah even after his death and why they assumed that their positive message about his death would have been understood by other Jews.[46] Paul directly identified his own gospel with Isaiah's preaching about the Suffering Servant.[47]

But why did the disciples link Jesus to these ancient prophecies? Did they misguidedly, and without good reason, apply popular traditions of suffering and atonement to their dead leader? This does not seem likely against the background of Jewish beliefs of the time:

- First-century Jewish messianism was dominated by expectations of a triumphant warrior-king, not a suffering victim.[48]
- Judaism did have a tradition of heroic martyrdom, as in First Maccabees, but this was not linked to vicarious atonement or resurrection

44. Hengel, "History of Isaiah 53," 81.

45. Stuhlmacher, "Isaiah 53," 147.

46. See Hengel, "History of Isaiah 53," 146.

47. Paul quoted from Isaiah 53:1 when he wrote, "But not all the Israelites accepted the good news. For Isaiah says, 'Lord, who has believed our message?' Consequently, faith comes from hearing the message, and the message is heard through the word about Christ" (Rom 10:16–17).

48. See Collins, *Scepter*, 68. Randall Price points out that in the Qumran Scrolls, "the overriding theme is one of royal messianic expectation" ("Eschatology of Dead Sea Scrolls," 25).

of the dead.[49] Vicarious suffering does appear in Second Maccabees 7, but this is very rare in Second Temple literature, and Daniel McClennan suggests this chapter might be a post-Christian addition from the first or second century AD.[50]

- Regarding three texts from the first century AD: the "son of man" in the Parables of Enoch does not suffer; a messianic figure does die in Four Ezra, but this might reflect Christian influence, and his death provides no atonement; the righteous do suffer in Wisdom of Solomon, but there is no vicarious suffering to cover the guilt of others.[51]
- As discussed in chapter 4.4, "neither the suffering of the Messiah, nor his death and resurrection, appear to have been part of the faith of first-century Judaism."[52] Joseph Klausner claimed that "all the references to the suffering Messiah in Rabbinic literature . . . belong *without exception* to the post-Tannaitic period, when Christian influences cannot be wholly discounted."[53]

After a comprehensive survey of the relevant literature, Martin Hengel concludes that there is little evidence of vicarious suffering in the Jewish sources,[54] there are only extremely rare traces of a pre-Christian suffering messiah, and in messianic Old Testament texts, the motif of end-time victory predominates.[55] This evidence suggests that it would not have been an obvious step for Jesus's followers to associate Jesus with Isaiah's suffering, atoning servant of God. In general, there does not seem to have been any clear-cut category that the disciples could have applied to Jesus, and Jewish scholar Alan Segal instead argues that New

49. See Hengel, "History of Isaiah 53," 96.

50. In Second Maccabees, one of seven martyred brothers prays "that in me and my brethren the wrath of the Almighty, which is justly brought upon our nation, may cease" (2 Macc 7:38 KJV). McClennan argues, "It has long been thought that 2 Macc 7 provided the foundation for the development of Christian beliefs about martyrdom, resurrection, and the doctrine of vicarious expiation . . . Far more parsimonious is later borrowing on the part of the author of 2 Macc 7 from the milieu of the Judeo-Christian battles for identity and orthodoxy" ("Function of 2 Maccabees 7," 94). On the other hand, if 2 Maccabees 7 was a pre-Christian text, it would help to explain why Jesus's followers could have interpreted his death as having atoning value.

51. See Hengel, "History of Isaiah 53," 132.

52. Vermes, *Jesus the Jew*, 38.

53. Klausner, *Messianic Idea*, 405 (original emphasis).

54. Hengel, "History of Isaiah 53," 119.

55. Hengel, "History of Isaiah 53," 89.

Testament Christology was developed rather than borrowed from any preexisting model.[56]

Jesus's followers came to believe that he fulfilled ancient Jewish predictions of a suffering and a triumphant figure. But there was no precedent for this in contemporary thought, and no other messianic group adopted this approach.[57] The New Testament depiction of Jesus's messianic atonement is therefore unique.[58] One explanation for this exceptional development would be that Jesus did make significant claims that were confirmed when he rose from the dead.

7.2 SEVEN ANCIENT HOLY FESTIVALS

The Judaic calendar was structured around the number seven, which symbolized perfection and completion: the seventh day was a day of rest (Exod 16:23), the land lay fallow every seventh year (Lev 25:4), and after seven times seven years was the fiftieth Jubilee year of renewal. There were also seven annual feasts when God's people appeared before him for holy purposes. Jesus's work has strong connections with these ancient festivals: three in spring, one in summer, and three in the fall.

Three Spring Feasts in Nisan

1. Passover/*Pesach*—The first Passover was instituted on Nisan 14 in Egypt when each Israelite family used a hyssop branch to apply the blood of an unblemished lamb to the door lintels as protection against the death of all first-born males (Exod 12:5–12).[59] The sac-

56. Segal writes, "According to rabbinic description, it does not seem necessary to believe that early Christians merely associated Jesus with some pre-existent savior model who came equipped with a fixed title and job description . . . Rabbinic debate makes it possible to see christology build through exegesis rather than through hypothetical, pre-existent titles" (*Two Powers*, x–xi).

57. Post-Christian rabbinic Judaism developed the concept of two future messiahs: a dying Messiah ben Joseph and a reigning Messiah ben David. Klausner suggested that the expectations of a slain messiah developed partly in response to the death of the messianic Bar Kokhba in AD 135 (*Messianic Idea*, 496). For the late date of the dual-messiah concept, see also Mitchell, "Messiah bar Ephraim," 222 n. 2; Edersheim, *Life and Times*, 54.

58. See Stuhlmacher, "Isaiah 53," 161; Hengel, "History of Isaiah 53," 132.

59. Hyssop was closely associated with cleansing rituals (Lev 14:4, 52; Num 19:18;

rificial lamb was then eaten, and on Nisan 15, Israel was released from slavery.

2. The Feast of Unleavened Bread—From Nisan 15 to 21, no leaven (yeast) was consumed, as this symbolized impurity and sin. The first day included a sacrificial sin offering (Num 28:22).
3. The Festival of Early Firstfruits—On the first Sunday after Passover, the priest waved a sheaf of the first (barley) harvest before God, and the sacrifice included a male lamb (Lev 23:10–12; Num 28:16–17).

Jesus was directly associated with themes and images of this Passover feast week. He was crucified during Passover and was the flawless sacrifice that provided redemption and purification:

> For you know that it was not with perishable things such as silver or gold that you were redeemed from the empty way of life handed down to you from your ancestors, but with the precious blood of Christ, a lamb without blemish or defect. (1 Pet 1:18–19)

> Get rid of the old yeast, so that you may be a new unleavened batch—as you really are. For Christ, our Passover lamb, has been sacrificed. (1 Cor. 5:7)

Jesus's death also provided freedom and an *ex-hodus* ("road out") from slavery:

> They spoke about his departure [*exodon*] which he was about to bring to fulfillment at Jerusalem. (Luke 9:31)

> Jesus replied, "Very truly I tell you, everyone who sins is a slave to sin. Now a slave has no permanent place in the family, but a son belongs to it forever. So if the Son sets you free, you will be free indeed." (John 8:34–36)

Jesus's tomb was found empty on the first Sunday after the Passover, which was the day when the firstfruits of harvest were offered to God. In the Old Testament, Israel represented the future harvest for God: "Israel was holiness to the Lord, the firstfruits of His increase" (Jer 2:3a). This imagery now applies to Jesus and his followers:

Ps 51:7), and it is a significant detail that a hyssop stalk was used to offer wine and vinegar to Jesus on the cross (John 19:29).

> But Christ has indeed been raised from the dead, the firstfruits of those who have fallen asleep. (1 Cor 15:20)

> Of his own will he brought us forth by the word of truth, that we should be a kind of firstfruits of his creatures. (Jas 1:18)

> It is these who follow the Lamb wherever he goes. These have been redeemed from mankind as firstfruits for God and the Lamb. (Rev 14:4b)

The traditional Orthodox Jewish Passover meal also contains some highly symbolic elements that seem surprisingly relevant to Jesus:

- Unleavened bread (*matzah*)—Before Passover, each house is searched to remove all traces of leaven. Unleavened dough is pierced to prevent rising, and three cooked matzot are then placed into separate compartments of a specially designed bag, forming a unity of three. At one stage of the ritual meal, the middle matzah is taken out and broken—one half is replaced (to be eaten as the "bread of affliction"), and the other half is wrapped in a cloth and hidden. At a later stage, this half is brought back to the table and eaten as the last food of the night. The matzot are said to possibly represent Abraham, Isaac, and Jacob, or the priests, Levites, and Israelites, but the unity of the three matzot has distinctly Trinitarian echoes. There is no explanation for why one of these pierced breads is broken, wrapped, hidden, and brought back a second time to complete the sacramental meal, but it is powerfully reminiscent of Jesus's broken body buried in a linen cloth, his claim: "This bread is my flesh, which I will give for the life of the world" (John 6:51b), and the expectation of his second coming.
- A lamb bone called the *zeroa*—This word was used for the shoulder of the sacrifice (Num 6:19; Deut 18:3) and also for God's arm of deliverance, as in Isaiah's prophecy of the Suffering Servant (Isa 53:1) who was associated with Jesus. So this Passover bone is linked to sacrifice and God's redemptive work through his Son.
- The Hallel (praise) Psalms 113 to 118—These ancient psalms are sung during the Passover meal. The hymns that Jesus and his disciples sang at the end of the Last Supper (Mark 14:26) would probably have included the following highly significant verses: "The right hand of the Lord does valiantly. I shall not die, but live . . .

This is the gate of the Lord, through which the righteous shall enter. I will praise You, for You have answered me, and have become my salvation" (Ps 118:16b–22).

The Summer Festival of Pentecost/*Shavuot*/Feast of Weeks

Fifty days, or seven weeks, after the firstfruits of Passover was the summer Shavuot feast of the second firstfruits (wheat) harvest (Lev 23:15–17; Exod 23:16; 34:22).[60] The earlier firstfruits celebration in Nisan involved one sheaf of barley, but this celebration used two loaves made with leaven, perhaps symbolizing a future harvest of both Jew and Gentile.

The Old Testament prophet Jeremiah associated this summer harvest with God's salvation: "Listen! The voice, the cry of the daughter of my people from a far country . . . The harvest is past, the summer is ended, and we are not saved" (Jer 8:19–20). And Jesus regarded himself as performing God's harvesting work: "'My food,' said Jesus, 'is to do the will of him who sent me and to finish his work . . . Open your eyes and look at the fields! They are ripe for harvest'" (John 4:34–35).

The feast of Shavuot was traditionally linked to the renewal of God's covenant, and it commemorated the day that Moses delivered God's laws on stone tablets.[61] We are told that when Jesus's followers were celebrating this ancient feast, the Holy Spirit came upon them and their preaching increased the harvest for God and established the church (Acts 2). This recalls God's promises in the Old Testament that his people would receive a new spirit, and his law would no longer be written in stone but on their inner being:

> I will give you a new heart and put a new spirit within you; I will take the heart of stone out of your flesh and give you a heart of flesh. (Ezek 36:26)

> But this is the covenant that I will make with the house of Israel after those days, says the Lord: I will put My law in their minds, and write it on their hearts. (Jer 31:33a)

60. The word "Pentecost" is from the Greek *pentékonta* (fifty).

61. See Jubilees 1.1, 6.17.

Three Fall Feasts in Tishri

The fall feasts were the Feast of Trumpets, the Day of Atonement, and the final Feast of Tabernacles.

The Feast of Trumpets/Rosh Hashanah

The first day of Tishri was celebrated by the blowing of trumpets (Lev 23:24b). Trumpets were associated with God's salvation (Num 10:9), the release of slaves on the Yom Kippur of each Jubilee year, and the future coming of God to Earth (Isa 27:12–13). Trumpets will also proclaim Jesus's return:

> And he will send his angels with a loud trumpet call, and they will gather his elect from the four winds, from one end of the heavens to the other. (Matt 24:31)

> For the Lord himself will come down from heaven, with a loud command, with the voice of the archangel and with the trumpet call of God, and the dead in Christ will rise first. (1 Thess 4:16)

> But in the days when the seventh angel is about to sound his trumpet, the mystery of God will be accomplished, just as he announced to his servants the prophets. (Rev 10:7)

The Day of Atonement/Yom Kippur

God's presence was said to take the form of a cloud in the Holy of Holies of the tabernacle, above the *kapporet* of the ark of the covenant (Exod 25:22; Lev 16:2). The Hebrew *kapporet*, translated as "atonement cover" or "mercy seat," is from the root *kaphar* (cover) and was associated with God's forgiveness of sin.[62] Only once a year, on the Day of Atonement (Tishri 10) could the high priest enter the Holy of Holies to provide annual atonement for Israel.

On this day, lots were drawn to choose between two goats. One was sacrificed as a sin offering to the Lord, and its blood was sprinkled seven times on the mercy seat to atone for Israel's transgressions (Lev

62. "And the *kohen* [priest] shall make *kapporah* [covering/atonement] for his *chattat* [sin] that he hath sinned, and it shall be forgiven him" (Lev 4:35 OJB).

16:14–16). (It has been suggested that Jesus would have bled seven times: when he sweated blood, at his scourging, from the crown of thorns, at three points on the cross, and when his side was pierced.) The high priest then laid his hands on the other living "scapegoat" to transfer onto it the sins of the nation, which it bore away when it was driven into the wilderness (Lev 16:21–22). Jesus was associated with this high-priestly ceremony of atoning sacrifice and ritual purification:

> He is the atoning sacrifice for our sins, and not only for ours but also for the sins of the whole world. (1 John 2:2)

> God made him who had no sin to be sin for us, so that in him we might become the righteousness of God. (2 Cor 5:21)

> Christ came as high priest . . . The blood of goats and bulls and the ashes of a heifer sprinkled on those who are ceremonially unclean sanctify them so that they are outwardly clean. How much more, then, will the blood of Christ, who through the eternal Spirit offered himself unblemished to God, cleanse our consciences. (Heb 9:11–14a)

As a side note, a rabbinic text records unusual phenomena in the first century Yom Kippur ceremonies: "Our Rabbis taught: During the last forty years before the destruction of the Temple, the lot ["For the Lord"] did not come up in the right hand; nor did the crimson-coloured strap become white; nor did the westernmost light shine; and the doors of the Hekal [temple] would open by themselves."[63] Josephus recorded one incident of the opening doors,[64] and the temple was destroyed in AD 70, so these strange events would have started around the time of Jesus's death.

63. *b*. Masechet Yoma 39b. The custom of a red strap turning white might have developed from Isaiah's verse, "'Come now, and let us reason together,' Says the Lord, 'Though your sins are like scarlet, they shall be as white as snow'" (Isa 1:18a).

64. Josephus wrote about an incident that took place not long before the destruction of the temple: "Moreover, the eastern gate of the inner [court of the] temple, which was of brass, and vastly heavy, and had been with difficulty shut by twenty men, and rested upon a basis armed with iron, and had bolts fastened very deep into the firm floor, which was there made of one entire stone, was seen to be opened of its own accord about the sixth hour of the night. Now those that kept watch in the temple came hereupon running to the captain of the temple, and told him of it; who then came up thither, and not without great difficulty was able to shut the gate again" (*Wars* 6.5.3).

The Feast of Ingathering/Tabernacles/Sukkot

This last festival of the year, from Tishri 15 to 21, was a joyful celebration of final harvest, during which time people lived outside in booths (*sukkot*) of branches to symbolize Israel's time in the desert (Lev 23:33–43). The weekly sacrifice was highly symbolic: thirteen animals were sacrificed on the first day, twelve on the second, eleven on the third, and so on, until seven were slaughtered on the seventh day (Num 29:13–34). The total of seventy represented the Gentile nations, and it was prophesied that the Feast of Tabernacles will be the only feast that the nations observe at the end times (Zech 14:16).

This festival week ended with a final eighth-day feast of rest, with the number eight representing a new beginning.[65] On this last day, a priest carried a golden jar of water from the pool of Siloam to pour out in the temple.[66] God's Spirit was traditionally described as living water,[67] and God had promised a future pouring out of his Spirit: "For I will pour water on him who is thirsty, and floods on the dry ground; I will pour My Spirit on your descendants, and My blessing on your offspring" (Isa 44:3). Jesus linked himself directly to this ancient symbolism and promise:

> On the last and greatest day of the festival [of Tabernacles], Jesus stood and said in a loud voice, "Let anyone who is thirsty come to me and drink. Whoever believes in me, as Scripture has said, rivers of living water will flow from within them." By this he meant the Spirit, whom those who believed in him were later to receive. (John 7:37–39a)

Overview

Judaism's seven ancient, holy convocations are structured around motifs and themes that have close connections with Jesus's teachings, death, resurrection, and second coming:

65. For example, a boy was circumcised eight days after birth, and the new week started on the eighth day (Sunday).

66. *m.* Sukka 4.9.

67. "For My people have committed two evils: They have forsaken Me, the fountain of living waters, and hewn themselves cisterns—broken cisterns that can hold no water" (Jer 2:13).

Ancient Feast	Date	Shared Theme in the New Testament
Passover and Exodus	Nisan 14	Jesus's sacrifice provides liberation and protection
Unleavened Bread	Nisan 15–21	Purification and sanctification
Firstfruits	First Sunday after Pesach	Jesus's resurrection is a promise of the future harvest for God
Pentecost	50 days after Firstfruits	Second harvest—the church
Trumpets	Tishri 1	Triumphant arrival of Christ at the second coming
Day of Atonement	Tishri 10	Repentance, forgiveness, and reconciliation
Tabernacles	Tishri 15–21	Final harvest and ingathering
Eighth Day of Assembly	Tishri 22	Pouring out of God's Spirit, and dwelling with God—a new beginning.

Either Jesus's followers had astounding skill in inventing details about Jesus to fit in with ancient practices and rituals, or these connections indicate something remarkable and highly significant. The symmetry of the seven feasts indicates that the three spring feasts are associated with events that have taken place, the present time is associated with the summer feast of second harvest, and events associated with the last three feasts of autumn have yet to occur.

7.3 THE BIG PICTURE FROM GENESIS TO REVELATION

The Old Testament sustains consistent themes of humanity's rejection of God's will, and God's promise to implement a future atonement and bring about the perfection of creation. The New Testament depicts Jesus as being instrumental in bringing these promises to fruition.

Revelation, the last book of the Bible and the only prophetic book in the New Testament, is thought to have been written towards the end of the first century by the aged disciple John. It describes John's vision of Jesus's return and, like Paul's Damascus encounter, it shares some features with Ezekiel's vision of God. For example, both John and Ezekiel are carried up by God's Spirit to see the glory of God in Jerusalem (Ezek 8:3–4; Rev 21:10–11); they both eat a scroll that tastes like honey (Ezek 3:3; Rev 10:10) and are both sent to prophesy for God—in Ezekiel's case, to Israel (Ezek 3:4) but in John's case, to "many peoples, nations, languages and kings" (Rev 10:11). This final vision of Judeo-Christian Scripture echoes ancient biblical motifs and depicts the fulfillment of God's plan for humanity. The New Testament therefore extends and completes the Old Testament in the following ways.

In the Beginning

In Genesis, God declares his creation to be very good (Gen 1:31) and places Adam in the garden of Eden to cultivate it and "be *shomer* over it" (Gen 2:15b OJB). This word, from the root word *shamar* (to keep, guard, or preserve), is also used in God's instructions for his people to keep his covenant (Gen 17:9), observe his feasts (Exod 12:17), and keep his commandments (Exod 16:28). God's instruction to Adam therefore had important covenantal implications. Theologian Gregory Beale even suggests that humanity was intended to play a central role in bringing God's creation to perfection.[68]

But instead of cooperating with God's plans, humanity both then and afterward rejected his authority, which called down God's curses on mankind (Gen 3:16–19) and on nature: "Cursed is the ground for your sake; In toil you shall eat of it all the days of your life. Both thorns and thistles it shall bring forth for you" (Gen 17–18a).[69] Humanity was evicted from the garden of Eden, from God's presence, and from the tree of life.

68. Beale writes, "In Eden there was a beginning establishment of a priest-king in a sinless world order who was to be faithful and obedient to God *until that first creation was consummated* . . . [Eden would] be brought to eschatological completion by God escalating the conditions and blessings of the prefall state into a permanent, indestructible creation" (*Unfolding of the Old Testament*, 88, original emphasis).

69. The Old Testament also records later curses following the infidelity of God's chosen people: "Even the land was defiled; so I punished it for its sin, and the land vomited out its inhabitants" (Lev 18:25). "Yet the land shall be desolate because of

The first Adam failed to obey God's instructions, but Paul calls Jesus the last Adam and teaches that through his obedience even unto death (Phil 2:8), Jesus has finally restored mankind to God.[70] The book of Revelation also teaches that Jesus will be instrumental in inaugurating the perfected new earth.

Promises of Atonement and a New Covenant

The Hebrew *sheba* means seven (symbolizing perfection) as well as oath or covenant. God instituted seven covenants: through Adam (Gen 2:15), Noah (Gen 9:11), Abraham (Gen 15:18), Moses (Deut 11:22–23), all Israel (Deut 30:15–16), David (2 Sam 7:16), and finally, Jesus Christ.[71] However, God's chosen people broke his covenants time after time, and alongside his many warnings,[72] God repeatedly expressed yearning for his people to repent, be spared suffering, and receive his blessing. It is important to hear how his voice of appeal speaks consistently through different prophets:

> I have nourished and brought up children, and they have rebelled against Me . . . Seek justice, rebuke the oppressor; Defend the fatherless, plead for the widow. Come now, and let us reason together . . . If you are willing and obedient, you shall eat the good of the land. (Isa 1:2b–19)

> Cast away from you all the transgressions which you have committed, and get yourselves a new heart and a new spirit. For why should you die, O house of Israel? For I have no pleasure in the death of one who dies . . . Therefore turn and live! (Ezek 18:31–32)

---

those who dwell in it, and for the fruit of their deeds" (Mic 7:13).

70. "For as in Adam all die, so in Christ all will be made alive" (1 Cor 15:22). "So it is written: 'The first man Adam became a living being'; the last Adam, a life-giving spirit" (1 Cor 15:45).

71. "This cup is the new covenant in my blood, which is poured out for you" (Luke 22:20b). "For this reason Christ is the mediator of a new covenant, that those who are called may receive the promised eternal inheritance—now that he has died as a ransom to set them free from the sins committed under the first covenant" (Heb 9:15).

72. "I will not go up in your midst, lest I consume you on the way, for you are a stiff-necked people" (Exod 33:3b). "Thus says the Lord: 'Behold, I am against you, and I will draw My sword out of its sheath and cut off both righteous and wicked from you'" (Ezek. 21:3).

> It may be that the house of Judah will hear all the adversities which I purpose to bring upon them, that everyone may turn from his evil way, that I may forgive their iniquity and their sin. (Jer 36:3)

> How can I give you up, Ephraim? How can I hand you over, Israel? . . . My heart churns within Me; My sympathy is stirred. (Hos 11:8)[73]

> But My people would not heed My voice, and Israel would have none of Me. So I gave them over to their own stubborn heart, to walk in their own counsels. Oh, that My people would listen to Me, that Israel would walk in My ways! (Ps 81:11–13)

Jesus wept at the thought of Jerusalem's impending destruction (Luke 19:42), and he echoed God's cries in his own words: "Jerusalem, Jerusalem, you who kill the prophets and stone those sent to you, how often I have longed to gather your children together, as a hen gathers her chicks under her wings, and you were not willing" (Matt 23:37).[74]

Through his prophets, God also promised that despite the fickleness of his people, he would provide a final atonement that would make a lasting, unbreakable covenant with humanity possible:

> I will establish an everlasting covenant with you . . . Then you shall know that I am the Lord, that you may remember and be ashamed, and never open your mouth anymore because of your shame, when I provide you an atonement for all you have done. (Ezek 16:60b–63)

> The days are coming . . . when I will make a new covenant with the people of Israel and with the people of Judah. It will not be like the covenant I made with their ancestors when I took them by the hand to lead them out of Egypt, because they broke my covenant, though I was a husband to them." (Jer 31:31–32)

> I will put My Spirit within you and cause you to walk in My statutes, and you will keep My judgments and do them. (Ezek 36:27)

73. See also Amos 5:21–24; Jer 30:11; 9:23–24; Lam 3:31–33; Isa 55:1–7. Ephraim was one of Joseph's sons, and the name referred to the northern tribes.

74. God was also associated with protective wings: "In the shadow of Your wings I will make my refuge" (Ps 57:1b).

> I, even I, am He who blots out your transgressions for My own sake; And I will not remember your sins. (Isa 43:25)

However, a holy God cannot simply overlook sin. As Emil Brunner explained, "The wrath of God is not a mood, it is an actual force . . . an objective necessity" in response to rebellion.[75] Even human repentance is not sufficient to remove the need for punitive action, in the same way that remorse cannot negate the judicial consequences of one's actions. Human rebellion against God's authority therefore has paradoxical implications: humanity must atone for its defiance, but no person is able to provide an immaculate sacrifice, and only God can reach across the rift. The resolution of this problem is an even greater paradox—the required atonement is made by one who is both God and man. As C. S. Lewis explained,

> Supposing God became a man—suppose our human nature which can suffer and die was amalgamated with God's nature in one person—then that person could help us. He could surrender His will, and suffer and die, because He was man; and He could do it perfectly because He was God. You and I can go through this process only if God does it in us; but God can do it only if He becomes man . . . That is the sense in which He pays our debt, and suffers for us what He Himself need not suffer at all.[76]

It seems illogical and unjust to claim that the suffering and death of one man could atone for the transgressions of others. However, in his divine-human nature and according to the ancient Hebrew concept of corporate identity, Jesus could choose to suffer as God for all of humanity. Like the nation of Israel, Jesus is described as God's beloved firstborn son and servant, and where Israel was God's vineyard, Jesus is now the root vine (John 15:5): as Paul explained, Jesus's atoning work has made it possible for anyone to be "grafted in" to the new Israel (Rom 11:17). From our perspective, Jesus's death might seem to have been pointless because the world is still wracked by pain and disorder. But although two thousand years seems like a long time, considering it has taken more than thirteen billion years to get to this point, it is just the blink of an eye.[77]

75. Brunner, *Mediator*, 482.

76. Lewis, *Mere Christianity*, 56.

77. "You turn man to destruction, and say, 'Return, O children of men.' For a thousand years in Your sight are like yesterday when it is past, and like a watch in the night" (Ps 90:3–4).

A New Heaven, New Earth, and New Jerusalem

In the Old Testament, God promised to provide a new creation, a perfected Jerusalem, and an end to suffering:

> See, I will create new heavens and a new earth. The former things will not be remembered, nor will they come to mind. But be glad and rejoice forever in what I will create, for I will create Jerusalem to be a delight and its people a joy. I will rejoice over Jerusalem and take delight in my people; the sound of weeping and of crying will be heard in it no more. (Isa 65:17–19 NIV)

John's vision in Revelation depicts the fulfillment of this ancient promise when the returning Jesus receives the new Jerusalem as a bride:

> Then I saw "a new heaven and a new earth," for the first heaven and the first earth had passed away, and there was no longer any sea. I saw the Holy City, the new Jerusalem, coming down out of heaven from God, prepared as a bride beautifully dressed for her husband . . . He will wipe every tear from their eyes. There will be no more death or mourning or crying or pain, for the old order of things has passed away. He who was seated on the throne said, "I am making everything new!" (Rev 21:1–5a)

Jewish expectations of end-time redemption included the restoration of the Jerusalem temple, but it is significant that the temple was designed to represent the natural world. It contained an enormous basin called the "sea," there were carved images of lions, oxen, palm trees, flowers, and pomegranates, and ten lampstands were branched like trees with seven lamps each, providing a total of seventy lamps to represent the Gentile nations (1 Kgs 6–7; Exod 25:33; 2 Chron 4:7). These natural elements suggest that ancient traditions of the future restored temple symbolized the redemption of the entire creation.

The inside of the temple would have looked like a garden, and it also shared the following specific features with the garden of Eden and with the final redemption of creation as depicted in Revelation:

- The temple and garden were the only biblical places associated with cherubim.[78]

78. Two cherubim guarded the entrance to the garden of Eden after Adam and Eve were evicted (Gen 3:24). In the temple, cherubim adorned the doors and walls (1 Kgs 6:29–32) as well as the curtains that concealed the Holy of Holies (Exod 26:31), and two cherubim were carved on the mercy seat of the ark of the covenant (Exod 25:22).

- Adam was placed in the garden to serve and keep it (Gen 2:15) in the same way that priests were keepers of the temple (Ezek 44:14).
- A river flowed from Eden to water the garden (Gen 2:10), and Ezekiel had a vision of a river flowing from the future temple (Ezek 47:1).
- In Ezekiel's vision, the river provided water to trees that have healing leaves (Ezek 47:12), and in John's vision in Revelation, a river flows from the throne, and the tree of life with its healing leaves is again available to humanity (Rev 22:1–3).

In the Revelation vision, the curse on Earth is finally lifted, and death is eliminated (Rev 22:3; 20:14; 21:4). God's cosmic plan for a perfected creation can therefore be thematically traced from the garden of Eden in Genesis, to the Jerusalem temple, through Old Testament visions of the perfected end-times temple, to its fulfillment in the final vision of Jesus's return in Revelation.

Old Testament expectations of the end times also included the reuniting of the twelve tribes of Israel (Ezek 37:21; Isa 49:6). It is significant that in Revelation, the names of the tribes that were once inscribed on the breastplate of the high priest are now inscribed on the twelve gates of the new Jerusalem (Rev 21:12), and the names of the twelve apostles are on the city's foundations (Rev 21:14) so that God's people of the Old and New Testaments together provide the basis of his perfected holy city.

Humanity Is Perfected

In the Old Testament, God expressed the desire for his entire people to form a holy priesthood (see Exod 19:6; Lev 11:44), and the concept of a perfected humanity is still a messianic expectation in Judaism.[79] In his vision, John was told that Jesus's sacrificial death has fulfilled this plan:

> And they sang a new song, saying: "You are worthy to take the scroll and to open its seals, because you were slain, and with your blood you purchased for God persons from every tribe and language and people and nation. You have made them to be a kingdom and priests to serve our God, and they will reign on the earth." (Rev 5:9–10)

79. According to Joseph Klausner, "The Messianic expectation of spiritual welfare includes the idea of *human perfection and the perfection of humanity* in the Age to Come" (*Messianic Idea*, 240, original emphasis).

Jesus's atoning death was therefore a vital part of God's plan to bring humanity to perfection. The first Adam defied God's will but as the last Adam, Jesus has perfected human nature through his obedience.[80] As a result, he has entered God's presence, "wearing our redeemed humanity . . . gathering our human existence into oneness with himself . . . [in] a movement which restores humanity to communion with God but far transcends the original creation in the nature of the union."[81] As Otfried Hofius explains,

> Christ has not simply come alongside the sinner in order to take away something—namely, guilt and sin; he has rather become identical with the sinner, in order through the surrender of his life to lead sinners into union with God and thus to open them to fellowship with God for the first time. Christ thus dies not only "in place of" the sinner; he dies "for" him in such a way that his death is as such the sinner's death and his resurrection is as such the sinner's "coming to God." Therefore no restitution takes place here, but rather new creation . . . a *new* being that the sinner never before possessed.[82]

Jesus's redeeming work also affects the entire creation.[83] In the words of C. S. Lewis,

> Our species, rising after its long descent, will drag all Nature up with it because in our species the Lord of nature is now included . . . For God is not merely mending, not simply restoring a status quo. Redeemed humanity is to be something more glorious than unfallen humanity would have been.[84]

If this is true, it is a profoundly exhilarating, liberating, reassuring, and inspiring message.

80. "Son though he was, he learned obedience from what he suffered and, once made perfect, he became the source of eternal salvation for all who obey him" (Heb 5:8–9).

81. Torrance, *Space, Time and Incarnation*, 77.

82. Hofius, "Fourth Servant," 174–75 (original emphasis).

83. Paul wrote, "For God was pleased to have all his fullness dwell in him, and through him to reconcile to himself all things, whether things on earth or things in heaven, by making peace through his blood, shed on the cross" (Col 1:19–20).

84. Lewis, *Miracles*, 198.

God's Wrath Is Poured Out

Jesus is the epitome of compassion, but he is not "meek and mild." His final judgment will implement God's righteous response to evil. These are God's words in the Old Testament:

> I have trodden the winepress alone, and from the peoples no one was with Me. For I have trodden them in My anger, and trampled them in My fury; Their blood is sprinkled upon My garments, and I have stained all My robes. (Isa 63:3)

In Revelation, Jesus warns, "Those whom I love I rebuke and discipline. So be earnest and repent" (Rev 3:19). And John's vision of the returning Jesus contains echoes of God's words:

> He is dressed in a robe dipped in blood, and his name is the Word of God . . . He treads the winepress of the fury of the wrath of God Almighty. (Rev 19:13–15)

This end time will also be a testing time for God's people:

> [The beast] was given power to wage war against God's holy people and to conquer them . . . This calls for patient endurance and faithfulness on the part of God's people. (Rev 13:7–10)

> And I saw the souls of those who had been beheaded because of their testimony about Jesus and because of the word of God. (Rev 20:4b)

These words bring to mind grim martyrdoms like those of the twenty-one Christians beheaded by ISIS on a Libyan beach in 2015 for refusing to renounce their faith.[85]

In his son-of-man vision, Daniel predicted the opening of the books for end-time judgment (Dan 7:10–11). Revelation similarly depicts a time when all of resurrected humanity will be judged according to their deeds (Rev 20:12). But those who accept the *kaphar* mercy-covering of Jesus's atoning work will not experience the second, spiritual death (Rev 2:11), which results in eviction from God's presence, echoing the expulsion of Adam and Eve from the garden and the chosen people from the promised land, but this time, for eternity.

85. The distressing yet inspiring story of these Christians is told in Martin Mosebach's book, *The 21: A Journey into the Land of the Coptic Martyrs.*

God Dwells with All Nations

God promised that he would one day openly tabernacle (dwell) with Israel and all nations.[86] The New Testament links this promise directly to Jesus's incarnation: "And the Word became flesh, and did tabernacle among us" (John 1:14a YLT) and also to his second coming: "Look! God's dwelling place is now among the people, and he will dwell with them" (Rev 21:3b).

The temple curtain that barred humanity from God's presence was said to tear at the time of Jesus's death (Mark 15:38; Matt 27:51). The New Testament regarded this as a symbol of Jesus's body: "We have confidence to enter the Most Holy Place by the blood of Jesus, by a new and living way opened for us through the curtain, that is, his body" (Heb 10:19b–20). It seems significant that the curtain was woven from blue, red, and purple threads (Exod 26;1): if blue represents heaven and red is the color of humanity (*adamah:* earth; *adom*: red), then purple, as the combination of both colors, would symbolize Jesus's human-divine (and royal) nature. The Most Holy Place was built in the form of a golden cube (1 Kgs 6:20), which symbolizes perfection and the cosmos.[87] The new Jerusalem is also depicted as a golden cube (Rev 21:16–18), signifying the extension of God's presence and sovereignty throughout creation.

God used to meet with his people in the temple. But the New Testament depicted Jesus and his followers as forming the new spiritual temple,[88] and even the furnishings of the ancient tabernacle and later temple seem to be relevant to Jesus.[89] Nicholas Perrin suggests that "Jesus

86. "I will set My tabernacle among you, and My soul shall not abhor you. I will walk among you and be your God, and you shall be My people" (Lev 26:11–12). "'Sing and rejoice, O daughter of Zion! For behold, I am coming and I will dwell in your midst,' says the Lord. 'Many nations shall be joined to the Lord in that day, and they shall become My people. And I will dwell in your midst'" (Zech 2:10–11a).

87. Interestingly, a cross made of six squares forms this important symbol.

88. "[You are] built on the foundation of the apostles and prophets, with Christ Jesus himself as the chief cornerstone. In him the whole building is joined together and rises to become a holy temple in the Lord" (Eph 2:20a). "You also, like living stones, are being built into a spiritual house to be a holy priesthood" (1 Pet 2:5a). "Jesus answered them, 'Destroy this temple, and I will raise it again in three days' . . . But the temple he had spoken of was his body" (John 2:19–21).

89. For example, Jesus is the only gate into God's presence (John 10:7), and there was only one gate into the tabernacle. Believers are purified and saved through his death and Spirit (living water), and the tabernacle contained a sacrificial altar and a laver of water. Jesus came as a servant to be the light of the world, and an eight-branched

of Nazareth saw himself and his movement as nothing less than the decisive embodiment of Yahweh's eschatological temple."[90] Jesus is therefore now the meeting place between God and humanity. N. T. Wright agrees that "Jesus acted and spoke as if he was in some sense called to do and be what the Temple was and did," and he suggests that "God will indeed dwell with his people, allowing his glory and mystery to 'tabernacle' in their midst, but the most appropriate way for him to do this will not be through a building but through a human being."[91] Hence, at the end of John's vision, there is no longer a temple building "because the Lord God Almighty and the Lamb are its temple" (Rev 21:22b).

The Alpha and Omega—God's Work Is Complete

In the Old Testament, Yahweh is called "Lord of Lords" (Deut 10:17) and "First and Last" (Isa 44:6). In Revelation, Jesus is given these same divine titles:[92]

> On his robe and on his thigh he has this name written: king of kings and lord of lords. (Rev 19:16)

> I am the Alpha and the Omega, the First and the Last, the Beginning and the End . . . I, Jesus, have sent my angel to give you this testimony for the churches. I am the Root and the Offspring of David, and the bright Morning Star. (Rev 22:13–16)

Alpha and omega are the first and last Greek letters, which correspond to the Hebrew aleph and tau, and aleph is spelled using the letters aleph, lamed, and peh. These letters are highly symbolic:

- The pictograph for aleph is an ox head, representing authority and power. Its symbol is a unity of three letters: two yods (which

candleholder was always lit in the tabernacle; the special Hanukkah lamp was lit by a ninth candle set on a separate plane from the others and called the *shamash*, which means helper or servant. Jesus is the bread of life (John 6:35), and the tabernacle contained twelve loaves of the bread of God's presence (literally, "Bread of the Face"), which was arranged in two piles, perhaps symbolic of the future Jewish and Gentile followers of Jesus.

90. Perrin, *Jesus the Temple*, 12.

91. Wright, *Challenge of Jesus*, 65, 110.

92. It might be significant that Jesus's Aramaic name, Yehoshua, is similar to YHWH, with the insertion of the Hebrew letter *shin*, which is shaped like three branches of flame that represent spiritual transformation: YH-sh-WH.

represent hand or God) connected by a vav, which means "hook." In esoteric Judaism, the upper yod is said to represent the hidden aspects of God and the lower represents God revealed to humanity.

- Lamed is associated with spiritual learning, and its pictograph is a shepherd's staff.
- Peh represents the power of the spoken word and is associated with holiness and prayer.
- Tau means mark or seal, and its pictograph is two crossed sticks. It symbolizes truth, perfection, and completion.

As the Alpha and Omega (aleph and tau), the returning Jesus will complete God's work. Old Testament predictions of this redemptive work used the standard phrase, "he has done it":

> All the ends of the earth will remember and turn to the Lord, and all the families of the nations will bow down before him . . . They will proclaim his righteousness, declaring to a people yet unborn: He has done it. (Ps 22:27–31 NIV)

> Sing, O heavens, for the Lord has done it! . . . For the Lord has redeemed Jacob, and glorified Himself in Israel. (Isa 44:23)

Jesus prayed to God, "I have brought you glory on earth by finishing the work you gave me to do" (John 17:4), and his dying words on the cross were: "It is finished/done" (John 19:30). Revelation uses this same phrase to teach that Jesus's second coming will usher in the final stage of God's redemptive work:

> He said to me: "It is done. I am the Alpha and the Omega, the Beginning and the End. To the thirsty I will give water without cost from the spring of the water of life." (Rev 21:6)

Overview

Judeo-Christian Scripture from Genesis to Revelation provides a consistent message about God's cosmic plan for humanity from creation, through mankind's rebellion, the formation of Israel, the promise of a future atonement, the drawing in of all nations, and the final redemption of creation:

Genesis—The Fall	Revelation—Final Restoration
God creates heaven and earth (Gen 1:7).	God establishes a new heaven and new earth (Rev 21:1).
God brings a wife to the first Adam (Gen 2:22).	God brings down the new Jerusalem as a bride for the last Adam (Rev 21:1–5).
Humanity defies God: "she took of its fruit and ate" (Gen 3:6b).	Jesus reconciles people to God: "Take, eat; this is My body" (Matt 26:26b).
Humanity hides from God's face (Gen 3:8).	"They will see his face, and his name will be on their foreheads" (Rev 22:4).
Humanity is barred from the tree of life (Gen 3:24).	The tree of life is available for the healing of all nations (Rev 22:2).
The ground is cursed (Gen 3:17).	The curse is lifted (Rev 22:3).
Humanity suffers.	All tears are wiped away (Rev 21:4).
Humanity experiences death.	There is no more death (Rev 21:4).
Humanity is evicted from God's presence (Gen 3:24)	God dwells with humanity (Rev 21:3).

CONCLUSION 7
WHAT LIGHT DOES THE OLD TESTAMENT SHED ON JESUS?

The Old Testament contains scattered but repeated themes that flash like light off the facets of a diamond. These sustained motifs and images include references to unleavened bread, trumpets, living water, sacrifice, atonement, a final covenant, and a perfected creation.[93]

93. Jacob Neusner offers the intriguing suggestion that we should not approach this extensive Scripture using linear, logical analysis because it functions in a fractal way: it describes "how things are, whether large or small, whether here or there, whether today or in a distant past or an unimaginable future. Fractal thinking finds sameness without regard to scale, from small to large—and so too in the case of events.

When Jesus's followers were trying to comprehend his nature and work, they would have found that he was somehow prefigured in these Old Testament themes. Messianic prophecies depicted a highly exalted agent who would suffer vicariously for others and accomplish God's redemptive work. Judaism's seven holy feasts had strong thematic links with Jesus's death, resurrection, and promised return. And Revelation depicts the realization of God's promises of an eternal covenant and a redeemed creation, achieved through Jesus's work. N. T. Wright argues that Jesus understood his actions to be "the fulfilment, not of a few prophetic-texts taken atomistically, but of the entire story-line which Israel had told herself, in a variety of forms, over and over again."[94]

Old and New Testament Scripture therefore forms a coherent and unified whole. And here we face a situation as irrational and "impossible" as any miracle: did Jesus teach his followers that Moses and the prophets wrote about him in the Old Testament because he *really was* the culmination and fulfillment of these ancient prophecies and themes? If this is not the case, then his followers must have enthusiastically tacked these details from the Hebrew Bible onto his memory, as in Burton Mack's myth-making scenario. However, the overall consistency in the New Testament materials argues against this suggestion. And would it really have been feasible to invent details of Jesus's acts, claims, teachings, and death to tie in so well with so many ancient images, prophecies, festival dates, and rituals? The theory of fabrication also does not explain why Jesus's followers were the only messianic group to claim that their leader fulfilled all these ancient themes and promises.

Christianity has been accused of being intolerant of alternative beliefs. But according to its Scripture, Jesus's work *is* the only redemption that God has provided, and his work was foreshadowed throughout the ancient Old Testament.

Fractal thinking therefore makes possible the quest for a few specific patterns, which will serve this and that, hither and yon, because out of acknowledged chaos they isolate points of regularity or recurrence" ("Contexts of Comparison," 57–58).

94. Wright, *Victory*, 130.

Final Overview

Implications of the Findings for Faith and Christianity

THIS BOOK HAS COLLATED and analyzed a wide range of evidence relevant to the debate between atheism and faith. Now that the entire picture has been drawn, it is worth revisiting some major decision points of each investigation.

Investigation	Decisions
1	Was Jesus a historical figure?
2	Was Jesus a human teacher who was only worshiped later outside Palestine?
3	Do existing New Testament gospel manuscripts largely preserve Jesus's most significant acts and teachings?
4	Could Jesus have regarded himself as more than an ordinary man?
	Do gnostic texts provide a more convincing picture of Jesus and his teachings than the New Testament?
	Does the report that Jesus was resurrected fit the relevant facts?
5	Can we be certain that no higher power can intervene in our world and supersede natural laws?

Investigation	Decisions
6	Can we be certain that there is no guiding power behind the arising of the universe and human life?
7	Do the Old and New Testaments form a coherent whole?

What is the implication of the evidence and the answers to these questions? Was Jesus a purely mythological construct, a fantastically embellished historical figure, a deluded megalomaniac, or the unique Son of God? Was Orthodox Christianity a later false development, or does it represent the beliefs of Jesus's first followers, which were the result of his teaching and resurrection? How should we interpret the fact that the New Testament has such extensive connections with the Old Testament? If these connections are not authentic, then this collection of Scripture would be a uniquely brilliant fraud or a spectacularly well-structured exaggeration. But if it records Jesus's life and teachings with any fidelity, then it is evidence of a Creator who desires to be known and who is implementing a far-reaching cosmic plan with profound implications for humanity.

We can choose to reject the Christian message of human rebellion and Jesus's atoning work, but it is important to be clear about our motives. For example, when atheist journalist Josh McDowell gathered evidence with the aim of discrediting Christianity, he came to realize that he was avoiding the implications of his findings:

> [I tried] to refute the overwhelming evidence I was accumulating that Jesus Christ was God's Son. I began to realize that I was being intellectually dishonest. My mind told me that the claims of Christ were indeed true, but my will was being pulled in another direction. I had placed so much emphasis on finding the truth, but I wasn't willing to follow it once I saw it . . . Becoming a Christian seemed so ego-shattering to me. I couldn't think of a faster way to ruin all my good times.[1]

But Christianity is not about throwing out rock music, adopting a pious attitude, and rejecting old friends, nor is it about blindly repeating a creed, learning to speak "Christianese," and pretending to love

1. McDowell, *New Evidence*, xxv.

everyone—it is simply about choosing a relationship with God through his Son, which McDowell finally did.[2]

Philosopher John C. Wright, who rejected the concepts of God and the supernatural, was also troubled by the implications of his logical analysis, and he shares the unexpected and dramatic result of his skeptical prayer to a non-existent God:

> Each time I followed the argument fearlessly where it led, it kept leading me, one remorseless rational step at a time, to a position the Church had been maintaining for more than a thousand years. That haunted me . . . But it was impossible, logically impossible, that I should ever believe in such nonsense as to believe in the supernatural. It would be a miracle to get me to believe in miracles. So I prayed. "Dear God, I know (because I can prove it with the certainty that a geometer can prove opposite angles are equal) that you do not exist. Nonetheless, as a scholar, I am forced to entertain the hypothetical possibility that I am mistaken. So just in case I am mistaken, please reveal yourself to me in some fashion that will prove your case . . . If you do not exist, this prayer is merely words in the air, and I lose nothing but a bit of my dignity. Thanking you in advance for your kind cooperation in this matter, John Wright."

John quips that God must have a sense of humor because he had a heart attack two days later. He describes his profound experiences while awaiting surgery in hospital:

> A sense of peace and confidence, a peace that passes all understanding, like a field of energy entered my body. I grew aware of a spiritual dimension of reality of which I had hitherto been unaware. It was like a man born blind suddenly receiving sight. The Truth to which my lifetime as a philosopher had been devoted turned out to be a living thing. It turned and looked at me. Something from beyond the reach of time and space, more fundamental than reality, reached across the universe and broke into my soul and changed me . . . I became aware of the origin of all thought, the underlying oneness of the universe, the nature of time: the paradox of determinism and free will was resolved for me. I saw and experienced part of the workings of a mind

2. Christian love is not an emotion but a deliberate attitude of compassion. Theologian Karl Barth described Christian love for one's fellow man in this frank way: "Love cannot alter the fact that he gets on my nerves . . . [but] the Christian cannot become an antagonist of his neighbour . . . The man who loves does not compile a dossier against his neighbour" (*Doctrine of Reconciliation*, 834).

> infinitely superior to mine, a mind able to count every atom in the universe, filled with paternal love and jovial good humor.[3]

John joined the church in 2008.

God issued an invitation through the Old Testament:

> And you will seek Me and find Me, when you search for Me with all your heart. (Jer 29:13)

Jesus repeats this offer in the New Testament:

> Here I am! I stand at the door and knock. If anyone hears my voice and opens the door, I will come in and eat with that person, and they with me. (Rev 3:20)

> Anyone who loves me will obey my teaching. My Father will love them, and we will come to them and make our home with them. (John 14:23)

If there is any truth in Judeo-Christian Scripture, it contains the most important question in anyone's life:

> "But what about you? Who do you say I am?"

3. These extracts are reproduced here with John's kind permission. His account is available in full at https://strangenotions.com/wright-conversion/. Buddhist Nilus Stryker shares his own unusual spiritual experience when every night for a week, a voice in his consciousness kept saying, "I miss Jesus." He finally asked, "Who are you?" and he experienced a profound impression of Divine Love and Light entering him, which could not be explained from his Buddhist background. Stryker writes movingly about his conversion to Christianity and his experience of a spiritual presence that he calls "A Light That Is Not Light That Knows My Name." http://journeytoorthodoxy.com/2010/07/through-the-eastern-gate-nilus-stryker/.

Appendix 1

Personal Accounts of the Unusual

There is nothing more convincing than personal experience. My exposure to the unusual is by no means earth-shattering, and books about miracles contain far more dramatic stories. But these few events in my life and the lives of those close to me seem strongly out of the ordinary. I humbly offer them as possible evidence that not every event can be scientifically explained.

PROTECTED BY WINGS?

Armed men burst into a friend's kitchen while the family was eating dinner, and they shot her husband. (Tragically, he passed away after a lengthy period in intensive care.) The intruders were extremely agitated and aggressive and continually threatened to rape and kill my friend and her teenage daughter. Her daughter slid beneath the kitchen table and was praying intensely, although I don't think she was religious in a conventional way.

While my friend was being manhandled into different rooms, her daughter suddenly felt enveloped by something soft and feathery and was flooded with a deep sense of peace. Her mother later spoke about how the atmosphere of the house changed—the intruders calmed down and even apologized for harming her husband. After collecting a few items, they told the two women to remain on the floor and they left the house. Both women were convinced that some supernatural presence had responded to desperate prayers that night. This verse from the psalms comes to mind: "He shall cover you with His feathers, and under His wings you shall take refuge" (Ps 91:4a).

AN ASTOUNDING RECOVERY

My cousin's two daughters and husband were involved in a devastating head-on collision that impacted the driver's side, instantly killing her husband. The younger daughter was in the seat behind her father and experienced horrific damage: the impact shattered her left leg and damaged her head, breaking four vertebrae of her neck. The doctor who operated on her stated later that throughout the surgery, he wondered why he was bothering, as she had such a slim chance of surviving, and even if she did, she was sure to be severely brain-damaged, and he knew she would never walk again. Her family prayer group was informed and there was an intense time of prayer.

The young girl did survive the operation. During the early days in rehabilitation, her mother would recite their favorite poem about an angel who stands at the foot of each child's bed. One afternoon when she reached the familiar line about the angel, as soon as she said "He . . . ," her daughter spoke for one of the first times, shouting out, "It's a she! It's a she!" Although the young girl no longer remembers this recovery period, it would seem she had a vivid impression of a female angelic presence. She made a complete recovery—even the doctors called her their miracle girl.

RELEASED FROM PAIN

A few years ago I started to suffer from agonizing cramps. It would strike at any time, and there would be no way I could stretch my foot that would ease the excruciating pain. Every attack was an anguishing experience—it felt as though sawing the foot off could not be worse. One night, when the muscles in my foot started to pull, I mentally called out in dread for God to help me because I knew that what was coming would be unbearable. I had absolutely no expectation of relief—I was just desperate.

Immediately, I felt a warm sensation on the top of my foot and to my total amazement, the impossible happened—the muscles relaxed and the excruciating cramp that always followed the tensing did not happen. I don't think it could have been my mind controlling my muscles as I was in a state of total panic and did not feel at all calm, or in control, or confident of avoiding the coming pain. Since then, I still have had many incipient cramping incidents, but each time I mentally reach out to God for help and the tingling, pulling, threatening sensation fades away.

FREED FROM ADDICTION

A close friend was a long-time user of heroin which severely impacted her health. She was desperate to give up the habit, but each time she tried, the pain was so intense and unremitting that she would be forced to take the drug again. She finally prayed in desperation for God to take away the pain so that she could detoxify and break the habit. Immediately after that prayer, she went "cold turkey" with no pain at all and is still drug-free.

A PHYSICAL CHANGE

A relative by marriage recently got a tattoo of an impressive, rampant dragon with a roaring head that reached up the back of her neck, clearly visible above her collar. Soon afterward, she became concerned about the impression this might give others about her Christian faith, but she could not afford to have it removed or altered. Instead, she asked God to take care of her problem.

A few months later, a friend pointed out that the tattoo had changed! They called me over and I took a photograph. What I had seen as a dragon head raised above wings was completely transformed into a smaller, peculiar, bound creature that did not show above the collar line (figure 14). If I was told this story, I would not believe it. But if a miracle is an event that does not conform to physical laws, this is a documented miracle.

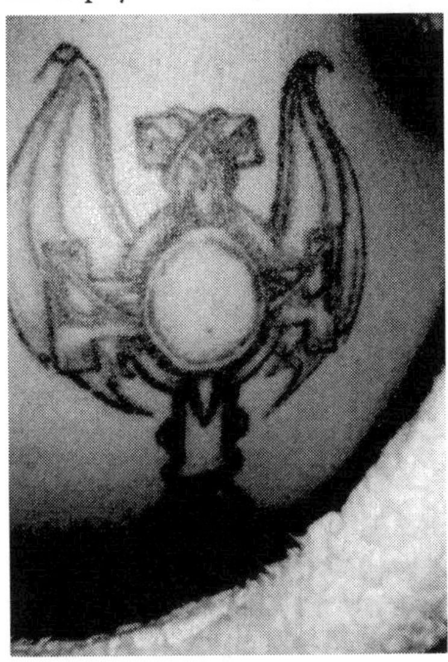

Figure 14: A transformed tattoo.

Appendix 2

Archaeological Confirmation of Biblical Events

ARCHAEOLOGY CONTINUES TO CONFIRM events recorded in the Old Testament, as is illustrated by these examples.

EXISTENCE OF HITTITES

The biblical tribe of Hittites (Gen 23:16; 2 Sam 11:2–4) used to be regarded as fictitious. But in the early twentieth century, archaeologists discovered the ruins of the ancient Hittite capital (present-day Boghazkoy), which contained written records from the second millennium BC.

DESTRUCTION OF SODOM AND GOMORRAH

According to Genesis, "the Valley of Siddim was full of tar pits" (Gen 14:10) and Sodom and Gomorrah were destroyed by a rain of burning sulfur (Gen 19:24). Geological evidence now indicates that these two cities (and Jericho) lay along a major fault line and were destroyed by earthquakes and volcanic activity involving bitumen, natural gas, and sulfur.[1]

1. See Neev and Emery, *The Destruction of Sodom, Gomorrah, and Jericho: Geological, Climatological, and Archaeological Background*; Harris and Beardow, "The Destruction of Sodom and Gomorrah: A Geotechnical Perspective."

INVASION OF PALESTINE BY PHARAOH SHESHONK I

The Bible records the invasion of Palestine by the Egyptian Shishak in the reign of King Rehoboam, around 925 BC (1 Kgs 11:40; 14:25–26; 2 Chron 12:2–9). Some scholars identify this leader with Pharaoh Sheshonk I.[2] A relief in the Egyptian Amun-Re temple complex contains a list of conquered towns, including the Palestinian cities of Arad, Beth-Horon, Beth-Shean, Gibeon, Mahanaim, Megiddo, and Rehob.

REBELLION OF THE MOABITE KING MESHA AGAINST ISRAEL

According to Scripture, King Mesha of Moab paid tribute to Israel but rebelled after the death of Ahab, the son of Omri (2 Kgs 3:4–6). The Mesha Stele (Moabite Stone) confirms this report: "I am Mesha . . . Omri was king of Israel, and oppressed Moab during many days . . . And Chemosh said to me, Go take Nebo [Moab] against Israel, and I went in the night and I fought against it from the break of day till noon, and I took it . . . and I took from it the vessels of Jehovah."[3]

EARTHQUAKE DURING THE REIGN OF KING UZZIAH

Amos 1:1 recorded an earthquake during Uzziah's reign (ca. 783–42 BC). Geologists have found evidence of a major earthquake around 750 BC, with its epicenter north of Israel.[4]

THE SIEGE OF JERUSALEM BY ASSYRIAN KING SENNACHERIB

Scripture records Sennacherib's campaign against Israel and Judah in the time of King Hezekiah (2 Kgs 18:13–15; 2 Chron 32:9–10). These events are confirmed in the Sennacherib Annals (Taylor Prism, col. 3): "As for Hezekiah the Judahite, who did not submit to my yoke: forty-six of his strong, walled cities . . . I besieged and took them . . . Himself, like

2. See Sagrillo, "Shoshenq I and biblical Šîšaq."
3. Taken from the translation by James King.
4. See Austin et al., "Amos's Earthquake."

a caged bird I shut up in Jerusalem, his royal city."[5] Second Chronicles 32:9fnames Lachish as one of the besieged cities, and a relief from Sennacherib's palace at Nineveh reads, "Sennacherib King of the Universe, King of Assyria, sits on a throne and the spoils of Lachish are paraded before him." Scripture also records that Sennacherib's son Esarhaddon reigned after his murder (2 Kgs 19:37; Isa 37:38), which has been confirmed by the Prism of Sennacherib.

EXISTENCE OF TWO MINISTERS

The book of Jeremiah names two royal ministers of the sixth century: Jehukal, son of Shelemiah, and Gedaliah, son of Pashhur (Jer 38:1). On the site of ancient Jerusalem, archaeologist Eilat Mazar has discovered two clay seal impressions dated to the sixth century that are inscribed, "Yehuchal ben Shelemyahu," and "Gedalyahu ben Pashur."

NEBUCHADNEZZAR'S CONQUEST OF JUDAH

The Babylonian Chronicles confirm the report in the book of Jeremiah that King Nebuchadnezzar II of Babylon defeated Egypt at the Battle of Carchemish[6] and conquered the city of Hamath.[7] According to Scripture, when King Jehoiachin would not pay tribute, Nebuchadnezzar took him captive to Babylon and replaced him with his uncle, which is also confirmed by the Babylonian Chronicles.[8]

Jeremiah recorded that Nebuchadnezzar "fought against Jerusalem and all the cities of Judah that were left, against Lachish and Azekah; for only these fortified cities remained of the cities of Judah" (Jer 34:7). At the site of Lachish, letters on pottery shards have been found, one of which (Letter 4) is addressed to an officer and contains these chilling words of concern: "May (my lord) be apprised that we are watching for the fire signals of Lachish according to all the signs which my lord has given, because we cannot see Azeqah."[9] Lachish was destroyed around 586 BC and its inhabitants taken captive to Babylon.

5. Translation by Daniel D. Luckenbill (*Annals of Sennacherib*).
6. See Babylonian Chronicles Obverse 1–4; Jer 46:2.
7. See Babylonian Chronicles Obverse 5–8; Jer 49:23.
8. See Babylonian Chronicles Reverse 11–13; 2 Kgs 24:8–17.
9. See Aḥituv, *Echoes from the Past*, 70.

KING CYRUS'S RELEASE OF JEWISH CAPTIVES

According to the Old Testament, after Cyrus the Great conquered Babylon, he permitted exiled Jews to return to Jerusalem and rebuild the temple (2 Chron 36:23; Ezra 1). This is consistent with the sixth-century clay Cyrus Cylinder, which reports Cyrus's policy of allowing captives to return home to reconstruct their religious buildings.

As Theodor Seidl notes, "Even highly marked theological texts such as Isaiah 10, Jeremiah 46 and 2 Chronicles 35 betray a certain connection to the Ancient Near Eastern politics and political affairs. The various proper names and dates in the texts are not fictitious, but are confirmed by non-biblical sources, at least in part."[10]

10. Seidl, "Carchemish," 658.

Bibliography

WORKS OF ANTIQUITY

Cassius Dio. *Roman History*. Vol. 4. Translated by Herbert Baldwin Foster. Troy, NY: Pafraets, 1905.

Celsus, A. Cornelius. *Of Medicine*. Translated by James Greive. London: Wilson and Durham, 1756.

Diodorus Siculus. *Library of History*. Vol 2 of *Diodorus of Sicily*, translated by C. H. Oldfather. London: Heinemann, 1967.

Josephus, Flavius. *The Works of Flavius Josephus*. Translated by William Whiston. Auburn, NY: Beardsley, 1895.

Lucian of Samosata. *Alexander: Or the False Prophet*. In *Translations from Lucian*, translated by Augusta M. Campbell Davidson, 172–206. London: Longmans and Green, 1902.

Pausanias. *Description of Greece*. Translated by W. H. S. Jones. London: Heinemann, 1918.

Philostratus. *The Life of Apollonius of Tyana*, 2 vols. Translated by F. C. Conybeare. London: Heinemann, 1912.

Pliny. *The Letters of the Younger Pliny*. Translated by John Delaware Lewis. London: Trübner, 1879.

Suetonius Tranquillus. *The Lives of the Twelve Caesars: To Which are Added His Lives of the Grammarians, Rhetoricians, and Poets*. Translated by Alexander Thomson. Revised by Thomas Forester. London: Bell, 1896.

Tacitus. *The Annals and the Histories*. Translated by Alfred John Church and William Jackson Brodribb. Edited by Moses Hadas. New York: Modern Library, 2003.

Wright, Wilmer C., trans. *The Works of the Emperor Julian*. Vol. 3. Loeb Classical Library 157. Cambridge, MA: Harvard University Press, 1913.

Yonge, Charles Duke. *The Works of Philo Judaeus, the Contemporary of Josephus, Translated From the Greek*. London: Bohn, 1854–1855.

WORKS OF JUDAISM

Epstein, Rabbi Dr I, ed. *Contents of the Soncino Babylonian Talmud*. Translated by Jacob Schachter et al. London: Soncino, 1935–1948.

Etheridge, J. W. *The Targums of Onkelos and Jonathan Ben Uzziel on the Pentateuch with the Fragments of the Jerusalem Targum from the Chaldee*. London: Longmans, 1862.

Pauli, C. W. H. *The Chaldee Paraphrase: The Prophet Isaiah*. London: London Society's House, 1871.

GENERAL WORKS

Abbot, Edwin A. *Flatland: A Romance of Many Dimensions*. New York: Dover, 1992.

Abegg Martin Jr., et al. *The Dead Sea Scrolls Bible: The Oldest Known Bible Translated for the First Time into English*. New York: HarperCollins, 1999.

Acocella, Joan. "The Typing Life." *The New Yorker*, April 9, 2007. https://www.newyorker.com/magazine/2007/04/09/the-typing-life.

Aḥituv, Shmuel. *Echoes from the Past: Hebrew and Cognate Inscriptions from the Biblical Period*. Jerusalem: Carta, 2008.

Allen, James P, trans. *The Ancient Egyptian Pyramid Texts*. Edited by Peter Der Manuelian. Writings from the Ancient World 23. Atlanta: Society of Biblical Literature, 2005.

Armstrong, Karen. *The Case for God*. London, Vintage, 2010.

Arnold, Bill T., and David B. Weisberg. "A Centennial Review of Friedrich Delitzsch's 'Babel Und Bibel' Lectures." *Journal of Biblical Literature* 121 (2002) 441–57.

Austin, Steven A., et al. "Amos's Earthquake: An Extraordinary Middle East Seismic Event of 750 B.C." *International Geology Review* 42 (2000) 657–71.

Baguñà, Jaume, and Jordi García-Fernàndez. "Evo-Devo: The Long and Winding Road." *The International Journal of Developmental Biology* 47 (2003) 705–13.

Bailey, Kenneth E. "Informal Controlled Oral Tradition and the Synoptic Gospels." *Themelios* 20 (1995) 4–11.

———. *Jesus through Middle Eastern Eyes: Cultural Studies in the Gospels*. Downers Grove, IL: InterVarsity, 2008.

Bale, John. *The Pageant of Popes*. Translated by I. Studley. London: Thomas Marshe, 1574.

Ball, Warwick. *Rome in the East: The Transformation of an Empire*. London: Routledge, 2001.

Barber, Richard. *The Holy Grail: Imagination and Belief*. Cambridge, MA: Harvard University Press, 2004.

Barnes, Luke A. "The Fine-Tuning of the Universe for Intelligent Life." *History and Philosophy of Physics* (2011) 1–76.

Barr, James. "Theophany and Anthropomorphism in the Old Testament." *Supplements to Vetus Testamentum* 7 (1960) 31–38.

Barth, Karl. *The Doctrine of Reconciliation*, part 2. Vol. 4 of *Church Dogmatics*. Translated by G. W. Bromley, edited by G. W. Bromley, and T. F. Torrance. 1956. Reprint, Peabody, MA: Hendrickson, 2010.

Basser, Herbert W. "The Gospels and Rabbinic Halakah." In *The Missing Jesus: Rabbinic Judaism and the New Testament*, edited by Bruce Chilton et al., 77–100. Boston: Brill, 2002.

Bauckham, Richard. *Jesus and the God of Israel*. Grand Rapids, MI: Eerdmans, 2009.

Bauer, Walter. *Orthodoxy and Heresy in Earliest Christianity*. Translated by Paul J. Achtemeier. Edited by Robert A. Kraft and Gerhard Krodel. 1934. Reprint, Philadelphia: Fortress, 1971.

Beale, Gregory K. *A New Testament Biblical Theology: The Unfolding of the Old Testament in the New*. Grand Rapids, MI: Baker, 2011.

Beck, Roger. "Merkelbach's Mithras." *Phoenix* 41 (1987) 296–316.

Bellamy, James A. "Textual Criticism of the Koran." *Journal of the American Oriental Society* 121 (2001) 1–6.

Bergeron, Joseph, and Gary R. Habermas. "The Resurrection of Jesus: A Clinical Review of Psychiatric Hypotheses for the Biblical Story of Easter." *Irish Theological Quarterly* 80 (2015) 157–72.

Beskow, Per Erik. "Branding in the Mysteries of Mithras." In *Mysteria Mithrae: Proceedings of the International Seminar on the "Religio-historical Character of Roman Mithraism, with Particular Reference to Roman and Ostian Sources,"* edited by Ugo Bianchi, 487–501. Leyden: Brill, 1979.

Bieberich, Erhard. "Recurrent Fractal Neural Networks: A Strategy for the Exchange of Local and Global Information Processing in the Brain." *Biosystems* 66 (2002) 145–64.

Bird, Michael F. *Jesus the Eternal Son: Answering Adoptionist Christology*. Grand Rapids, MI: Eerdmans, 2017.

Birdsall, J. Neville. "Review of *Orthodox Corruption*, by Bart Ehrman." *Theology* 97 (1994) 460–62.

Black, Matthew. "Aramaic Barnāshā and the 'Son of Man.'" *Expository Times* 95 (1984) 200–206.

Blomberg, Craig L. *The Historical Reliability of John's Gospel: Issues and Commentary*. Downers Grove, IL: InterVarsity, 2002.

———. *Interpreting the Parables*. Downers Grove, IL: InterVarsity, 1990.

———. *Jesus and the Gospels: An Introduction and Survey*. 2nd ed. Nashville, TN: B. and H., 2009.

Bock, Darrell L. "Blasphemy and the Jewish Examination of Jesus." *Bulletin for Biblical Research* 17 (2007) 53–114.

Bohm, David. *Wholeness and the Implicate Order*. London: Routledge and Kegan Paul, 1980.

Bond, Helen K. *Pontius Pilate in History and Interpretation*. SNTSMS 100. Cambridge: Cambridge University Press, 2004.

Borde, Arvind, and Alexander Vilenkin. "Eternal Inflation and the Initial Singularity." *PRL* 72 (1994) 3305–309.

Boring, M. Eugene. *Mark: A Commentary*. London: Westminster John Knox, 2006.

Born, Irene, trans. *The Born Einstein Letters*. London: Macmillan, 1971.

Borsch, Frederick. H. "Further Reflections on 'The Son of Man': The Origins and Development of the Title." In *The Messiah: Developments in Earliest Judaism and Christianity; The First Princeton Symposium on Judaism and Christian Origins*, edited by James H. Charlesworth et al., 130–44. Minneapolis: Fortress, 1992.

Bousset, Wilhelm. *What is Religion*? Translated by F. B. Low. London: Putnams, 1907.

Bowersock, G. W. *Hellenism in Late Antiquity*. Jerome Lectures 18. Ann Arbor: University of Michigan Press, 1990.

Boyarin, Daniel. *The Jewish Gospels: The Story of the Jewish Christ*. New York: New Press, 2012.

———. *A Radical Jew: Paul and the Politics of Identity*. Berkeley: University of California Press, 1997.

Bremmer, Jan N. "Attis: a Greek God in Anatolian Pessinous and Catullan Rome." *Mnemosyne, A Journal of Classical Studies* 4 (2004) 534–73.

Brown, Dan. *The Da Vinci Code: A Novel*. New York: Doubleday, 2003.

Brown, Raymond E. *The Semitic Background of the Term "Mystery."* Facet Biblical Series 21. Philadelphia: Fortress, 1968.

Brubaker, Daniel Alan. *Corrections in Early Qur'ān Manuscripts: Twenty Examples*. Lovettsville, VA: Think and Tell, 2019.

Bruce, F. F. "The Background to the Son of Man Sayings." In *Christ The Lord: Studies in Christology presented to Donald Guthrie*, edited by H. H. Rowdon, 50–70. Leicester: InterVarsity, 1982.

———. *Paul: Apostle of the Heart Set Free*. Grand Rapids, MI: Paternoster, 2000.

Brunner, Emil. *The Christian Doctrine of God*. Vol. 1 of *Dogmatics*. Translated by Olive Wyon. London: Lutterworth, 1949.

———. *The Mediator: A Study of the Central Doctrine of the Christian Faith*. Translated by Olive Wyon. London: Lutterworth, 1959.

Budge, E. A. Wallis. *Legends of the Gods*. London: Kegan Paul, 1912.

Bultmann, Rudolf. "Is Exegesis without Presuppositions Possible?" In *Existence and Faith: Shorter Writings of Rudolf Bultmann*, translated by Schubert M. Ogden, 291–92. Cleveland: Meridian, 1960.

Byrskog, Samuel. *Story as History, History as Story: The Gospel Tradition in the Context of Ancient Oral History*. WUNT 123. Tübingen: Mohr Siebeck, 2000.

Carey, George. *The Great God Robbery*. London: Fount, 1989.

Castro, Carlos. "Fractal Strings as the Basis of Cantorian-Fractal Spacetime and the Fine Structure Constant." *Chaos, Solitons, and Fractals* 14 (2002) 1341–351.

Chalupa, Aleš. "The Origins of the Roman Cult of Mithras in the Light of New Evidence and Interpretations: The Current State of Affairs." *Religio Revue pro Religionistiku* 24 (2016) 65–96.

Chancey, Mark A. *The Myth of a Gentile Galilee*. SNTSMS 118. Cambridge: Cambridge University Press, 2002.

Charlesworth, James H. "From Messianology to Christology: Problems and Prospects." In *The Messiah: Developments in Earliest Judaism and Christianity; The First Princeton Symposium on Judaism and Christian Origins*, edited by James H. Charlesworth et al., 3–35. Minneapolis: Fortress, 1992.

Chester, Andrew. *Messiah and Exaltation: Jewish Messianic and Visionary Traditions and New Testament Christology*. WUNT 207. Tübingen: Mohr Siebeck, 2007.

Chilton, Bruce D. *The Glory of Israel: The Theology and Provenience of the Isaiah Targum*. Journal for the Study of the Old Testament Supplement Series 23. Sheffield: Journal for the Study of the Old Testament, 1983.

Clauss, Manfred. *The Roman Cult of Mithras: The God and his Mysteries*. Translated by Richard Gordon. 1903. Reprint, New York: Routledge, 2001.

Collins, Adela Yarbro. "The Charge of Blasphemy in Mark 14:64." *JSNT* 26 (2004) 379–401.

Collins, John J. *The Scepter and the Star: The Messiahs of the Dead Sea Scrolls and Other Ancient Literature.* New York: Doubleday, 1995.

Conway Morris, Simon. *The Runes of Evolution: How the Universe Became Self-Aware.* West Conshohocken, PA: Templeton, 2005.

Cotter, Wendy. "Greco-Roman Apotheosis Traditions and the Resurrection Appearances in Matthew." In *The Gospel of Matthew in Current Study: Studies in Memory of William G. Thompson, S. J.*, edited by David E. Aune, 127–53. Grand Rapids, MI: Eerdmans, 2001.

Cross, Frank Moore. "Fragments of the Prayer of Nabonidus." *Israel Exploration Journal* 34 (1984) 260–64.

Cumont, Franz. *The Mysteries of Mithras.* Translated by Thomas J. McCormack. Chicago: Open Court, 1903.

Dahia, F., and C. Romero. "The Embedding of the Spacetime in Five Dimensions: An Extension of Campbell-Magaard Theorem." *International Journal of Modern Physics* 17 (2002) 4287–295.

Dahl, Nils H. "Messianic Ideas and the Crucifixion of Jesus." In *The Messiah: Developments in Earliest Judaism and Christianity; The First Princeton Symposium on Judaism and Christian Origins*, edited by James H. Charlesworth et al., 382–403. Minneapolis: Fortress, 1992.

Daniélou, Jean. *The Theology of Jewish Christianity.* Vol 1 of *The Development of Christian Doctrine before the Council of Nicaea.* Translated and edited by John A. Baker. Chicago: Regnery, 1964.

Davies, Paul. *The Cosmic Blueprint: New Discoveries in Nature's Creative Ability to Order the Universe.* New York: Simon and Schuster, 1988.

———. *The Goldilocks Enigma: Why is the Universe Just Right for Life?* London: Penguin, 2007.

———. *The Mind of God: Science and the Search for Ultimate Meaning.* London: Penguin, 1992.

Davies, Paul, and John Gribbin. *The Matter Myth.* London: Penguin, 1992.

Davies, W. D. *Paul and Rabbinic Judaism: Some Rabbinic Elements in Pauline Theology.* 4th ed. Philadelphia: Fortress, 1980.

Dawkins, Richard. *The Blind Watchmaker: Why the Evidence of Evolution Reveals a Universe Without Design.* New York: Norton, 1987.

———. *Climbing Mount Improbable.* Penguin: London, 1996.

———. *The God Delusion.* New York: Mariner, 2008.

———. *The Selfish Gene.* Oxford: Oxford University Press, 1989.

Decker, Rodney. "The Bauer Thesis: An Overview." In *Orthodoxy and Heresy in Early Christian Contexts: Reconsidering the Bauer Thesis*, edited by Paul A. Hartog, 6–33. Eugene, OR: Wipf and Stock, 2015.

de Duve, Christian. "The Beginnings of Life on Earth." *American Scientist* 83 (1995) 428–37.

Dempster, Stephen G. *Dominion and Dynasty: A Biblical Theology of the Hebrew Bible.* New Studies in Bible Theology 15. Downers Grove, IL: InterVarsity, 2003.

Derrett, J. Duncan M. *Law in the New Testament.* 1970. Reprint, Eugene, OR: Wipf and Stock, 2005.

Doriani, Daniel. "The Deity of Christ in the Synoptic Gospels." *JETS* 37 (1994) 333–50.

Douady, S., and Y. Couder. "Phyllotaxis as a Dynamical Self Organizing Process: Part 1 The Spiral Modes Resulting from Time-Periodic Iterations." *Journal of Theoretic Biology* 178 (1996) 255–74.

———. "Phyllotaxis as a Physical Self-organized Growth Process." *PRL* 68 (1992) 2098–2101.

Drews, Arthur. *The Christ Myth.* 3rd ed. Translated by C. Delisle Burns. London: Fisher Unwin, 1911.

Driver, Samuel Rolles, and Adolf Neubauer, trans. *The Fifty-third Chapter of Isaiah According to the Jewish Interpreters.* London: James Parker, 1877.

Dunn, James D. G. *Jesus Remembered.* Vol 1 of *Christianity in the Making.* Grand Rapids, MI: Eerdmans, 2003.

———. "Messianic Ideas and Their Influence on the Jesus of History." In *The Messiah: Developments in Earliest Judaism and Christianity; The First Princeton Symposium on Judaism and Christian Origins*, edited by James H. Charlesworth et al., 365–81. Minneapolis: Fortress, 1992.

Dupuis, Charles François. *The Origin of All Religious Worship.* 1795. English translation, New Orleans, 1872.

Durant, Will. *Our Oriental Heritage.* Vol. 1 of *The Story of Civilization.* New York: Simon and Schuster, 1954.

Durant, Will, and Ariel Durant. *Caesar and Christ: A History of Roman Civilization and of Christianity from their Beginnings to AD 325.* Vol. 3 of *The Story of Civilization.* New York: Simon and Schuster, 1944.

Duthoy, Robert. *The Taurobolium: Its Evolution and Terminology.* EPROER 10. Leiden: Brill, 1969.

Dyson, Freeman J. *Disturbing the Universe.* New York: Harper and Row, 1979.

Easton, Burton Scott. *Christ in the Gospels.* New York: Scribner, 1930.

Eberlin, Marcos. *Foresight: How the Chemistry of Life Reveals Planning and Purpose.* Seattle: Discovery Institute, 2019.

Eddington, Arthur Stanley. *The Nature of the Physical World.* Cambridge: Cambridge University Press, 1929.

Eddy, Paul Rhodes, and Gregory A. Boyd. *The Jesus Legend: A Case for the Historical Reliability of the Synoptic Gospels.* Grand Rapids, MI: Baker, 2007.

Edersheim, Alfred. *The Life and Times of Jesus the Messiah.* Peabody, MA: Hendrickson, 2009.

Ehrman, Bart D., ed. and trans. *The Apostolic Fathers.* Vol. 1. Loeb Classical Library 24. 2nd ed. London: Harvard University Press, 2005.

———. *Did Jesus Exist? The Historical Argument for Jesus of Nazareth.* New York: HarperCollins, 2013.

———. *How Jesus Became God: The Exaltation of a Jewish Preacher from Galilee.* New York: HarperOne, 2014.

———. *Jesus, Apocalyptic Prophet of the New Millennium.* New York: Oxford University Press, 1999.

———. *Misquoting Jesus: The Story Behind Who Changed the Bible and Why.* New York: HarperCollins, 2005.

———. *The New Testament: A Historical Introduction to the Early Christian Writings.* New York: Oxford University Press, 1997.

———. *The Orthodox Corruption of Scripture: The Effect of Early Christological Controversies on the Text of the New Testament.* 2nd ed. New York: Oxford University Press, 2011.

———. *Truth and Fiction in the Da Vinci Code: A Historian Reveals What We Really Know about Jesus, Mary Magdalene, and Constantine.* New York: Oxford University Press, 2004.

Einstein, Albert, and Leopold Infeld. *The Evolution of Physics: The Growth of Ideas from Early Concepts to Relativity and Quanta.* London: Cambridge University Press, 1938.

Eisenman, Robert, and Michael Wise. *The Dead Sea Scrolls Uncovered: The First Complete Translation and Interpretation of 50 Key Documents Withheld for Over 35 Years.* New York: Penguin, 1993.

Ellis, E. Earle. "Reading the Gospels as History." *Criswell Theological Review* 3 (1988) 3–15.

Ellis, George F. R. "The Evolving Block Universe and the Meshing Together of Times." *Annals of the New York Academy of Sciences* 1326 (2014) 26–41.

Ellis, George F. R., et al. "Multiverses and Physical Cosmology." *Monthly Notices of the Royal Astronomical Society* 347 (2004) 921–36.

Endsjø, Dag Øistein. *Greek Resurrection Beliefs and the Success of Christianity.* New York: Macmillan, 2009.

Erwin, Douglas H. "Macroevolution is More Than Repeated Rounds of Microevolution." *Evolution and Development* 2 (2000) 78–84.

Eve, Eric. *Behind the Gospels: Understanding the Oral Tradition.* Minneapolis: Fortress, 2014.

Farrer, A. M. "On Dispensing with Q." In *Studies in the Gospels: Essays in Memory of R. H. Lightfoot,* edited by D. E. Nineham, 55–88. Oxford: Blackwell, 1955.

Fee, Gordon D. *Pauline Christology: An Exegetical-Theological Study.* Grand Rapids, MI: Baker, 2007.

———. "Review of *The Orthodox Corruption of Scripture*, by Bart D. Ehrman." *Critical Review of Books in Religion* 8 (1995) 203–206.

Feinberg, John S. *The Many Faces of Evil: Theological Systems and the Problems of Evil.* Wheaton, IL: Crossway, 2004.

Ferrini, Paul. *Reflections of the Christ Mind.* New York: Doubleday, 2000.

Feynman, Richard P. *QED: The Strange Theory of Light and Matter.* Princeton: Princeton University Press, 1985.

Fitzmyer, Joseph A. "The Aramaic Language and the Study of the New Testament." *Journal of Biblical Literature* 99 (1980) 5–21.

Fletcher-Louis, Crispin. *Jesus Monotheism.* Vol. 1 of *Christological Origins: The Emergence Consensus and Beyond.* Eugene, OR: Cascade, 2015.

Flew, Antony, and Roy Abraham Varghese. *There Is a God: How the World's Most Notorious Atheist Changed His Mind.* New York: Harper Collins, 2007.

Forster, Roger, and Paul Marston. *Reason, Science, and Faith.* Crowborough, Sussex: Monarch, 1999.

France, Richard T. "The Worship of Jesus: A Neglected Factor in Christological Debate?" *Vox Evangelica* 12 (1981) 19–33.

Francis, James A. "Truthful Fiction: New Questions to Old Answers on Philostratus' Life of Apollonius." *American Journal of Philology* 119 (1998) 419–41.

Funk, Robert W., et al. *The Five Gospels: What Did Jesus Really Say? The Search for the Authentic Words of Jesus.* New York: Macmillan, 1993.

Galison, Peter Loius. *Minkowski's Space-Time: From Visual Thinking to the Absolute World.* In *Historical Studies in the Physical Sciences* 10, edited by Lewis Pyenson, 85–121. Berkeley, CA: California University Press, 1979.

Gamow, George. *One, Two, Three—Infinity: Facts and Speculations of Science.* New York: Dover, 1988.

García Martínez, Florentino, and Eibert J. C. Tigchelaar, eds. *The Dead Sea Scrolls Study Edition.* Leiden: Brill, 1999.

Gasparro, G. Sfameni. *Soteriology: Mystic Aspects in the Cult of Cybele and Attis.* EPROER 103. Leiden: Brill, 1985.

Gentry, Peter J. "The Septuagint and the Text of the Old Testament." *Bulletin for Biblical Research* 16 (2006) 193–218.

Gerdmar, Anders. *Roots of Theological Anti-Semitism: German Biblical Interpretation and the Jews, from Herder and Semler to Kittel and Bultmann.* Studies in Jewish History and Culture 20. Leiden: Brill, 2009.

Gerhardsson, Birger. *Memory and Manuscript: Oral Tradition and Written Transmissions in Rabbinic Judaism and Early Christianity; With Tradition and Transmission in Early Christianity.* Translated by Eric J. Sharpe. 1961. Reprint, Grand Rapids, MI: Eerdmans, 1998.

Gibson, Shimon. "The Excavations at the Bethesda Pool in Jerusalem: Preliminary Report on a Project of Stratigraphic and Structural Analysis (1999–2009)." *Proche-Orient Chrétien Numéro Spécial* (2011) 17–44.

Glattfelder, James B. *Information—Consciousness—Reality: How a New Understanding of the Universe Can Help Answer Age-Old Questions of Existence.* Cham, Switzerland: SpringerOpen, 2019.

Goldberger, A. L., et al. "Bronchial Asymmetry and Fibonacci Scaling." *Experientia* 41 (1985) 1537–538.

Gould, Stephen Jay. "Is a New and General Theory of Evolution Emerging?" *Paleobiology* 6 (1980) 119–30.

Grant, Michael. *Greek and Roman Historians: Information and Misinformation.* New York: Routledge, 1995.

———. *Jesus: An Historian's Review of the Gospels.* New York: Scribner, 1977.

Graves, Kersey. *The World's Sixteen Crucified Saviors: Or Christianity Before Christ.* 6th ed. Boston: Colby and Rich, 1875.

Green, Garett. *Theology, Hermeneutics, and Imagination: The Crisis of Interpretation at the End of Modernity.* Cambridge: Cambridge University Press, 2000.

Green, Glenda. *Love Without End: Jesus Speaks.* Sedona, AZ: Spiritis, 2009.

Greene, Brian. *The Fabric of the Cosmos: Space, Time and the Texture of Reality.* London: Penguin, 2005.

Greenstein, George. *The Symbiotic Universe: Life and Mind in the Cosmos.* New York: William Morrow, 1988.

Gribbin, John. *In Search of Schrödinger's Cat.* London: Black Swan, 1991.

Grosberg, A., et al. "Crumpled Globule Model of the Three-Dimensional Structure of DNA." *Europhysics Letters* 23 (1993) 373–78.

Grushina, N. V., et al. "Special Features of the Diffraction of Light on Optical Fibonacci Gratings." *Moscow University Physics Bulletin* 63 (2008) 123–26.

Gundry, Robert H. *The Use of the Old Testament in St. Matthew's Gospel.* Leiden: Brill, 1967.

Guthrie, Donald. *New Testament Introduction.* Downers Grove, IL: InterVarsity, 1990.

Guthrie, W. K. C. *Orpheus and Greek Religion: A Study of the Orphic Movement.* London: Methuen, 1952.

Habermas, Gary R., and Anthony G. N. Flew. *Did Jesus Rise from the Dead? The Resurrection Debate.* Edited by Terry L. Miethe. San Francisco: Harper and Row, 1987.

Hamming, Richard W. "The Unreasonable Effectiveness of Mathematics." *The American Mathematical Monthly* 87 (1980) 81–90.

Hannah, Darrell D. "The Elect Son of Man of the *Parables of Enoch.*" In *"Who is This Son of Man?" The Latest Scholarship on a Puzzling Expression of the Historical Jesus*, edited by Larry W. Hurtado, and Paul L. Owen, 130–58. New York: Bloomsbury T. and T. Clark, 2011.

Harris, G. M., and A. P. Beardow. "The Destruction of Sodom and Gomorrah: A Geotechnical Perspective." *Quarterly Journal of Engineering Geology and Hydrogeology* 28 (1995) 349–62.

Hartog, Paul A. "Walter Bauer and the Apostolic Fathers." In *Orthodoxy and Heresy in Early Christian Contexts: Reconsidering the Bauer Thesis*, edited by Paul A. Hartog, 34–59. Eugene, OR: Wipf and Stock, 2015.

Hawking, Stephen W. *A Brief History of Time: From the Big Bang to Black Holes.* New York: Bantam, 1989.

———. "Gödel and the End of Physics." Dirac Centennial Lecture 2002. http://www.hawking.org.uk/godel-and-the-end-of-physics.html.

Head, Peter M. "The Nazi Quest for an Aryan Jesus." *Journal for the Study of the Historical Jesus* 2 (2004) 55–89.

———. "Scribal Behaviour and Theological Tendencies in Singular Readings in P. Bodmer II (P66)." In *Textual Variation: Theological and Social Tendencies? The Fifth Birmingham Colloquium on New Testament Textual Criticism*, edited by H. A. G. Houghton, and D. C. Parker, 55–74. Texts and Studies 3. Piscataway, NJ: Gorgias, 2008.

Heinrich, A. "Dionysos." In OCD, 479–82.

Heisenberg, Werner. *Physics and Philosophy: The Revolution in Modern Science.* 1958. Reprint, New York: HarperPerennial, 2007.

Hengel, Martin. *The Atonement: The Origins of the Doctrine in the New Testament.* Translated by John Bowden. London: SCM, 1981.

———. "Christological Titles in Early Christianity." In *The Messiah: Developments in Earliest Judaism and Christianity; The First Princeton Symposium on Judaism and Christian Origins*, edited by James H. Charlesworth et al., 425–48. Minneapolis: Fortress, 1992.

———. *Crucifixion in the Ancient World and the Folly of the Message of the Cross.* London: SCM, 1977.

———. "The Effective History of Isaiah 53 in the Pre-Christian Period." Translated by Daniel P. Bailey. In *The Suffering Servant: Isaiah 53 in Jewish and Christian Sources*, edited by Bernd Janowski, and Peter Stuhlmacher, 75–146. Grand Rapids, MI: Eerdmans, 2004.

———. *The Four Gospels and the One Gospel of Jesus Christ: An Investigation of the Collection and Origin of the Canonical Gospels.* Translated by John Bowden. Harrisburg, PA: Trinity, 2000.

———. *The "Hellenization" of Judaea in the First Century after Christ.* Translated by John Bowden. London: SCM, 1989.

———. *Judaism and Hellenism: Studies in their Encounter in Palestine during the Early Hellenistic Period.* Vol 1. Translated by John Bowden. 1973. Reprint, Philadelphia: Fortress, 1974.

———. *The Septuagint as Christian Scripture: Its Prehistory and the Problem of Its Canon.* Edited by David J. Reimer. Translated by Mark E. Biddle. Edinburgh: T. and T. Clark, 2002.

———. *The Son of God: The Origin of Christology and the History of Jewish-Hellenistic Religion.* Translated by John Bowden. 1975. Reprint, Philadelphia: Fortress, 1976.

Herbert, Nick. *Quantum Reality: Beyond the New Physics.* New York: Anchor, 1987.

Heschel, Susannah. *The Aryan Jesus: Christian Theologians and the Bible in Nazi Germany.* Princeton: Princeton University Press, 2010.

Higgins, Godfrey. *Anacalypsis: An Attempt to Draw Aside the Veil of the Saitic Isis.* Vol. 1. New York: Macy-Masius, 1927.

Hijmans, Steven. "*Sol Invictus, the Winter Solstice, and the Origins of Christmas.*" *Mouseion* 47 (2003) 377–98.

Hilbert, David. "On the Infinite." Translated by Ema Putnam, and Gerald J. Massey. 1925. In *Philosophy of Mathematics: Selected Readings*, edited by Paul Benacerraf and Hilary Putnam, 134–51. Reprint, Englewood Cliffs, NJ: Prentice Hall, 1964.

Hofius, Otfried. "The Fourth Servant in the New Testament Letters." Translated by Daniel P. Bailey. In *The Suffering Servant: Isaiah 53 in Jewish and Christian Sources*, edited by Bernd Janowski, and Peter Stuhlmacher, 163–88. Grand Rapids, MI: Eerdmans, 2004.

Hooker, Morna D. *The Son of Man in Mark: A Study of the Background of the Term "Son of Man" and its Use in St Mark's Gospel.* London: SPCK, 1967.

Hoyle, Fred. "The Universe: Past and Present Reflections." *Engineering and Science* 45 (1981) 8–12.

Hultgren, Arland J. *The Rise of Normative Christianity.* Minneapolis: Fortress, 1994.

Hume, David. *An Enquiry Concerning Human Understanding.* Edited by Peter Millican. Oxford: Oxford University Press, 2007.

Hurtado, Larry W. *Lord Jesus Christ: Devotion to Jesus in Earliest Christianity.* Grand Rapids, MI: Eerdmans, 2003.

———. "New Testament Christology: A Critique of Bousset's Influence." *Theological Studies* 40 (1979) 306–17.

———. *One God, One Lord: Early Christian Devotion and Ancient Jewish Monotheism.* 3rd ed. London: Bloomsbury T. and T. Clark, 2015.

———. "Paul's Messianic Christology." In *Paul The Jew: Rereading the Apostle as a Figure of Second Temple Judaism*, edited by Gabriele Boccaccini, and Carlos A. Segovia, 107–32. Minneapolis: Fortress, 2016.

Jaffee, Martin S. *Torah in the Mouth: Writing and Oral Tradition in Palestinian Judaism 200 BCE–400 CE.* Oxford: Oxford University Press, 2001.

Jeans, James. *The Mysterious Universe.* New York: Macmillan, 1943.

Jenkins, Philip. *Hidden Gospels: How the Search for Jesus Lost Its Way.* Oxford: Oxford University Press, 2002.

———. *The Many Faces of Christ: The Thousand Year Story of the Survival and Influence of the Lost Gospels*. New York: Basic, 2015.

———. *The New Anti-Catholicism: The Last Acceptable Prejudice*. Oxford: Oxford University Press, 2003.

Jipp, Joshua W. "Ancient, Modern, and Future Interpretations of Romans 1:3–4: Reception, History and Biblical Interpretation." *Journal of Theological Interpretation* 3 (2009) 241–59.

Johansson, Daniel. "'Who Can Forgive Sins but God Alone?' Human and Angelic Agents, and Divine Forgiveness in Early Judaism." *JSNT* 33 (2011) 351–74.

Jones, Arnold H. M. *Studies in Roman Government and Law*. Oxford: Blackwell, 1960.

Juel, D. H. "The Origin of Mark's Christology." In *The Messiah: Developments in Earliest Judaism and Christianity; The First Princeton Symposium on Judaism and Christian Origins*, edited by James H. Charlesworth et al., 449–60. Minneapolis: Fortress, 1992.

Julsgaard, Brian, et al. "Experimental Long-lived Entanglement of Two Macroscopic Objects." *Nature* 413 (2001) 400–403.

Kaiser, Walter C. Jr. *The Messiah in the Old Testament*. Grand Rapids, MI: Zondervan, 1995.

Keener, Craig S. *The Historical Jesus of the Gospels*. Grand Rapids, MI: Eerdmans, 2009.

Keith, Chris. "Memory and Authenticity: Jesus Tradition and What Really Happened." *ZNW* 102 (2011) 155–77.

Kennedy, H. A. A. *St. Paul and the Mystery-Religions*. London: Hodder and Stoughton, 1913.

Kim, Seyoon. *The Origin of Paul's Gospel*. 1981. Reprint, Eugene, OR: Wipf and Stock, 2007.

Kimball III, Charles A. "Jesus' Exposition of Scripture in Luke 20:9–19: An Inquiry in Light of Jewish Hermeneutics." *Bulletin for Biblical Research* 3 (1993) 77–92.

Kitadai, Norio, and Shigenori Maruyama. "Origins of Building Blocks of Life: A Review." *Geoscience Frontiers* 9 (2018) 1117–153.

Kittel, Charles, and Herbert Kroemer. *Thermal Physics*. 2nd ed. San Francisco: Freeman, 1980.

Klausner, Joseph. *From Jesus to Paul*. Translated by William F. Stinespring. New York: Macmillan, 1943.

———. *The Messianic Idea in Israel: From its Beginning to the Completion of the Mishnah*. Translated by W. F. Stinespring. New York: Macmillan, 1955.

Knight, Peter. *Conspiracy Culture: From Kennedy to the X-Files*. London: Routledge, 2000.

Knight, Robin D., and Laura F. Landweber. "The Early Evolution of the Genetic Code." *Cell* 101 (2000) 569–72.

Koester, Helmut. "*GNOMAI DIAPHOROI*: The Origin and Nature of Diversification in the History of Early Christianity." In *Trajectories through Early Christianity*, edited by James M. Robinson, and Helmut Koester, 114–57. 1971. Reprint, Eugene OR: Wipf and Stock, 2006.

Kohler, George Y. "Renewed Messianic Thought in Nineteenth Century Germany: A Dispute Between Moses Hess and Leopold Loew." *DAAT: A Journal of Jewish Philosophy and Kabbalah* 84 (2017) 5–23.

Kolomiytsev, Nikolay P., and Nadezhda Ya Poddubnaya. "The Diffuse Organism as the First Biological System." *Biological Theory* 5 (2010) 67–78.

Komoszewski, J. Ed, et al. *Reinventing Jesus: How Contemporary Skeptics Miss the Real Jesus and Mislead Popular Culture*. Grand Rapids, MI: Kregel, 2006.

Koonin, Eugene V. "The *Origin* at 150: Is a New Evolutionary Synthesis in Sight?" *Trends in Genetics* 25 (2009) 473–75.

Köstenberger, Andreas J., and Michael J. Kruger. *The Heresy of Orthodoxy: How Contemporary Culture's Fascination with Diversity has Reshaped Our Understanding of Early Christianity*. Wheaton, IL: Crossway, 2010.

Köstenberger, Andreas J., et al. *The Cradle, the Cross, and the Crown: An Introduction to the New Testament*. Nashville: B. and H., 2009.

Laland, Kevin N., et al. "Does Evolutionary Theory Need a Rethink?" *Nature* 514 (2014) 161–64.

Lampe, Peter. *From Paul to Valentinus: Christians at Rome in the First Two Centuries*. Translated by Michael Steinhauser. 1989. Reprint, Minneapolis: Fortress, 2003.

Lapide, Pinchas. *The Resurrection of Jesus: A Jewish Perspective*. Translated by Wilhelm C. Linss. 1982. Reprint, London: SPCK, 1984.

Lee, K. C., et al. "Entangling Macroscopic Diamonds at Room Temperature." *Science* 334 (2011) 1253–256.

Lenstra, Reijer. "Evolution of the Genetic Code Through Progressive Symmetry Breaking." *Journal of Theoretical Biology* 347 (2014) 95–108.

Lewis, C. S. *Mere Christianity*. 1952. Reprint, London: Collins, 1969.

———. *Miracles*. 1947. Reprint, London: Harper Collins, 2002.

Lewontin, Richard. "Billions and Billions of Demons: A Review of *The Demon-Haunted World*, by Carl Sagan." *New York Review of Books* 44 (1997) 28–30.

Licona, Michael R. *The Resurrection of Jesus: A New Historiographical Approach*. Downers Grove, IL: InterVarsity, 2010.

Lieberman, Saul. *Hellenism in Jewish Palestine: Studies in the Literary Transmission, Beliefs, and Manners of Palestine in the I Century BCE—IV Century CE*. Texts and Studies of the Jewish Theological Seminary of America 18. 2nd ed. New York: Jewish Theological Seminary of America, 1962.

Lieberman-Aiden, Erez, et al. "Comprehensive Mapping of Long-Range Interactions Reveals Folding Principles of the Human Genome." *Science* 326 (2009) 289–93.

Linde, Andre. "The New Inflationary Universe Scenario." In *The Very Early Universe*, edited by G. W. Gibbons et al., 205–49. Cambridge: Cambridge University Press, 1983.

Lindner, John F., et al. "Strange Nonchaotic Stars." *PRL* 114 (2015) 054101:1–5.

Linnemann, Eta. *Is There A Synoptic Problem? Rethinking the Literary Dependence of the First Three Gospels*. Grand Rapids, MI: Baker, 1992.

Litfin, Bryan M. "Apostolic Tradition and the Rule of Faith in Light of the Bauer Thesis." In *Orthodoxy and Heresy in Early Christian Contexts: Reconsidering the Bauer Thesis*, edited by Paul A. Hartog, 141–65. Eugene, OR: Wipf and Stock, 2015.

Livio, Mario. *The Golden Ratio: The Story of Phi, the World's Most Astonishing Number*. New York: Broadway, 2003.

Luckenbill, Daniel David. *The Annals of Sennacherib*. Chicago: University of Chicago Press, 1924.

Lüdemann, Gerd. *The Resurrection of Jesus: History, Experience, Theology*. Translated by John Bowden. Minneapolis: Fortress, 1994.

Mack, Burton L. "The Christ and Jewish Wisdom." In *The Messiah: Developments in Earliest Judaism and Christianity; The First Princeton Symposium on Judaism and*

Christian Origins, edited by James H. Charlesworth et al., 192–221. Minneapolis: Fortress, 1992.

———. *The Lost Gospel: The Book of Q and Christian Origins*. San Francisco: HarperCollins, 1994.

Mackie, J. L. "Evil and Omnipotence." *Mind New Series* 64 (1955) 200–212.

Maeir, Aren M. "Israel and Judah." In *EAH*, 3523–27.

Maier, Paul L. *Josephus: The Essential Works*. Grand Rapids, MI: Kregel, 1995.

Malament, David B. *Topics in the Foundations of General Relativity and Newtonian Gravitation Theory*. Chicago: University of Chicago Press, 2012.

Marchand, Suzanne L. *German Orientalism in the Age of Empire: Religion, Race, and Scholarship*. Cambridge: Cambridge University Press, 2009.

Margulis, Lynn. "The Conscious Cell." *Annals of the New York Academy of Sciences* 929 (2001) 55–70.

Mason, Steve. *Josephus and the New Testament*. Peabody, MA: Hendrickson, 1993.

Massey, Gerald. *Ancient Egypt the Light of the World: A Work of Reclamation and Restitution in Twelve Books*. Vol. 1. 1907. Reprint, Leeds: Celephais, 2008.

———. *The Natural Genesis*. Vol. 2. 1883. Reprint, Leeds: Celephais, 2008.

Mastrocinque, Attilio. *The Mysteries of Mithras: A Different Account*. Orientalische Religionen in der Antike 24. Tübingen: Mohr Siebeck, 2017.

Mazar, Eilat. *The Complete Guide to the Temple Mount Excavations*. Jerusalem: Shoham, 2002.

McClellan, Daniel O. "A Reevaluation of the Structure and Function of 2 Maccabees 7 and its Text-Critical Implications." *Studia Antiqua* 7 (2009) 81–95.

McCue, James F. "Orthodoxy and Heresy: Walter Bauer and the Valentinians." *Vigilae Christianae* 33 (1979) 118–30.

McCullagh, C. Behan. *Justifying Historical Descriptions*. Cambridge: Cambridge University Press, 1984.

McDowell, Josh. *The New Evidence that Demands a Verdict*. Milton Keyes: Authentic Media, 2012.

McGrath, Alister E. *Heresy: A History of Defending the Truth*. New York: HarperOne, 2009.

McGrew, Timothy J. "Inference, Method, and History." *STR* 3 (2012) 27–39.

Meier, John P. *The Roots of the Problem and the Person*. Vol. 1 of *A Marginal Jew: Rethinking the Historical Jesus*. New York: Doubleday, 1991.

Mendels, D. "Pseudo-Philo's *Biblical Antiquities*, the Fourth Philosophy, and the Political Messianism of the First Century CE." In *The Messiah: Developments in Earliest Judaism and Christianity; The First Princeton Symposium on Judaism and Christian Origins*, edited by James H. Charlesworth et al., 261–75. Minneapolis: Fortress, 1992.

Millard, Alan R. *Reading and Writing in the Time of Jesus*. Biblical Seminar 69. Sheffield: Sheffield Academic, 2000.

Mitchell, David C. "Messiah bar Ephraim in the Targums." *Aramaic Studies* 4 (2006) 221–41.

Mitchison, G. J. "Phyllotaxis and the Fibonacci Series." *Science* 196 (1977) 270–75.

Moreval, Ekaterina, et al. "Time From Quantum Entanglement: An Experimental Illustration." *Physics Review A* 89 (2014) 052122.

Mournet, Terence C. *Oral Tradition and Literary Dependence: Variability and Stability in the Synoptic Tradition and Q*. WUNT 2.195. Tübingen: Mohr Siebeck, 2005.

Müller, Gerd B. "Why an Extended Evolutionary Synthesis is Necessary." *Interface Focus* 7 (2017) 20170015.

Nagel, Thomas. *The Last Word*. Oxford: Oxford University Press, 1997.

———. *Mind and Cosmos: Why the Materialist Neo-Darwinian Conception of Nature Is Almost Certainly False*. Oxford: Oxford University Press, 2012.

Neev, David, and K. O. Emery. *The Destruction of Sodom, Gomorrah, and Jericho: Geological, Climatological, and Archaeological Background*. Oxford: Oxford University Press, 1995.

Négadi, Tidjani. "A Mathematical Model for the Genetic Code(s) Based on Fibonacci Numbers and their q-Analogues." *NeuroQuantology* 13 (2015) 259–72.

Neil, James M. A. *Everyday life in the Holy Land*. London: Cassell, 1913.

Neusner, Jacob. "Contexts of Comparison: Reciprocally Reading Gospels' and Rabbis' Parables." In *The Missing Jesus: Rabbinic Judaism and the New Testament*, edited by Bruce Chilton et al., 45–68. Leiden: Brill, 2002.

Newport, G. C. "A Note on the 'Seat of Moses' (Matthew 23:2)." Andrews University Seminary Studies 28 (1990) 53–58.

Noble, Denis. "Evolution Beyond Neo-Darwinism: A New Conceptual Framework." *The Journal of Experimental Biology* 218 (2015) 7–13.

———. "Physiology Is Rocking the Foundations of Evolutionary Biology." *Experimental Physiology* 98 (2013) 1235–243.

Nock, Arthur Darby. *Early Gentile Christianity and its Hellenistic Background*. New York: Harper and Row, 1964.

Norris, Frederick W. "Ignatius, Polycarp, and 1 Clement: Walter Bauer Reconsidered." *Vigiliae Christianae* 30 (1976) 23–44.

Ordway, Holly. *Not God's Type: An Atheist Academic Lays Down Her Arms*. San Francisco: Ignatius, 2014.

Orgel, Leslie E. "The Implausibility of Metabolic Cycles on the Prebiotic Earth." *PLOS Biology* 6 (2008) 5–13.

———. "Prebiotic Chemistry and the Origin of the RNA World. *Critical Reviews in Biochemistry and Molecular Biology* 39 (2004) 99–123.

Pagels, Elaine, H. *Beyond Belief: The Secret Gospel of Thomas*. New York: Random House, 2003.

———. *The Gnostic Gospels*. New York: Vintage, 1989.

———. *The Gnostic Paul: Gnostic Exegesis of the Pauline Letters*. London: Continuum, 1992.

Painter, John. *Just James: The Brother of Jesus in History and Tradition*. Edinburgh: T. and T. Clark, 2005.

Pannenberg, Wolfhart. *Jesus: God and Man*. Translated by Lewis L. Wilkins, and Duane A. Priebe. Philadelphia: Westminster, 2002.

Pavšič, Matej. *The Landscape of Theoretical Physics: A Global View From Point Particles to the Brane World and Beyond, in Search of a Unifying Principle*. Fundamental Theories of Physics 119. Dordrecht, Netherlands: Kluwer, 2002.

Payne, Philip B. "Jesus' Implicit Claim to Deity in His Parables." *Trinity Journal* 2 (1981) 3–23.

Pellionisz, Andras J. "The Principle of Recursive Genome Function." *Cerebellum* 7 (2008) 348–59.

Penrose, Roger. *The Emperor's New Mind: Concerning Computers, Minds and the Laws of Physics*. Oxford: Oxford University Press, 1989.

Perez, Jean-Claude. "Codon Population in Single-stranded Whole Human Genome DNA are Fractal and Fine-tuned by the Golden Ratio 1.618." In *Interdisciplinary Sciences: Computational Life Sciences* 2 (2010) 228–340.

Perrin, Nicholas. *Jesus the Temple*. Grand Rapids, MI: Baker, 2010.

Petkov, Vesselin, ed. *Space and Time: Minkowski's Papers on Relativity*. Translated by Fritz Lewertoff, and Vesselin Petkov. Montreal: Minkowski Institute, 2012.

Pines, Schlomo. *An Arabic Version of the* Testimonium Flavianum *and its Implications*. Jerusalem: Israel Academy of Sciences and Humanities, 1971.

Plantinga, Alvin C. *God, Freedom, and Evil*. Grand Rapids, MI: Eerdmans, 1977.

Pletzer, Belinda, et al. "When Frequencies Never Synchronize: The Golden Mean and the Resting EEG." *Brain Research* 1335 (2010) 91–102.

Polkinghorne, John C. *The Faith of a Physicist: Reflections of a Bottom-up Thinker*. Minneapolis: Fortress, 1996.

———. *Science and Creation: The Search for Understanding*. London: SPCK, 1997.

———. *Serious Talk: Science and Religion in Dialogue*. Harrisburg, PA: Trinity, 1995.

Popper, Karl R. "Scientific Reduction and the Essential Incompleteness of All Science." In *Studies in the Philosophy of Biology: Reduction and Related Problems*, edited by F. J. Ayala, and T. Dobzhansky, 259–84. Berkeley: University of California Press, 1974.

Price, J. Randall. "The Eschatology of the Dead Sea Scrolls." *Eruditio Ardescens* 2.2 (2016) Article 1.

Prigogine, Ilya, et al. "Thermodynamics of Evolution." *Physics Today* 25 (1972) 23–28.

Quispel, G. "The Discussion of Judaic Christianity." *Vigiliae Chistianae* 22 (1968) 81–93.

Rakočević, Miloje, M. "The Genetic Code as a Golden Mean Determined System." *Biosystems* 46 (1998) 283–91.

Rawlinson, A. E. J. *The New Testament Doctrine of the Christ*. London: Longmans, Green and Co., 1926.

Reed, Jonathan L. *Archaeology and the Galilean Jesus: A Re-Examination of the Evidence*. Harrisburg, PA: Trinity, 2000.

Rembaum, Joel E. "The Development of a Jewish Exegetical Tradition Regarding Isaiah 53." *Harvard Theological Review* 75 (1982) 289–311.

Ricardo, Alonso, and Jack W. Szostak. "Life on Earth." *Scientific American* 301 (2009) 54–61.

Riesenfeld, Harald. *The Gospel Tradition and its Beginning: A Study in the Limits of 'Formschichte.'* London: Mowbray, 1957.

Rist, John M. *On The Independence of Matthew and Mark*. SNTSMS 32. Cambridge: Cambridge University Press, 1978.

Roberts, Alexander, and James Donaldson, eds. *The Apostolic Fathers with Justin Martyr and Irenaeus*. Vol. 1 of *ANF*. Buffalo, NY: Christian Literature, 1886.

Roberts, Alexander, and James Donaldson, eds. *Fathers of the Third Century*. Vol. 4 of *ANF*. Buffalo, NY: Christian Literature, 1886.

Robertson, Michael P., and Gerald F. Joyce. "The Origins of the RNA World." *Cold Spring Harbor Perspectives in Biology* 4.5 (2012) a003608.

Robinson, James M., ed. *The Nag Hammadi Library: The Definitive New Translation of the Gnostic Scriptures, Complete in One Volume*. 3rd ed. New York: Harper Collins, 1990.

Robinson, Thomas A. *The Bauer Thesis Examined: The Geography of Heresy in the Early Christian Church.* Studies in the Bible and Early Christianity 11. Lewiston, NY: Edwin Mellen, 1988.

Rodríguez, Rafael. *Structuring Early Christian Memory: Jesus in Tradition, Performance and Text.* Library of New Testament Studies 407. London: T. and T. Clark, 2010.

Ross, David, ed. and trans. *The Works of Aristotle.* Vol. 12. Oxford: Clarendon, 1952.

Rubin, David C. *Memory in Oral Traditions: The Cognitive Psychology of Epic Ballads and Counting-out Rhymes.* Oxford: Oxford University Press, 1995.

Rummel, R. J. *Death by Government: Genocide and Mass Murder Since 1900.* 1994. Reprint, New York: Routledge, 2017.

Ruse, Michael. "Curb Your Enthusiasm." *Aeon*, October 1, 2012. https://aeon.co/essays/how-humanism-lost-its-way-in-a-charismatic-crusade.

Sadeghi, Behnam, and Mohsen Goudarzi. "Ṣan'ā' 1 and the Origins of the Qur'ān." *Der Islam* 87 (2012) 1–129.

Sagrillo, Troy Leiland. "Shoshenq I and Biblical Šîšaq: A Philological Defense of Their Traditional Equation." In *Solomon and Shishak: Current Perspectives from Archaeology, Epigraphy, History and Chronology*, edited by Peter J. James, and Peter Gert van der Veen, 61–81. Oxford: Archaeopress, 2015.

Sandage, Allan. "A Scientist Reflects on Religious Belief." *Truth: An Interdisciplinary Journal of Christian Thought* 1 (1985) 56–57.

Sanders, E. P. *Paul and Palestinian Judaism: A Comparison of Patterns of Religion.* London: SCM, 1977.

———. *The Tendencies of the Synoptic Tradition.* SNTSMS 9. Cambridge: Cambridge University Press, 1969.

Sanders, James A. *Canon and Community: A Guide to Canonical Criticism.* Philadelphia: Fortress, 1984.

Sarovar, Mohan, et al. "Quantum Entanglement in Photosynthetic Light Harvesting Complexes." *Nature Physics* 6 (2010) 462–67.

Schermer, Michael, and Alex Grobman. *Denying History: Who Says the Holocaust Never Happened and Why Do They Say It?* Berkeley: University of California Press, 2000.

Schrödinger, Erwin. "Discussion of Probability Relations between Separated Systems." *Mathematical Proceedings of the Cambridge Philosophical Society* 31 (1935) 555–63.

Schwartz, Jeffrey H. *Sudden Origins: Fossils, Genes, and the Emergence of Species.* New York: Wiley, 1999.

Schweitzer, Albert. *Paul and His Interpreters: A Critical History.* Translated by W. Montgomery. London: A. & C. Black, 1912.

Segal, Alan F. "Conversion and Messianism: Outline for a New Approach." In *The Messiah: Developments in Earliest Judaism and Christianity; The First Princeton Symposium on Judaism and Christian Origins*, edited by James H. Charlesworth et al., 296–340. Minneapolis: Fortress, 1992.

———. *Two Powers in Heaven: Early Rabbinic Reports about Christianity and Gnosticism.* 2nd ed. Leiden: Brill, 2002.

Seidl, Theodor. "Carchemish in Near Eastern Historiography and in the Old Testament." *Old Testament Essays* 22 (2009) 646–61.

Shapiro, James, A. *Evolution: A View from the 21st Century.* Upper Saddle River, NJ: Pearson, 2011.

Shapiro, Robert. "Small Molecule Interactions Were Central to the Origin of Life." *Quarterly Review of Biology* 81 (2006) 105–26.

Sheldon, Henry C. *The Mystery Religions and the New Testament*. New York: Abingdon, 1918.

Shipman, P. D., et al. "How Universal are Fibonacci Patterns?" *The European Physical Journal D* 62 (2011) 5–17.

Skarsaune, Oskar. *In the Shadow of the Temple: Jewish Influences on Early Christianity*. Downers Grove, IL: InterVarsity, 2008.

Smit, Peter-Ben. "The End of Early Christian Adoptionism? A Note on the Invention of Adoptionism, its Sources, and its Current Demise." *International Journal of Philosophy and Theology* 76 (2015) 177–99.

Smolin, Lee. *The Trouble with Physics: The Rise of String Theory, the Fall of a Science, and What Comes Next*. New York: Houghton Mifflin, 2006.

Sokal, Alan. "Transgressing the Boundaries: Toward a Transformative Hermeneutics of Quantum Gravity." *Social Text* 46/47 (1996) 217–52.

Sokal, Alan, and Jean Bricmont. *Fashionable Nonsense: Postmodern Intellectuals' Abuse of Science*. New York: Picador, 1998.

Srinivasan, T. P. "Fibonacci Sequence, Golden Ratio, and a Network of Resistors." *American Journal of Physics* 60 (1992) 461–62.

Stanton, Graham N. *Jesus and Gospel*. Cambridge: Cambridge University Press, 2004.

Stapp, Henry P. *Mindful Universe: Quantum Mechanics and the Participating Observer*. 2nd ed. Heidelberg: Springer, 2011.

Stein, Robert H. "An Early Recension of the Gospel Traditions?" *JETS* 30 (1987) 167–83.

———. *The Method and Message of Jesus' Teachings*. Philadelphia: Westminster, 1978.

Streeter, Burnett Hillman. *The Four Gospels: A Study of Origins, the Manuscript Tradition, Sources, Authorship, and Dates*. London: Macmillan, 1930.

Stuhlmacher, Peter. "Isaiah 53 in the Gospels and Acts." Translated by Daniel P. Bailey. In *The Suffering Servant: Isaiah 53 in Jewish and Christian Sources*, edited by Bernd Janowski, and Peter Stuhlmacher, 147–62. Grand Rapids, MI: Eerdmans, 2004.

Sukenik, Eleazar L. *Ancient Synagogues in Palestine and Greece*. Oxford: Oxford University Press, 1934.

Taylor, Vincent. *The Formation of the Gospel Tradition: Eight Lectures*. London: Macmillan, 1933.

Tegmark, Max. "The Mathematical Universe." *Foundations of Physics* 38 (2008) 101–50.

Thomas, Edward J. *The Life of Buddha as Legend and History*. New York: Alfred Knopf, 1931.

Thomassen, Einar. "Orthodoxy and Heresy in Second-Century Rome." *Harvard Theological Review* 97 (2004) 241–56.

Thornton, Joseph W., and Rob DeSalle. "Gene Family Evolution and Homology: Genomics Meets Phylogenetics." *Annual Review of Genomics and Human Genetics* 1 (2000) 41–73.

Torrance, Thomas F. *Space, Time and Incarnation*. Edinburgh: T. and T. Clark, 1997.

Trebilco, Paul. "Christian Communities in Western Asia Minor into the Early Second Century: Ignatius and Others as Witnesses against Bauer." *JETS* 49 (2006) 17–44.

Trevors, Jack T., and David L. Abel. "Chance and Necessity Do Not Explain the Origin of Life." *Cell Biology International* 28 (2004) 729–39.

Turner, Henry E. W. *The Pattern of Christian Truth: A Study in the Relations between Orthodoxy and Heresy in the Early Church*. London: Mowbray, 1954.

Tzaferis, Vassilios. "Crucifixion: The Archaeological Evidence." *Biblical Archaeology Review* 11 (1985) 44–53.

Ulrich, Eugene. *The Dead Sea Scrolls and the Origins of the Bible*. Grand Rapids, MI: Eerdmans, 1999.

Ulrich, Eugene, and Peter W. Flint. *Qumran Cave 1. II: The Isaiah Scrolls*. Discoveries in the Judaean Desert 32. Oxford: Clarendon Press, 2010.

VanderKam, James C. *The Dead Sea Scrolls and the Bible*. Grand Rapids, MI: Eerdmans, 2012.

———. "Righteous One, Messiah, Chosen One, and Son of Man in 1 Enoch 37–71." In *The Messiah: Developments in Earliest Judaism and Christianity; The First Princeton Symposium on Judaism and Christian Origins*, edited by James H. Charlesworth et al., 169–91. Minneapolis: Fortress, 1992.

VanderKam, James, and Peter Flint. *The Meaning of the Dead Sea Scrolls: Their Significance for Understanding the Bible, Judaism, Jesus, and Christianity*. London: T. and T. Clarke, 2002.

Vansina, Jan. *Oral Tradition as History*. Madison: University of Wisconsin Press, 1985.

van Voorst, Robert E. *Jesus Outside the New Testament: An Introduction to the Ancient Evidence*. Grand Rapids, MI: Eerdmans, 2000.

Vasas, Vera, et al. "Lack of Evolvability in Self-sustaining Autocatalytic Networks Constraints Metabolism-first Scenarios for the Origin of Life." *Proceedings of the National Academy of Sciences* 107 (2010) 1470–475.

Vermaseren, M. J. *Mithras: The Secret God*. Translated by Therese and Vincent Megaw. 1959. Reprint, London: Chatto and Windus, 1963.

Vermes, Geza. *The Complete Dead Sea Scrolls in English*. London: Penguin, 2004.

———. *Jesus the Jew: A Historian's Reading of the Bible*. Minneapolis: Fortress, 1981.

Vitiello, Giuseppe. "Coherent States, Fractals and Brain Waves." *New Mathematics and Natural Computing* 5 (2009) 245–64.

Volney, C. F. *The Ruins, or Meditation on the Revolutions of Empires; and The Law of Nature*. Translated by Joel Barlow. 1792. Reprint, New York: G. Vale, 1853.

Wallace, Daniel B. "Challenges in New Testament Textual Criticism for the Twenty-first Century." *JETS* 52 (2009) 79–100.

———. "The Gospel According to Bart: A Review Article of *Misquoting Jesus* by Bart Ehrman." *JETS* 49 (2006) 327–49.

———. "The Textual Reliability of the New Testament: A Dialogue." In *The Reliability of the New Testament: Bart D. Ehrman and Daniel B. Wallace in Dialogue*, edited by Robert B. Stewart, 13–60. Minneapolis: Fortress, 2011.

Wallace, J. Warner. *Cold Case Christianity*. Colorado Springs: David C. Cook, 2013.

Wasserman, Tommy. "The 'Son of God' Was in the Beginning (Mark 1:1)." *Journal of Theological Studies* 62 (2011) 20–50.

Wershler-Henry, Darren. *The Iron Whim: A Fragmented History of Typewriting*. New York: Cornell University Press, 2007.

Westcott, Brooke Foss. *Introduction to the Study of the Gospels*. New York: Macmillan, 1882.

Whitesides, George M. "Revolutions in Chemistry: Priestley Medalist George M. Whitesides' Address." *Chemical and Engineering News* 85 (2007) 12–17.

Wigner, Eugene. "The Unreasonable Effectiveness of Mathematics in the Natural Sciences." *Communications in Pure and Applied Mathematics* 13 (1960) 1–14.

Wilber, Ken. *The Spectrum of Consciousness*. Wheaton, IL: Quest, 1993.

Wilczek, Frank. "On Absolute Units, III: Absolutely Not?" *Physics Today* 59 (2006) 11.

Willoughby, Harold R. *Pagan Regeneration: A Study of Mystery Initiations in the Graeco-Roman World*. Chicago: University of Chicago Press, 1929.

Wise, Michael, et al., trans. *The Dead Sea Scrolls: A New Translation*. New York: HarperCollins, 2005.

Woit, Peter. *Not Even Wrong: The Failure of String Theory and the Search for Unity in Physical Law*. New York: Basic, 2006.

Wrede, William. *Paul*. Translated by Edward Lummis. London: Philip Green, 1907.

Wright, N. T. *The Challenge of Jesus: Rediscovering Who Jesus Was and Is*. Downers Grove, IL: InterVarsity, 1999.

———. "Jesus and the Identity of God." *Ex Auditu* 14 (1998) 42–56.

———. *Jesus and the Victory of God*. COQG 2. Minneapolis: Fortress, 1996.

———. *The Resurrection of the Son of God*. COQG 3. Minneapolis: Fortress, 2003.

Yamauchi, Edwin M. "The Gnostics and History." *JETS* 14 (1971) 29–40.

Yu, Daqiu, et al. "Golden Ratio and Bond-valence Parameters of Hydrogen Bonds of Hydrated Borates." *Journal of Molecular Structure* 783 (2006) 210–14.

Zacharias, Ravi, and Norman Geisler. *Who Made God? And Answers to Over 100 Other Tough Questions on Faith*. Grand Rapids, MI: Zondervan, 2003.

Zugibe, Frederick T. *The Crucifixion of Jesus: A Forensic Inquiry*. New York: Evans, 2005.